EGYPT, The Stalled Society

Written
after Modernization theory
Ansari = student of Binder
    Second stratum — (sometimes religious → secular)
            traditional societies moving toward modernization
            In process of movement conflict bet. tradition
            and modern, movement is unidirectional development,
            Problem w/ modernization is that it assumes
            clearly defined - tradition Ns Modern
        Co-existent: In Reality, tradition in Modernity, modernity as tradition
        thesis
        Elite ~~approach~~:
    Ansari: pwr diffused throughout society
            Nat'l struggle can be to seen at a local level
            use local: Kemshist to get nat'l to
            support regime policies
        Second stratum: is not just one variable
    Sadat uses retraditionalization to undue Nasserism
    Islamic Fundal. movement from above - part / retradition
        Kibar Al A'yan: prominent   كبار الأعيان
            land owning families
            no loyalty - self-interested
            kinship binds them
        └─ crude power - economic control over
            peasantry non-hegemonic (no-coercion)

SUNY Series in Near Eastern Studies
Said Amir Arjomand, Editor

EGYPT,
The Stalled Society

Hamied Ansari

State University of New York Press

In Memory of My Parents

Published by
State University of New York Press, Albany

Printed in the United States of America

For information, address State University of New York
Press, State University Plaza, Albany, N.Y., 12246

Library of Congress Cataloging-in-Publication Data
Ansari, Hamied.
  Egypt, the stalled society.

  (SUNY series in Near Eastern studies)
  Bibliography: p.
  Includes index.
  1. Egypt—Politics and government—1952-
2. Egypt—Rural conditions.   3. Social classes—Egypt.
I. Title.
DT107.827.A57 1986   962′.05   86-14524
ISBN 0-88706-183-4
ISBN 0-88706-184-2 (pbk.)

10 9 8 7 6 5 4 3 2

Contents

Figures

Tables

List of Abbreviations

AFRACT	Fractions of Family Members in the ASU Committees
ASCBU	Arab Socialist Union Basic Unit Officers
ASU	Arab Socialist Union
ASUDO	Arab Socialist Union District Officers
DAGCP	Director of Agricultural Cooperative
DS	Descendancy Status (Prerevolutionary Parliamentary Elites)
DSO	No Descendancy Status (Families without Prerevolutionary Parliamentary Elites
FP	Family Adult Population
GODE	The Gulf Organization for the Development of Egypt
GVCMP	ASU's Governorate Committees
HADITU	The Democratic Movement for National Liberation
HCLF	The Higher Committee for the Liquidation of Feudalism
IMF	International Monetary Fund
LOWN	Landownership
LRL	Land Reform Law
MCI	Military Criminal Investigation
MEMGC	Member of Governorate Council
MP	Member of Parliament
MPNU	Members of Parliament in the National Union
NDP	National Democratic Party
NSHK	Number of Shaykhs
NU	National Union
NUDO	National Union District Officeholding
NUFRACT	Fractions of Family Members in the NU Committees
NUMDA	Number of 'Umdas
ODC	Officeholding in District Councils
RCC	Revolutionary Command Council

RDIFF	Difference in Family Fractions in Comparing ASU Committees with NU Committees
RMC	Rural Middle Class
Tajamu'	National Progressive Unionist Party
TOTFLOS	Total Family Landownership
UAR	United Arab Republic
UPLOW	Lower/Upper Egypt

Exchange rates, weights, and measures

E£ = $2.87 (1948)
E£ = $1.40 (1979)
1 faddan = 1.038 acres

Preface

A CONSERVATIVE WIND HAS SWEPT over the Middle East, sharply contrasting with the radical trends of the 1960s. In Egypt, the secular ideas underlying Pan-Arabism and socialism have given way to religious beliefs and sectarian attitudes. Order, stability, and legitimacy have assumed a higher priority than egalitarianism and redistribution. This manuscript examines the effects these ideological and policy changes have had on individuals and classes divided by a century of lopsided development in the social and economic sectors.

My source of inspiration lies in the Kamshish Affair, which gave fresh impetus to the radical trend of the 1960s. To the untutored mind, Kamshish—a small village in the heart of the Delta—appeared to be at the threshold of a socialist revolution that should have engulfed the whole country, if not the whole region. The village Kamshish became the Mecca of the left to which such luminaries as Che Guevara, Jean Paul Sartre, and Simon de Beauvoir paid personal homage. But the imminent revolution failed to materialize. The state, weary and exhausted by defeat and foreign adventures, turned off the socialist revolution just as it had started it. A new beginning was announced by President Sadat soon after he came to power in 1970. The new beginning meant, in essence, placating his predecessors' rightist victims while meeting out punishment to leftist elements.

Kamshish serves as a clue for understanding the social history of Egypt as well as the evolving relations between Egyptian rulers and the masses from the middle of the nineteenth century to the present. My main aim is to relate the events that took place in Kamshish to the larger social and economic history of Egypt, from which I derive conclusions on the effects of ideological changes on local community relations, the impact of social and economic transformations on political stability under successive regimes, the response of the peasantry towards limited reforms, and the more recent growth of Islamic militancy.

I am indebted to all the individuals who have shared with me their sweet and bitter memories about events in their lives, which I have endeavored to present as fairly and objectively as possible. I am particularly indebted to Shahinda Maqlad, Aziz al-Fiqqi, and Abdel Fattah Abu al-Fadl, whose candid views helped me write about the Kamshish Affair, although I must emphasize that I alone am responsible for my interpretation.

In the course of my research in Cairo, I met with individuals who gave generously of their time and effort. Space, however, does not permit me to mention all of them by name. I would like to express my thanks to my students at the American University in Cairo, where I taught for three years, and at the Johns Hopkins' School of Advanced International Studies. The following students were very helpful in their criticisms: Reem Mikhail, Khalida Ahmad Zaki, Lawrence Fioretta, Geoffrey Hathaway, Roya Hakimzadeh, and David Weinstein. My gratitude also goes to Monica Allen, Zilla Bristol, Theresa Simmons, and all the staff at the School of Advanced International Studies for typing the manuscript and making several copies available for reviewers and editors.

My gratitude also goes to Helen Knapp for preparing the Index and to Nancy Sharlet for editing the manuscript and readying it for the press.

My final words of gratitude go to Professor Leonard Binder for his constant guidance and support, and for his encouragement to me to hold onto my own independent views.

Washington, D.C.
June 1985

Introduction

R ULING ELITE MODELS HAVE helped a generation of scholars concerned with Middle East studies, but nowhere have they been so extensively applied as in studies of Egypt. A great deal of reformulation and adaptation has been made in the various approaches for unraveling the secrets of a society whose history and politics continue to fascinate scholars and laymen alike. For the purpose of analysis, however, these approaches may be divided into two major models: the elite-mass model and the second stratum approach.

Each model emphasizes an important aspect of the social and political reality and ignores another. The elite-mass model stresses the ruling elites' autonomy, while the second stratum model emphasizes the social base of support for the ruling elites. I will argue here that greater insights into the problems of development can be gained by observing the interaction between ruling elites' autonomy and the limits of that autonomy, as illustrated by the second stratum model. I will further explain the limitations of these approaches and suggest possible ways to overcome them in light of my analysis of the social and economic factors behind the shifts in ruling elite ideology and policy.

The elite-mass model has dominated the field without any rival. Consequently, the literature is replete with concepts such as the "unincorporated society,"[1] the "praetorian state,"[2] "patrimonial"[3] and "neo-patrimonial"[4] rule, and the "elite will"[5]—all conveying a near consensus on the autonomous character of the state and the absence of social restraints on the exercise of power by the ruling elites. By contrast, the second stratum approach presents a minority view on the links between the social and political orders and posits important questions concerning sources of political stability for which the dichotomous approach has no adequate answers.

The dichotomous elite-mass approach to Middle East studies does not deviate significantly from the classic ruling elite model, which divides societies into rulers and ruled. The rulers constitute a small minority that dominates an undifferentiated mass. The instrument of rule for the dominant ruling elites is

1

the military and government bureaucracy. Groups and classes, both of which are fundamental in the liberal and Marxist theories of development, respectively, are not considered influential, given their immature stages of development. In the majority of cases, they are excluded from consideration because of the underlying assumption that they do not constitute a threat to the ruling elites nor do they exercise control over policy making in any effective way. Thus, the dichotomous elite-mass approach, in its extreme form, reduces politics to the uncomplicated pattern of a small minority controlling and directing an undifferentiated mass.

Military intervention in Middle Eastern societies has generally reinforced the view of the autonomy of the ruling elites on the basis of assumptions drawn largely from the Latin American literature. For example, it has been observed that army officers intervene in politics autonomously and in accordance with their corporate interests. The invariable impression is that Middle Eastern rulers, particularly the rulers drawn from the military ranks, are above the society, unconstrained by its structure and untouched by the consequences of their decisions. It is further assumed that the authoritarian tendencies of the ruling elites are reinforced by a cultural disposition that teaches blind obedience to authority.[6]

In contrast, the second stratum approach assumes that power in its most rudimentary form originates from dependence on traditional support. Thus, a fundamental point in this approach is the assumption that state and civil societies are not separated, as the conventional, dichotomous approach dictates. Rather, it is assumed that the state and the society are linked by a social stratum, an idea whose intellectual origins can be traced back to the Italian thinker, Gaetano Mosca. In the words of Leonard Binder, "for Mosca, the second stratum is the necessary mediating instrument without which the ruling class or the ruling oligarchy cannot rule. The political function of the second stratum extends from representation through expressive identification to the exercise of authority."[7] In a slightly modified version of Mosca's thesis, Binder points out that the "second stratum, it must be remembered, is not the ruling class. The second stratum does not rule but is the stratum without which rulers cannot rule."[8]

To understand fully the concept of the second stratum and its operational principles, it is important to bear in mind that its political significance does not stem from its functional indispensibility. It is rather its particular situation in the society that lends it political significance. Egypt, along with a number of Middle Eastern countries, has experienced an uneven pattern of regional development in the diffusion of modernization. The major differences are between the urban and rural areas, and these differences continue to exist despite recent demographic changes evidenced by high rates of urbanization and rural migration into the cities.[9]

The cultural-geographical bisector has been traditionally bridged by the intermediary role of locally influential individuals, the heads of villages, the landlords, or the tribal chieftains. In Algeria and Tunisia, this role has traditionally been fulfilled by the *Qa'id*, while in Egypt it has been carried out by the *'Umdas* or by the rural notables, the *A'yan*. In Iraq and Morocco, it was the tribal chieftains who acted as mediators and as the initiators of national integration by acting as representatives at the central government. In Syria, the *Zu'ama* and the *Mukhtars* mediated with the central authority using their local influence. What unites these individuals is their traditional role as instruments of national integration. They are generally resident cultivators, and, since they are more closely tied to the soil than the urban *dhawat* and *effendi* classes, they regard themselves as the carriers of national culture and as its most authentic representatives. Despite their localism, these mediators have succeeded in forging kinship links with the urban areas, as more and more of their members attain a higher education and come to occupy high positions in the military and government bureaucracy. Although they are conscious of their economic interests, these elements do not constitute a cohesive class in the classical Marxist definition of the term.

The conditions I seek to explain by using the ruling elite models are very complex, and the following is only a brief summary of what I examine in full in subsequent chapters. Perhaps most salient is the persistence of the political order in many countries of the Middle East, despite the failure of reforms and the shifting orientations of the ruling elites. This observation is valid even for countries that have suffered chronic instabilities and recurrent military coups. By contrast, the experience of many countries in the region reveals that the policies aimed at establishing socialist or liberal-capitalist orders have failed, although many scholars in the past expressed optimism that these goals were realizable. Today, most societies in the region have a wide gap between the minority at the top of the socioeconomic scale and the majority in the subordinate classes. The main source of tension for these societies, however, is the persistence of traditional patterns of authority in conflict with social and economic changes. Fouad Ajami sums up the Middle Eastern and Latin American situations with these insightful words.

> The prospects for redistribution—within and among nations—are not particularly bright, the prospects for "stalled societies"—like Mexico or Egypt—are more problematic still. Stalled societies escape the grim horrors of great crusades and—given the record of great crusades in our

time—that must be judged a positive thing. What they suffer is what Barrington Moore has aptly called the "appalling costs of stagnation."[10]

A few words are necessary to explain what I mean by the persistence of the political order despite the failure of reforms and redistribution. I have chosen to concentrate on Egypt because I believe Egypt presents a pattern of development being duplicated elsewhere, albeit on a larger scale. I will draw comparisons whenever possible in the course of this introduction.

As to the persistence of the political order, obviously the political order established by the Egyptian army officers in 1952 has lasted until today, give or take a few changes in the political institutions, including the recent emergence of the New Wafd in alliance with the Muslim Brotherhood under a controlled, multiparty system. The Egyptian political order has survived at least two major military defeats and numerous diplomatic setbacks. The last unsettling event was the assassination of President Anwar Sadat. Despite these setbacks, the political order has demonstrated an extraordinary resiliency. The Egyptian continuity, however, is not unique. The same kind of continuity can be observed in countries such as Syria under Hafiz Al-Assad and Iraq under Saddam Hussein. I have mentioned these countries in particular because of their past histories of recurrent military coups. The regime of Qadhafi in Libya will this year observe the fifteenth anniversary of the military coup that brought him to power. This continuity is rather extraordinary considering the continuing domestic and interstate instabilities, which make efforts to seek an explanation more compelling.

What do I mean by the failure of reforms? Again, the example of Egypt may serve as a model for countries with a radical past. The economic policies during the Nasserist regime shifted in the 1960s from relying heavily on limited agrarian reforms, domestic savings, and investment in the private sector to a socialist strategy, whose aim was to maintain equity through redistribution based on dispossessing the urban and landed bourgeoisie. Growth and equity, however, proved difficult to maintain simultaneously. This fact became evident in the failure to raise sufficient revenues to finance the first five year plan in the 1960s. During this period, the Nasserist regime faced the inevitable choice of further squeezing the dominant class or maintaining social peace by sacrificing equity. Nasser chose the latter course, but not before taking some repressive measures against the landed and urban bourgeoisie.

The reverses that resulted from the socialist crisis of the Nasserist regime became a general trend under Sadat. The latter went further than his predecessor by offering political rehabilitation to the prerevolutionary political elites most affected by Nasser's socialist decrees and policies of confiscation. In the countryside, desequestration was carried out at the expense of small peasants, the main beneficiaries of the agrarian reforms. The climax of these efforts was the "Open Door" policy, *siyasat al-infitah*, which laid the cornerstone for a free market economy. This open policy envisaged lifting the restrictions that impeded the growth of the private sector at the cost of the public sector, removing the controls on foreign exchange, and providing incentives to attract foreign investments.

The Open Door policy, however, met its first crisis during the Food Riots of January 1977. The immediate cause of the rioting was the attempt by the government to gradually eliminate subsidies. These subsidies were meant to aid the poor in buying essential commodities, but they were thoroughly abused since they became freely available to everyone, including the well-to-do. In addition to the pressing need for reforming this system, there was also mounting pressure on the government by the International Monetary Fund to rationalize the economy. This rationalization meant, in essence, doing away with the worst abuses of the socialist system. Nevertheless, the authorities were thoroughly convinced that any reforms aimed at reversing some of the socialist principles would meet with immediate resistance from the subordinate classes. The liberal order reached crisis situation with the suppression of political opposition in September 1981. Thus, in the span of slightly more than one decade, the authorities influenced by opposite ideologies of development decided to halt progress along the preferred course due to complex circumstances this book attempts to explain.

The net result of the shift in policy orientation from the socialist to the free market economy was the emergence of a mixed economy that combined the worst features of both systems. Egypt today gives the impression of affluent urban society amid massive poverty. Growth in the commercial and construction sectors contrasts sharply with the increasing impoverishment of the majority of the people. Industrialization has lagged behind, while importation of goods, including one-half of Egypt's food requirements, has continued apace, thus putting a heavy burden on the country's foreign exchange earnings and pushing its external debt even higher.

Several countries in the Middle East seem to be undergoing or are at the threshold of undergoing the Egyptian experience. States such as Algeria, Tunisia, Syria, and Iraq, which have maintained the reformist-cum-socialist pretensions, have adopted the policy of *infitah*, despite its Egyptian trademark. Apparently these states are not only similar to Egypt in the continuity of their political orders, but also share with Egypt the failure of reforms and the radical past. In addition, they have also experienced rapid urbanization and massive rural migration into the cities, both of which lend strength to Islamic militancy.

The paradoxical phenomena of a persistent political order versus the failure of reforms cries out for an explanation. The interpretation derived from the elite-mass approach sheds little light on the persistence of the political order, for it predicates ruling elite autonomy and ignores the social base of support for the central authority and the limitations such support imposes on the ruling elites. Inevitably, under this approach, the bureaucracy or the party, devoid of its extrasocietal character, becomes an instrument of control. The argument is strengthened by proclaiming the prevalence of a cultural disposition that inculcates blind obedience to authority. In contrast, the second stratum approach takes a step in the right direction by emphasizing the social base of support for the ruling elites.

In Leonard Binder's intepretative scheme based on the second stratum approach, the political formula devised by the military officers who seized power in Egypt in 1952 reflected an alliance with the rural middle class (RMC).[11] In his view, the RMC is a class of locally influential landowners of moderate means (owners of ten to fifty faddans) who constitute the backbone of the second stratum. Through the medium of the single party, the military oligarchy mobilized the RMC while excluding the outlawed, urban-based, prerevolutionary parties and political movements from participation.[12] Similarly, one could argue that sources of political stability for the Syrian and Iraqi regimes lie in efforts to mobilize the support of the small and middle peasantry through the B'ath Party. In Libya, the People's Bureaus mobilized the supportive elements and excluded the disloyal individuals or persons whose loyalties were suspected.

Parallel to the mobilizational efforts using the single party were the agrarian reforms, whose purposes worked in tandem with the purposes that had motivated the creation of the political apparatus. The reforms were meant to strip the traditionally dominant classes of their economic privileges and to isolate them politically. In Egypt, agrarian reforms were implemented gradually, the landownership ceiling being lowered each time until it reached fifty faddans per individual or one hundred faddans per family. This ceiling was in addition to the famous socialist decrees that deprived the wealthy classes of their huge, urban-based resources.

The Ba'th regime in Syria implemented a much more radical agrarian reform than the one adopted by the Egyptians, although the latter actually implemented the first agrarian reform in the history of Syria in 1958. As pointed out by Ziad Keilany, the Ba'th Party made strenuous efforts to extend its authority into the villages after removing the rural power of the landlords through agrarian reforms. "In fact the land reform program itself was used as a vehicle to establish political linkage extending between the revolutionary elite and the masses in the villages and neighborhoods."[13] The regime of Colonel Qadhafi went to the extreme of refusing to recognize private property, although his extremist outlook was influenced more by the need to deprive the traditionally dominant class and men of the Sanusi order of their economic resources and, consequently, political power than by any egalitarian impulse.

The reforms, however, failed to satisfy the expectations of the peasant masses. On the contrary, the experience of both Syria and Egypt shows a rise in the influence of rich and middle-class peasants. Egypt is a prime example of a country whose agrarian reforms failed to stem the rise of rich and middle-class peasants to positions of influence. To indicate the extent of their influence, Batatu points out that they "control about 62% of the farming area and as high as 80% to 90% of the agricultural machinery. Their position has been further enhanced by the *infitah*, or open door."[14] Keilany, among others, has also shown that the traditional power of the landlords in Syria has persisted, creating a rival power to the peasant unions the Ba'th Party attempted to organize.

How do we explain the failure of these reforms? From the perspective of the elite-mass approach, the reforms failed because of the personal predilections of the rulers themselves, their political orientations, fears, and hesitations, that can be summed up as the "Elite Will." To John Waterbury, the reforms' failures were related to Nasser's own fears and hesitations.

> Nasser refused to use the iron fist, not because of signals from the countries of the core (they abounded) nor because of his class predilections, if he had any. Rather his course was set by his very real unwillingness to sacrifice, as he put it, the present generation for those of the future and to unleash potentially uncontrollable elements of class conflict.[15]

Waterbury, however, leaves unexplained why the rulers would be motivated to wear the egalitarian mask in the first place. If they were autonomous, why would they feel compelled to enact reforms or respond favorably to egalitarian demands? If there were no limits on the autonomy of the ruling elites, why would they retreat from more radical reforms once they initiated them? Finally, why assume that the abandonment of reforms would prevent class alienation and the exacerbation of class conflicts? Is it not more reasonable to assume the exact opposite, that is, that the failure of reforms would increase class alienation and conflicts?

Binder's explanation for the failure of reforms is congruent with his explanation of the attempts of the ruling oligarchy to mobilize RMC support and exclude from participation the prerevolutionary elites. According to his theory, the RMC was like "lucky Pierre, always seems to turn up as a beneficiary of the system."[16] He further points out that as a consequence of the agrarian reforms, "the great absentee landowners who were connected with the palace or with the Wafd were deprived of part of their wealth and most of their political influence, leaving the more traditional rural segment of the second stratum in virtually undisputed dominance."[17] It is not surprising, according to Binder, that the agrarian reforms did not affect landownership below the fifty-faddan limit—the threshold beyond which the interests of the RMC would have been directly affected.

The political significance of the link between political stability and limited agrarian reforms can be more fully appreciated in a situation where the second stratum does not exist. Iran under the Shah came close to resembling such a situation. It has been observed that a rural middle class in Iran was conspicuous by its absence. Furthermore, Iran is the only country in the Middle East that implemented agrarian reforms almost revolutionary in their consequences. A scholar has pointed out that "the two Pahlavi monarchs in Iran gradually broke the power of the tribal chiefs, local notables, the trade and merchant guilds, and eventually of the nationalist politicians who had acted as a bridge between the old politics and the new. This facilitated appeals to an undifferentiated mass, without traditional intermediaries."[18] Because of the agrarian policy adopted by the Shah, resulting in the removal of the traditional landlord class, the Shah was brought face to face with recalcitrant peasants. Thus, his reliance on the bureaucracy as an instrument of control was increased. By contrast, the agrarian reforms in Egypt had the opposite effect. They reversed the phenomenon of landlord absenteeism while consolidating the rural notables who have traditionally acted as mediators between the regime and the peasant mass. Thus, the agrarian reforms in Iran destabilized the countryside and set the stage for the revolutionary upheaval that engulfed the country shortly before the ouster of the Shah, whereas the reformist policies of Nasser produced the opposite effect of stabilizing the countryside and strengthening the power of the state.

The second stratum approach is based on strong empirical evidence, although it lacks a rigorous definition of the relations between the ruling oligarchy and its instrument of rule and of the second stratum itself. A rigorous definition of the second stratum is difficult to achieve because it does not constitute a cohesive class.[19] Although members of the second stratum give the appearance of a homogeneous class by virtue of their traditional outlook and their pervasive local and national influence, they are divided by wide gaps of wealth and prestige. It must be noted that neither the agrarian reforms or the party-bureaucratic penetration of the countryside eliminated the traditionally influential elites who constituted the wealthiest rural strata. In Egypt, the new leadership in the rural areas promoted by the central authorities and the traditional leadership overlap. In Syria, they coexist as rival centers of power, although party leaders are sometimes forced by the exigencies of circumstances to seek compromises with the traditional elites.

Binder's assumptions regarding the intermediary role of the RMC are based on an uncertain gradation of landownership arbitrarily drawn by the Bureau of Statistics.[20] Empirical evidence shows that the traditionally influential elites are highly stratified in terms of property ownership and the amount of influence exerted both at the national and subnational levels. Insofar as Egypt is concerned, the most influential nationally and subnationally are the wealthiest. But this fact does not mean that the small peasant with the proper kinship connections is without influence in his locality. The point here is that the second stratum extends above and below the RMC—the large landowners who were most influential in the prerevolutionary era and the small farmers.

The stratified character of the second stratum permits the ruling elites a flexibility often reflected by their shifting ideological and policy orientations, although a historical review would reveal that the upper stratum or *Kibar al-A'yan* continued to exercise political influence except for brief periods when the ruling elites put on the radical mask.[21] During the Khedival period, the British occupation, and the monarchy, *Kibar al-A'yan* dominated the political system through its intermediary role, as is reflected by the representative institutions, the various parties, and the bureaucracy. Under Nasser, Iliya Harik's study of power relations within a village community under the impact of the center's party-bureaucratic penetration revealed the dynamic nature of the social base of power at the local community level.[22] During the period that preceded the radical trends of the mid-1960s, the rich farmers, who may be regarded as equivalent to Binder's RMC, displaced the traditionally dominant elites who were most closely identified with the ancien régime in the local party and bureaucratic organs. In the radical period that coincided with the Kamshish Affair and lasted until the outbreak of the June War, 1967—the so-called mobilizational period—the rich farmers suffered a setback, while the small farmers rose to positions of influence thanks to the Leadership Groups organized by the central authorities and to the various party organs, whose main aim was to mobilize the small farmers. This change took place at a time when the urban areas were seething with discontent and when the left emerged on the political scene as a counterforce to the underground movements of the Wafd and the Muslim Brotherhood.

The Kamshish Affair was followed by the investigations of the Committee for the Liquidation of Feudalism (HCLF). The latter represented the last stage in the radical attitude of the central authorities toward the rural elites. The Kamshish Affair arose from the killing of Salah Husain Maqlad in April 1966. He was then serving as the local secretary for the propagation of socialism in the village Kamshish in Minufiyya—Lower Egypt. Members of the Fiqqi family, who traditionally dominated village affairs for over a century, were suspected of plotting the murder. Like the majority of rural migrants from Minufiyya, the Maqlads had lost their lands in the village because of economic pressures in the decade preceding the army seizure of power. Salah Maqlad and his wife Shahinda migrated to Alexandria. There they were exposed not only to the travails of city life but also to its alluring ideas. Salah Maqlad's biography renders some intelligibility to the ideologies successive rural generations came to embrace: in the early 1950s as hosts to the ideas of the Muslim Brotherhood, and in the early 1960s as Nasser's foot soldiers on the march to fulfill the socialist imperative. The latter provided the opportunity for Salah Maqlad not only to renew contact with his village but also to challenge the traditional authority of the Fiqqis. He began to expose to the central authorities the various attempts by the Fiqqis to circumvent illegally the agrarian reforms.

Salah Maqlad was killed at a time when the rhetoric about the socialist transformation was most intense. Kamshish itself seemed to have been transformed and on the verge of a revolutionary change. There was a great deal of enthusiasm among the peasants for the future Salah Maqlad vividly described in numerous speeches. He essentially described a future without the oppressive presence of the privileged Fiqqis. But what started as a local conflict ended up becoming a national cause of far-reaching proportions. The Egyptian left was searching for a cause and found it in the death of Salah Maqlad. Nasser appeared to respond to the pressure by ordering the formation of the HCLF. All the institutions of the state—the provincial bureaucracy, the secret police, the army, the party, and the office of the president—became involved in collecting information on the illegal activities of the feudalists. The HCLF included Marshal 'Amer, Vice President 'Ali Sabri, and Minister of the Interior Sha'rawi Gom'a, among other top-ranking elite. Throughout the sixteen agricultural provinces, the HCLF brought charges against the so-called feudalists that led in many cases to banishment from villages, land expropriation, and dismissal from government services.

The question is, What motivates the ruling oligarchy to put on the egalitarian mask? An important element missing in the elite-mass approach is the sociopolitical implications of the social origins of the ruling oligarchy. Egypt shares with Syria, Iraq, and Libya the fact that its ruling elites are drawn from the lower middle classes and generally have appealed to the sentiments and values of their class origins. In fact, the leaders of Syria and Libya come from the most downtrodden classes. In the words of Hanna Batatu, the 'Alawis, from which the Syrian ruling military officers are drawn,

> constituted the most numerous and poorest peasants to the west, south and east of Alawi Mountains. Under the Ottomans, they were abused, reviled, and ground down by exactions, and, on occasion, their women and children were led into captivity and disposed of by sale. Their conditions worsened with the deepening commercialization of agriculture and after the First World War became so deplorable that they developed the practice of selling or hiring out their daughters to affluent townspeople. It is such conditions that drove them to enroll in great numbers in the state armed forces, a fact which eventually was instrumental in their rise to political dominance which they now enjoy.[23]

In Libya, to quote Colonel Mu'amar al-Qadhafi,

> the officers have the conscience to recognize the people's claims better than others. This depends on our origin which is characterized by humbleness. We are not rich people; the parents of the majority of us are living in huts. My parents are still living in a tent near Sirte. The interests we represent are genuinely those of the Libyan people.[24]

Iraq is also no exception to what is apparently a general pattern. Again, according to the numerous documents presented by Hanna Batatus, the ruling officers represent the rise of inferior tribal and small town elements to positions of power.[25]

The Egyptian officers who captured power in 1952, by contrast, did not come from a homogeneous socioeconomic background. Among them were officers who were the sons of the rich *'Umda* class, as, for example, Marshal 'Abdel Hakim 'Amer. Others were closely connected to the landed aristocracy with close associations with the palace, such as 'Ali Sabri. Nevertheless, Nasser and Sadat, the two Egyptian leaders who controlled their country's destiny successively in the last three decades, came from the class of small landowners. It has been pointed out that Nasser's father owned less than five faddans, while Sadat's father owned two and a half faddans. It is not surprising, therefore, that Nasser turned out to be the nemesis of the landed elites and the champion of the downtrodden *fallahin*, or the small and landless peasants.

Social origins, however, do not always explain political behavior. In contrast to Nasser, Sadat showed a preference for Parisian clothes and the easy, luxurious life, with thirty-five resthouses spread around the country. In his late years, Sadat's opulence contrasted sharply with his social origins, which Heikal has described in the *Autumn of Fury*. How do we explain the contradictory behavior of Nasser and Sadat? How do we explain the shifting sociopolitical orientations of the ruling elites, which sharply contradicted the influence social origins might have had on their perceptions of political reality?

A significant consideration missing in both the elite-mass and the second stratum approaches is that of the pressure exerted by the very small farmers and landless peasants. It has generally been assumed that Middle Eastern peasants are politically acquiescent. The image of the peasant as a submissive and conservative individual has not changed since W. Blunt made the following remark, a few years before the British occupation of Egypt in 1882: "In spite of the monstrous oppression of which they are the victims, we have heard no word of revolt, this is not from any superstitious regard for their rulers, for they are without political prejudice, but because revolt is no more in their nature than it is in a flock of sheep."[26]

It has further been assumed that the agrarian reforms were implemented from above and that the peasants played no part in them. Waterbury, for example, conveys the impression that the agrarian reforms had a "tunnel effect" on the peasants, meaning, the accommodation of one stratum of peasants while the rest of the rural population awaited their turn patiently. Waterbury goes further by asserting there has been no sign of peasant involvement in Egyptian political life since 1952.[27] On the other hand, Binder maintains the view that the ruling elites were more keen on keeping the lid on social change than on hotly pursuing egalitarian principles. Egalitarianism was sacrificed in the interest of maintaining the alliance with the RMC.

History, however, conveys a different impression. The peasants have been able to bring pressure upon the ruling elites from time to time, although they failed to change the social order. Peasant rebellions coincided with major historical events, such as the French invasion in 1798, the 'Urabi revolt that led to the British occupation in 1882, and the 1919 revolt for national independence. Finally, the rebellious spirit of the peasants manifested itself in isolated incidents of violence in some villages before and after the army seized power in 1952. It has even been suggested that the limited agrarian reforms carried out in 1952 were to prevent further polarization in the countryside and to stem the revolutionary tide among the peasants.[28] Accumulated evidence thus reveals that the submissiveness of the peasant is only skin-deep and that given circumstances such as a major reshuffling of power at the center, the propensity to rebel may be manifested.[29] Perhaps nowhere in the Middle East has the revolutionary consciousness of the peasant been more revealed than in the Algerian war of independence. It would have been hardly possible for the leaders of the Algerian revolution to persist in a long and protracted struggle against the French colonialists without the support of the Algerian peasantry.[30]

But both the Algerian revolution and the 1919 nationalist revolt in Egypt were turned on and off by the elites. In both instances, the elites turned out to be more conservative than the peasants despite the former's rhetoric about revolutionary change and the egalitarian outlook. Nonetheless, Nasser and the leaders of the Algerian revolution learned that it was difficult to contain the revolutionary impulse of the peasants once they were stirred by the hope of reform.

A crisis of state was reached when the ruling elites were forced to give up the egalitarian outlook in the interest of preserving the stability of the political system by seeking a compromise with the traditional sources of power. As explained by Kalecki in his leftist critique of the Nasserist experiment, the alliance between the ruling elites, on the one hand, and the lower middle classes and the rich farmers, on the other, was not free from the pressures caused by the multiplicity of interests in the society.[31] The problem is more acute in the underdeveloped countries, where the ruling elites are under pressure to increase productivity, raise the level of investments and savings, and, simultaneously, carry out reforms intended to alleviate the conditions of the poor. According to Kalecki, the ruling elites in the initial stage nationalize big business and carry out extensive agrarian reforms, but soon these efforts reach a stage where a contradiction arises between state interests and the requirements of egalitarian development. In the opinion of Kalecki, the regressive phase of state capitalism begins when the contradiction is resolved in favor of the alliance with the traditional elites, at the expense of the majority of the population. In contrast to Kalecki, I use the concept of retraditionalization to refer to the dynamic nature of the relations between crises of development and the stabilizing roles of traditional elites.

The socialist crisis of the Nasserist regime had its origin in 1964 when, due to lack of capital, the regime halted the socialist transformation, whose avowed aims were economic growth and equity. The deepening of the socialist crisis was reflected by the events that followed the defeat during the June War of 1967. The HCLF was dissolved, and all its activities were reversed. The feudalists were allowed to return to their villages, and the ousted officials and local government employees were reinstated.

The new magic formula adopted by President Sadat under the Open Door policy failed to relieve Egypt of her economic and social ills. On the contrary, Egypt seems to have plunged into a worse dependence than ever before. By all accounts, the Open Door policy led to more cumbersome bureaucratic controls, price distortions, and an unbridled appetite for luxury goods that catered to the wealthy and, hence, sharpened the differences between a privileged minority and the majority. On the other hand, welfare and distribution policies suffered a major setback. Very few observers failed to make the connection between the Open Door policy and the Food Riots of January 1977. Thus, the ideological concerns of the regimes of Nasser and Sadat, represented by the polar extremes of egalitarianism and economic growth, clashed at critical historical junctures with social and economic realities.

This work analyzes the circumstances leading to the crises of the state under two opposite political and economic systems: the socialist era under Nasser and the Open Door policy or the *infitah* era under Sadat. I use Kamshish's lopsided social and economic development to explain the origins of these crises and their resolutions. The socioeconomic history of the village Kamshish fits with some of the general trends that have been taking place in the rural areas since the nineteenth century. One of these trends was the emergence of an indigenous but thin stratum of big landowners at the top of the social pyramid. These were mostly government officials, rural notables, and Bedouin Shaykhs who together constituted a new aristocracy that must be distinguished from the nonindigenous elements of Turco-Circassian origins. Secondly, Kamshish reflected another general trend in that landownership played a significant part in the process of social differentiation, both locally and at the national level of institutional representation. Finally, Kamshish showed how incongruent and asymmetrical were the reformist tendencies of the Nasserist regime and the revolutionary expectations of the peasant masses after the overthrow of the monarchy and the implementation of three successive agrarian reforms.

I intend to examine concepts such as ruling elite autonomy, second stratum, retraditionalization and political mobilization, crises of political development, peasant revolution, and Islamic militancy, in light of the interactions between sets of variables, including the ruling elites, the urban bourgeoisie and the professional classes, the lower middle classes and rural migrants, the large landowners, the rural middle class, the small farmers, and the landless peasants. My analysis of the data is based on the following propositions:

1. Ruling elite autonomy is reflected by the absence of cohesive classes and groups able to influence decision-making.
2. The second stratum explains not only sources of political stability and continuity for the existing regime, but also some of the important factors behind the arrested development of competitive urban interests.
3. Relations between the ruling elites and the second stratum are characterized by harmony of interests and by conflicts.

4. Conflicts are generated by pressures from below for social and economic reforms.
5. The second stratum is highly stratified, including the large landowners, the rural middle class, and the small farmers.
6. Retraditionalization through political mobilization of one or more of the above rural classes reflects different stages in the evolution of the political orientations of the ruling class.
7. Crises of political development occur when the responses to egalitarian requirements or, vice versa, when economic and political liberalization come into direct conflict with sources of political stability.
8. The revolutionary attitude of the landless and small peasants is determined not only by consciousness of the need to alter local power relations but also by accessibility to committed and organizing elites. In the absence of the latter, the revolutionary consciousness of the peasants remains isolated and its political impact limited.
9. The Islamic militant phenomenon can be explained by rural migration into provincial cities and major urban centers. Migrants' integration into the traditional left or right of the political spectrum remains an open possibility.

The organization of the data in this manuscript was guided by the principle that the human aspects of the Kamshish Affair must not be sacrificed at the altar of abstract conceptual analysis. The problem I confronted in organizing the data was in keeping a balance between the Kamshish Affair and the wider social and historical picture. It is impossible to make sense of the struggle in Kamshish without first becoming acquainted with the respective roles of the antagonists in the formation of large estates and the opposite act of property fragmentation. These roles are fundamental in the history of landownership and made agrarian reforms inevitable. Furthermore, little can be understood about the internal organization of the local community in Kamshish during the Nasserist period without first sketching in broad details the intricate and complex relations resulting from ideological diffusion and the extension of party-bureaucratic control. Also, the significance of Kamshish might not be fully appreciated unless the formation and the results of the investigations of the Higher Committee for the Liquidation of Feudalism are brought to the attention of the reader. Finally, it is unlikely that one can appreciate or even understand the twists and ironies in which the Kamshish antagonists became involved without fully comprehending the reverses suffered by Nasserism at the hands of Sadat.

Chapter 1 deals with the history of the conflict in Kamshish and the impact the intervention of central authority had on social reforms and land distribution within the village community. The aim of the chapter is to reveal the local response to the diffusion of ideology and party-bureaucratic penetration.

Chapter 2 examines the social origins of the rural upper stratum families and the formation of large estates in the middle of the nineteenth century. It will be observed that, despite the interpenetration of commerce and industry with landed interests, the upper stratum families, unlike the absentee owners, continued to maintain local connections. This distinction is crucial in light of the evolving links between the political order and the traditional order. The chapter further elucidates the widening of the rural gap between a small minority of large landowners and the majority of small and landless peasants. The chapter traces the political ascendancy of the large landowners under the Khedival administration, the British occupation, and the constitutional monarchy. It examines the attitudes of the large landowners toward the political struggle in the capital represented by the king, toward the last vestiges of British presence in Egypt, and toward the Wafd party. The chapter concludes by focusing on the deteriorating conditions of the peasantry and the consequent rural migration to urban areas as preludes to the military coup of 1952.

Chapter 3 focuses on the gradual radicalization trends in the political orientation of the military rulers and the means used to divest the prerevolutionary political elites of their political and economic power. The agrarian reforms, the single-party organization, the left, and the socialist Vanguard are all brought into focus to reveal the gradual unfolding of Nasser's leftward radicalism.

Chapter 4 examines by means of statistical analysis the extent of influence exerted by the rural elite families as revealed by the HCLF investigations. Party, bureaucratic structure, landholdings, and representation in the central institutions are some of the indicators used to measure influence. The formation, the composition, and the means by which the HCLF carried out its investigations, plus the geographical distribution of the families investigated constitute an important part of this chapter.

Chapter 5 focuses on the first symptoms of change in the ideological and political orientations of the ruling elites after the June War defeat in 1967. The beginnings of deradicalization is demonstrated at the regional, national, and subnational levels.

Chapter 6 provides fresh insights into the factional struggle among the ruling elites after Nasser's death, leading to the Corrective Movement in May 1971. The aim of this chapter is to expose the various strategies devised by

Sadat, including the cultivation of elements on the right to combat the Nasserists and the left in general.

Chapter 7 looks at the deNasserization trends by examining the various desequestration laws and their effects on both Nasser's beneficiaries and his erstwhile victims. The aim of the chapter is to reveal how Sadat unwittingly set the stage for the return of the prerevolutionary elites centered around the New Wafd.

Chapter 8 focuses on the exacerbation of social conflicts both at the national and subnational levels. The second trial of Kamshish to condemn those responsible for the tortures committed in 1966, the People's Assembly's hearings on the atrocities committed against the rural elites during the HCLF's investigations, the Food Riots in 1977, and the conflict between landlords and tenants over rent controls are all part of my explanation of the extent and limits of the deradicalization trends.

Chapter 9 traces the developments that led to the emergence and self-dissolution of the New Wafd under government pressure. This discussion is followed by an examination of the factors behind the suppression of the Council of the Bar Association, as part of my general analysis of the general crackdown on secular and religious opposition in September 1981.

Chapter 10 examines the social origins of the Islamic militants responsible for Sadat's assassination and the areas where Islamic militancy found most appeal. My purpose is to show that Islamic militancy lacks institutional mediation, and its integration through mobilization of opposition groups in the traditional left or right of the political spectrum remains a possibility.

Chapter One
Power and Ideology in the
Life of a Local Community

It is difficult to avoid the conclusion that the government was not very interested in pressing for changes at the village level. Rather than exploit the Kamshish affair to create substantial political awareness at the base, the government was still far more concerned with keeping the lid on and with increasing production. No one suggested that the Committee to Liquidate Feudalism accomplished anything of enduring political significance.

Leonard Binder, *In a Moment of Enthusiasm*, 342–43.

There are several versions of how the whole incident was trumped up, perhaps even staged, and that it almost certainly revolved about an unsavory tale of cuckolds and philanderers, including the President's brother. But whatever else it was, it became the pretext for a wholesale settling of accounts.

John Waterbury, *The Egypt of Nasser and Sadat*, 340.

T HE EVENTS IN KAMSHISH in the 1960s assumed dramatic proportions of far-reaching political significance. Many individuals ascended the Kamshish stage to enact their roles before the unsuspecting *fallahin*. It was not apparent then that the whole affair, except for the murder of the peasant leader Salah Husain Maqlad in April 1966, was being stage-managed by the state. The chief villains in the Kamshish drama were the influential members of the Fiqqi family, which had dominated the village for over a century at least. Urban intellectuals, observing the agitations provoked by the murder, declared confidently that the peasants were finally aroused from their deep slumber and were now ready to usher in the brave new world. Then an abrupt change occurred in the central government that gave a new twist to the lives of the individuals on the Kamshish stage. Nasser was replaced by Sadat, a rhetoric about social change gave way to rhetoric about liberalization atmosphere, the villains were transformed into the victims of a re order, while the latter's heroes and heroines assumed the status of misguided and ill-bred peasants who were misled by starry-eyed intellectuals consumed by class hatred.

The Kamshish drama raises two fundamental, theoretical questions: Is it possible to rationally explain historical evolution by examining the ruling class's shifting strategies, which often appear to be arbitrary exercises of power? Conversely, is there ground for interpreting social change in isolation from the irreconcilable interests and feelings found in a local community and from the community's intertwined relations with ruling strategies? The Kamshish drama reveals that strategies of power and parochial interests determine each other, although they appear to be a world apart.

Salah Husain Maqlad was murdered when leading a faction of peasants in response to the socialist rhetoric of the ruling class. He cleverly turned the socialist ideals into an instrument of opposition to fight the last vestiges of power and influence exerted by the Fiqqi family in the village. The ideology diffusing from the center created much confusion in the minds of the peasants, who were divided in their support to Salah Maqlad. The murder was preceded by heated debates and even physical encounters by rival peasant factions. Nonetheless, given the prevailing conditions and the influence of the socialist rhetoric, it was inevitable that suspicion would hang over the heads of the influential faction of the Fiqqi family, not present in the village at the time of the murder. The leftist organs reacted to the murder by reporting in gruesome and vivid details the evils perpetrated by the traditional elites. No one at that time dared challenge the revolutionary claims of the Nasserist regime or question its responsibility for the wide social and economic inequality in the rural areas, as pictured by the intellectual left.

The government responded to the Kamshish Affair by demonstrating its revolutionary sincerity with the formation of the Higher Committee for the Liquidation of Feudalism (HCLF) and its massive witch hunt against traditional influence in hundreds of villages. The investigations lasted for a few months, but most of the HCLF activities were rescinded. After the 1967 June War defeat, the Kamshish Affair appeared to be almost a thing of the past; it evoked some bitter memories only in the minds of those deeply touched by it. The HCLF itself was dissolved after the June War defeat in 1967. Its only traces were the results of its investigations, which largely confirmed the leftist criticism that the revolutionary claims of the ruling class were unsupported by conditions in the countryside.

At first glance, Kamshish is indistinguishable from other Egyptian villages in the Delta. It lies in the heart of Minufiyya or roughly forty miles north of Cairo. But first impressions do not accord with the past history of the village.

There are few Egyptians who do not recall the chain of events set in motion by the murder of Salah Husain Maqlad. The path alongside the canal passing through the village leads to a large open space surrounded on three sides by mud houses. At my visit to Kamshish, a few peasants were huddled together there, seemingly oblivious of my presence. At the far end of the yard, separated from us by a new, six-foot-high wall, stood a dilapidated but imposing building reminiscent of the palaces the provincial elites built around the turn of the century. Behind the wall I could catch glimpses of modern houses, hidden behind thick orchards.

The villagers could no longer contain their curiosity and hesitantly approached me to ask if I needed help. I pointed to the mansion and asked if it belonged to the Fiqqi family. One of the village elders remarked that indeed it did during feudal times; however, after pondering my question for a while, he added there was a good reason to believe those times had returned. President Sadat, a villager explained, liquidated all the socialist gains achieved by his predecessor. In subdued voices and with sad expressions on their faces, the villagers recounted the gradual steps by which Sadat—who happened to come from the next village—reversed the socialist trends.

I learned from peasants and unrepentant socialists, from the rural elites subjected to the HCLF's investigations, and from those directly involved in the investigation of the murder of Salah Husain Maqlad that social reality is seen through several prisms, all conflicting with each other. Nearly fourteen years after the Kamshish Affair erupted on the national scene, the main antagonists continue to believe in the justice of their causes, and alternately praise or condemn the ruler's interference in their affairs. The peasants echoed the sentiments of a bygone era when redistribution had such an alluring appeal, inevitably drawing them close to the ruler. But although the sentiment of the past overwhelmed their minds, they were also afraid of deradicalization, symbolized by the wall opposite which they stood, and its effects on their "socialist inheritance." The leading figure among the peasants of Kamshish remains Shahinda, the widow of Salah Husain Maqlad. She has survived Sadat's witch hunt against Marxists and former communists and now occupies the post of secretary of Peasant Affairs in the Nationalist Progressive Unionist Party—a minority party consisting of the survivors of the socialist path and those once misled into the belief that the struggle in Kamshish reflected a much-heralded class struggle.

The restoration did not even produce a happy ending for the traditionally influential elites, because nothing could heal their wounded pride or mitigate the sense of loss resulting from property dispossession. I met Aziz al-Fiqqi at his home in what was once an upper-class section of Cairo. He was polite and hospitable, and his general appearance exuded an aristocratic bearing in remarkable contrast to that of the humble peasants dominated by his ancestors for over a century. Some efforts were made by Sadat to assuage the feelings of the influential *A'yan* through undermining his leftist political rivals. But his power was not potent enough to wipe out the memory of tortures perpetrated by the military and security forces during the HCLF's investigations or to take away from the beneficiaries all they had come to regard as their own.

The cast of characters in the Kamshish drama also included members of the HCLF, who were responsible for selecting and prosecuting the influential *A'yan*. Most of the HCLF's members, however, are now in prison, dead, or in permanent exile. Nevertheless, I was fortunate enough to secure several interviews with Muhammad Abdel Fattah Abu al-Fadl, the key person in the investigation of, first, the Kamshish Affair and, then, the rural elite families in all the agricultural provinces. During these investigations, he was serving as the secretary of membership affairs in the Arab Socialist Union (ASU). He was chosen for this post because of his wide experience in all matters related to intelligence gathering. This is not surprising since his last post was as deputy director of the Bureau of Intelligence. His major responsibility in the ASU was to keep close watch over the activities of members and to report directly to Nasser on urgent matters. This charge may explain why he was the first among officials of the central government to arrive at the murder scene in Kamshish. As a member of the HCLF, a major responsibility that devolved upon Abu al-Fadl was to investigate violations of the agrarian reforms by the landed elites. For all these reasons, his testimony is valuable for understanding not only the motives behind the murder in Kamshish but also for providing a rare opportunity to observe how the bureaucracy attempted to cope with the demands for social change. The not too surprising discovery is that this bureaucracy had a different conception about how to bring about social change than the one upheld by Marxists and communists. Abu al-Fadl was keen to impress upon me that he was neither a communist nor a Marxist. Nonetheless, he carried out his duties because he believed in the socialist brand advocated by Nasser and embodied as a general principle by the ASU. It is useful to remember that class struggle was not part of the official doctrine when socialism became the new gospel of the political order.

Is it possible to impart some coherence to social reality when its constituent elements are so far apart from each other, not only by irreconcilable interests but also by diametrically opposed conceptions of that reality? The question is further complicated by the ambivalence of the rulers themselves, as was evident in their constantly shifting strategies while in pursuit of power. The Kamshish drama shows that the only possibility for achieving some clarity in presenting events, with all their paradoxes and ambiguities, is to consign them to their historical contexts, but without losing sight of the fact that they are part of a continuity reflected in the biographies of the individuals we are about to discuss in detail. A simplified procedure is to present the Kamshish drama in chronological order, but this method would risk elimination of the twilight zones that defy any classificatory scheme.

The first act in the Kamshish drama has no definable beginning, since the dualism of oppression and subjection is as ancient as the land itself. A useful beginning, however, can be found in the emergence of private property in the second half of the nineteenth century. With this act, the individuals marked by the distinction of property or by the absence of it make their appearance on the landscape of history. The concentration of property in only a few hands and its fragmentation into the hands of the majority is the major theme behind the struggle for privilege or for simple existence. The second act opens with the military seizure of power, armed by the will to change the social order. But the expressed will appears to be less constitutive of a new reality than as a reaction to the train of events which appeared to upset social hierarchies in the local community. The third act signals a shift from a reactive will to a constitutive will, reflected in the discovery of the socialist "truth." This transformation in the ruling elite coincides with the Kamshish murder. The peasants come to occupy center stage, and the influential *A'yan* give the illusionary appearance of making their final exit. The fourth act reveals a much chastised ruler, who attempts to revert to the old tactics of power consolidation after a massive defeat in the 1967 June War and in response to the irrepressible demands raised by both supporters and enemies of the regime. In the fifth and final act, the Kamshish drama becomes an illusion for repentant adherents of the socialist order, a symbol of infamy to its embittered victims, and a source of betrayal for those foolish enough to believe and trust.

THE FIRST ACT: LAND AND LOCAL POWER

The root of all evil is not private property but its concentration into few hands. This lesson is the first one derived from Kamshish. The origins of the large estate of the Fiqqis in Kamshish and those in surrounding villages can be traced to the second half of the nineteenth century, when private property became an established right. Before then, an ancestor controlled an *'Iltizam* (tax farming), granted during Muhammad 'Ali's reign (1805–1848), that, as in the case of many of the *Kibar al-A'yan* families, was one of the major sources of local differentiation.[1] The ancestor who became the focus of attention during the Kamshish Affair was al-Sayyid al-Kabir (the great), a graduate of al-Azhar who rose to political prominence upon his election to the Chamber of Consultative Deputies, the Majlis Shura al-Nuwwab (1870–1873). Subsequently, he assumed the post of Ma'mur (district commissioner) in Minuf, the capital of Minufiyya before its replacement by Shibin al-Kom.[2]

Al-Sayyid al-Kabir was reelected to the Majlis in 1881, and thus was at the center of the political storm that led to the 'Urabi revolts against Khedive Tawfiq and to the country's occupation by British forces in 1882. I will examine in chapter 2 the central political upheaval and the ambivalent position of the *Kibar-al-A'yan*. Suffice it now to say that, under the impact of the Kamshish Affairs, historians tended to exaggerate the betrayal of nationalist causes at the hands of the opulent rural notables.[3] Barakat, for example, singles out al-Sayyid al-Fiqqi, the *'Umda* of Kamshish, and Ahmad 'Abdel Ghaffar, the *'Umda* of Tila, for the role they played in the defeat of the nationalist cause by the British forces.[4]

The betrayal of 'Urabi by *Kibar Al-A'yan* was highlighted by the press during the Kamshish Affair in 1966. Historical data was unearthed to show how deeply embedded was the reactionary feelings within the notable families. One writer, for example, published an article in *al-Musawwar* supported by photostatic pictures of pages from 'Urabi's memoirs exposing the persons responsible for his defeat.[5] Another source remarked that al-Sayyid al-Kabir, along with a number of rural notables, moved about in the rural areas calling on peasants to put down their arms and to rally behind the Khedive.[6] The apparent improvement in the political position of al-Sayyid al-Kabir under the British occupation added fuel to the later wholesale condemnation of the Fiqqis. He became one of forty six deputies elected to the General Assembly, which replaced the Majlis Shura al-Nuwwab between 1885–1889, as part of the British policy to encourage the participation of the largest landowners. Most historians agree that this assembly was composed of the wealthiest representatives of the rural notables. Revisionist historians, however, maintain that the largest landowners acquired these large amounts of land because of their reactionary role. For example, it has been pointed out that in return for his betrayal of 'Urabi, al-Sayyid al-Kabir "received large amounts of land from the Mudir (governor) of Minufiyya."[7]

The inheritance records show that al-Sayyid al-Kabir left 1375 faddans (roughly two-thirds of the *zimam* of Kamshish). This estate was divided among his descendants (see Figure 1) in accordance with the Islamic laws of inheritance. The male descendants received 171 faddans, and the daughters and wives received 85 faddans each. The records further show that Abdullah, one of the three sons of al-Sayyid al-Kabir, left upon his death 116 faddans, which were divided equally between his two sons — Sayyid and Ahmad. Thus it can be assumed that the Fiqqis were destined to join the ranks of small owners through

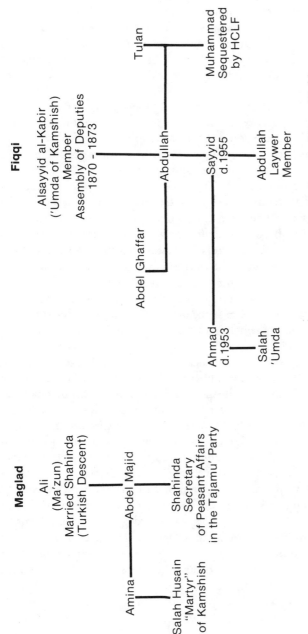

Figure 1. Abridged Genealogies of the Fiqqi and the Maglad families.

1. Abridged Geneologies of the Fiqqis and the Maqlads.

intergenerational division of lands as a result of the Islamic inheritance laws. This land division would be tantamount to loss of political and administrative privileges, which went hand in hand with the amount of land rural notables had at their disposal. The pattern of property fragmentation among the Fiqqis, however, was reversed in the mid-1930s. Both Sayyid and Ahmad emerged as large landowners and unchallenged masters of the villages in which they had extensive property.

The reason for the countervailing effects of property fragmentation is fairly clear. The cotton-growing areas in the mid-1930s bore the brunt of the Great Depression, but the medium and small owners suffered most and were forced to dispose of their meager holdings. In contrast, the fortunes of the Fiqqis took an upward swing, as reflected in the considerable expansion of their landholdings. Ahmad consolidated his hold over the *'Umda* post in Kamshish, while his landholdings amounted to one-third of the village *Zimam* or 735 faddans in accordance with the property division carried out by family members in 1947.[8] Sayyid's landholdings were as impressive as those of his brother. As of 1947, his holdings amounted to 700 faddans scattered throughout Minufiyya. According to one source, most of the expansion was carried out at the expense of middle and small farmers, who were driven by indebtedness into selling their holdings.[9] One of these families was the Maqlads, whose descendant Salah Husain was depicted in 1966 as the hero of Kamshish. At the time of the incident, though, it was not widely known that the hostility between the Fiqqis and the Maqlads laid deeply rooted in history.

In keeping with the social manners and habits of the wealthy rural elites, al-Sayyid al-Kabir took as his lawfully wedded wife a woman of Turkish descent.[10] Her name was Shahinda (she should not be confused with her namesake and granddaughter who became famous during the 1960s). After Sayyid's death, Shahinda married Shayk 'Ali Maqlad who was the son of the village Ma'zun—a respectable local dignitary whose religious and social duties included officiating at wedding ceremonies. Because of his marriage to Shahinda, 'Ali Maqlad suddenly became a relatively rich landlord, since he came to control his wife's share of the inheritance from her former husband's estate. The conflict with the Fiqqi family began when the latter contested Shahinda's share on the grounds that her marriage had been annulled by their father. According to one source, the inheritors produced a "forged document" to prove that Shahinda was divorced by their father and therefore not entitled to possess the land now under the control of the Maqlads.[11] But the courts upheld Shahinda's right to her share of the inheritance.

The seeds of discord, however, had been sown, so that relations between descendants on both sides broke into open hostility two generations later. In the meantime, the property 'Ali Maqlad acquired through marriage was divided into small parcels among his thirteen children. During the 1930s, most of these parcels reverted to the control of the original owners—the Fiqqis. Under the harsh economic conditions of the depression, some of the medium and small farmers were reduced to the ranks of landless peasants. A large number of destitute peasants, including the Maqlads, emigrated to Cairo and Alexandria, where the fortunate ones found jobs in the government bureaucracy and in the army and police. But the pull of the land, even if only a memory, was strong. Such feelings certainly stayed with Salah Hasain Maqlad, who continued to nurse bitter feelings against the Fiqqis even though he had emigrated to Alexandria. It is not surprising, then, that when the army seized power in 1952, Salah Husain Maqlad and his wife Shahinda—named after her Turkish ancestor—became the principal organizers of the Kamshish peasants against the Fiqqis.

These peasants had less personal grievances against the Fiqqis than the Maqlads.[12] Nonetheless, their feelings are important for understanding why they resorted to violence when misled into thinking the army officers seized power in 1952 with the main objective of bringing about a revolutionary transformation in the countryside. One grievance was the Fiqqis' control of the agricultural cooperatives, established in the village in 1936. The cooperative was meant to provide credit to small owners as well as to supply seeds and fertilizer. Through their control of the agricultural cooperative, however, the Fiqqis were able to exert pressure on any small owner who resisted their demands. The Fiqqis often resorted to the Muqabala (exchange of land) practice, whereby farmers were forced to exchange good quality land with whatever land the Fiqqis chose, which was often of poor quality. Occasionally, as some peasants claimed, they were forced to sell. The Fiqqis were able to exert such pressure because they were fully backed by family members occupying key posts in the provincial government. Furthermore, peasants complained that although forced labor (corveé) was officially abolished, the Fiqqis continued to demand free labor on family estates through their control of the *'Umda* post in the village. Another major irritation for farmers was the Fiqqis control over the canal that brought water to the village. Because of this control, peasants and farmers were completely at the mercy of the Fiqqis. It is no wonder, then, that as soon as they heard that army officers had seized power and overthrown the monarchy, the peasants began to prepare for deliverance from the Fiqqis' control.

ACT II: THE UNFULFILLED PROMISE

The checkered political career of Salah Husain Maqlad leads us to conclude that strategies of power and mass ideology do not always change symmetrically. Salah Husain started his political career as a member of the Muslim Brotherhood and died as the socialist advocate for his village. In between, he was repeatedly imprisoned or banished from the village, until considerations of power began to coincide fitfully with parochial concerns. These events, however, came much later and only when the Nasserist regime began to take a critical look at its own traditional basis of support. Let us take one step at a time.

Like most rural migrants in the urban sprawl, Salah Husain was exposed to confusing ideological signals from different directions. The Muslim Brotherhood was asking for volunteers in the early 1950s to join the holy struggle against the newly created state of Israel. The testimony of Abu al-Fadl states that Salah Husain sold his gold-plated Qur'an to buy passage to Palestine, although his affiliation to the Muslim Brotherhood was omitted in this testimony because, by that time, he was already a socialist martyr.

Salah Husain turned his attention from the holy crusade under the banner of the Muslim Brotherhood to the crusade against the landed elites when the Revolutionary Command Council of the military regime announced the enactment of agrarian reforms. In the rush of enthusiasm that followed the announcement, there was little questioning about whether the military regime had seized power in the name of the workers and peasants. Nor did Salah Husain have any apprehensions about his previous political affiliation, since the army officers themselves avidly sought membership in the Muslim Brotherhood and even made some effort to offer them a share in the power. Who could predict the temporary nature of the alliances forged under the pressure of power consolidation?

The first peasant rebellion in Kamshish coincided with the announcement of agrarian reforms in September 1952. Salah Husain reacted by declaring to a gathering of the *fallahin* that the army movement on 23 July represented the revolution of the peasants and that usurped lands would soon be restored to its rightful owners. He appealed to them to "refuse forced labor (*Sukhra*) and to live freely on their lands."[13]

The first violent confrontation between the Fiqqis and peasants led by Salah Husain took place in January 1953.[14] The reason for the confrontation was the canal the Fiqqis had dug across lands some small farmers claimed as their own. During his attack on the canal, Salah Husain was confronted by the Fiqqis and their armed guards. Sixteen persons, including several women, died as a result of the clashes. Security forces from the district arrived on the scene and arrested Salah Husain along with other participants in the clashes. Salah Husain, however, was released the next day upon the arrival of the public prosecutor to investigate the causes of the dispute. After lengthy deliberations, Salah al-Fiqqi persuaded the committee set up by the public prosecutor that the lands through which the canal passed belonged to his family.[15] However valid the claims of the Fiqqis, this outcome was the first shock in a series of disappointments the small farmers and peasants began to experience with a regime that claimed to be revolutionary.

The next confrontation took place in June 1953 over the Fiqqis' monopoly over water resources in the village. Some peasants, armed with shovels and pick axes, decided to let the water flow through a canal controlled by the Fiqqis. The site of the dam was protected by armed guards, who fled as soon as they saw peasants advancing towards them. The discomfiture of the armed guards sent a wave of jubilation among the peasants led by Salah Husain. The Fiqqis retaliated by hiring Bedouins from Manfalut and other outlying desert areas to protect their property. The presence of outside elements sparked yet another violent confrontation. Once again, Salah Husain led another attack on the Bedouin guards, which resulted in the death of two guards while those remaining fled from the village. Security forces arrived on the scene and immediately imposed a curfew.[16] Salah Husain was ordered to leave the village. His place of residence was restricted to Shibin al-Kom by a military order issued in November 1953. Following the crackdown on the Muslim Brotherhood in March 1954, Salah Husain was detained between November 1954 and February 1956 by a military on suspicion of belonging to the dissolved Muslim Brotherhood. He was also placed on the list of political disenfranchisement (*al-'Azl al-Siyyasi*),[17] which remained in force until November 1965. The leadership of the discontented peasants passed on to his cousin and wife Shahinda.

The rebellious peasants were very disappointed that the agrarian reforms did not affect property distribution in the village. In response to the reforms, both Ahmad and Sayyid Abdullah al-Fiqqi had submitted depositions to the Bureau of Agrarian Reforms indicating that each possessed only 250 faddans.[18] They also indicated that the 50 faddans each held in excess of the limit set by law would be disposed of by selling them to their children, in accordance with the agrarian reform law. The law did not limit ownership by the family unit; therefore, any property bequeathed to a family member before 1941 was not subject to expropriation if the possessor owned less than 200 faddans. Sayyid and Ahmad showed testaments dated 1923 and 1931 proving that more than 200 faddans had already been bequeathed to their children. The authenticity of the testaments was disputed by peasants, but, for the time being, the Fiqqis convinced the authorities that the property had been divided among family members long before the adoption of the agrarian reforms. Following the submission of the despositions, an inspector from the Department of Land Survey studied the claims and attested to their validity.

Thus, the gap between the Fiqqis and the peasants in their village persisted despite the agrarian reforms. An additional source of friction included frequent peasant allegations that the Fiqqis were not complying with rent control. The law fixed rental rates at seven times the tax rate. It was alleged that the Fiqqis were flouting rent controls by charging much more. In fact, some peasants charged that the Fiqqis forced them to sign blank promissory notes to keep them under perpetual debt.

Most distressing to peasants was that traditional authority in the village did not change with the death of Ahmad al-Fiqqi, the *'Umda* of the village. His son, Salah al-Fiqqi, succeeded him in February 1953. Complaints and protests were sent to the authorities at the district level and at the central government. According to one source, all complaints fell on deaf ears because the Fiqqis were protected by their connections in the provincial bureaucracy.[19]

Nonetheless, because of the recurrent clashes, the *'Umda* post was abolished and replaced by a police station in May 1955. Salah al-Fiqqi was also politically disenfranchized. It thus appeared that the military government had stamped out the causes of violence in the village by politically isolating the main figures in the conflict. There was nothing to disturb the calmness that prevailed in the village until the Nasserist regime called for general elections to the committees of the National Union (NU), which replaced the Liberation Rally as the country's single political organization.

In the brief period during which the NU was established, Nasser had emerged as the undisputed leader. He was at the height of his prestige both at home and abroad. Internationally, he won a great political victory over Britain, France, and Israel after their invasion of Egypt and the withdrawal of their troops under strong American pressure. Nasser's prestige was further enhanced when he successfully united his country with Syria in 1958. At home, Nasser consolidated his hold over the government and over the RCC officers who had participated in the overthrow of the monarchy. Power strategies dictated the mobilization through the NU supportive urban and rural populations as the regime's answer to the problem of participaton. There was no reason to suspect that the needs and aspirations of peasants and lower urban classes were anything but identical with the purposes and objectives by which the NU was cast. In due course, however, a major discrepancy began to surface between the peasants' perception of the NU's role and how it was defined by the authorities at the center.

Peasant participation in the NU elections was motivated by the desire to use local committees as transmission belts to communicate their demands upward to the authorities.[20] These demands included control of local agricultural cooperatives by small farmers, the establishment of a union for agricultural workers, and the formation of health clinics in the villages. The Kamshish peasants further demanded the reconstruction of a linen factory, allegedly burned down by the Fiqqis because it was draining much needed workers for picking cotton and was hiking wages due to labor shortages during the harvest season.[21] The main reason for joining the NU and for participating in the elections of the local committee of ten, however, was the compelling desire to use the NU as a vehicle to pass information to the authorities about persons who contravened the agrarian reforms either by not declaring lands in their possession in excess of the ceiling or by violating rent controls.

Shahinda's political career in the village began during the preparations for the NU elections. On the eve of the elections to the local NU committee, Shahinda gathered the peasants for an election sit-in. According to one source, district officers and security men came to the village to keep an eye on the elections and to prevent electoral tension from escalating into armed conflict.[22] It was reported that security officers detained Shahinda briefly on charges of intimidating the *fallahin*. In the meantime, representatives of the authorities at the district capital made frequent calls at the home of the Fiqqis to demonstrate their support. The result of the election was an equal division of the ten committee seats between the opposing sides. The five seats won by the Fiqqis were attributed less to the votes of the villagers than to the extensive control of the big landowners over the police and provincial administration. Shahinda, however, made history with her election to the NU committee.

The NU was used to vent local grievances from the moment it was constituted. This method of appeal to the authorities appeared to be more effective than individual attempts to bring local problems to the notice of the authorities. Earlier, the Ministry of Agrarian Reforms had received a complaint from Salah Husain in which he alleged the Fiqqis held land in excess of the limits stipulated by the 1952 agrarian reform law. In response, the ministry formed a committee comprised of officials from the Department of Expropriation, the Land Survey Department, and local officials in Shibin al-Kom. The committee established that there were no grounds for the complaints submitted by Salah Husain. The issue was shelved on the recommendation of the committee. It was revived, however, at the first National Conference of the National Union, held in Shibin al-Kom and attended by representatives of the central authorities, including the minister of agrarian reforms. At this conference, Shahinda declared that the Fiqqis were violating the first agrarian reforms, since Ahmad and Sayyid each held lands amounting to 800 faddans. Once again a committee was formed headed by a new chairman, who was zealous enough to conduct on the spot investigations assisted by the *'Umdas* in the area. The committtee disclosed in a memorandum submitted to the Department of Expropriation that the Fiqqis held 350 faddans in excess of what had been reported by Ahmad and Sayyid in 1952. The Department of Expropriation, however, did not proceed to requisition the land, since the inheritors held testamentary rights to it that fell outside the enforcement of the 1952 agrarian reform law. The peasants disputed these rights and claimed they were based on forged documents. There could be no conclusive decision, therefore, in whether the Fiqqis had contravened the agrarian reforms until a decision could be made by the legal department on the authenticity of the documents. In the meantime, the chairman of the committee who discovered the amount of land in excess was taken off the case.

ACT III: THE RULER AS A BENEFACTOR

A sudden transformation took place in Kamshish when its inhabitants came under the influence of socialism. However, the new ideology exacerbated social divisions, not only because it could take on different meanings for competing parochial concerns but also because official goals and local interests were often at odds with each other. Nasser discovered the socialist "truth" when he suffered a heightened sense of insecurity because of the Syrian secession and his fear of bourgeois reaction in 1961. Thus the radical steps he took against traditional landed elites in the same year were stimulated by external factors. At any rate, Nasser's socialist measures and his avowed intention to reorganize the party apparatus in order to eliminate bourgeois influence were cast in the name of peasants and workers. The Arab Socialist Union (ASU) replaced the NU with a brand new doctrine, which advocated the alliance of the classes interested in preserving the revolutionary order. Naturally peasants and workers headed the list, while only the "nonexploiting" national bourgeoisie would be tolerated. At this stage in the evolutionary radicalization of Nasser's position, property sequestration was used in addition to agrarian reforms as means to limit the economic power of the landed bourgeoisie. Nasser's socialist rhetoric left no doubt that the traditional order was on its way out, at least, such was how the situation appeared when Kamshish came under the impact of the constitutive will of the central authority.

The Fiqqis' property was put under sequestration in 1961, and the land discovered to be in excess of the limits set by the agrarian reform laws was seized and distributed among small farmers. The family was ordered out of the village and its place of residence was restricted to Alexandria. The family's ancestral home—known locally as the palace—was left empty. Some of the less well-to-do Fiqqis remained in the village, including Muhammad al-Fiqqi whose property remained largely intact until 1966. The net effect of land redistribution was its parcellization into small holdings controlled by the small farmers. Table 1 shows that a high proportion of the village land became holdings of one to five faddans. Of 576 small farmers, 200 benefited from the agrarian reforms—or the dispossession of the Fiqqis—and the area they held amounted to four hundred faddans, that is, two faddans on the average per family.

The important conclusion to be drawn from the redistribution of land in Kamshish is that the concentration of large amounts of land in a few hands—the endemic pattern of landownership before the agrarian reforms— apparently vanished. The small landowners who held one to five faddans emerged not only as the most numerous but also as the holders of roughly two-thirds of the village *Zimam*. The position of the small landowners seemed to be assured given their success in bringing the local agricultural cooperative under their control following the election held in 1962. By comparison, the very small landowners, who held less than one faddan, and the landless peasants were not satisfied with the new realities. Their main complaint was that the expropriated land was distributed among the former tenants of the Fiqqis, who managed to expand their holdings at the expense of everyone else.[23]

The changes in land distribution were accompanied by changes in traditional authority relations within the village. We observed earlier that the Fiqqis had lost control over the *'Umda* post and that local authority had come under direct central control with the establishment of a police station. The for-

TABLE 1   Land Distribution in Kamshish in 1966

Categories (in Faddans)	No. (owners)	%	Size[a]	%
(15 maximum)	12	1.3	150	7.8
5 - 10	22	2.4	165	8.7
1 - 5	576	63.3	1440	75.6
<1	300	33.0	150	7.9
TOTALS	910	100.0	1905	100.0

SOURCE: *al-Tali'ah*, September 1966, p. 46.

[a]Based on estimates calculated by taking the average holding per category and multiplying it by the number of owners in each category. The estimate total is 200 faddans short of the actual *Zimam* of the village. Part of the discrepancy can be explained in that not all the Fiqqis' property was parcelled out to small farmers.

mation of a local committee for the ASU did not alter the peasants' perception of the actual source of authority in the village. Most peasants expressed the opinion that the police station rather than the ASU committee was where one ought to defer for resolving local disputes.[24]

The changes in Kamshish during the postsecession era created the illusion that the long struggle of the peasantry against the big landowners had finally come to an end. Kamshish became the model of revolutionary change and an object of curiosity for both true believers and skeptics. The village scene was peaceful, and there was nothing to shatter its tranquility. The election to the ASU committee was held in 1963, which more or less confirmed the new social reality in the village. In March 1965, Nasser and Che Guevara visited Kamshish while on their way to see Sadat at his home in the adjacent village of Mit Abu al-Kom. Shahinda described the visit of the legendary hero from Latin America and his revolutionary comrade, President Nasser: Banners were hoisted and the solemn proclamation that "the revolution of Kamshish greets the leader of the mother revolution" was posted at the village gate. Nasser and Che Guevara were serenaded with folk songs that told the saga of the village struggle against feudalism and how the feudalists tried to isolate the leader from the peasant masses.[25]

Beneath this calm surface, however, there were deep seated divisions among the peasantry, concealed by the tranquility that pervaded the village atmosphere. These divisions coincided with the lifting of restrictions on Salah Husain, allowing him to resume his political activities. The action was the prelude to his murder in April 1966 and the subsequent formation of the HCLF under Marshal 'Amer to eliminate feudalism in the countryside. Let us first trace the checkered political career of Salah Husain.

From the records of the Section for Combating Communism of the General Bureau of Investigation, we learn that Salah Husain was a member of the Muslim Brotherhood and was placed under house confinement in November 1953. He was arrested by military order in November 1954 and was released in February 1956. He was also arrested in September 1965 and released in the same month. The last record of arrest was related to the discovery of a Muslim Brotherhood plot to assassinate President Nasser. Salah Husain was fully rehabilitated by the end of the year, as is evident by his resumption of political activity as a socialist *Da'ya* (proselytizer). The official use of the word *Da'ya* shows the irony in Salah Husain's new role in light of his political past. It further reveals a source of confusion in the language, meant to express the new social reality.

The Ideological Affairs Committee of the ASU to which Salah Husain belonged apparently came to life upon the sudden arrival at the village of the exiled Fiqqis on the occasion of the death of a close relative. The occasion left the peasants who had benefited from the misfortunes of the Fiqqis deeply anxious. Salah Husain expressed this anxiety in a letter addressed to Abu al-Fadl, the ASU's secretary for membership affairs, in which he tried to give wide social and political significance to a local problem and the concerns it had aroused. He pointed out that the "reactionary forces of feudalists and capitalists were acting as fifth columnists for world imperialism and the reactionary forces in the Arab world."[26] He praised the support of the regime for the progressive movements in Yemen, Vietnam, and Cuba, and expressed the view that the biggest challenge to the regime was the unholy alliance between the United States and Saudi Arabia—the two countries impeding the realization of peace in Yemen. (His special reference to Yemen might be related to his attempt to establish his revolutionary credentials, since his brother, an air force major, was killed there.) He also condemned the Muslim Brotherhood because it constituted part of the reactionary alliance, whose objective was to undermine the regime. He ended the letter by reminding the authorites of the rumors feudalists and capitalists were spreading about the terrible fate awaiting the revolution. He warned that the latter were behaving as if its failure was foregone conclusion. He therefore proposed to the authorities that they arrest all feudalists and capitalists and put an end to their ambitions by opening labor camps to make them work as ordinary workers and peasants.

If there was any doubt about Salah Husain's revolutionary credentials, they were completely dispelled by the local ASU committee. In a memorandum dated 21 March 1966, the local ASU Committee informed the ASU's secretary for membership affairs that the feudalists, under cover of mourning, had converged on Kamshish in eight hundred cars from all over the country. They had tried to oppose the activities of the Ideological Affairs Committee by using the same tactics used by reactionary forces in the Arab world, that is, by asserting religious values and authenticity over the adoption of the experiences of other countries (meaning the socialist countries). The committee further alleged that an officer from the secret service, *al-Mabahith*, was present during the funeral to lend support to the feudalists and to intimidate the peasants. The committee called on the authorities to expropriate the deserted mansions of the Fiqqis so they could be used as educational and health facilities. It ended the memorandum by demanding that the exiled Fiqqis not be allowed to return to the village.

The activities of Salah Husain were immediately brought to the attention of the dreaded internal security apparatus (see appendix C). Salah Husain, in a memorandum dated 27 March written by the security director, General Hasan Talaat, to the ASU secretary for membership affairs, was accused of con the minds of the inhabitants of Kamshish. It was stated he was disseminating information that contradicted the official position on socialism, since he was informing peasants that the official version of socialism was influenced by Marxist thoughts. In an earlier memorandum dated 2 March, al-Mabahith had informed the ASU's secretary about the contradictions between the information disseminated by Salah Husain and the official socialist doctrine. This memorandum said that Salah Husain and his associates in Kamshish were calling for the collectivization of agriculture and the abolishment of private property. They were also calling for cooperative farming, following the model adopted by the communist countries. Secondly, according to the memorandum, Husain was maintaining that the socialist ideology in the United Arab Republic was very close to the Marxist ideology and that its recognition of private property was temporarily dictated by the circumstances of the present stage. Al-Mabahith asserted that Salah Husain had formerly been affiliated with the Muslim Brotherhood, which added to the ideological confusion, and informed the ASU's secretary of his record of arrests.

Internal Security expressed concern over the consequences of this paradoxical position of Salah Husain to social harmony in the village community. The 27 March memorandum stated that the activities of Salah Husain created a split in the village. Heated arguments occurred during consciousness-raising seminars, during which opposite camps accused each other of being either communists or reactionaries. As a consequence, the memorandum said, the camp opposing Salah Husain had begun to boycott the seminar under his control. They boycotted the socialist consciousness-raising seminar held on 18 March since it was used by Salah Husain to attack them. It was further stated that Salah Husain's followers were resorting to violence to intimidate their opponents. For instance, Salah Husain allegedly fired a shot from inside one of the houses to scare his opponents. It is interesting to note that, in another brief statement, al-Mabahith stated that Salah Husain and his associates exploited the hatred of village inhabitants for the Fiqqis to draw village youths toward the communist movement. The recommendation of al-Mabahith was to confine the socialist consciousness-raising seminars to the Executive Bureau in the district capital and to the General Secretariat of the Governorate. The Al-Mabahith warned that if Salah Husain was allowed to continue his activities unrestrained the escalation of the conflict would endanger internal security.

On the last day of April, 1966, while returning from Cairo where he had made a strong plea to the authorities at the ASU's Secretariat for Peasant Affairs to confiscate the deserted mansions of the Fiqqis, Salah Husain was shot dead. According to witnesses, the shots were fired during an altercation he was having with villagers opposing him. The killer was apprehended almost immediately.

Thus ended in violent death a checkered political career that would have had no impact on the central authorities had not circumstances converged to arouse the interest of President Nasser and Marshal 'Amer. According to Shahinda, Salah Husain's brother, the major in the air force who had died in Yemen, was a friend and classmate of Husain Abdel Nasser, the President's brother and Marshal 'Amer's son-in-law. Through him, Nasser was promptly informed of the killing in Kamshish. Nasser's personal interest in the murder was behind the prompt despatch of both government officials and 'Amer's dreaded arm of the Military Criminal Investigation to Kamshish.

The ASU's secretary for membership affairs, Muhammad Abu al-Fadl, was among the first to arrive in Kamshish for the investigation. He was ideally suited for rebutting the confusing but deadly indictment for which al-Mabahith was famous. In a long memorandum he personally gave Nasser, Abu al-Fadl rejected the charges levied by al-Mabahith against Salah Husain. We learn from Abu al-Fadl's memorandum that Salah Husain was neither a Muslim Brother nor a communist; rather, he was a nationalist hero who came from a poor family. Despite his poverty, however, he had volunteered to join the fight for the liberation of Palestine, and he was able to do so only after selling his gold-plated Qur'an. Early in his youth, he was shaken by the mighty presence of the reactionary feudalists in the village, represented by the Fiqqi family. The outbreak of the revolution in 1952 offered a glimmer of hope for deliverance from the oppression of feudalism and reactionism. The memorandum continued this saga of heroism by pointing out that, during the Suez Canal crisis of 1956, Salah Husain had raised an army of volunteers to take part in the national struggle against foreign aggression.

Abu al-Fadl further pointed out that the enactment of the reforms strengthened Salah Husain's resolve to work hard for the realization of revolutionary aims. He continued his efforts by organizing peasants to confront the Fiqqis and by exposing some of the deviant elements in the local government. He pursued these aims despite the harassments he encountered because of his alleged connections with the Muslim Brotherhood. The information supplied by him on the attempts of the Fiqqis to circumvent the agrarian reform laws had led to the sequestration of their property and the distribution of 230 faddans among the poor farmers in the village in 1965.

Abu al-Fadl described the final stage in the political career of Salah Husain as a member of the local Ideological Affairs Committee. He praised Husain's effectiveness in attracting peasants to the socialist cause. Abu al-Fadl pointedly remarked, however, that the activities of Salah Husain caused others to accuse him of being a communist, while earlier he had been accused of belonging to the Muslim Brotherhood. Abu al-Fadl added that these charges emanated from the Fiqqis, who influenced "deviant elements in the local government." The last battle Salah Husain had fought against the Fiqqis was his call for the complete liquidation of feudalism. He had requested, through the local ASU committee, the expropriation of the deserted mansions of the Fiqqis.

In the same memorandum Abu al-Fadl praised Shahinda. He wrote that he had seen in Shahinda the heroism of the Egyptian woman. Without bemoaning the death of her husband , she declared she had unflinching faith in the revolutionary struggle to liquidate the reactionaries, not only in Minufiyya, but also in the whole of the United Arab Republic. To complete the picture of the heroic struggle of the family of Salah Husain, Abu al-Fadl reminded the authorities that Husain's brother had already sacrificed his life at the altar of the revolutionary cause in Yemen. The ASU secretary for membership affairs concluded his memorandum by pointing out that the perpetrator of Salah Husain's murder acted under the influence of the Fiqqis, including their head, Salah Ahmad; but, he added as an afterthought, this guilt would be difficult to prove in a court of law.

The government bureaucracy was aroused from its deep slumber and began to act on Salah Husain's previous allegations. In a letter dated 10 May 1966, the director of administrative control (*al-Raqaba al-'Idariyya*) informed the ASU's secretary for membership affairs that officials in the local government had not acted on the information conveyed to them by Salah Husain and Shahinda concerning the violations of agrarian reforms by members of the Fiqqi family. He pointed out that complaints had been received by his office as far back as 1960. The Office of Administrative Control had investigated the complaints and had established the possible existence of collusion between the Fiqqis and officials in the Ministry of Agrarian Reforms. This finding had been submitted in a report to the state prosecutor in July 1961. A copy of the report was sent to the minister of state, Kamal Rif'at, for information and necessary action. The director further pointed out that another complaint had been received from Salah Husain and Shahinda, which had been forwarded in October 1961 to the Ministry of Agrarian Reforms for investigation. But there was no response, despite several reminders in 1962. Somehow, in his efforts to absolve himself, it escaped the notice of the director of administrative control that the Fiqqis' lands were by then under sequestration order.

The most telling effect of the murder of Salah Husain was in the reaction of the Egyptian left. The "real left," as opposed to the pseudo-leftism of 'Ali Sabri and subordinates in the Executive Bureaus, mounted a press campaign that received offical blessings. Two journals in particular, *al-Tali'ah* and *Rose al-Yusif*, poured forth articles and commentaries that described the savagery of the feudalists in lurid details. The tone of the writings gave the impression that the countryside was ripe for radical change, the like of which was never experienced under the Nasserist era. The left appeared to be fully resolved to use the opportunity offered by Kamshish to vent their anger and frustration for the limited role they had played so far. In their view, fundamental obstacles prevented the revolutionary penetration of the countryside, including the continuing presence of the feudalists who, although shorn of their political influence on the national level, still enjoyed local influence. The persistence of their influence was explained by their ability to adapt to new conditions; thus, in the case of the Fiqqis, although their land was sequestered and their place of residence restricted to urban areas, they were quick to establish a dairy farm in Alexandria and to enter into cattle-sharing relationships with their former tenants in Kamshish. The old relationship was maintained through new means of exploitation.[27]

The left further maintained that behind the persistence of local influence despite agrarian reforms was the kinship and friendship between officials in the local government and the feudalists. Some leftists pointed out that violations of agrarian reforms and criminal activities by the feudalists were often reported to the press and to authorities, but no action was taken because of the protective attitude of government officials. Thus, in outlining the lessons of Kamshish, the Marxist intellectuals demonstrated that the influence of feudal families persisted despite the agrarian reforms, the property sequestration of the "landed aristocracy," and the political disenfranchisement of the prerevolutionary party leaders. The historian Mohammad Anis wrote that the death of Salah Husain was "primarily a political event linked to social struggle and to the forces of progress battling the remnants of feudalism. The struggle goes on in many villages the like of Kamshish."[28] The chief editor of *Al-Tali'ah*, Lutfi al-Kholi expressed the optimism that the struggle in Kamshish revealed the emergence of class struggle.

In response to the Kamshish Affair, Nasser ordered the formation of the Higher Committee for the Liquidation of Feudalism (HCLF), composed of the heads of various branches of the government bureaucracy, the ASU, and the military establishment. With this step, Nasser signaled his aversion to any changes except those carried out under state. The formation and composition of the HCLF will be discussed in chapter 4. For the time being, let us remember that, by forming the HCLF, Nasser sustained the illusion that the bureaucracy could be transformed into a revolutionary instrument.

ACT IV: THE LIMITS OF THE RULING ELITE WILL

The paradox between power and ideology revealed itself when the ruling class fell behind the masses it had aroused by its revolutionary rhetoric. The murder of Salah Husain and the subsequent HCLF's investigations against the traditional elites aroused peasant expectations. But, as happens to all chastised leaders, stability and order later assumed a higher priority over change and social violence. The June War defeat in 1967 shattered the confidence of the ruling class and forced them to revert to time-honored strategies of retraditionalization as a bulwark against an uncertain future. The problem confronting Nasser in the post–June War period was how to reverse the socialist trend while coping with the masses who remained insensitive to the new rhetoric of law and order.

Following the killing of Salah Husain, army personnel belonging to the Military Criminal Investigation, the army counterpart of al-Mabahith, took charge of the situation in Kamshish. All suspects, including some of the dependents and distant relatives of the Fiqqis who remained in the village, were subjected to physical torture.[29] Some of the exiled Fiqqis were brought from Alexandria to Shibin al-Kom so that punishment could be meted out to them in front of peasants. After the vengeful spirit of the outraged peasantry was temporarily quenched, some members of the Fiqqi family and suspects continued to be held on various charges including the murder of Salah Husain. In the meantime, Shahinda assumed her husband's mantle. On the recommendation of Abu al-Fadl, allowances were ordered to be paid to her regularly. Moreover, Salah Husain's wish to turn the Fiqqis' palace into the local ASU headquarters was granted. Thus, an ancient struggle between two families unequal in wealth and influence seemed to have ended in favor of the poor and the downtrodden. The peasants, however, were wise enough not to rush to premature conclusions.

As revealed by Shahinda, the local authorities wanted to restrain peasants moved by Salah Husain's death by preventing them from holding a memorial service for Salah Husain at the conclusion of the forty days of mourning.[30] The governor, the director of security and the governorate's ASU secretary made personal pleas to Shahinda to stop the preparation for the traditional memorial service. They even claimed they were acting on orders received from the central authorities. When local officials insisted on their demands, hundreds of villagers decided to converge on Cairo to put pressure on the central authorities. They were halted by the police as the trucks transporting them reached the city outskirts. They were told only a delegation of a few individuals would be allowed to proceed and that the rest must return to their village. One hundred deputies were selected to meet with the authorities. As explained by Shahinda, the large number of deputies was intended as a subterfuge to conceal the identity of the real leaders and also to act as a deterrent if the authorities decided to arrest them. The deputies emerged from the meeting with Marshal 'Amer, 'Ali Sabri, and Shams Badran with the satisfaction of ~~~ ing personally communicated their grievances to the highest authorities. They were permitted to return home and to hold the memorial service for Salah Husain as planned.

The friction between the local government and the Kamshish peasants reached a climax in January 1967 when a protest was organized over the dismissal of the local ASU secretary at the governor's order. Security forces reacted by rounding up the ringleaders, 37 of whom were still in jail when Nasser delivered his speech on Labor Day (1 May 1968) in which he paid tribute to the memory of Salah Husain who fell while resisting the feudalists. One could not mistake the irony in Shahinda's tone when she related this episode to me.

The reverses the Kamshish peasants began to encounter with the central authorities took an ominous twist with the first announcement of property desequestration in July 1967. The announcement was limited to properties put under sequestration as a consequence of the HCLF's investigations — not the properties sequestered in the early 1960s when socialism was still a novelty. Nonetheless, the move was sufficiently alarming to those who had come to believe firmly in the "socialist inheritance."[31] More alarming still was the fact that the desequestration decree was passed on to Sayyid Mar'i, the new minister of agrarian reforms, whose return to power was symbolic of the changes in the political orientations of the ruling class.

The measures undertaken under the desequestration order (by Sayyid Mar'i) affected forty farmers, all of whom were former tenants of Muhammad Abdullah al-Fiqqi — the poor branch of the Fiqqis, as Shahinda liked to refer to him and his children to distinguish them from the opulent Fiqqis whose maternal connections were superior (see Figure 1). Muhammad al-Fiqqi arrived in the village accompanied by a police force to challenge the legitimacy of peasant claims over his land. There was a great deal of ambiguity regarding the status of the land — eighty faddans in all — which was divided into small parcels of two faddans each. Unlike the land distributed after the implementation of the agrarian reform laws, the distribution of land under sequestration did not give the recipient full possession. Nonetheless, under the influence of revolutionary change, the farmers had come to regard the small plots they had received as their own. One can imagine their disappointment when Muhammad al-Fiqqi arrived in the village with an eviction order from a district court. The March 30 Statement of 1968, in which Nasser reiterated the supremacy of laws, added weight to the claims of Muhammad al-Fiqqi and to all claims by individuals who lost their lands because of the activities of the HCLF. His former tenants, however, decided to resist. Muhammad al-Fiqqi was forced to take recourse to law. In the meantime, a new drama began to unfold in the trial of those accused of the murder of Salah Husain.

The trial was delayed until May 1968 because, as alleged by Shahinda, the authorities could not make up their minds whether or not it should be held before a revolutionary court due to the political nature of the crime. She added that it was symptomatic of the times that it was finally decided to let a court concerned with ordinary criminal cases try the case, contrary to the wishes of the majority in Kamshish who wanted the trial to go before a "revolutionary court." Shahinda concluded that the decision of the authorities during the political climate of the postwar period robbed the peasants of the opportunity to dramatize the plight of the victims of feudalism. She did not anticipate a favorable decision because the June War defeat lent strength to the forces seeking to undo the decisions of the HCLF behind the mask of the supremacy of law, as announced in the March 30 Statement.

Twenty-one persons, the majority of whom were small farmers from Kamshish and dependents of the Fiqqis, were tried on a variety of charges, some of which were only indirectly connected with the killing of Salah Husain. Only two of the accused, Salah and Abdullah, belonged to the traditionally influential branch of the Fiqqi family. They were charged with complicity in the murder of Salah Husain and also with bribing government officials in an effort to circumvent the agrarian reform laws. The trial lasted two months, at the end of which all but four of the accused were acquitted. None of the convicted were closely related to the influential branch of the Fiqqi family. The convicted were small farmers, and only one person had any kinship connections with the wealthy Fiqqis. The latter was given a three-year term for illegal possession of arms. Both Salah and Abdullah were acquitted. In his explanation of the court decision, the judge stated that "although circumstantial evidence shows that the peasants of Kamshish suffered for long under the tyrannical and harsh authority of the feudalists in the village, the court in passing its judgment must adhere to the letter of the law. In this case there is no evidence to indict the feudalists."[32] The judge, however, acknowledged that political motives were behind the murder, as was revealed by Muhammad 'Abdel Fattah Abu al-Fadl, the ASU's secretary for membership affairs, who stated unequivocally that "Salah Husain died while exposing the attempts by feudalists to circumvent the agrarian reforms."[33]

The acquittal of the Fiqqis came as a severe shock to Shahinda, although she had sensed the unfavorable change in the political climate at the center. She believed "the Fiqqis should have at least been penalized for possession of arms, for forgeries and bribes to escape from the agrarian reform laws in which government officials themselves were guilty of complicity."[34] Shahinda, however, did not take the court decision passively. She decided to appeal to the higher authorities in Cairo. She met with Sha'rawi Gom'a, to whom she delivered a long letter addressed to Nasser in which she called for a new trial held by a "revolutionary court." Gom'a informed Shahinda that Nasser was a sick man and must not be disturbed, but promised to see to it that justice was done. Looking retrospectively at those unhappy days, Shahinda wistfully remarked that, despite all the pressures upon Nasser to give up championing the small peasant cause, he never ratified the court decision establishing the innocence of the Fiqqis. It was left for Sadat to do precisely what Nasser refused to do.

The peasants of Kamshish were not simply seeking retribution for a murder committed two years before. They were more concerned about their own plight once the exiled Fiqqis were restored to their former privileges and status in the village. Establishing the Fiqqis' innocence was only one step in a process, the ultimate end of which the peasants dreaded most. The return of Muhammad al-Fiqqi with the eviction order in his pocket sent waves of alarm among peasants, for it opened their eyes about what to expect from a regime that apparently had surrendered their cause. They began to mark time.

Muhammad al-Fiqqi's appeal for the eviction of his former tenants now claiming his land was granted by a court in Shibin al-Kom in early 1969.[35] Thus, armed with the eviction order from a higher court and with a contingent from the police force, Muhammad al-Fiqqi once again proceeded to claim his property.

The Kamshish peasants were divided on how to prevent the eviction order from being carried out. The majority favored taking recourse to official channels by appealing to the central authorities to rescind the eviction order. Only a small minority favored resistance if force was applied. The majority prevailed because, as stated by Shahinda, it was impossible to arouse the revolutionary consciousness of peasants resigned to their fate and to Nasser's good will. The beneficiaries felt they would be deprived if they were moved to act in their own interests.

While peasants gathered on the land of Muhammad al-Fiqqi in a show of force, reinforcements from the district capital were brought in to help the local contingent restore order. The confrontation lasted for fifteen days in February 1969. In the meantime, delegations were sent to draw the attention of journalists and writers who had championed the cause of Kamshish in May 1966. The ASU leadership in Cairo was alerted, while a campaign of protest cables addressed to Nasser was launched. Shahinda said that delegations from all over the country came to Kamshish to show solidarity with the peasant cause. Local ASU leaders in Kamshish voted to form a delegation to meet with government and party leaders in Cairo. The delegation met with Minister of the Interior Sha'rawi Gom'a, who was unable to promise anything concrete. The situation was summed up by Shahinda: The regime was weak and vulnerable, while its enemies, the feudal elements, were on the rise. Her remark correctly diagnosed the political situation of the Nasserist regime in its death throes, but failed to convey the meaning behind the rise of the traditionally influential elites. The assumption of power by Sadat left no doubt about the intimate connections between the rising influence of the traditional elites and the quest for political stability.

ACT V: THE RESTORATION

Retraditionalization under Sadat was carried out under the ideology of *infitah* or liberalization. There was no alternative to this course because the socialist path had taxed the ruling elite will, threatened the stability of the political order, and aroused the hostility of the traditionally influential families. It was inevitable, then, that the persecuted would become the persecutors. They represented themselves as the victims of a capricious and arbitrary power and sought justice and retribution for all the pains inflicted upon them in the name of socialism. Sadat, however, soon discovered the limits of deradicalization under pressure from subordinate classes in almost the reverse order of the pressures caused by the socialist transformation.

Shahinda's troubles with the authorities began a few days after the Corrective Movement, wherein Sadat liquidated his so-called socialist rivals centered around 'Ali Sabri in May 1971. The following month, she, along with several peasant leaders, junior officials, and teachers sympathetic to her cause, was ordered out of the village Kamshish. From this point onwards, her place of residence alternated between a small apartment in Alexandria and a prison cell. Nonetheless, over the years she faithfully held memorial services to mark the anniversary of her husband's death to remind villagers of his sacrifices and the socialist past. The authorities often suspected Shahinda was linked to an underground communist organization. She was arrested during a labor strike in Alexandria in January 1975 and was released for lack of evidence. There were occasions when she went into hiding, and she learned how to cope with frequent official harassments.

The restrictions on the Fiqqis were lifted. The mansion, which had become the village school in the socialist era, was handed back to the family, plus one hundred faddans of orchards. But the restoration of this property was not considered satisfactory since the family lost roughly four hundred faddans in land distributed to the *fallahin* in small plots during the early 1960s. The family found the opportunity to press for compensation and redemption of its lost influence when Sadat launched the liberal experiment in a multiparty system in 1976, the success of which was paradoxically dependent upon traditional support. As will be revealed in chapter 8, the reenactment of the Kamshish Affair in a form of trial wherein the prosecuted became the prosecutors was intended to indict the Nasserist regime, expose its cruelties, and publicize the personal tragedies of its victims. It was further intended to give a sense of purpose and resolution to the faltering steps of the Sadat regime along its chosen rightist direction.

The trial of twenty defendants accused of torturing prisoners during the interrogations of suspects in the killing of the socialist Salah Husain was held in a small and crowded room in Cairo.[36] It lasted two years, during which the witnesses described in vivid details all the cruel means used by the interrogators to extract confessions. The majority of the accused belonged to the special branch of the armed forces known as the *al-Mabahith al-Jina'iyya al 'Askariyya* or the Military Criminal Investigations. The leading figure among the accused was retired Colonel Riad Ibrahim, the chief interrogator of the suspects in the killing of Salah Husain. The list also included former army officers, indicted earlier by another court for their part in the torture of members of the Muslim Brotherhood. As many as 120 senior government officials and police officers were called to the witness stand by the public prosecutor. It was like putting the state on trial for its past misdeeds. Shahinda was one of the few witnesses for the defence. On the other side of the aisle sat the plaintiffs, led by the redoubtable members of the Fiqqi family.

On the opening day of the trial, the public prosecutor said that the death of Salah Husain on 30 April 1966 was an ordinary murder exploited by the highest authorities and the left for purely political reasons. One of the witnesses pointed out that the normal course of investigation through the judiciary and the security apparatus was interrupted upon the arrival of retired Colonel Riad Ibrahim in Kamshish, at the head of a force drawn from the military police and with orders from Marshal 'Amer to conduct an on-the-spot investigation to ascertain the motives behind the killing of Salah Husain.

During the trial, it was revealed that Colonel Ibrahim extracted confessions from suspects under duress and that some were then found guilty at the trial held in 1968 for crimes ranging from evasion of the agrarian reforms to duplicity in the killing of Salah Husain. Nevertheless, as told by the public prosecutor, the prevarications surrounding the Kamshish episode had been exposed, since the presiding judge in the same trial declared the innocence of members of the Fiqqi family. The prosecutor added that this disclosure would not have occurred had not the former regime committed itself to the supremacy of laws and political liberalization in the March 30 Statement. Nonetheless, the suspects remained in custody despite their acquittals, and only after Sadat assumed power and launched the Corrective Movement did they gain total freedom.

The tales of torment and torture as told by plaintiffs and their witnesses bore a close resemblance to an exaggerated drama enacted in a medieval torture chamber. Mahmoud 'Issa was a small farmer from Kamshish accused in 1966 of acting as an accomplice in the murder of Salah Husain at the behest of his chief benefactor, Salah al-Fiqqi. He said that three days after the incident, he and the rest of the suspects were brought back to Kamshish from Shibin al-Kom, where they were held in custody. They were beaten with clubs by the military police as soon as they arrived in the village in front of excited and hostile spectators who urged their tormentors to go on beating them. He also said in his testimony that Colonel Ibrahim threatened to molest his wife if he did not confess that Salah Husain's murder was instigated by a member of the Fiqqi family. In fact, his wife was brought in and was ordered to undress. 'Abdel Qadir al-Shazli was Kamshish's Shaykh al-Balad at the time of Salah Husain's murder. He, too, was whipped until his skin was broken in several places. The confession demanded of him was that Salah al-Fiqqi plotted to kill Salah Husain. Several witnesses testified to the means used to extract confessions, including the administration of electrical shocks to the nerve centers of the body and the extraction of fingernails.

Most humiliating for the Fiqqis was the confrontation with Shahinda, the distraught wife of Salah Husain, a meeting Marshal 'Amer's men had forced upon them. According to one testimony, Shahinda was ordered to avenge her husband's death by slapping and spitting in the faces of the suspects.[37] Later, the suspects were put behind bars where, as most of the witnesses testified, they were subjected to constant beatings and even sexual abuse. The attorney of the plaintiffs, Abdel Aziz al-Shourbaji, the president of the Bar Association and a close friend of the Fiqqi family, demanded a compensation payment to the victims amounting to E£350,000. He also demanded that Shahinda and Husain 'Abdel Nasser, President Nasser's brother and the son-in-law of Marshal 'Amer be prosecuted for their part in the tortures. (The president's brother was in Kamshish during the interrogation of the suspects.)

Shahinda's testimony was overwhelmed by the hostile public opinion outside the courtroom, influenced by the innuendoes, hints, and suggestions Mustafa Amin's *al-Akhbar* had spread, particularly about her questionable relations with the president's brother.[38] Mustafa Amin, among other journalists, lost no opportunity under the *infitah* to expose the crimes committed in the name of socialism. Nonetheless, undaunted, she stood before her accusers to say that her husband had led a movement that demanded the fulfillment of peasant rights as recognized by the agrarian reforms, which members of the Fiqqi family had tried to evade.[39] Shahinda reminded the audience, prosecutors, and judges that in 1966 the whole village was calling for the conversion of the Fiqqis' palaces into public facilities to serve peasant needs. She reminded the crowded court that her husband's death sparked a popular demonstration and a general call for the liquidation of feudalism in Egyptian villages. Peasants had then demanded that the murder of her husband be treated as a political matter and that the suspects be tried in the village itself by a revolutionary court. "Except for the timely intervention of the authorities, the suspects would have been liquidated instantly."[40] Further, to dispel the rumors about her relations with the president's brother, Shahinda explained that his presence in the village in May 1966 was to offer condolences to the family, since he was a friend of the deceased. She and others who followed her to the witness stand completely denied any knowledge of tortures carried out against the suspects in the killing of Salah Husain.

Abdel Aziz Shourbaji summed up his case on behalf of the plaintiffs by recalling the evils perpetrated in Kamshish in 1966. He accused Shahinda of turning into a communist agent and an instrument for torturing the inhabitants of Kamshish and of sabotaging the Egyptian system. Another attorney for the plaintiffs called for the demolition of the war prison where his clients had been incarcerated and for erecting in its place a memorial to the injustices committed in the name of socialism.

The defence attorneys rebutted each one of the allegations made by the public prosecutor and the attorneys for the plaintiffs. They rejected the belief earnestly inculcated by senior government officials, including the president himself, that sequestration and confiscation under the agrarian reforms were expressions of Nasser's class hatred, *al-hiqd al-tabaqi*. They reaffirmed the belief that these methods were sound means to protect the majority of peasants against an exploitative minority. It is interesting to note that the defence attorneys invoked the four schools of Islamic laws in defence of Nasser's reforms without mentioning socialism.[41] In the era of *infitah*, socialism had become suspect, and any reference to it was avoided even by word of mouth because it was easily confused with communism and with heretical beliefs.

After long deliberations and a trial that lasted roughly two years, during which all the pent-up emotions for and against the Kamshish Affair were let out, the court committed Colonel Riad Ibrahim to fifteen years of imprisonment at hard labor, and gave prison terms of twenty years to an aide and of five years to eleven defendants. Only three defendants were acquitted. The court further demanded that the convicted individuals, jointly with the former minister of war in his personal capacity, pay compensations to the victims totaling E£ 720,000. The Fiqqis were to receive E£ 420,000 in compensation, and the balance was to be distributed among sixty-three inhabitants of Kamshish. The verdict of the court was echoed in Mustafa Amin's daily column in *al-Akhbar*. He wrote that the final judgment

> of the court recorded for posterity that the period in which the events of this exciting case [the Kamshish Affair] took place was the worst in the long history of Egypt, ancient and modern. During this period human dignity was trampled upon. The court, while recording these events, is overcome by sorrow for what the Egyptian man had to endure: the loss of his liberty, and humanity, the stifling of his potentialities and loss of his security, property and honor.[42]

The verdict as uttered by Mustafa Amin provided the ideological justification for Sadat's political liberalization. It also reflected the convergence of interests between the authority and the traditional influence behind the liberal mask and its outraged morality. During the elections to the People's Assembly, the ruling party won an overwhelming majority thanks to traditional support in the rural areas. By comparison, the die-hard Nasserists, Marxists, and former communists who together had formed the Nationalist Unionist Progressive Party, Tajamu', failed miserably to win the popular vote. Shahinda, who joined the Tajamu' as the party's secretary of the Peasant Affairs Committee, failed to win the elections against the scion of the 'Abdel Ghaffar family—the family that had extensive kinship links with the Fiqqi family and also stood condemned in the eyes of revisionist historians in the 1960s. The cementing of relations between the authority and the traditional elites was symbolized by the marriage ties between Sadat's and 'Abdel Ghaffar families.

The pressures against deradicalization did not subside and reached a climax in the Food Riots of January 1977. Shahinda, together with her comrades in the Tajamu', found themselves either behind prison bars or in hiding. The gathering of the storm against the Sadat regime, however, was stimulated by the unintended consequences of retraditionalization disguised by the liberal mask. Urban protest widened with the resurrection of the Wafd and the Muslim Brotherhood, both of which attempted to show the liberal limits of the *infitah*. Ironically, Abdullah al-Fiqqi, who had just won his case against the tortures of Kamshish, joined in the formation of the Wafd. Islamic militancy also emerged, questioning the seriousness of Sadat's appeal to traditional and Islamic values. Nonetheless, Sadat was still basking in the confidence of traditional support when his security forces made their wide sweep through most urban areas cracking down on urban protesters across the political spectrum and putting their leaders in jails. The Wafd, the Muslim Brotherhood, and a large number of opposition groups and associations were dissolved. Shahinda was arrested, as well as some of her eloquent bourgeois detractors. There were very few detainees who belonged to the *Kibar al-A'yan* families; nonetheless, the sons of two such families — the Zomor and Islambuli — were sufficiently motivated to plot the assassination of Sadat in October 1981, and to set free all the detainees, including Shahinda and her leftist comrades.

For Shahinda, the Kamshish story as yet remains unfinished. She continues to entertain the hope of turning the small farmers and peasants into an autonomous movement able to exert pressure on the authorities. She did not hesitate to form a union of small peasants under the wing of the Tajamu' shortly after her release from prison. The formation of the union was announced in 1983 on the anniversary of her husband's death. It is doubtful, however, that it will receive the official sanction of the Mubarak regime. The Wafd Party and the Muslim Brotherhoood reemerged on the political spectrum, but as urban-based movements with little support in the rural areas. The Mubarak regime has fully reaped the harvest from the seeds implanted by Sadat, for its ruling party enjoys unchallenged mastery over the rural areas.

What can be learned from the local community, which we tend to lose in making generalities and abstractions during an aggregate analysis? It is tempting to say that any separation between national and subnational politics is an illusion. Their links exist in the minds of the rulers, whose strategies of power dictate the promotion of some interests while stifling others. In this long historical description we have seen that the processes of radicalization and retraditionalization are part of the strategy of rule aimed at securing political stability. In both instances, there are limits on how much change is desirable. Nonetheless, neither these strategic shifts nor the ironies and contradictions arising from them can be fully understood or appreciated in isolation from sheer existence, of which studies of the local community can reveal varied meanings and conflicting significance.

Furthermore, strategic shifts demand the diffusion of ideology. Contrary to current belief, the diffusion of ideology does not create a coherent view of the outside world. Local rivalries and ancient prejudices come into full play, twisting and bending the new language to fit parochial concerns and local interests. Nor do strategies of power go unresisted whenever rulers face the difficult task of suppressing the passions they have aroused or of limiting the expectations of those to whom they have appealed. Let us now see whether these conclusions, derived from the study of a local community, can bear the weight of aggregate analysis.

2. Patrol duties to maintain order in Kamshish on 8 August, 1953.

3.   Frontier forces in Kamshish after the curfew imposed on 8 August, 1953.

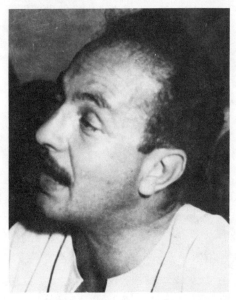

The "Martyr of Kamshish", Salah Husain Maqlad, shortly before his death on 30 April 1966.

5.   The widow of Salah Husain, Shahinda, in a state of mourning.

6.   Confrontation between Shahinda and the accused killers of her husband among the Fiqqi family on 5 May, 1966.

7.   Members of the Fiqqi family, Salah. Aziz and Husam, showing reporters the chains used by the military police to tie them up like animals on 5 May, 1966.

8.   The inhabitants of Kamshish occupying one of the mansions belonging to the Fiqqi family on 29 May, 1966.

9. Court scene during the trial of the accused in the killing of Salah Husain Ma-qlad on 21 May, 1968.

10. Scene from the second trial of Kamshish in which retired officers from the Military Criminal Investigation, "the torturers of Kamshish," are held behind bars on 16 January, 1978.

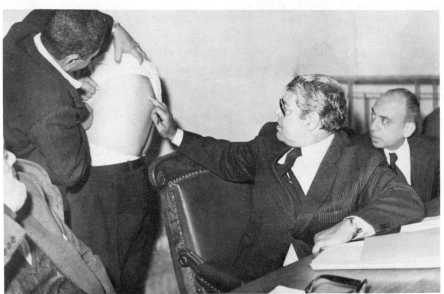

11. The presiding judge over the trial of the "torturers of Kamshish" viewing evidence of tortures inflicted on members of the Fiqqi family on 23 January, 1978.

Chapter Two
The Widening Rural
Gap during the
Prerevolutionary Era

I N THE HEADY ATMOSPHERE of the 1960s, removing all obstacles in the way of equity and social justice became the battle cry of the state and its leftist allies. Only a few individuals asked whether the fulfillment of justice for some would deprive others of inherited or acquired rights. On the contrary, the dominant concern was that the reforms failed to narrow the wide social gap, whose unsettling effects left deep impressions on the rural areas in the decade preceding the army seizure of power and the overthrow of the monarchy in 1952.

The protagonists of social change and the main critics of the existing social order were the Marxists and former communists. Their social criticisms emphasized the persistence of extreme inequalities in the distribution of wealth and influence. Neither regime changes throughout the many generations nor the assumption of power by army officers belonging to rural, lower middle-class origins seemed to alter this social and political reality. The ideological recipe now called for a radical solution to free the peasants from their immediate oppressors.

Causes, however, tend to simplify conflicts and render complex situations less ambiguous. Any existing contradictions and ambiguities that might subvert the ideological premise tend to disappear from political discourse under ideological influences. Intellectuals on the left expected peasant militancy, as manifested in the village Kamshish, to bring about social transformation in the countryside and, consequently, to destroy the traditional basis of the political order. The temptation to link peasant militancy to the revolutionary pretensions of the ruling class proved to be much stronger than the desire to question the paradox inherent in the latter's attempt to undermine the traditional basis of its support. A different outcome would have been expected were the intellectuals in the 1960s inclined to regard the conflict in Kamshish and the subsequent HCLF (The Higher Committee for the Liquidation of Feudalism) investigations as part of a historical pattern, in which peasant militancy was the unintended consequence of the expanding power of the state in conflict with traditional local authority. This chapter tries to reveal this conflict and how its resolution through retraditionalization was effected at critical historical junctures in the interest of preserving the stability of the political order.

THE SOCIAL ORIGINS OF KIBAR AL-A'YAN

Traditional influence at the subnational level was exercised by *Kibar al-A'yan*, the rural upper stratum, from generation to generation. They survived the vicissitudes of autocratic sultans, foreign occupation, and military intervention because their local power and prestige came from internal differentiation within the local community rather than being externally imposed. They must, therefore, be distinguished from the landed elites, whose influence originated at the center, and from the absentee owners, who preferred urban life over drab and dreary existence in the rural areas.[1] Unlike the latter, the resident *Kibar al-A'yan* derived their influence from a hierarchical structure of local authority in which kinship was the dominant factor. The more extensive the kindship connections, the greater the opportunities for expanding traditional influence throughout several generations. Therefore, it is not surprising to note that the evidence turned up by the HCLF showed that the rural elites, whose influence originated in the tribal community or in the most traditional areas in Upper Egypt, were the ones having greater resiliency and adaptability in their relations with the central authority over the last century at least.

The most ubiquitous among the wielders of local influence was the *'Umda* class. Owing to the weakness of the central administration, the rulers of Egypt since Muhammad 'Ali's reign (1805–1848) had relied heavily on the *'Umdas* to collect taxes, reallocate lands among peasants within the village community, maintain order, administer justice, and select individuals to provide compulsory services for road building and constructing canals. Some of these functions were taken away from the *'Umdas* with the expansion of the central authority. During the reign of Viceroy Sa'id (1854–1863), important changes were introduced into the village community that deprived the *'Umdas* of some of their important functions and, consequently, weakened their hold over peasants. They lost important functions such as the periodical reallocation of lands and tax collection, as these functions came directly under the control of the central government. The introduction of private ownership, tenurial system and individual responsiblity in the collection of taxes added further to the erosion of the local power of the *'Umdas*.[2]

The *'Umda* class continued, though, to remain the mainstay of traditional power at the local community level, despite administrative reforms and the expansion of the central authority. 'Ali Pasha Mubarak (1824–1893) described in his late nineteenth-century chronicles, the power and influence of the family that held the *'Umda* post in al-Hawatka (Upper Egypt).

> The family of Abi Mahfuz is famous for many generations. It possesses many properties and cultivates thousands of fertile acres. The village inhabitants are under its control to the extent that the death of a family member causes the whole village to mourn him. No man dared to sleep inside his home, marry or perform circumcision. I perchance a woman became pregnant in that year, she and her husband would suffer.[3]

Mubarak's chronicles reveal that there was no check on traditional authority and that some *'Umdas* became famous for their excessive cruelty against peasants. He also recorded his impressions of another family by the name of Fawaz in a village in Sohag, whose head used to "whip people in the village without rhyme or reason."[4] The British administrative reforms prohibited the use of the *korbaj* (whip) in law enforcement and brought the *'Umdas* under the strict control of district officers. Recent evidence also shows that the *'Umdas* have lost much of their local power and prestige. Nonetheless, opportunities for reversing the decline of traditional authority became available whenever a shift occurred in the balance of forces at the center that required the stabilizing influence of the *'Umda* class. This dependency will become apparent when we examine the impact of the 'Urabi revolt, the 1919 nationalist revolt, and the emergence of a competitive party system under the constitutional monarchy. Suffice it now to say that the local power of the *'Umda* class rose and fell in direct proportion to the expansion and contraction of the central authority.

Opportunities for *Kibar al-A'yan* to exert influence outside local communities were limited, since positions of prestige and influence in the higher ranks of the provincial administration were reserved for the Turco-Circassians. Nevertheless, opportunities for the upward mobility of the indigenous elites improved with the recruitment policy of Muhammad 'Ali. Some of the nineteenth-century *'Umdas* and tribal chieftains were promoted to high positions in the provincial administration, including the post of *Mudir* or provincial governor. During the first years of Khedive Isma'il's reign (1863–1879), a large number of elites belonging to the *'Umda* class were appointed to the highest provincial office of *Mudir*. These elites included Muhammad Sultan, Hasan Shari'i, Muhammad Minshawi, Ayyub Jamal al-Din, and Atrabi Abu al-'Izz. More were appointed between 1869–1871, including Muhammad al-Sairafi, Ahmad al-Sharif, Sulaiman Abaza, Ahmad Mustafa, Hilal, Amir al-Zomor, 'Umar Jami'i, Sulaiman 'Abd al-'Al, Ahmad 'Ali, al-Sayyid Abaza, Muhammad

Hamadi, 'Umar Ahmad, Muhammad al-Shawaribi, Muhammad 'Afifi, and Hamid Abu Satit. However, the Turco-Circassian elements reasserted their hegemony during the turbulent era coinciding with the deposition of Khedive Isma'il and the succession of his son Tawfiq. This event was accompanied by a proportionate decline in the influence of indigenous elites.

The same trends were reflected in the military bureaucracy. The foreign conquests of Muhammad 'Ali as part of his grand ambition to extend Egypt's influence in Africa, the Levant, and the Arabian Peninsula led to the recruitment of a large number of native Egyptians. This policy was discontinued under the reactionary government of Khedive 'Abbas (1848–1854) and was completely reversed in the first year of Khedive Tawfiq's (1879–1892) rule, which provoked the 'Urabi revolt in 1881. Interestingly, in contrast to the provincial administration, the military bureaucracy became the means for the upward mobility of indigenous elites who belonged to rural, lower middle-class origins. 'Urabi himself belonged to such a class — his father owned eight faddans.[5] Despite these reversals, the provincial administration remained one of the main sources of traditional influence for *Kibar al-A'yan*. These rural elites continued to occupy positions of influence, even when recruitment of Egyptians reached its nadir during the turbulent era of Tawfiq.

The majority of the notables appointed to the provincial administration belonged to the class of large landowners. For example, Mubarak observed that the Shawaribi family in Qalub held the *'Umda* post for many generations. Its property included shops, orchards, and a cotton-ginning factory, while its landed property totalled 4,000 faddans, more than half the village *Zimam* or the total acreage belonging to Qalub.[6] Another example was Hamad al-Basil. As pointed out by Barakat, al-Basil, who rose to political prominence during the 1919 revolt, owned 1,200 faddans in Qasr al-Basil in al-Fayyum.[7] Mubarak also wrote about Hamid Abu Satit, a simple fallah who rose during Khedive Isma'il's reign to the position of governor of Sohag and later of Qena. His cultivated lands amounted to 7,000 faddans, apart from 100 faddans of palm tree plantations in various parts of the country.[8] Another example cited by Mubarak was Ahmad 'Ali Abu Krishah, who was appointed Nazir Qism or district officer in Sohag by Muhammad 'Ali. In his estimation, the Abu Krishah family cultivated 16,000 faddans.[9] Gabriel Baer draws our attention to the Abazas while producing evidence to show the strong relationship between landownership and higher administrative and political influence. The Abazas, who held on several occasions spanning at least one century the post of provincial governor, controlled more than 6,000 faddans in fifteen villages in the Sharqiyya province.[10] Sayyid al-Fiqqi, the subject of the controversy during the Kamshish Affair, was a district officer in Minufiyya during the 'Urabi revolt. He owned at that time 1375 faddans or roughly two-thirds of the village *Zimam*.

National prominence for *Kibar al-A'yan* coincided with the transformation of Egyptian agriculture during the reign of Khedive Isma'il. One of the lasting impacts left by Khedive Isma'il's predecessor, Sa'id, was the promulgation of laws whose cumulative effects were reflected in the security the rural notables came to enjoy over land and tenure. Furthermore, the area under cultivation expanded tremendously during this period, stimulated by a capitalist transformation due to the increasing European demand for cotton because of the famine caused by the American Civil War. There is no doubt that Egypt's integration into the world economy was behind the new prosperity of the rural notables. Nonetheless, this development made them dependent on external forces, whose adverse effects were reflected in the vicissitudes of cotton prices on the world market.

The capitalist transformation of Egyptian agriculture left its deepest impact on the provincial cities, to which *Kibar al-A'yan* were drawn in increasing numbers in pursuit of new economic gains. There, the traditionalist lifestyles were displaced by a cosmopolitan outlook. Some of the mansions the *Kibar al-A'yan* built in the provincial cities and even amid the mud houses of the *fallahin* in the villages stand as tangible evidence of the transformation that took place in the second half of the nineteenth century. The cities that attracted the largest landowners were those centrally located and in close proximity to means of transportation. Tanta, for example, attracted the largest landowners due to the centrality of its location in the cotton-producing provinces of Beheira, Daqahliyya, and Minufiyya. As noted by Mubarak, the mansions built in Tanta belonged to individuals who were most prominent in their own provinces, but who converged on Tanta to avail themselves of new economic opportunities.[11] Similar trends led to the emergence of Asyut as the trading and crop-processing center in Upper Egypt.

Proximity to one another in the provincial cities and the consequent social intercourse had a homogenizing effect on *Kibar al-A'yan*. Part of the homogenizing process was determined by the frequency of intermarriages among members of the upper stratum. As can be observed in the case of the Fiqqi family, marriage ties among the rural *A'yan* were widespread, covering almost the entire delta and parts of Upper Egypt. The Fiqqi family had marriage ties with 'Abdel Ghaffar, Abu Hussein, Ghazi, Jundi, Qadi, 'Abdel 'Al, and Bilal in Minufiyya; Hammad, Abu Gazya, Abu Basha, al-Kholi, Sherif, and Nassar in Gharbiyya; 'Issawi and Abu Na'im in Kafr al-Shaykh; Jayyar, Misri, Mahmoud, and Muhanna in Beheira; Atrabi and Hilal in Daqahliyya; Ma'mun in Qalubiyya; Sayyid Jalal in Cairo; Latif in Bani Suwayf; and Abu Hasanain, Makhluf, and 'Attar in Minya. Prosperity enabled the biggest landowners to marry Turkish and Circassian women, especially favored because of their fair complexion and due to the hidden desire to bridge the gulf separating *A'yan* from the ruling class. Thus wealth apparently transcended all barriers and rose the socially inferior native Egyptians to the level of the Turkish aristocracy.

The prevasive practice of maintaining a second residence, either in Cairo or in Alexandria, in addition to fusing large, landed properties with large-scale commerce, industry, transportation, banking, and other branches of the urban economy, produced rampant absenteeism — one of the worst features of the agrarian structure before the army seized power in 1952. But there is also no doubt that, despite the numerous temptations of city life, the rural notables were less inclined to sever links with sources of their traditional authority in the local communities. Only a small proportion of the traditionalists among *Kibar al-A'yan* were content to pocket the surplus from agricultural production and settle down permanently in urban areas. The reason for the majority's attachment to the native soil and to its cultural milieu was the strong correlation between land and local power relations within an extended kinship structure. In the following discussion, we will observe that political factors intervened to offset the effects of urbanism and the forces that tended to weaken the kinship bond.

POLITICIZATION OF THE TRADITIONAL ORDER

The continuity of the parliamentary history of some of the prominent rural elite families since the inception of representative institutions in the second half of the nineteenth century became an issue of major concern during the Kamshish Affair and the investigations of the HCLF in 1966. This continuity resulted from the ongoing interdependence between the political process and the traditional order, which began after the convocation of the first Chamber of Consultative Deputies, Majlis Shura al-Nuwwab, in 1866. Since its institutionalization, parliamentary representation reflected a rural bias. The first Majlis (1866–1870) consisted of seventy delegates, out of whom only five deputies represented Cairo and Alexandria while the majority of the delegates (83 percent) came from the *'Umda* class. The opulent *'Umdas* continued to dominate all subsequent assemblies with little decline in their numbers.

The reorganization of the parliamentary institutions under direct British influence (1882–1922) had negligible effects on the representative character of these institutions. In fact, the colonial power was inclined toward consolidating traditional authority and mobilizing the wealthiest rural strata, as was reflected in the legislative assemblies. The legislative assembly convened in 1913 contained forty-nine large landowners out of a total of sixty-five deputies (76 percent).

The establishment of the constitutional monarchy after Egypt gained her nominal independence from Britain in 1922 further reflected the growing power and influence of the traditional landed elites. The commission responsible for drafting the constitution consisted of eighteen members, eleven (61 percent) of whom were large landowners. Also, the Constituent Assembly, which debated and approved the draft constitution, consisted of twenty large landowners among a total of thirty-two members (62 percent). The clauses in the constitution consolidated traditional influence, as can be observed in the electoral procedure of the Chamber of Deputies, Majlis al-Nuwwab. Deputies were to be elected in two-member districts by majority vote. This procedure favored entrenched local interests with strong local connections. Property qualifications of fifty to sixty faddans or its equivalent of an annual property tax of E£ 30 limited candidacy to *Kibar al-A'yan*.

Property qualifications for the Senate, Majlis al-Shuyukh, were even higher. To qualify, a candidate must pay annual taxes of E£ 150 or possess a minimum of two hundred faddans. The constitutional committee also approved a resolution that allowed candidates to run for elections only in districts in which they were registered. A proposal introduced by an absentee owner that would allow candidates to run for elections in any electoral district was soundly defeated. In the opinion of a resident owner, the Burkean form of representation would have infringed local rights had it been approved. The electoral procedures thus preserved the traditional basis of representative institutions despite the large-scale absenteeism that became most evident in the decade preceding army seizure of power.

Contemporaries and historians question the motives behind Khedive Isma'il's convocation of the first Majlis Shura al-Nuwwab as the official representative body of the Egyptian people. Wilfred Blunt expressed the belief that Isma'il intended to "repudiate his whole debt (to European creditors) and to shelter himself in doing so by proclaiming a constitutional government in Egypt."[12] Schölch, however, maintains there was no compelling reason for Isma'il to convene the Majlis: "Whatever Isma'il granted to his subjects, he granted graciously, not yielding to pressure from below."[13] He consistently argues that the Majlis Shura al-Nuwwab was an appendage of power and its existence was tolerated as long as it suited the purposes of the Khedive. He argues further that the growth in the power of the deputies toward the end of Isma'il's rule, which Rafi'i mistook as a sign of opposition, was the result of coincidence of interests between the Khedive and the rural notables, since both sides were burdened by the intolerable demands imposed by the European powers through their representatives in the "independent" Council of Ministers.[14] Contrary to the argument of Schölch, the power of the *Kibar al-A'yan* toward the close of Isma'il's rule grew in direct proportion to the increasing dependence of Isma'il on the representatives in the Majlis. Isma'il's aim was to reduce the pressure of the European creditors and to repay the debt, which amounted to E£90 million.

The enactment of the Muqabala law in 1871 was one of a number schemes to which Isma'il resorted in order to squeeze the surplus from the opulent rural notables. The law imposed the payment of a sum equal to the total amount of taxes paid over six years, in addition to the yearly contributions. The government in return pledged to reduce taxes by one-half in perpetuity and to recognize the legal ownership of lands held as usufruct rights (Kharajiyya) for which the Muqabala had been paid. More than one-half of the foreign debt, which amounted to E£ 30 million in 1871, was collected by this means. However, the Muqabala law was abandoned subsequently without the payment of compensation to those who fell victim to the Khedivial fraud. In 1875, while facing an unavoidable state of bankruptcy, Khedive Isma'il was forced to sell to Britain Egypt's share in the Suez Canal Company. But neither the amount of money raised in this manner nor the imposition of additional taxes in the same year was sufficient to satisfy the incessant demands of foreign creditors. A year later, a commission known as the Caisse de la Dette Publique was established to protect the interests of European bondholders. This action was followed two years later by the establishment of a dual Anglo-French control over Egyptian finances through representatives in the Council of Ministers.

The Muqabala law was only one instance of a myriad number of taxes and duties whose burdens fell heavily on the shoulders of the *Fallahin*. As a consequence, peasants in arrears were forced to flee their villages in alarming numbers. The situation deteriorated even further when agricultural production declined in the same period due to a drop in the water level of the Nile. Thus, under conditions of famine and increasing rural restlessness, Cairo early in 1879 witnessed a constant flow of delegates from the provinces, who came to the capital to complain officially about increased taxes. These conditions led a group of officials, army officers, and rural notables to form the National Party, *Hizb al-Watani*. The party called for a constitutional government, under which no taxes would be raised without consulting the representatives of the nation. The National Party presented a weak challenge to the autocratic Khedive and was deeply divided along ethnic lines. Nonetheless, its emergence struck a responsive cord with Khedive Isma'il, whose brief flirtations with the constitutionalists were designed to reassert his absolute authority. Although ultimately he failed to secure his aims and was forced to abdicate in favor of his son, Tawfiq, Khedive Isma'il left a deep and abiding legacy reflected in the resurgent power of the *Kibar al-A'yan*. Thus, when Tawfiq reversed the policies that sought the cooperation of native Egyptians and instead relied on the Turco-Circassian elites, he found himself facing the combined opposition of both the *Kibar al—A'yan* and the army.

THE 'URABI REVOLT AND THE COLONIAL ERA

To the revisionist historian, the 'Urabi revolt stands as a symbol of nationalist defiance against foreign control and the autocratic Khedive. During the Kamshish Affair, the revolt gained a larger social significance since Marxist historians explained the defeat of 'Urabi and the failure of the army movement to safeguard the country's independence with the treacherous conduct of the large landowners.[15] The intellectuals who tried to provide an ideological justification for the activities against the rural elites in 1966 wasted no time in identifying with the purposes behind the 'Urabi revolt and the Free Officers' Movement in 1952. The similarities, superficial as they were, appeared to be persuasive, and from them inferences were drawn about the real identity of the enemy. Both 'Urabi and the Free Officers predominantly belonged to rural, lower middle-class origins, and their nationalist aims were thwarted by the landed elites in alliance with royal authority and foreign intervention. But history seen through nationalist eyes is necessarily a history free of contradictions and ambiguities.

As pointed out by Schölch, the army movement under 'Urabi did not aim to revolutionize the society.[16] Its social outlook reflected rigid social hierarchies — no call was made for the redistribution of wealth or privilege. Nor did its aims and purposes transcend the political structure of the Ottoman Empire, and its ideology upheld traditional Islam, which exalted the patriotic spirit behind the Ottoman Sultan. Conditions of instability and social turmoil, however, had forced the *Kibar al-A'yan* to act at cross-purposes and to support conflicting causes.

At the outset, the *Kibar al-A'yan* identified their interests with those of the army movement, but when conditions of instability threatened local privileges, the majority decided to throw its weight behind the Khedive and foreign intervention. In the first instance, the aims of the *Kibar al-A'yan* and the 'Urabi movement coincided, since both were motivated by the desire to displace the Turco-Circassian ruling aristocracy. Both were strongly inclined toward restricting the power of the Khedive and stemming the tide of foreign intervention, especially in areas touching upon local privileges and economic interests. Nonetheless, the stakes were much too high for the rural notables, or at least for the representatives of the upper stratum in the fourth Majlis elected in 1881, to throw their whole weight behind the army officers. Instead, the leading members of the Majlis opted for a cautious approach, reflected at first by their attempt to appear neutral by offering to mediate the conflict between the Khedive and the army-dominated council of Ministers.

When all attempts to contain the conflict failed and the army movement turned into an open rebellion against the Khedive, the prominent members of the rural elite threw their weight behing the latter. To borrow Schölch's words, the revolutionary ineptitude of the leading members of the rural notables had been exposed.[17] "The maintenance of peace and order was the thing nearest to their hearts."[18] The *Kibar-al-A'yan* stopped short of committing themselves to the revolutionary bonfire in 1882 because the 'Urabi revolt was turning into a movement that seemed to grow in popularity in direct proportion to peasant unrest and their rebellious behavior toward immediate oppressors. In the words of Afaff Lutfi al-Sayyid, "the fallahin, thinking the military would rid them of the money lenders, and scrap their debts, supported them."[19]

Lord Cromer summed up the situation of the rural notables who found themselves torn between the patriotic impulse and the need to protect their ancient privileges: "[The] manner in which Arabist ['Urabist] principles were put in practice led the most intelligent among the Shiekhs to doubt whether it was wise to hand themselves and their cause over to a mutinous army."[20] Historians agree with Lord Cromer. Barakat, for example, stresses that the support of the notables for Khedive Tawfiq reflected the growing concern of *Kibar al-A'yan* about peasant attacks against large estate holders.[21] Other historians revealed the identities of the *Kibar al-A'yan* whose political ambivalence ruined whatever chances 'Urabi had to assert the constitutional rights of the Egyptians. Afaff Lutfi al-Sayyid observes that notables like Sultan Pasha—a onetime 'Urabist, president of the Majlis, and one of the founders of Hizb al-Watani—"had not scrupled to defect to the Khedive's side after the bombardment of Alexandria." Interestingly, among the rural notables who "betrayed 'Urabi Pasha,"[22] Rif'at al-Sa'id mentions, in particular, Ahmad 'Abdel Ghaffar and his close relative, Sayyid al-Fiqqi—two prominent rural elites whose direct descendants were involved in the Kamshish Affair.[23]

The cry of "Egypt for the Egyptians" died after the crushing defeat of 'Urabi. Nonetheless, the rural notables emerged socially and politically ascendant. In the Majlis, the passage of the Basic Law in 1881 gave the deputies control over part of the finances and fiscal policy. The law also endeavored to protect their economic interests in the rural areas. Neither the restoration of the Khedive nor the imposition of direct British control had any lasting effects on the growing influence of the indigenous rural elites. On the contrary, a weakling Khedive under foreign occupation provided the opportunity for further advancement. After the unsettling conditions caused by the army rebellion, a process of retrenchment in which the rural notables played a major part seemed to govern the activities of Egypt's new rulers.

The Egyptian administration under colonial rule was modeled on the British Raj in India. The net result was mixed blessing. The British authorities instituted order and were able, in less than one decade, to create a surplus in the budget, despite the 50 percent allocation of state revenues to the foreign debt. Also, reforms were implemented notwithstanding the privileges granted to foreigners under the Capitulations. Taxes were kept low, while the irrigation system was improved through the construction of new canals, dykes, and dams—thereby expanding the area under cultivation. The reforms, according to Lord Cromer, were aimed at winning the gratitude of all classes. Nonetheless, the major beneficiary of colonial rule turned out to be the *Kibar al-A'yan*.

This result is not surprising given the British colonial record in India and elsewhere, where the imperial authorities showed lack of concern in bridging social and economic gaps. As stated by Lord Cromer, the main purpose of British rule in Egypt was not to "shatter the edifice which, rotten as it was, had still kept Egyptian society together for centuries past."[24] In the interior, members of the *A'yan* were recruited in refurbishing the local government. The village council (al-Majlis al-Baladi) and the provincial council (Majlis al-Mudiriyya) all led to the formal institutionalization and broadening of the *A'yan's* power at the local level.[25] Lord Cromer himself encouraged the appointment of native Egyptians to high offices. Sa'd Zaghlul, who had achieved national prominence during the 1919 revolt for independence, was appointed a cabinet member on two occasions under the British Protectorate. Furthermore, the legislative assemblies between 1882–1914 became large gatherings of opulent landowners, the majority of whom were drawn from traditionally influential families.[26] Finally, improvements in agricultural production and the sale of state lands vastly expanded the holdings of the *Kibar al-A'yan*, helped along by the availability of credit offered by mortgage banks, which infiltrated the land market in large numbers.

With the newly acquired wealth came honors and high titles. More native Egyptians came to hold the titles of *Pasha* and *Bek*. Eric Davis, for example, shows that between 1866–1914 there was a noticeable increase in the number of title holders among delegates in the Egyptian parliament.[27] According to his figures, while the notables constituted only 4 percent of the holders of the title *Bek* in 1866, they amounted to 66 percent in 1914. He further points out that no rural delegate held the title of *Pasha* prior to 1881. By 1914, eleven such titles could be found among the rural delegates. The number of rural delegates holding the title of *effendi* rose from 8 percent in 1866 to its highest point of 58 percent in the upper and lower houses in 1914.

Despite the benefits accruing to the *Kibar al-A'yan*, conflicts began to emerge between them and the colonial power. Ironically, the conflict with Britain was led by the very class upon which the imperial power tried to bestow immense privileges. Davis draws attention to the fact that members of the *A'yan* grew resentful over their dependent state of development. In his view, the infusion of foreign capital was the decisive factor not only in the formation of the agrarian bourgeoisie, but also in "creating the contradictions and class consciousness which led the large landowners to challenge foreign domination of Egyps."[28] The history of the period, however, fails to reveal the existence of a cohesive class behind the nationalist struggle for independence. For the second time in less than three decades, we witness the political ambivalence of *Kibar al-A'yan*.

Most economic historians have pointed out the unbridled appetite of the *Kibar al-A'yan* for foreign capital to finance their land deals. As a consequence, they became heavily dependent on foreign banks, whose mortgage deals used land as security. Ramadan demonstrates the extent to which foreign banks entered the land market by pointing out that the mortgages amounted to one-half the crop value in 1907, estimated to be E£ 120 million. These operations probably would not have caused friction between creditors and lenders under stable cotton prices. Such stability, however, was not to be. The crash in cotton prices during 1907 caused many big landowners to incur huge debts. It has been pointed out that no less than 1,100,000 faddans were forcibly seized as a result of the debts incurred between 1907 and 1913.[29] Admittedly, however, the majority who suffered foreclosures were small holders, a fact that prompted the passage of the Five-Faddan-Law to protect the latter.

This period sharpened the *A'yan's* political awareness of their dependent status, to which they gave full expression in the organ of the 'Umma party, *al-Jarida*.[30] Disuqi provides the names of some of the party leaders among the *A'yan* who accumulated huge debts. These leaders included 'Adli Yegen, 'Abdel Latif al-Shufani, 'Abdel Majid Sultan, 'Ali al-Manzalawi, Muhammad Shiri'i, Othman Satit, Hamad al-Basil, Wasif Ghali, 'Ali Sha'rawi, Qilini Fahmi, and Mustafa 'Amru.[31] Opposition to British rule among the *A'yan* gathered momentum as they increasingly felt that foreigners were encroaching on what they had come to regard as their ordained rights. The expansion in the area under cultivation held by foreigners was one example. Ramadan's figures show that foreign-owned estates of over 50 faddans constituted roughly 13.2 percent (720,000 faddans) of the cultivated land in 1910.[32] Foreign competition was also felt in the provincial administration as a result of the increasing number of British advisers sent to outlying areas. Some of these advisers were quite ignorant of native customs and traditions and consequently damaged local sensibilities.

It is doubtful whether these sources of irritation would have caused the *A'yan* to throw all caution to the wind and actively pursue a policy of open hostility toward the British presence were it not for the harsh conditions caused by World War I. The restrictions imposed on the cultivation of cotton in pursuance of a wartime policy to increase the production of grains, the recruitment of the labor force, which drained the interior of manpower but which enabled Britain to cary out her war aims in Palestine, the limited importation of luxury goods to which the *A'yan* had grown accustomed—all caused the moderate elements in the rural areas to join forces with urban radicals to oppose the occupation. According to Rafi'i, the *Kibar al-A'yan*, who rarely opposed authority and often showed keen interest in cultivating strong connections with the government to advance their aims, were swept up by the nationalist movement in 1919.[33]

The revolutionary temper of the *A'yan* proved to be a transient affair however. One of the few exceptions was the stand of Sa'd Zaghlul, whose popularity among the peasant masses was behind the uncompromising position he took during negotiations with British officials for independence. By contrast, the majority of *Kibar al-A'yan* were inclined to show moderation because of the escalation of violence and disorderly conduct among peasant masses. This caution is to be expected since, unlike the absentee owners and the urban radicals, the rural *A'yan* bore the brunt of mob violence. Peasants, aroused by the revolutionary rhetoric of the urban elites—Azharites were sent by the droves to incite the peasant population—attacked the large estates in their areas because they reminded them of their poverty. In Asyut, for example, peasants attacked the home of Mahmoud Sulaiman, the largest landowner of Sahil Salem, whose son Muhammad Mahmoud was exiled to Malta with Sa'd Zaghlul when negotiations failed. The writer Fikri Abaza related how he personally witnessed enraged peasants attacking the property of Mahmoud Sulaiman because he refused to "distribute bread among the needy."[34]

The violence and disorder reached a climax in March 1919 after the news had spread about the detention of Sa'd Zaghlul and his later exile. The moderate *A'yan* reacted by forming pacification committees to contain mob hysteria and prevent further damage to private and public properties. For example, the pacification committee of the Sharqiyya Province was composed of the largest landowners in the province, including the famous Abaza, Hijazi, and Raslan families. In Minya, Muhammad Shiri'i appealed to the populace to maintain calm. Some of the *A'yan* formed delegations to appeal directly to the authorities in Cairo to contain mob violence.

The unity of the nationalist movement was dealt a heavy blow when some of the moderate *Kibar al-A'yan* decided to reach a modus vivendi with the British authorities. The direct cause for this step was the failure of the negotiations conducted by Sa'd Zaghlul in June 1920 and his rejection of the so-called Milner proposals because they fell short of the nationalist demand for complete independence. The moderates opted for an independent course through use of the newly constituted Liberal Constitutionalist Party, whose leadership was largely composed of former Wafdists (as the group led by Sa'd Zaghlul came to be known). The formation of this party in October 1922 led Gabriel Baer to comment that the big landowners "showed a tendency during the 1920s to create an organizational vehicle opposed to the popular mass-Wafd movement."[35] The big landowners referred to by Baer were for the most part members of the rural *Kibar al-A'yan*.

THE CONSTITUTIONAL MONARCHY

The emergence of competitive political interests at the center under the constitutional monarchy and the failure of big landowners to develop an organizational vehicle to address their common interests determined the political process in the two decades preceding the army seizure of power. The defects of the constitution were in the amount of power granted to the king at the cost of the elected representatives of the people. Both the cabinet and parliament became pawns in the hands of an autocratic king. He appointed and dismissed cabinets at will and often intervened in the legislative process or simply prorogued the parliament if it displeased him. The authoritarianism of the king was further strengthened by the support of the *'Ulama* in the Azhar and the apparent willingness of some of the big landowners to lend support to the king during his constant struggle with the Wafd. Some of the big landowners joined the palace-inspired minority parties in an unsuccessful bid to undermine the electoral successes of the Wafd, which were due to the latter's massive popular support. The Itihad Party and Isma'il Sidqi's People's Party were conceived with this purpose in mind in 1925 and 1930, respectively. Splinter groups that broke away from the Wafd as they grew disenchanted with the latter's repeated flirtations with urban radicals and formed their own parties became the willing tools of the king. For example, the Sa'dist Party was formed in 1937 by Ahmad Mahir and Mahmud Nuqrashi in reaction to the constant radicalization of the Wafd, as was evident by the creation of paramilitant cadres known as the "Blue Shirts."

The Wafd remained the only political force that withstood the authoritarianism of the king and his interference in the constitutional process. It participated in the first elections held in 1924, which it won overwhelmingly. The electoral successes of the Wafd were repeated in 1925, 1926, 1929, 1936, 1942, and 1950, meaning that the Wafd won every election held during the monarchy with the exception of the 1931 and 1945 elections, which it had boycotted because of government tampering in the electoral procedures (the most flagrant of which was carried out by Sidqi Pasha's government in 1931). The only time the Wafd entered an election and was defeated was in 1938, a result of the split that led to the formation of the Sa'dist Party.[36]

A review of the distribution of parliamentary seats in relation to the Wafdist electoral performance and the proportion of seats held by the big landowners, as shown in Table 2, reveals that the latter were divided in their support to the Wafd. They apparently contributed to the electoral successes of the Wafd during the 1924, 1926, and 1942 elections. Paradoxically, the big landowners were among the anti-Wafdist forces, as was obvious, during the 1931 and 1945 elections. In neither instances did they heed the Wafdist call for boycotting the elections.

TABLE 2   Electoral Performance of the Wafd and Big Landowners during the Monarchy

Year of Parl.	Total Seats	No. of Wafdists	% Wafdists	No. Big Landowner	% Big Landowner
1924	214	181[a]	84.6	93[b]	43.5
1925	214	113	52.8	95	44.4
1926	214	172	80.4	105	49.1
1929	235	212	90.2	108	45.9
1931	150	0	0.0	58	38.7
1936	232	180	77.6	112	48.3
1938	264	14	5.3	131	49.6
1942	264	203	76.9	93	35.2
1945	285	0	0.0	123	43.2
1950	317	157	49.5	119	37.5

[a]John Anderson, "Representative Systems and Ruralizing Elections" (M.A. thesis, University of Chicago, 1976).

[b]Asim al-Disuqi, *Kibar Mullak al-Aradhi al-Zira'iyya wa dawruhum fi al-Mujtama' al-Misri* (Cairo: Dar al-Thaqafah, 1975) p. 212.

The support of the big landowners for the anti-Wafdists was also condi-
tioned by the depression in the early 1930s, which knocked the bottom out of
cotton prices. Many cotton producers and merchants were ruined and their only
hope was to secure government help. According to Quraishi, the Sidqi government was installed by the palace to deal with the effects of the crisis. He further
asserted that the landowning faction of the Liberal Constitutionalist Party extended their support to Sidqi's government because "they thought that Sidqi
could help the rich and the middle landowners in their economic difficulties on
the one hand and protect them from the wrath of peasantry on the other."[37]

A large number of the big landowners who supported the anti-Wafdist
forces were rural *A'yan* families, whose descendants were subjected to the
investigations of the HCLF in 1966. Table 23 shows that their level of representation in parliament was consistent throughout the years, regardless of which
force had the upper hand at the center. Nevertheless, there is some evidence indicating that they were most enthusiastic in their support of the palace-
installed government of 1931. This enthusiasm is to be expected since the
Kibar al-A'yan in rural areas felt especially vulnerable in the 1930s, during
which the peasant masses grew very restless. *Kibar al-A'yan* were not party
loyalists; however, they were more inclined to support the Liberal Constitutionalist Party than were the absentee owners. Their proportion in parliament

TABLE 3   Percentage of Resident Upper Stratum Ancestors among All Big Landowners
Elected to Parliament

Year of Parl.	No. of Big Landowners	No. of Rural A'yan Ancestors[a]	% of Big Landowners
1924	93	16	17.2
1925	95	15	15.8
1926	105	21	20.0
1929	108	20	18.5
1931	58	14	24.1
1936	112	19	17.0
1938	131	23	17.6
1942	93	18	19.4
1945	123	29	23.6
1950	119	30	25.2

[a] Data on the number of ancestors in the prerevolutionary parliaments were drawn from
Muhammad Subhi's *Ta'irkh al-Hayat al-Niyabiyya Fi Misr* (Cairo: Dar al-Kutb, 1967), and from
the reports submitted to the Committee for the Liquidation of Feudalism in 1966.

declined only when the Wafd either won a massive majority, as in 1929, or when it returned to power with a substantial majority, as in 1936 and 1942. The HCLF data further show that the majority of liberal constitutionalists came from Upper Egypt. Many of the rural *A'yan* also benefited from the electoral difficulties of the Wafd. For example, some of the *A'yan* who joined Sidqi's People's Party were not represented in the pre-1931 parliaments and failed to return to subsequent parliaments. This fact suggests that Sidqi enlisted the support of new and less established *A'yan* in his effort to undermine the rural support of the Wafd. The emergence of the Sa'dists as a strong parliamentary group in the mid-1940s was another opportunity for the rural *A'yan* to promote their political interests through the use of minority parties opposing the Wafd. This opposition was apparent in the 1945 elections, which the Wafd refused to contest. Nevertheless, the Wafd retained in large part the support of absentee owners, who contributed to the Wafdist electoral victory in 1936 and joined the Wafdist cabinet that became famous for successfully concluding the Anglo-Egyptian Treaty in the same year.[38] Among the prominent absentee owners who joined the Wafd during this year was Fouad Siraj al-Din Shahin, whose family hailed from Gharbiyya and was linked in marriage with another famous family in the province, the Badrawi-'Ashur family. Fouad Siraj al-Din rose quickly in the ranks of the Wafd to become the party secretary general and, long after the party was banned by the military regime, the party's unofficial leader. Furthermore, toward the close of the 1940s, the Wafd came to rely heavily on some of the rural *A'yan* families, who contributed to the party's electoral victory in 1950. This support resulted from changes in the Wafd's electoral strategy, which offset its long neglect of the rural areas. This change in electoral strategy, however, came much too late since, like the majority of the urban-based parties, the Wafd could not extricate itself from the iron grip of urban anarchy and violence.

PRELUDE TO THE MILITARY COUP

One consequence of a system dominated by large landowners was the widening of the gap between them and the small owners. Statistics indicate that before the overthrow of the monarchy fewer than 12,000 owners (0.5 percent) held 2.0 million faddans (32.2 percent), while the small owners numbered 2.6 milion (94.3 percent) and their share of cultivated land was 2.1 million faddans (35.4 percent). Between these two strata were 148,000 (5.2 percent) middling owners, cultivating an area of 1.8 milion faddans (30.4 percent).[39] How can we explain the persistence of this gap from the last quarter of the nineteenth century until the overthrow of the monarchy in 1952?

Economic historians provide several explanations for the persistence of large, individually owned estates through the first half of the twentieth century, despite the natural fragmentation that results from Islamic laws of inheritance. The chief explanation is that state land (Da'ira Saniya and Domain land) was sold to the largest landowners because of their access to credit.[39] Another explanation is that the area under cultivation was expanded through land reclamation, the newly arable land being divided into large parcels and sold to the largest landowners. An explanation more pertinent to the longest cultivated areas was that the expansion of the large estates was carried out at the cost of the small owners who were forced to sell because they incurred huge debts.

Government intervention in times of economic crisis and the availability of credit for the big landowners preserved not only the large estates but also helped expand them. During the Great Depression, the Sidqi government saved many big landlords who had contracted huge debts under the so-called *taswiyya* (settlement) law. The government assumed their debts, lowered their interest rates, and reduced their annual payments; however the medium and small owners bore the full brunt of the depression. Baer remarks that "the only possible explanation for the relatively low rate of fragmentation of large landed property during the 1930's appears to be the sequestration of small properties and their concentration in the hands of the big landowners."[40]. In addition, the conversion of property into *Waqf* (religious or family endowed property) and the inequitable rates of taxation allowed the more privileged stratum of owners to preserve and increase their holdings at the expense of the *fallah*. According to Abdel-Fadil, the number of owners holding over fifty faddans remained steady at 12,000, constituting 1.0 percent of all owners in 1900 or 0.5 percent in 1952.[41] Using the family as a unit of analysis, Asim al-Disuqi revealed that the total number of families whose properties ranged between 100 and 10,000 faddans, excluding foreigners and members of the royal dynasty, between 1914 and 1952 was 2,500.[42] By contrast, the majority of the small owners, who constituted roughly 94 percent of all landowners, suffered a steady decline in the size of their holdings from an average of 1.8 faddans in 1894 to 0.8 faddan in 1952. Subsistence for a family of four is estimated to require three faddans, therefore the majority of the *fallahin* were living below subsistence levels before the outbreak of the revolution.

Hand in hand with the trend toward concentrating lands into only few hands was the spiral increase in land prices. Land speculations in the 1940s pushed the price per faddan to unprecedented levels. By 1950–1951, according to Ramadan, the artificially induced price per faddan jumpted to E£ 800, although its real value was E£ 200.[43] Land prices were even higher in some of the densely populated provinces such as Minufiyya, where the price per faddan reached the preposterous level of E£ 1,000. As a natural corollary of rising land prices, rents skyrocketed from an average E£ 5 in 1896 to an average E£ 25 to E£ 50 per fadden shortly before the overthrow of the monarchy in 1952. In the same period, the yield per faddan did not amount to more than E£17, therefore, the tenant not only failed to make two ends meet but also incurred huge debts that made him prey to the whims of the landlord.

More and more big landowners were tempted to rent their lands because of the spiral increase in rental rates. By 1952 the amount of land rented reached 75 percent of the land under cultivation, whereas it did not exceed 1.7 percent in 1900.[44] The big absentee landowners rented their lands to middlemen who divided them into small parcels and auctioned them in the village market, a procedure that often drove up rental prices due to the ignorance of the small tenants and their hunger for lands. Absenteeism was also encouraged by the availability of cheap labor. Many big landowners handed their estates to the *Nazir* while they retired to the cities.

The rural *Kibar al-A'yan* families faced the same temptations as the absentee owners, but they did not totally succumb because of their extended local kinship networks from which they derived support and sustenance. They followed a mixed tenurial system to take advantage of the market situation, particularly the high rental prices and the availability of cheap labor. They were part cultivators, depending on hired cheap labor, part sharecroppers, often usurping four-fifths of the produce, and part rentiers, leasing out their lands to the highest bidders. In addition to the mixed tenurial system, the resident *A'yan* continued to maintain absolute control over village affairs through kinship connections in the provincial administration and the agricultural cooperatives. It is no surprise then that, given their extensive control over the *fallahin*, the rural *A'yan* were retrospectively described as feudal.

The pauperization of the *fallah* was acute in the provinces that had been cultivated the longest, of which Minufiyya stands as a prime example. There is good reason why, of all the agricultural provinces, this province gave rise to the Kamshish Affair and the HCLF investigations. Minufiyya is the longest cultivated province, surrounded by fully developed and exploited lands. There was no possibility for expansion in any direction here, unlike the provinces bordering the desert such as Sharqiyya and Beheira. Moreover, state lands whose sale helped preserve large estates in Middle Egypt, such as in Bani Suwayf and Minya, were not available in Minufiyya. Under these circumstances, only a small minority was able to preserve its large estates. The small owners as well as the majority of the medium owners were faced with two forces that led to property fragmentation. The first of these forces was the

Islamic inheritance law. Second, the vicissitudes of the cotton market during the depression rendered small farmers insolvent and forced them to sell their lands. A contemporary of the period described the conditions of small farmers in Minufiyya in the mid-1930s:

> The soil is divided into many small properties either rented or privately owned. These small holdings only accentuate the overcrowding which causes them. Help is wanted as cheap as possible; children can provide it. Thus the *fellah* is forced by the exigencies of the land to have children, and as many as possible. This for him is the meaning of marriage and the family. Where all these conditions exist together, as in the province of Menoufiya in the Upper Delta where the land has been longest cultivated and irrigated, where cotton is the chief crop and small holdings are the most numerous, a density of over 2,000 to the square mile is to be found.[45]

There is not doubt that the conditions described above by Father Ayrout were behind the mass exodus of peasants to Cairo and Alexandria, where they joined the ranks of the unemployed and where only the lucky ones were able to secure government jobs or join the lower echelons of the army and police. Minufiyya was by far the most populous province and was outstanding in its number of rural emigrants. According to one study, nearly one-fifth of the rural migrants who settled in Cairo came from Minufiyya.[46]

The rebellious spirit of peasants began to surface shortly before the outbreak of the revolution and was largely manifested in local disturbances over rising rents. Baer writes that the sharpest disputes over rising rents took place on the estates of the Badrawi-'Ashur family in the village of Buhut (Gharbiyya).[47] Sayyid Mar'i issued the following warning to members of his class when justifying the agrarian reforms launched by the military regime in 1952.

> We all remember the days preceding the revolution of July 1952; we remember how the Egyptian village became restless as a result of dangerous agitation; we remember the events which led to bloodshed and destruction of property—for the first time in the history of Egyptian village [sic]. Would the large landowners have preferred to be left exposed to the wind blowing through this unrest, and endangering, perhaps, the peace of our entire fatherland.[48]

The warnings issued by Sayyid Mar'i came too late for the big landowners, who never seriously countenanced any reforms that would have alleviated the conditions of the peasant masses. All through the 1940s, voices in favor of reforms were raised, but to no avail. Some of the reformists, influenced by Fabian thought, advocated a program of agrarian reforms whose implementation could have brought some stability to small holdings. Mirrit Butros Ghali proposed in 1945 a twenty-five-year program of agrarian reform, which called for a "ban on new acquisition of land by the large landowners, noninterference with the fragmentation of the large estates through inheritance, establishment of a three-faddan minimum for the division of arable land and, finally, redistribution among the poor *fallahin* the holdings of the Waqf."[49]

The radical advocates of reform believed that land fragmentation in the hands of majority and land concentration in the hands of a few landlords were two sides of the same coin. But the radicals were divided over the means that must be adopted to prevent concentration. One group favored putting a ceiling on individual ownership. Muhammad al-Khattab proposed at parliament in 1944 a ceiling of fifty faddans on all lands newly possessed either through sale or inheritance. The proposal raised an uproar in the Senate, where all the principal parties opposed it. Another group advocated a graduated tax to encourage big landowners to divert their surpluses into the more profitable channels of commerce and industry instead of buying more lands. This proposal also fell on deaf ears.

The countryside continued to seethe with discontent, while the urban centers gravitated toward extremism in which urban-based movements such as Misr al-Fattah and the Muslim Brotherhood took an active part. Even the Wafd found itself compelled to resort to extremism because of the growing popular hostility against the British presence in the Canal Zone. The defeat of the Arab armies in Palestine in 1948 and the creation of the State of Israel exacerbated internal conflicts. At this time, echoes were heard of Tawfiq al-Hakim's clarion call for "the man who would unite all in one."[50] The anxiety that had forced al-Hakim to issue this call in the early 1930s reached a climax in the burning of Cairo by "unknown" persons on 26 January 1952. A few months later, army officers led by Gamal Abdel al-Nasser brought down the monarchy and began a new chapter in the history of Egypt.

Tawfiq al-Hakim's call for a strong man at the helm reflects a historical pattern in which authoritarianism depended on the support of the traditional order. There is no dearth of historical material for substantiating the views of the nationalist historian about how traditionalist *A'yan* thwarted nationlist aspirations and impeded Egypt's progression toward independence and liberalism.

History, however, does not provide monocausal explanations, nor is it free of contradiction and ambiguity. There were occasions when the rural *A'yan*, including the wealthiest and the most established, behaved in a manner opposite the self-imposed view of the revisionist historian. This inconsistency stemmed from the political ambivalence of the *A'yan* themselves due to the opposite pressures to which they were subjected — the expanding power of the state and peasant unrest at certain critical, historical junctures. They resisted the encroachments of the central authority and foreign intrusion into their zones of influence. They became recalcitrant and demanding whenever rulers grew dependent upon their support to contain social violence, thwart foreign intervention, or frustrate the electoral strategies of competitive urban interests vying for rural support. Thus, relations between the state and the traditional order were not as harmonious as the nationalist historian would like us to believe.

Nonetheless, the interests of rulers and traditionalist *A'yan* coincided whenever peasant militancy threatened to undermine local privileges or uproot the system of domination that persevered until the outbreak of the military coup in 1952. The question now arises whether the amry officers, in their response to egalitarian demands, succeeded in demolishing the old order and, consequently, the political process it had determined.

Chapter Three
Closing the Social Gap
1952.1966

R EVOLUTIONARY CONSCIOUSNESS CAME TO Nasser by stages, but, for reasons I shall explain in this chapter, Nasser ultimately failed to create a new social order. The army officers seized power without a plan or an ideology to guide their actions. They stumbled upon power with little experience in how to excercise it and with little idea of the purposes for which power might be applied. Internal and external circumstances often intervened to deflect the ruling elites from pursuing their social and economic objectives. Nonetheless, some meaning can be found in Nasser's leftward radicalism by observing the dialectical relationships between policy choice and the contradictions inherent in the objective situation.

The first agrarian reform law in 1952 was quite generous toward the big landowners. The law limited individual ownership to 200 faddans, with an additional 100 faddans allowable for a family of two or more children. Property in excess of these limits was allowed to be sold to small farmers or tenants. Interest-bearing bonds at 3 percent and redeemable in thirty years were issued to the big landowners whose properties were confiscated by the state. All expropriated lands were meant for distribution among the small farmers and tenants rather than among landless peasants. The logic behind this decision was that the latter had no experience in tilling the land or how to take care of it. The truth was that the first agrarian reform law was quite moderate, involving no more than 8.4 percent of the cultivated land. Roughly only 365,000 faddans were available for redistribution among 146,500 families in small parcels ranging from between three and five faddans.[1] The only revolutionary aspect of the law was the imposition of strict controls over the tenurial system. Cash rents were fixed at seven times the land tax and sharecropping arrangements were fixed at an equal division of crops between landlords and tenants. Thus one of the worst abuses of the agrarian system, which affected 75 percent of the cultivated land, was eliminated.

The hasty implementation of the agrarian reform law produced many loopholes, which became obvious much later on. The rural gap persisted due to the failure to limit landownership by the extended family unit.[2] As shown by Abdel-Fadil, many big landowners evaded the agrarian reforms by producing fictitious bequests, and others fabricated evidence to prove that property transfers had been made to other family members.[3] Gadalla has also pointed out that similar motives were behind the rise in the number of marriages on the large estates.[4] On the other hand, there were many instances of outright resistance to the implementation of the agrarian reforms. The landowners in some instances resisted the reforms by refusing to declare the extent of their holdings and by resorting to acts of sabotage, which included actually damaging property seized by the state and even poisoning animals. The only incident of real violence took place in Maghagha in Minya, when the Lamlums led their tribal members in an attack on the local police station. Nonetheless, the first agrarian reforms did produce some lasting effects in the countryside, the most significant of which was the reversal of absenteeism. In the words of Abdel-Malek,

> the big landowners who clung to the land would thereafter take the trouble to manage it themselves, and little by little give up absentee ownership. Their social weight in the rural areas no longer crushed the group of medium owners (five to fifty feddans) — the Egyptian kulaks — which the government was determined to consolidate and which it was to surround with an even larger class of small proprietors.[5]

By the big landowners, Abdel-Malek meant the *Kibar al-A'yan*, who exercised undue influence during the monarchy. Nonetheless, this action by the Revolutionary Command Council (RCC) had unintended consequences, later reflected in rural unrest. The military coup occurred in July 1952 amid urban violence instigated by Muslim Brotherhood, the extremist wing of the Wafd, and the workers and peasants in the provincial cities and on the large estates. Labor strikes were occurring in al-Mahalla al-Kubra — a major industrial complex in Gharbiyya. In the same province, peasants on the large estates of the Badrawi-'Ashur family became violent because of the spiral increase in rents. In Kamshish, peasant agitation forced the government to call in reinforcements from the Frontier Force to help the local police restore order.

Ramadan observes that the enactment of agrarian reform laws allowed peasants to delude themselves into thinking they were entering a revolutionary stage in the agrarian structure. Many stopped paying dues to landlords a month before the agrarian reform took effect. He further observes that some peasants under the influence of the left prepared themselves to seize the lands they cultivated. Many declared that the army gave them the lands, that they would not allow the owners to set a foot on them, and that they would not pay rents nor give up the yields of the land.[6]

Peasant unrest distrubed the RCC officers. They immediately issued appeals to remain calm and to resist the extremists who were causing disorder.[7] The junta acted swiftly to bring about order and to maintain control in the countryside. The labor strike in Mahalla al-Kubra was crushed, and two of the labor leaders were summarily executed in August. This suppression led Abdel-Malek to remark that "from the outset the army's action smashed by terror the first attemp at popular revolution that emanated from a popular leadership and was capable, despite the confusion of its objectives and the weakness of its basic staff, of turning into a peasant insurrection of stature.'"[8]

The agrarian reform law was enacted not only to strip the politically dominant class of large landowners of their economic resources but also to mobilize urgently needed mass support. Following the announcement of the agrarian reform law, RCC members began to tour the countryside amid much publicity and fanfare. Sayyid Mar'i, the architect of the agrarian reform law and himself a descendant of rural notables with substantial landholdings in Sharqiyya, claims he was behind the plan to bring the RCC members closer to peasant masses. He observes in his memoirs that he sensed the wide gulf between the leaders of the revolution and the masses. The urgency in establihsing links with rural areas was underscored by the following remark:

> If the parties of the counter-revolution concentrated their activities in Cairo and put all their weight here, then why should not the RCC move out of Cairo and go directly to the peasants who benefited from the agrarian reforms. In my opinion, this is the only solution. Nasser ought to go to one of the villages and begin to distribute title deeds of lands seized from the big landowners.[9]

Vatikiotis points out that other RCC members were despatched to their home provinces on similar missions and with the same objectives in mind as mentioned by Sayyid Mar'i. Thus Kamal al-Din Hussein worked in Qalubiyya and Beheira, al-Baghdadi, in Daqahliyya and its capital Mansura, and 'Abdel Hakim 'Amer, in Minya.[10] They presented themselves as the sons of the people and identified their revolutionary cause with the aspirations of the masses.[11] Except for officers such as 'Abdel Hakim 'Amer and 'Ali Sabri, the majority of the officers belonged to the lower middle classes, and, therefore, their attempt to identify with their social origins did not appear to be forced or unnatural. Some went to the extent of drawing similarities between Nasser and his nineteenth-century predecessor, 'Urabi, both of whom claimed to be real sons of Egypt and from the same class of small landowners. Vatikiotis further points out that eight of the eleven RCC members had been enrolled in the military academy in

1936.[12] This year was when the Wafd forced open the doors of the academy to the lower middle classes. Prior to this date, it had been the exclusive reserve of the upper classes.

In the urban areas, it was perfectly natural for the RCC and the Muslim Brotherhood Movement to forge an alliance against the bourgeoisie in the Wafd and in the palace-created parties. Both members of this alliance appealed to the same constituency and drew support from the lower middle classes and peasants. The RCC officers even attempted to project an image of being devout Muslims. Sayyid Mar'i shows how even popular religion was used to harness traditional feelings to the state power machine. He reveals that when he made plans for Nasser to tour Sharqiyya, ostensibly to distribute title deeds from the lands seized from the royal family and big landowners, he requested Shaykh 'Alwan, the respected local leader of the Sufi order, to draw people to the streets. Mar'i remarks that Shaykh 'Alwan's efforts produced an overwhelming popular upsurge for Nasser and his entourage.[13] It also became a common practice for RCC members such as Kamal al-Din Hussein and Sadat to frequent mosques to deliver the Friday sermon. Furthermore, the Muslim Brotherhood leaders were encouraged into believing that the RCC needed their advice in order to pass legislation conforming with the spirit and letter of Islamic laws. The RCC contained officers who were either full members or sympathetic to the fundamentalist cause. The command council was even prepared to accept a Muslim Brotherhood member in the cabinet headed by General Nagib. It was not obvious then that the RCC and the Muslim Brotherhood movement were rivals competing for the same constituency and using the same ideological weapons to appeal to the traditionally-minded segment of the population. A temporary alliance was necessary in order to deal with the bourgeois and secular-minded politicians centered around the Wafd and the other minority parties.

Early in September 1952, the RCC demanded that all parties purge themselves. No guidelines were set, and thus it was left to party leaders to make their own interpretations and to set their own standards for liquidating corrupt elements. Naturally, accusations and counteraccusations thoroughly weakened intraparty unity, aggravated by the passage of the agrarian reform law. Finally, by January 1953, the RCC was ready to put the parties out of their misery by ordering the dissolution of all parties. This action was followed by the establishment of a revolutionary tribunal, with Anwar al-Sadat as its leading member, to try the prominent members of the old regime. A number of legislative measures followed in quick succession. Many former party leaders were given long-term prison sentences, and all members of the cabinets from the last decade of the monarchy were prohibited from engaging in political activities.

The exclusion from political participation of the opponents of the regime came to be known as *al-'Azl al-Siyyasi*, or political isolation. Their disenfranchisement may be described as a reverse type of participation crisis. In other words, the new regime was not confronted with the problem of admitting into the political system members of lower classes, the problem Western democracies had to resolve to achieve full participation; rather, the major problem confronting the army officers was in restricting the participation of politically mature individuals, the majority of whom were experienced participants in the former political order. The second major problem was in preventing the waning of popular enthusiasm for the army movement.

These purposes were achieved by the creation of the Liberation Rally as Egypt's single-party organization with Nasser as the secretary general. The only political movement allowed to continue was the Muslim Brotherhood. The official explanation for this exception was that the movement was not a party in the traditional sense of the term; rather, it was an organization devoted to the proselytization of Islamic values. The pretense that the Muslim Brotherhood was not a political movement and was devoid of political objectives could not be kept up for too long however.

Having cleared the scene of the secular opposition — the prerevolutionary parties — the RCC turned its attention towards the Muslim Brotherhood. The Brotherhood's honeymoon with the RCC officers ended when Hasan al-Hudaibi, the Supreme Guide of the movement, became thoroughly convinced that the government was unwilling to share the power, let alone consider the passage of legislation in accordance with Islamic laws. The RCC officers also realized that a confrontation with the Muslim Brotherhood was inevitable. The first clashes occurred between followers of the movement and students mobilized by the Liberation Rally in February 1953, sparked by the conclusion of an agreement with Britain over the Sudan. The Muslim Brotherhood interpreted the agreement as a betrayal of the national cause because it led to the destruction of the unity of the Nile Valley. The conflict between the majority of the RCC members and General Nagib, the nominal leader of the RCC, which climaxed in February 1954, provided the opportunity for the Muslim Brotherhood as well as for the defunct prerevolutionary parties to reassert themselves temporarily.

The rivalry between Nagib and the majority of the RCC officers has been retold by many authors, and for this reason it is sufficient to reiterate only that the split within the military ranks occurred over the issue of the restoration of democracy. General Nagib and some of the junior officers, principally those around Khalid Muhi al-Din in the armored corps and some in the Cairo garrison, were in favor of the restoration of liberal democracy and the return of the military to the barracks. Nasser and the majority of the RCC officers believed Egypt needed a military dictatorship for at least three years to eliminate political corruption. In a series of tactical moves in the spring of 1954, Nasser was able to disarm Nagib and his supporters among the junior officers by mobilizing the officers who, having tasted power, were reluctant to relinquish it. Nevertheless, it would be a mistake to assume that the military dictatorship under Nasser was placed in power by the support of the army alone. Part of the responsibility must rest with the Liberation Rally.

In a well-documented study, the historian Abdel Azim Ramadan has revealed the orchestrated plans Nasser worked out with two junior army officers in the Liberation Rally to mobilize the transportation workers.[14] At the height of the crisis in March, the transportation workers launched a major strike that completely paralyzed the city. This strike was followed by rallies in support of Nasser's faction in the RCC, organized by labor and student leaders affiliated with the Liberation Rally. Nagib was ousted, while 450 dissident officers were purged. The purged officers including leftist elements as well as some of the known members of the Muslim Brotherhood. The suppression of the Muslim Brotherhood was completed in the fall of 1954. Following an assassination attempt on Nasser, more than seven thousand members of the Muslim Brotherhood were arrested. A military tribunal found eight hundred members guilty of conspiring against the state and sentenced them to long-term imprisonment. Six leaders were put to death. The regimentation of society was complete with the suppression of *al-Misri*, the organ of the Wafd. The syndicates whose loyalties could not be bought, including the Bar Association, which condemned the military dictatorship, were cowed into silence. RCC members emerged to occupy cabinet posts, while Nasser combined the roles of premier and leader of the revolution.

Until the promulgation of the constitution in January 1956, Egypt was governed without a clearly formulated ideology nor institutions to mediate the transition to republican order. The statement announced at the beginning of the revolution was rather nebulous. It contained six principles, including the elimination of imperialism, the destruction of feudalism, the fight against monopolies and capitalist control of government, the establishment of a strong army, and the achievement of social justice.[15] The constitution reaffirmed the republican order under which Nasser was elected as the country's first president. The constitution further established the National Assembly and called for the reorganization of the Liberation Rally under the name of the National Union (NU). It also declared that candidates for the assembly must also be NU members. A committee consisting of three former RCC officers was created to screen candidates.

The structure of the NU was formulated according to the communist party model of the Easten bloc. It was shaped like a pyramid, organized on a hierarchical order with commands flowing from the top to the bottom. At the bottom were the basic committees, whose size were determined by population at the primary unit. The basic units elected members of the NU committees for the district level, whose activities were supervised by a bureau of officers consisting of president, vice president, secretary, and treasurer. The same was repeated at the provincial level. A central committee controlled by an executive committee mainly of former RCC officers was established at the capital. Anwar al-Sadat was appointed the secretary general of the party.

Some efforts were exerted to reorganize local government. These efforts, however, did not apparently produce any tangible departure from the old provincial administration inherited from the monarchy. With the possible exception of the governors, the middle and lower officials were the same men who served during the ancien régime. They were the same *'Umdas* and the same district Ma'murs to whom the village heads had been directly responsible.[16] The continuity of the old order was further reflected by the composition of the National Assembly elected in 1956. Despite the screening procedures, Abdel-Malek observed that the assembly included a "large number of prosperous men, and most of the provincial delegates favored the old system of agrarian dominance."[17] The old order could also be found among the newly elected NU committees. Abdel-Malek again points out that "between 1952 and 1957 the single-party method put the men of the old order back into power in all areas."[18] Binder's thorough analysis of the 28,000 NU committee members from the sixteen agricultural provinces showed that the traditionally influential families elected two or more of their members to the local committees. More interesting was the revelation that the majority of the NU officers at the district level had ancestors who were *'Izba* owners and in the prerevolutionary parliaments.[19]

The political and administrative reorganization of the country coincided with significant changes in its regional and international relations, which in turn affected domestic policies. These changes were the Baghdad Pact, concluded in February 1955, the Israeli attack on the Gaza Strip in the same month, and the conclusion of the Czech arms deal, which broke the Western monopoly over arms supplies to the region in September 1955. These events were the beginnings of Egypt's gradual embroilment in regional conflicts and external rivalries, which sapped her energy and laid her economy to waste. Nevertheless, in 1956, Nasser, imbued with the spirit of nonalignment reached at Bandung, seemed to score one diplomatic victory after another, enhancing his popularity at home and making him less inclined to resolve the problem of participation and more determined to use the single party as a vehicle of mobilization and containment. His popularity emerged intact after the Suez Canal crisis, which came about as a result of Nasser's nationalization of all foreign assets in the Suez Canal Company, with its immediate repercussions in the form of a combined military action against Egypt by Britain, France, and Israel in October 1956.

Nasser also seemed to derive maximum benefits from the rivalry between the superpowers for a foothold in the region. Both powers were even prepared to ignore the aspects of his policies that were inimical to their interests. Western aid continued to flow with little interruption, despite Nasser's leading position in the anti-imperialist camp and his role in bringing about the collapse of the Baghdad Pact, a Western attempt to contain the Soviet Union. Soviet support to Egypt also seemed to persist, despite Nasser's persecution of Egyptian communists, especially during conflict with Iraq under Abdel Karim Qasim in 1959.

Nasser's biggest victory on the diplomatic front came with the Egyptian-Syrian merger. In February 1958, Nasser appeared to be transforming the quest for unity into a tangible reality. The price Syria had to pay for the merger was reorganization of its political institutions along Egyptian lines, which meant the suppression of the Syrian Ba'th Party. Nasser, however, committed a fatal error of appointing Marshal 'Abdel Hakim 'Amer the governor of the Northern Province (Syria), since he was unfit for the task of transforming the United Arab Republic (UAR) into an integrated political and economic entity.

A radical transformation in Nasser's outlook in the early 1960s began to direct domestic and foreign policies. This change in viewpoint preceded and in some respects precipitated the Syrian secession in September 1961. This ideology was the socialist imperative, developing after the Egyptian bourgeoisie had shown all kinds of resistance to becoming participants in the state's industrialization schemes. Ample opportunities had been provided for Egyptian capital to expand, including the Egyptianization of foreign companies and the nationalization of British and French assets as a consequence of the Suez Canal crisis. The Syrian-Egyptian merger had also led to an expansion of the market. But the Egyptian bourgeoisie preferred the safer ground of investing in real estate, construction, and bank deposits.

In some sense, it could be argued there was something inevitable about the development of the socialist trend, not simply because of the default of Egyptian private capital. The nationalization of the British and French assets was the first step toward a statist economy, which made its first appearance in the establishment of an Economic Agency and the adoption of centralized planning. In 1960, the government announced its intention to double national income in ten years. The first five-year (1960–1965) plan proposed to raise national income by 40 percent, with a growth rate of 81 percent in industry, electricity, and construction. To achieve this end, local production would have to be increased by 42 percent, and it would be necessary to invest a total sum of E£ 1.7 billion, including E£ 439 million for industry. The percentage of domestic savings in relation to the national income would be raised from 11 percent to 21 percent, thus ensuring the financing of at least 65 percent of the investment plan.[20] The balance would be secured by foreign aid and by forcibly seizing the assets of the Egyptian bourgeoisie.

In July 1961, the government announced the famous socialist decrees, which included the nationalization of all banks, insurance companies, and other firms operating in the area of heavy and basic industries. This action was followed by another decree that nationalized public works companies and public utilities. A third decree, which affected medium-sized industrial companies belonging to groups and families, established state participation through state ownership of all shares held by each stockholder in excess of E£ 10,000. The enactment of the second agrarian reform law reduced individual ownership of land from two hundred to one hundred faddans, but no limit imposed on ownership by the family unit beyond the 1958 amendment to the first agrarian reform law that had limited family ownership to three hundred faddans. The family unit referred to in this amendment was the nuclear and not the extended family. The amendment also applied only to future acquisition of property either through inheritance or contracts. In the same year, landholding, *al-hiyazah* (owned and leased land), was limited to three hundred faddans. This restriction was clearly aimed at the rich peasants who expanded their holdings by taking advantage of the reductions in rent.[21]

The Syrian secession led to a severe polarization in the Arab world, which complicated Egypt's relations with the superpowers and directly affected domestic politics. The conflict was mainly ideological, setting the progressive regimes against the conservative regimes, or the poor republics against the oil-rich monarchies. Undoubtedly, Nasser needed to consolidate his domestic position in order to strike back at the Saudis and the Jordanians, among other "reactionaries," for their alleged role in the Syrian secession. Indeed, it was during this critical period that Nasser made the ill-fated decision to intervene on the side of the revolutionaries in Yemen against the feudal monarchy.

Domestically, the immediate impact of the Syrian secession was to sound the death knell of the upper class, at least, such was the impression Nasser conveyed to 'Abdel Latif al-Baghdadi, as was revealed in the latter's published memoirs. Nasser said he recognized the necessity of socialist reforms for disarming the reactionaries. Baghdadi observes that the Bolshevik revolution and

Lenin's strategy in dealing with the bourgeoisie and rightist threats became Nasser's model and source of inspriation at this critical stage of Egypt's socialist transformation. Reflecting on his own past compromises with the bourgeoisie, Nasser took comfort in the thought that even Lenin at one time committed the grave error of seeking to cooperate with the bourgeoisie. After the Syrian break, though, Nasser declared in his conversation with Baghdadi, that error needed to be rectified: "We have no other alternative but to liquidate them by arresting all of them and putting them in Wadi al-Jadid."[22]

The new ideology of the regime was embodied in the *al-Mithaq* or the Socialist Charter—a document prescribing the socialist transformation—that received the approval of 1500 delegates from the so-called popular forces, representing professional syndicates, labor and trade unions, agricultural cooperatives, and a host of other groups, who gathered for a conference between May and July 1962. The *Mithaq* declared that Egypt was ready to enter a new stage in its revolutionary development by adopting a plan to bring about social change. Nasser declared at the conference that the 1919 nationalist revolt failed because the leadership fell into the hands of the big landowners or the feudalists who were adverse to the idea of social change. The *Mithaq* therefore declared that a socialist solution was inevitable and that the only means to carry it out was through the new political organization, the Arab Socialist Union (ASU), which would replace the National Union (NU) and would reflect the alliance of the popular forces that included peasants, workers, intelligentsia, the armed forces, and "nonexploitative" capitalists. Also, to ensure the socialist character of the alliance, the *Mithaq* decreed that, henceforth, 50 percent of the seats in all elective bodies, including the National Assembly, would be reserved for the delegates of peasants and workers (although neither the *Mithaq* nor Nasser's response to inquiries raised during the conference spelled out exactly what was meant by the terms peasants and workers.)[23]

An addition to the political formula for the socialist transformation was Nasser's recognition of the need to organize a socialist vanguard that would lead and direct the change on the Leninist model. But he did not envision the creation of an apparatus independent of the ASU. It became evident, too, that despite the radical impression conveyed to Baghdadi and Nasser's own remarks during the conference, apparently influenced by Marxist-Leninist thought, there was little inclination to bring about revolutionary change in the social structure. Nasser rejected class struggle as a means of eliminating class conflicts and preached, instead, peaceful solutions to class differences and coexistence. Notably, however, Nasser's remarks were confined only to the national forces represented in the ASU. Nasser declared there would be no dictatorship of one class over another and that there would be no attempt to sacrifice the present generation for future generations. The Stalinist method was reserved for the so-called feudalists and exploitative capitalists who dominated the politics of the ancien régime. Ironically, some "reactionary" elements who had earlier infiltrated the NU were also present at the congress as delegates from the agricultural cooperatives. Their presence there was discovered later, during the Kamshish Affair. In the meantime, Nasser seemed to be ideologically and psychologically prepared to take some radical steps against the upper classes. The nationalization measures were followed by sequestration laws 138/61 and 140/61, less than one month after the Syrian secession. These laws became the ultimate weapons for dispossessing the upper classes. Nasser remarked that sequestration was meant to deprive a whole class of its privileges. It must not, however, be confused with nationalization, since it did not deprive the property holder of his right to ownership as nationalization did. Those affected by the sequestration measures were allowed to keep their homes and a small plot of land to cultivate themselves. A fixed salary was also provided.[24]

Needless to say, the sequestration laws were politically motivated, since the majority of the individuals affected by them were officially regarded as subversive elements engaged in activities against the state. Nasser at that time was susceptible to all sorts of rumors about a counterrevolution. The secret service reported the activities of the outlawed Wafdists and members of the Muslim Brotherhood. It was suspected that these elements emerged after Nasser's prestige suffered a blow and were being encouraged by the propaganda campaign launched by the new military rulers in Damascus.

It must, however, be pointed out that there were varied motives behind the sequestration measures. One motive was to deprive *Kibar al-A'yan* of the right to manage their properties because of their failure to comply with the agrarian reform laws. It was also applied to individuals enriching themselves due to nepotism, bribery, and trafficking in illicit drugs and merchandise.[25] Consequently, the list included men of mixed social backgrounds. The sequestration list, announced in October 1961, included a former rector of al Azhar, journalists, writers, and newspaper publishers. It also included the most influential members of business and financial circles and families belonging to the rural upper stratum, as well as many *'Umdas* and Shaykhs. According to the figures provided by Waterbury, between 1961 and 1966 some 4,000 families (7,000 individuals) were affected by the sequestration measures. The total assets seized were close to E£ 100 million and included 122,000 faddans, 7,000 urban properties, about 1,000 business establishments, and over E£ 30 million in stocks and bonds. The second agrarian reform law led to the confiscation of a further 100,000 faddans scheduled to be redistributed among 45,800 families.[26]

Political reorganization and administrative reform were carried out side by side with sequestration measures and the political isolation of elements whose loyalties were in doubt. The organization of the ASU did not depart much from its predecessor, the NU. The ASU basic unit committees or local committees were divided into residential and work units. All committees, regardless of village size, were to have twenty members. Also, a novel departure from the NU was the election of officeholders at the local community level: ASU secretaries and assistant secretaries. The same pattern was followed in the organization of the party at the district and provincial levels. Each level was to elect its representatives to the next level, culminating in the National Congress that would elect a Central Committee and a Supreme Executive Committee.[27] The ASU elections were held in 1963; but, as pointed out by Binder, there was no significant change in the class basis of the regime, despite the trauma of the secession and the adoption of the Socialist Charter.[28]

Parallel to the attempts at party reorganization, efforts were made by the regime to rationalize the system of local government.[29] Actions during the post-1961 period were meant to improve the electoral system and to curtail the power of the wealthy families in the selection of 'Umdas. Officeholding in the local government was made contingent upon active party membership. To "democratize" village administration, Law No. 59/1964 was enacted to do away with property qualifications and to limit traditional village offices to five-year terms. Also, relatives of 'Umdas were prohibited from occupying the office of Shaykh. The new provision highlighted the government's awareness of the fact that more than one family member often dominated the village ad- ministration. Officeholding in the agricultural cooperatives was restricted to small landowners of five faddans or less. The object behind this new provision was to prevent the large landowners from exercising influence on the local agricultural cooperatives. Needless to say, the regime's action fell short of the demands of the left to abolish the 'Umda system because of its traditional ex- ploitation of the peasants.[30]

The socialist transformation of the Nasserist regime experienced its first crisis in 1964. During this crucial year, the regime came face to face with the difficult problem of weighing egalitarian requirements against economic growth, or of simultaneously maintaining redistribution as well as the savings and investment urgently needed to develop internal resources. The major obstacles hindering the latter were the harsh measures against the urban bourgeoisie and the landed elites. Nasser's difficult choices were complicated by two interrelated factors. The first was Egypt's First Five Year Plan, the objec- tives of which were unrealizable, as became apparent in light of the com- plicated international and domestic situations confronting the Nasserist regime in the mid-1960s. The second problem was Egypt's severe balance of payment deficits.

According to the economist Hazem el-Biblawi,[31] Egypt enjoyed relative economic independence until 1964 because it had sufficient reserves to draw upon between 1946 and 1958 and because of the policy of nonalignment that provided aid from both the Eastern bloc and the West. The figures provided by Biblawi showed that Egyptian reserves in the post-World War II era amounted to 430 million sterling pounds, which were exhausted in the 1950s. The policy of nonalignment between 1958 and 1964 produced the necessary external support for narrowing the gap between the country's resources and the requirements for economic growth. Since 1958, American aid through PL 480 became available to Egypt, through which wheat and agricultural products were imported. In the same period, several agreements were concluded with the Soviet Union to finance industrial projects. By 1965, Egypt's external debt amounted to $2 billion, of which $1.5 billion were actually paid. United States aid alone amounted to $530 million, as opposed to $320 million in aid from the Eastern bloc. The combination of foreign aid and internal resources through nationalization of foreign assets and confiscation and sequestration of properties belonging to the national bourgeoisie enabled the Nasserist regime to maintain both equity and a growth rate of 6.8 percent.

These favorable conditions could not be maintained after 1964, due to the withdrawal of United States aid by the Johnson administration and Egypt's shift to a total reliance on the Eastern bloc. Internally, more radical measures against the Egyptian urban and landed bourgeoisie would have produced a revolutionary situation the government wanted to avoid at all costs. The left was already disseminating information on reactionary elements who had infiltrated the ASU following the 1963 election while the socialist rhetoric of the central authorities unintentionally aroused the expectations of the peasants. In the urban areas, the Nasserist regime faced rightist threats from disgruntled members of the Muslim Brotherhood.

These changes in Egypt's international relations and in the domestic situation produced a major reorientation in the regime's radical policies. The first sign of the direction in which the regime was moving was the promulgation of the provisional constitution in 1964, which ended the state of emergency that had permitted the authorities to enforce the sequestration measures. A law enacted in March 1964 was intended to settle all outstanding claims related to sequestered properties. The law stipulated that the ownership of sequestered properties exceeding E£ 30,000 in value would revert to the state, with the payment of compensation to the owners in negotiable bonds redeemable in fifteen years at 4 percent interest. The appointment of Zakaria Muhi al-Din in October

1965 to replace 'Ali Sabri as prime minister was interpreted as an attempt by the Nasserist regime to mollify right-wing opinion.

These domestic changes produced some differences between the Nasserist regime and the recently rehabilitated left, composed of Marxists and communists, that became evident between 1965 and the flare-up during the Kamshish Affair. To understand the complex relations between the Nasserist regime and the left, it is important to bear in mind that the emergence of the left into local politics was part of the regime's shift to a pro-Soviet position and the latter's adoption of a new ideology to underline the progressive character of military-dominated governments.[32] Nonetheless, the official attitude toward leftists at home vacillated between repression and limited or controlled participation. The regime's history with the left began with the ruthless suppression of the labor movement and the emasculation of its leadership a few days after the military seized power in 1952.

Opportunities for leftist collaboration with the regime presented themselves during the post-1961 period when Nasser announced the famous "socialist decrees" and the Socialist Charter. The latter alluded to the creation of a vanguard, the *al-Jihaz al-Siyyasi*, within the ASU. This vanguard was seen by the left as the long-awaited opportunity for the creation of a party cadre on the Leninist model, which would represent the interests of the working class.[33] The official goal, however, as we will shortly observe, was entirely different.

The rehabilitation of the left began in 1963, and by the end of 1964, all Marxists and communists had been released from detention. In the wake of this development, Egypt's communist party, the Democratic Movement for National Liberation (*Haditu*), announced its self-dissolutionment. The regime, in fulfillment of its pledge to create a political apparatus within the ASU, announced the establishment of the Socialist Vanguard, and allowed former *Haditu* members to join as individuals. The Marxists intellectuals were further allowed to occupy key posts in the mass media. At this stage, also, the publication of *al-Tali-'ah* began, which soon turned into a leftist platform with critical articles on socioeconomic conditions, the bureaucracy, and the ASU.

The disillusionment of the so-called real left began with the realization that Nasser intended to allow them to participate in the political system only under state control and supervision.[34] Hamrush, a former *Haditu* member, revealed that the Vanguard was being organized into groups by men hand-picked by Nasser. The group in which Hamrush himself was a member had the largest number of former *Haditu* members.[35] Interestingly, this group was made answerable to the conservative Marshal 'Amer, first vice president and chief of the General Staff. The Vanguard's formation was the only instance, according to Hamrush, that real Marxists were integrated en masse.[36] No other candidates were allowed to join the Vanguard without first seeking the approval of the president himself through the secretary general of the ASU.[37]

Like the parent organization, which had Hussein al-Shafi'i, another conservative member of the original Free Officers Movement, as its secretary general, the Vanguard came under the control of former army officers drawn mostly from the intelligence services. Hamrush pointed out that when the first General Secretariat of the Vanguard was set up, Nasser appointed Hilmi al-Sa'id, Sha'rawi Gom'a, Abdel Ra'uf Sami Sharaf as its members, and with Gom'a as the secretary general. These men were second-string officers with intelligence backgrounds.[38]

Neither the Vanguard nor its parent organization, the ASU, had much impact on the rural areas. No serious attempt was made to create a party cadre, despite the repeated demands of the left, or to extend party control horizontally into the local communities. Evidence exists, however, indicating that some of the ASU leaders with somewhat leftist inclinations reported to higher authorities the dominant influence of some rural elite familes over local party organs. The authorities, however, did not act on the reports. The reports further disclosed that senior government officials and members of the National Assembly, including the House Speaker Anwar Sadat, were acting to prevent the ASU functionaries from inquiring into the political, social, and economic resources of rural elite families.[39]

The last stage in party mobilization was sparked by the renewed activities of the Muslim Brotherhood in 1965. A plot to assassinate President Nasser was discovered, some of the Muslim Brotherhood members were accused of conspiring with Saudi Arabia, and Sayyid Qutb's famous book *Ma'alim Fi al-Tariq* (Sign Posts on the Road) came to the attention of the authorities. The publication was seen by the authorities as a textbook calling for an armed rebellion against the state. The renewed activities of the Muslim Brotherhood sent the regime into a frenzy to find the means to confront the new challenge and to shore up its defenses. 'Ali Sabri, an ambitious, second-string officer with an aristocratic background and with leftist inclinations, became responsible for consolidating power through the use of a new mobilization drive to organize the Executive Bureaus. The organization of the Executive Bureaus began in October 1965 upon the appointment of 'Ali Sabri as the secretary general of the ASU. The Bureaus were staffed by full-time party cadres and were established in district and provincial capitals.[40] Attempts were also made to have the so-called "leadership groups" penetrate the local areas. The experiment was first started in Cairo, then spread to some of the villages of Lower Egypt. No clear organizational and functional distinctions can be drawn between 'Ali Sabri's Executive Bureaus and the Socialist Vanguard established some three years

before. It has been suggested that the Socialist Vanguard was actually functioning as the hidden arm of the Executive Bureaus. In fact, some members of the
Vanguard were recruited to serve as members of the Executive Bureaus. But it is
quite certain that the leadership of the Executive Bureaus and that of the
Vanguard tended to converge at the top. The Vanguard, because of the covert
nature of its operations, came to fulfill an important function as the conduit of
information on subversive elements.[41]

Some leftists were bitterly disappointed in the political apparatus, since
they questioned its revolutionary efficacy. Although 'Ali Sabri was identified
with progressive elements and with a pro-Soviet policy, the communists and
Marxists expressed dismay over the fact that the primary purpose of the
political apparatus was for information-gathering. They charged that the
cumbersome bureaucracy had taken over the Socialist Vanguard and the Executive Bureaus. It was pointed out that the provincial secretaries in the
Bureaus were receiving salaries equivalent to the deputy ministers and that
bureaucrats seconded to the Bureaus received additional renumerations.[42]
These incentives made the political apparatus organized by Sabri a lucrative
sinecure for petty bureaucrats. For these reasons, they considered Sabri's apparatus and the ASU as a whole a bureaucratic nightmare. Some elements of
the Egyptian left, who called themselves "real socialists" to distinguish
themselves from members of the Executive Bureaus, flocked to the High Institute for Socialist Studies and became active in the ASU's Secretariat for
Ideological Affairs, *Amanat al-Fikr wa-al-Da'wa*.[43] This branch of the ASU,
which was mainly responsible for the dissemination of socialist ideas, was headed by the former RCC officer Kamal Rif'at, whose commitment to socialism
received the grudging respect of most dedicated Marxist.

The "real socialists" organized public seminars and lectures and began to
train youths in ways to convert the masses to socialism. Some of the prominent
Marxists, such as the historian Mohammad Anis and Ibrahim Saad al-Din, were
involved in these activities. A new apparatus seemed to emerge from the decision to organize the socialists engaged in conversion activities. Ironically, the
model sought for mass conversion was the Muslim Brotherhood's *al-Da'wa*
(proselytization). The socialists responsible for carrying out the conversion activities also described themselves as *Du'a* (singular *Da'iya*). It was even claimed
that some of the socialist *Du'a* had already established themselves in villages,
especially in those villages where members of the Muslim Brotherhood were active. However, when the Ideological Affairs apparatus began to show greater
independence, 'Ali Sabri was ordered to bring its activities under control.

According to one source, Sabri's men began to infiltrate the Ideological
Affairs Secretariat after receiving a clearance from the latter's secretary, Kamal

Rif'at. The purpose of planting members of the Vanguard in the new apparatus was "to purge it of elements suspected of professing hostility toward the regime."[44] One of the group's members remarked that there was a genuine fear of them being accused of creating an organization outside the ASU. The same observer said that a conference of all socialist *Du'a* was held toward the middle of 1966 to discuss the obstacles impeding political activity. One of the these obstacles was that the undercover security branch of the Ministry of the Interior, *al Mabahith al-'Amah*, was allegedly subjecting the socialist *Du'a* to constant harassmment.[45]

From within this complex and bewildering maze of covert and overt apparatuses, an army of secret agents, and a general discontent to which the Egyptian left had given expression, the Kamshish Affair burst forth like a lightening bolt, momentarily revealing a factionalized, ruling elite with a heightened sense of insecurity. Kamshish apparently infused the leadership with a new sense of mission, and, for the left, it was the much-awaited opportunity to launch the socialist revolution.

Chapter Four
The Rural Elites
in Balance

IN JUNE 1966, IN an open self-criticism in Damanhur, Nasser admitted that, fourteen years after the revolution, feudalism in the countryside continued to exist. Large landownership had not ended despite the agrarian reforms. Nasser did not find faults in the agrarian policy, but in the fraudulent means the feudalist used to circumvent the agrarian reform laws and manipulate the authorities. The result was that some "feudal elements" continued to own up to seven hundred or eight hundred faddans. Nasser also disclosed another phenomenon of peasant exploitation, linked to monopolizing village administration rather than land per se. In his speech at Damanhur, Nasser pointed out instances of families holding only a few faddans, yet controlling the posts of 'Umda, Shaykh (section head), and Shaykh al-Ghafar (head watchman). Such families controlled the village administration to such an extent that no one dared raise his voice in opposition.

The feudalists held their peasants in perpetual debt. As Nasser explained, many peasants were forced to sign blank promissory notes that the feudalists kept in their safes by the hundreds. Other feudalists resorted to violence and crime (an obvious reference to Kamshish). In addition, many tenants or farmers on the large estates of the landed aristocracy had replaced their former masters on the social hierarchy in the village and begun also to exercise all these forms of oppression.

Nasser then went on to reveal that a Committee for the Liquidation of Feudalism (HCLF) had been formed under Field Marshal 'Abdel Hakim 'Amer, chief of the General Staff. The major objectives of the HCLF, as announced by Nasser, were to investigate all manifestations of peasant exploitation:

1. Contraventions of the agrarian reforms, including evasion of the ceilings on landownership or the limits imposed on lease holdings and violations of tenancy relations
2. Political influence in the villages as reflected by the composition of local ASU committees

97

3.   Socioeconomic influence over local agricultural cooperatives, including the control of credit facilities, agricultural supplies, and officeholdings
4.   Traditional influences as reflected by the occupation of administrative posts in the villages.

Nasser ended his speech by calling on all real socialists to participate actively in the regime's efforts to wipe out all forms of exploitation in the countryside. The composition of the HCLF, however, indicated that Nasser was not sincere about involving the real socialists, to use Hamrush's description of Marxists and former communists. As indicated by the list of HCLF membres (see Table 4), none of the Marxists were included in the investigations. In fact, Nasser's handling of the Kamshish Affair was strikingly similar to the way he disposed of the pressure from the left to form a party cadre. In both instances, Marxists and former communists were excluded from the highest level of decision making, and, in both instances, the military officers played a dominant role.

THE COMPOSITION OF THE HCLF

The activities of the HCLF were launched in May 1966, a few days after the Kamshish incident was brought to the attention of the authorities. The committee remained in session until September and was abruptly dissolved a few months thereafter. During this period, the top-ranking members of the army, the intelligence services with their military and civilian branches, the provincial administration, the ASU, and the Office of the President were brought together in a joint effort to fulfill Nasser's pledge to wipe out feudalism in the countryside.

Nasser's decision to let Marshal 'Amer assume the upper hand in the HCLF was most revealing of the regime's persisting efforts to exclude the Marxists and former communists from participation at the highest decision-making level. As indicated by Binder, the left was generally inclined to place heavy blame on 'Amer for their lack of progress in the 1960s.[1] A descendant of a rich *'Umda* class in Minya, 'Amer's conservatism was clearly revealed in his opposition to leftist solutions for Egypt's socioeconomic problems, as the minutes of the first session of the HCLF indicate. 'Amer's position in the HCLF was strengthened by the inclusion of his followers. His faction of the HCLF included Shams Badran, 'Abbas Radwan, Salah Nasr, and Hasan 'Ali Khalil. All four individuals owed their influence to 'Amer and were members of his inner circle in the Marshal's Office, *Maktab al-Mushir*. Shams Badran was the head of the Marshal's Office before he replaced 'Abdel Wahab al-Bishri as the war minister in September 1966. According to Dekmejian, the appointment of Badran as war minister represented a victory for Marshal 'Amer.[2]

Another powerful member of 'Amer's faction on the HCLF was Salah Nasr, the head of the General Intelligence Bureau, *al-Mukhabarat al-'Amah*. This bureau was the civilian branch of intelligence responsible for foreign and counterespionage activities. Under Salah Nasr, the General Intelligence Bureau earned a great deal of notoriety, which came to light only after the June War defeat and Nasser's decision to liquidate "centers of power," as 'Amer's faction and, later on, 'Ali Sabri's faction were called. Also, on the HCLF was Major Hasan Khalil, commander of the Military Criminal Investigation (MCI). The MCI maintained internal security when its civilian counterpart, the General Investigation Bureau, *al-Mabahith al-'Amah*, fell under suspicion for its failure to act on reports concerning the activities of the Muslim Brotherhood. A few months after the discovery in August 1965 of a plot to assassinate President Nasser, 'Abdel Azim Fahmi, the minister of the interior under whose control fell the General Investigation Bureau, was dismissed. Before he had become the minister of the interior in the cabinets of 'Ali Sabri and Zakariya Muhi al-Din between 1961 and 1965, 'Abdel Azim Fahmi was the head of the General Investigation Bureau.[3] He was succeeded to this post by General Hasan Tal'at, one of the powerful members of the HCLF.

Another political heavyweight, besides Marshal 'Amer, on the HCLF was 'Ali Sabri. He was a descendant of an aristocratic family influential during pre-revolutionary times. His uncle held the honorific title of *Pasha*, and his father was a senior government official. Sabri was generally identified with the left and with a pro-Soviet policy. However, much to the displeasure of the Egyptian left, the radicalization of the ASU did not take place when he assumed its leadership. Of 'Ali Sabri's faction on the HCLF, the most powerful figures were Sha'rawi Gom'a, the new minister of the interior and 'Abdel Muhsin Abu al-Nur, deputy premier for agriculture, irrigation and land reform. All four members were of the Cairo Committee of the Vanguard and were personally recruited by 'Ali Sabri.[4] This group, in addition to the other two HCLF members, Kamal al-Din al Hinnawi and 'Abdel Majid Shadid, the secretary general of the HCLF, formed a tight clique that played a crucial role in the struggle for power between President Sadat and 'Ali Sabri in May 1971.

Of the twenty-two members, the only civilian on the HCLF was 'Abdel Hamid Ghazi, the ASU's secretary for farmers' affairs. The only former officers with perhaps some leftist inclinations were Kamal al-Din Rif'at and Abdel Fattah Abu al-Fadl. Both these men were active in the Institute of Socialist Studies and the ASU's *Amanat al-Fikr wa-al-Da'wa*. As revealed by Hamrush,

TABLE 4   Members of the Higher Committee for the Liquidation of Feudalism (HCLF)

Name	Role in HCLF	Other Official Positions
'Abdel Hakim 'Amer	Chairman	First Vice President and Chief of the Army General Staff
'Abbas Radwan	Chairman of the Sub-Committee for Upper Egypt	Deputy Premier for Local Government and ASU Secretary for Upper Egypt
'Abdel Muhsin Abu al-Nur	Chairman of the Sub-Committee for Lower Egypt	Deputy Premier for Agriculture, Irrigation and Land Reform
'Abdel Majid Shadid	Secretary General	ASU Secretary for Financial Affairs and Executive Bureau Secretary for Cairo
'Ali Sabri	Member	Vice President and Secretary General of ASU
Kamal al-Din Rif'at	Member	Deputy Premier for Scientific Affairs and ASU Secretary for Propagation of Socialist Ideology
Sha'rawi Gom'a	Member	Minister of the Interior and ASU Secretary for Organization
'Abdel Fattah Abu al-Fadl	Member	ASU Secretary for Membership Affairs
Kamal al-Din al-Hinnawi	Member	ASU Secretary for Lower Egypt
'Abdel Hamid Ghazi	Member	ASU Secretary for Farmers' Affairs
Salah Nasr	Member	Director, General Intelligence Bureau
Ahmad Hamdi 'Ubayd	Member	(official position unknown)
Yusif Hafiz	Member	Deputy Minister, Ministry of the Interior
Abdel Ra'uf Sami Sharaf	Member	Secretary of the President for Information
Shams Badran	Member	War Minister
Hasan 'Ali Khalil	Member	Commander, Military Criminal Investigations

TABLE 4   Members of the Higher Committee for the Liquidation of Feudalism (HCLF)

Name	Role in HCLF	Other Official Positions
Sayyid Sayyid Jad	Member	Military Officer
Sa'd Zaghlul Abdel Karim	Member	Director, Military Police
Hasan Tal'at	Member	Director, General Invesitgation Bureau
Hasan 'Alish	Member	Director, Military Prison
'Abdel Khaliq Shawqi	Member	Military Officer
Ibrahim Mukhaymar	Member	Military Officer

however, former officers who dominated the ASU and the bureaucracy were less influential than the active military officers.[5]

THE SCOPE OF THE INVESTIGATIONS

On 19 May 1966, the HCLF held its first session to establish the proper guidelines for the provincial party and government officials to follow in meeting the objectives of the investigation. The session was attended by the provincial governors, secretaries of the ASU's Executive Bureaus, and police directors. In this session, 'Amer emphasized the social and political nature of the HCLF's activities and warned the provincial party and government officials against forming the impression that they were about to discharge one more bureaucratic responsibility.[6]

According to 'Amer, there were three causes of peasant exploitation and hardship: landownership, criminal behavior, and local control over village administration. 'Amer, however, was selective and specific about who was to be investigated. Small and medium landowners were not to be considered by the HCLF. Muhammad 'Ali Bashir, the Executive Bureau secretary in al-Sharqiyya Province, argued that the educated among the rural middle class who owned between ten to forty faddans and occupied administrative posts in the provinces were "ideologically inclined toward the reactionary forces."[7] Kamal al-Din Rif'at raised the same argument when he said that the behavior of the twenty-faddan owner was not les feudalistic than the owner of two hundred faddans or more.[8] 'Amer, in response, linked these arguments with the projected leftist solution of the problem of private property. He emphatically pointed out the regime's determination to consolidate the rural middle class by means of the mass organization. "Either we follow this solution or follow an absolute leftist solution to which we are opposed."[9] To silence his critis, 'Amer reminded them that it was the owner of two hundred faddans who used to be elected to the prerevolutionary parliaments, not the twenty-faddan landowner.[10] He went so far as to assert that the regime did not want to lose the support of owners of one hundred faddans or less. "Our struggle is with the large landowners and there is no justification for us to enter into conflict with others that might lead to the loss of all rural support."[11] Furthermore, to prevent misinterpretation of the objectives of the HCLF and to reassure the landowners of less than the one hundred-faddan limit, 'Amer asserted that the actions of the HCLF would not go beyond what the Socialist Charter had already pronounced.[12] Also, no new decrees limiting ownership were being contemplated.[13]

The investigations were to be directed against owners of large estates who qualified for the enforcement of the first agrarian reform. According to 'Amer, the large estate owners represented the dominant agrarian interest in prerevolutionary times and were "part of the rich class which held power and controlled the parties. They now constitute a counter revolutionary political force."[14] A thorough investigation was to be conducted of each person who had been dispossessed of part of his property in 1952. The extent of his present landownership and his current occupation, whether in the village, or the government, the army or the police, or the public sector of the economy, were to be examined. Information on the occupation of closely related family members was also to be included in the reports. "We must have complete information on these people, lest we leave in sensitive posts subversive elements working against the regime," 'Amer warned the HCLF members.[15]

The next step was to investigate landholdings (owned and leased land) beyond the limits prescribed by the agrarian decrees. The object of the investigation was to uncover those persons who were resorting to fraudulent means for circumventing the purpose of the agrarian reforms, which had set a ceiling on the amount of land a farmer or a tenant could own or rent. The investigations were to include all persons who were subjected to the first (1952) and second (1961) agrarian reforms.

A third problem was family influence over village administration and agricultural cooperatives. Dr. Fouad Muhi al-Din, then secretary of the Executive Bureau in al-Qalubiyyah Province, pointed out that kinship solidarity, *al-'Asabiyya al-'A'iliyya*, was deeply rooted in village life and was often reflected in the struggle for undisputed power and influence, although the family holdings might be modest, varying in size between ten to twenty faddans. Muhi al-Din's remark could be interpreted to mean the influence exerted by whole clans as revealed by Ammar in his study of the political expression of tribal solidarity in upper Egypt,[16] although I suspect that it was more narrowly defined and concentrated within what Henry Ayrout described as patriarchal families. According to Ayrout, patriarchal families were the backbones of the rural notables' power.[17] Binder's macrostudy of NU members revealed that the sociopolitical elite he had described as members of the second stratum possesed some characteristics differentiating them from kinship groups. These character-istics were (1) close relations among influential persons in kinship-based group, (2) a greater concentration of resources and opportunities within a sublineage structure, and (3) status and influence maintained in direct patrilineal descent.[18] These characteristics constituted the basis of the HCLF decision to impose collective family responsibility to evasions of the agrarian reforms or other offenses. The ruling elites, acting on their native political instincts, believed that power and influence laid with the family unit, not with the large kinship group, the individual, or the class. Although the application of collec-tive family responsibility aroused a great deal of controversy among HCLF members, as mentioned below, no serious attempt was made to challenge the official view—that the political and economic power of the few at the peak of the social pyramid laid in the wealth and social influence of their close relations in the local communities.[19]

The problem before the HCLF, however, was to establish the closeness of relations with the patriarchal head of the family—the main source of influence —to make the application of the principle of collective family responsibility possible. There was also a practical side to the problem, too, that is, to limit the scope of the HCLF investigations by excluding distant kinsmen. This problem would not have arisen had the HCLF members been content to stick to the nuclear family upon which the agrarian reforms were based. But given the ex-tensive social and political networks of the extended family, the HCLF decided to broaden the definition of the family unit by including collaterals. The scope of the investigation was to be determined by the degrees of proximity of rela-tionship to the family patriarch, *Rab-al-'A'ilah*.[20] A graduated pattern of rela-tionships to the family patriarch was therefore revealed by the HCLF: first degree (wife or wives, sons, grandsons, and unmarried daughters), second degree (brothers and their direct desendants), third degree (paternal uncles and cousins), and fourth degree (relatives by marriage). Thus, in the view of the HCLF, kinship relations within the traditionally influential family took the form of a series of concentric circles with the patriarch at the center.

To some extent, the degrees of punishment to be meted out were also determined by kinship proximity to the patriarch. The severest punishment was the imposition of sequestration and deportation from the rural areas. The

HCLF members, however, were openly divided on whether these extreme measures should apply only to the patriarchal heads or to all immediate family members (first degree relatives) as well.[21] A lesser form of punishment was dismissal from the security and administrative branches of the provincial government, including the police department, the provincial judiciary, agrarian reforms and agricultural departments, and village administration. This form of punishment was to apply to family members in the first and second degrees. However, in the most sensitive area of enrollment in the Military Academy, the process of exclusion was expanded to include paternal uncles and cousins (third degree relatives.)[22] As for those already in active military service, the dismissals were to apply only to first and second degree relatives (see Figure 17).

Although limited in its application, sequestration and deportation from rural areas put the principal of collective family responsibility to the test. Some HCLF members, representing a very small minority, balked at the thought of making children pay for offenses allegedly committed by their parents.[23] But the view of the majority was that wealth and influence were concentrated within the immediate family of the patriarch. Punishing only the individual, according to 'Ali Sabri's group and a few military officers of lower rank, would not eliminate the influence of the family as a unit. Extreme measures were therefore favored, despite the fact that some children and adult sons became landowners through legal means.

Marshal 'Amer was more inclined to use collective responsibility against the large landowners only. He reminded the HCLF members of the political purposes of their activities and that the primary objective of the HCLF was the neutralization of this segment of the rural population.[24] As stated by 'Amer, all the large landowners who were subjected to the first agrarian reform (individual ownership exceeding two hundred faddans) plus their immediate family members were to be placed under sequestration and removed from the rural areas, regardless of whether or not they had complied with the agrarian reforms. 'Amer's political stand, however, resulted in a heated argument on the validity of collective family responsibility. Interestingly, although Ali Sabri's faction supported 'Amer's position, some of the high-ranking army officers found the summary application of sequestration and deportation of large landowners unwarranted, if not harmful to the interests of the regime.[25] Shams Badran, the war minister, for example, attacked the assumption that all large landowners were disloyal to the regime. Badran argued that, although few in number, the plight of the loyal elements as a result of the summary application of sequestration and deportation might arouse the sympathy of the people.[26]

The final decision of the HCLF was highly ambiguous. Though the HCLF accepted 'Amer's political stand on the summary imposition of stiff measures against large landowners, including sequestration and deportation of the family head and immediate family members, it was decided to leave some room for exempting some individuals if sufficient evidence warranted such action.

THE METHOD OF INVESTIGATION

Information gathering fell upon the provincial administration and party apparatuses. The ASU's Executive Bureaus and the provincial administrative branches, acting under the governors of each province, were asked to forward independent reports to the General Secretariat of the HCLF (see appendix D). The Military Criminal Investigation Bureau (MCI) and the General Investigation Bureau were to check the reports of the ASU and the provincial administration; however, as indicated by our data, the MCI and its civilian counterpart carried out their own investigations and submitted independent reports to the HCLF. Furthermore, two subcommittees of the HCLF were created, one for Upper Egypt under 'Abbas Radwan and the other for Lower Egypt under 'Abdel Muhsin Abu al-Nur. The task of the subcommittees was to supervise the provincial committees drawn from the administrative branches, the representatives coming from the agricultural department, department of land reforms, department of land survey, department of taxation, and police department. The local ASU committees were excluded from representation on these provincial committees. 'Amer himself was against coordination of activities by the political apparatus at the grassroots level, overriding the objections raised by Executive Bureau members that this method of inquiry might lead to unnecessary duplication of work.[27]

'Amer singled out the ASU when explaining why other institutions were drawn into an activity that was regarded primarily as political and was, therefore, the responsibility of the mass party organization. In his meeting with the governors, ASU secretaries, and police directors of Upper Egypt on 2 June, 'Amer complained that the ASU had not penetrated the rural areas and that the power structure of the local communities was reflected in their existing ASU committees. 'Amer further declared that the ASU had lost the confidence of the *fallahin* and that the major obstacle in regaining that confidence was the dominant influence of feudal elements. Nevertheless, 'Amer added, the participation of the ASU in the HCLF activities as an independent entity would provide the political apparatus with the opportunity to penetrate the local community structure.[28] He did not explain how this goal was to be accomplished, except for vaguely mentioning that the formation of the new ASU committees was under way. There was no reference to the Leadership Groups, said to have been formed under 'Ali Sabri's mobilization drive. The elimination of the local ASU committees from the investigation thus deprived the Executive Bureaus in the district and provincial capitals of the means for gathering information at the local community level. They had to rely on villagers willing to act as informers.

'Ali Sabri also threw doubt on the ability of the local ASU committees to produce reliable information. In response to a comment made by Mustafa al-Jundi, the Executive Bureau secretary in Gharbiyya Province, that the local ASU committees ought to be the primary source of information, Sabri said, "We must be realistic, the local committees might have fallen under feudal control and any information forwarded by them might be misleading."[29] Sabri further declared that the existing committees would be dissolved and replaced by new committees, whose members would be appointed by the center. "Until then, the information gathered by the mass political organization must be checked by the HCLF against other sources of information drawn by the provincial administration, the Military Intelligence and the General Investigation Bureau."[30]

THE GEOGRAPHICAL DISTRIBUTION OF THE INVESTIGATED FAMILIES

The HCLF investigations into what it called "feudal conditions" in rural Egypt covered all the agricultural provinces. 'Ali Sabri estimated that, on the average, each province had twenty to thirty families whose members either evaded the agrarian reforms, controlled the village administration and party organs, or exercised oppressive influence. According to Sabri's estimation, the number of influential families in all the rural areas was in the range of 400 to 500.[31] However, the total number of families investigated by the HCLF was 334, of which we have complete data on only 198. Of these 198 families, only 100, with 1700 members, were found to be resident landowners whose influence extended from the village level upward to the center (see appendix E). The evidence contained in the reports forwarded to the HCLF on the resident families was confirmed by checking various lists—of National Union members in 1957 as reported by the *Golden Register*, of provincial and local ASU secretaries and assistant secretaries in 1963, and of the National Assembly members in 1957,

1960, and 1964. The effort yielded more information on the resident families, but no evidence of local or provincial influence was found for the remaining 98 families. Some of these latter families represented a long line of prerevolutionary parliamentary elite, frequently mentioned by the historians of the monarchical period as among the most prominent absentee owners.[32]

The resident families were found in 111 villages and 8 large towns in fifteen agricultural provinces. Some families had kinship ties in a number of villages, and in some cases the villages controlled by one family were not in the same district. However, the majority of the families held exclusive dominance in at least one village, as indicated by family members' occupations of positions of prestige.

Positions of prestige in the village communities are the posts of 'Umdas and Shaykhs. It has generally been assumed that, as a consequence of village expansion because of population growth, the traditional exercise of authority suffered a decline. Many of the villages with large population came under the direct influence of the central authority as a result of the conversion of the 'Umda post into a police station supervised directly by the higher organs of the provincial bureaucracy and the ministry of the interior.

The resident families that came under the HCLF investigations in 1966 included 74 'Umdas and 140 Shaykhs in 111 villages. As shown in Table 5 and in the graphic description in Figure 12, the families continued to exercise traditional influence in all villages even in large villages of 10,000 inhabitants. The HCLF data thus revealed that, despite the prohibition by a government order in 1964 against more than one family member occupying administrative posts

TABLE 5   Ratios of *'Umdas* and Shaykhs to Total Villages Under HCLF's Investigations Grouped by Population

Village Population[a] (.000)	*'Umda* per village	Shaykhs[b] per village
<2.5 (N = 31)	.75	.94
2.5 - 5.0 (N = 31)	.71	1.19
5.0 - 7.5 (N = 24)	.58	1.29
7.5 - 10.0 (N = 15)	.67	1.00
>10.0 (N = 10)	.40	1.00

[a] N = Number of Villages.

[b] Unlike *'Umdas*, a village may have more than one Shaykh.

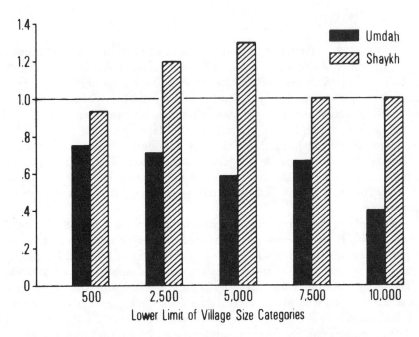

12.   Ratios of 'Umdas and Shaykhs to total villages grouped by population.

in the villages (see Chapter 3), the traditionally influential families continued to defy government restrictions.

The map in Figure 13 shows the number of villages by districts in which the families investigated by the HCLF held dominant status. We note that the districts of Fayyum in Upper Egypt and in the western sector of the Delta stand out most prominently. In contrast, we note fewer villages controlled by these families in the eastern sector of the Delta and south of Fayyum in Upper Egypt.

The provincial and regional variations in the distribution of families that came under HCLF investigation are shown in Table 6. The provincial distribution shows that the rural elite families were most prevalent in Beheira and Fayyum. Also, the number of villages under family control was greater in these provinces. The regional distribution shows that, although Lower Egypt held a large number of families coming under HCLF investigation, rural elite influence appeared to be more concentrated in Upper Egypt, as indicated by the higher number of villages controlled by each family.

Historical and social factors in part explain why a comparatively high number of families was found in Beheira and Fayyum. Briefly, the formation of large estates in the former province was associated with the level of agricultural development. Many families in the second half of the nineteenth century were

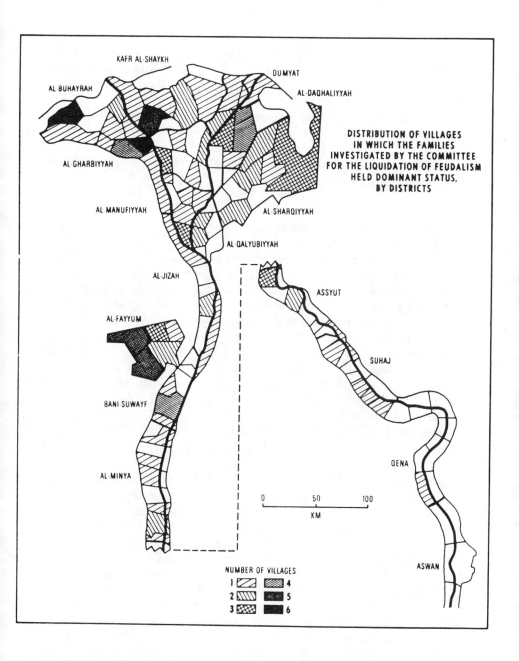

KAFR AL-SHAYKH

DUMYAT

AL-BUHAYRAH

AL-DAQHALIYYAH

AL-GHARBIYYAH

DISTRIBUTION OF VILLAGES
IN WHICH THE FAMILIES
INVESTIGATED BY THE COMMITTEE
FOR THE LIQUIDATION OF FEUDALISM
HELD DOMINANT STATUS,
BY DISTRICTS

AL-MANUFIYYAH

AL-SHARQIYYAH

AL-QALYUBIYYAH

AL-JIZAH

ASSYUT

AL-FAYYUM

SUHAJ

BANI-SUWAYF

QENA

AL-MINYA

0   50   100

KM

ASWAN

NUMBER OF VILLAGES

1   4
2   5
3   6

13. Distribution of villages in which the families investigated by the Committee for the Liquidation of Feudalism held dominant status in 1966.

granted large amounts of land by the Egyptian rulers as rewards for reclaiming desert land and bringing it under cultivation. Similarly, large amounts of land in Fayyum were granted to tribal chiefs during the same period in an effort to settle the Bedouins of the Western desert.[33]

The distribution of these influential families confirms the view that the rural elites were more prevalent in the more-developed region of Lower Egypt.[34] Nevertheless, it is clear from the distribution shown in Table 6 that rural elite influence was more concentrated in Upper Egypt, the less-developed and more traditional part of Egypt.

SOCIAL HIERARCHY AMONG RURAL ELITES

The HCLF investigations revealed three types of rural elite families at different stages of political development. The first type was the upper stratum, the descendants of the large landowners whose influence permeated the bureaucracy and parliamentary institutions before the military seized power in 1952. The second type lacked the political genealogy and the economic resources of the upper stratum families; but, after the takeover by the army officers, there was a coincidental rise in its influence, largely reflected in the local government and in the National Assembly elected in 1957, 1960, and 1964. The third type of family was still at the embryonic stage—its influence did not extend beyond the control of posts in the local government. The three types are referred to below as the upper stratum, the post-revolutionary elites and the locally-notable families. The fundamental criterion for this differentiation is accessibility to the center through parliamentary representation and its longevity.

The upper stratum was the main target of the HCLF investigations. This focus is not surprising, since families belonging to this category were identified with the ancien régime. Their influence extended from the village level upward, reaching to the center. Figure 14 gives an idea of how extensive and widespread the influence of an upper stratum family was. The combination of administrative and party influence is evident at local and higher levels. For example, the 'Umda of al-Qasr was also one of the forty-eight district representatives on the Governorate Council of Beheira Province, while his cousin, the 'Umda of Derut, held the post of health committee chairman in the rural or village council. It should also be noted that the central influence of the family had been maintained in direct lineal descent since 1876. The last family member to occupy a National Assembly seat was also the ASU secretary at the basic unit.

TABLE 6   Number of Villages Under Family Control, by Province and Region

Province	Number Families	Number Villages	Number of Villages Controlled Per Family
LOWER EGYPT			
Qalubiyya	5	4	0.80
Sharqiyya	9	12	1.33
Daqahliyya	10	11	1.10
Dumyat	2	2	1.00
Kafr al-Shaykh	8	10	1.25
Gharbiyya	5	7	1.40
Minufiyya	7	7	1.00
Beheira	19	23	1.21
TOTAL LOWER EGYPT	65	76	1.17
UPPER EGYPT			
Giza	3	4	1.33
Fayyum	11	16	1.45
Bani Suwayf	4	6	1.50
Minya	6	6	1.00
Asyut	6	5	0.83
Sohag	4	5	1.25
Qena	1	1	1.00
TOTAL UPPER EGYPT	35	43	1.23

The HCLF revealed that social hierarchy among the rural elites ran parallel to the institutional hierarchy in local government and party organization. A brief explanation of the latter may shed light on the former. As noted in chapter 3, both the administrative and party organizations were hierarchically structured. The highest positions in the local government were in the provincial capital directly supervised and directed by governors and their Councils. At the middle and low levels were the district Councils and the traditional 'Umda posts. With the exception of some attempts at administrative rationalization and decentralization in the 1960s, the hierarchical order of local government remained roughly the same since its inception in the middle of the 19 century. The party apparatus adopted in the 1950s was also conceived with the hierar-

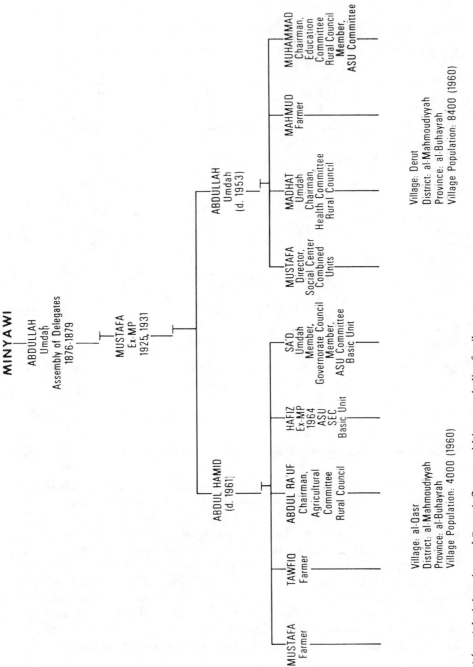

14.   Administrative and Party influence within a rural elite family.

chical order as the principal mode of organization. Furthermore, the reorganization of the single party in the guise of the Arab Socialist Union (ASU) to replace the National Union (NU) in the early 1960s did not deviate from the hierarchical order. The most influential positions were held at the governotate level, followed by district and village levels in a descending order.

Table 7 examines positions in the local government in relationship to social hierarchy among the families differentiated by their political genealogies. It will be observed that the highest positions were controlled by families that included descendants of prerevolutionary parliamentary elites or the upper stratum. By contrast, the postrevolutionary elite families and the locally notable families exerted greater influence over traditional administrative posts in village communities.

The establishment of the NU to fill the political gap resulting from the abolishment of the multiparty system increased the opportunities for rural elite families to augment their social positions. Although party status was largely ceremonial, it did serve to strengthen traditional influences over local sources of power while fulfilling the critical function of acting as intermediaries between the center and the periphery.

TABLE 7   Political Hierarchy Among the Families Investigated by the HCLF Correlated With Influence in the Local Government

Political Hierarchy	'Umda & Shaykh		District Council		Governorate Council	
	No	%	No	%	No	%
Locally Notable Families	33	52.4	0	0.0	2	11.8
Post Revolutionary Elite Families	10	15.9	0	0.0	3	17.6
Upper Stratum Families	20	31.7	5	100.0	12	70.6
TOTALS	63	100.0	5	100.0	17	100.0

SOURCE: Reports of the Committee for the Liquidation Feudalism.

The NU did not produce changes in local power relations. Family influence in the local government ran parallel to its influence in the party apparatus. Often the same individual held both administrative and parallel party posts. For example, the majority of the Governorate Council members were also district-level NU officers, while, at the local level, all 'Umdas and Shaykhs were also members of the local NU committees. In the light of our previous observation on the strong relationship between political hierarchy among the rural elites and positions held in the local government, it must not be surprising to find that of 34 NU district officers uncovered by the HCLF's investigations 24 (70.6 percent) belonged to the upper stratum families. The convergence between traditional influence in local government and party influence confirms the view that the single-party method brought men of the old order back into power.

The change in Nasser's political orientation following the Syrian secession of 1961 led to party reorganization under the influence of a radical socialist doctrine. This reorganization was accompanied by determined efforts by the regime to prevent reactionary elements from infiltrating the party apparatus. The ASU was elected in 1963 under tight screening procedures. The candidates to key posts in the party were subjected to close scrutiny, lest subversive elements find their way back into power. The results of the elections, however, showed an increase in the local committee representation among the families that became the target of subsequent investigations. Following the ASU elections, these families increased their representation from 269 to 399. This increase may be attributed to the expansion of all ASU local committees to 20 members, whereas under the NU organizaton committee size was determined by village population. The introduction of officeholding in the local party organization strengthened further traditional influence. In light of the HCLF data, the families included 71 ASU secretaries and 38 assistant secretaries.

Table 8 confirms the views of the regime's leftist critics, during the HCLF's investigations, on the lack of social change in the rural areas, despite the ASU's reorganization and the adoption of a socialist formula. The upper stratum families or the feudal families continued to dominate the higher organs of the ASU at both the district and governorate levels. Furthermore, the traditional influence of the notable families was reflected in the local communities, an important factor in the decision of the central authorities to bypass the local committees in their investigations of traditional influence.

The continuity underlying the social base of party organization, despite the ideological change at the center, may further be confirmed by comparing the different levels of influence exerted by all the resident families in the NU and ASU organizations. As shown in Table 9, the relationship between the two

TABLE 8   Political Hierarchy Among the Families Investigated by the HCLF Correlated
With Influence in the ASU

Political Hierarchy	Local Officer		District Officer		Governorate Committee	
	No	%	No	%	No	%
Locally Notable Families	24	57.1	2	22.2	0	0.0
Post Revolutionary Elite Families	5	11.9	2	22.0	6	28.6
Upper Stratum Families	13	31.0	5	55.6	15	71.4
TOTALS	42	100.0	9	100.0	21	100.0

SOURCE: Reports of the Committee for the Liquidation Feudalism.

scaled variables of the NU and the ASU was significant ($p = .0001$), indicating
continuity of rural elite influence at all levels. The families that included
district officers or members of the National Assembly in 1957 and 1960 captured more than the expected number of seats in the Governorate Committee
following the 1963 elections. As pointed out earlier, the majority of these
families belonged to the upper stratum or the descendants of the prerevolutionary parliamentary elites.

All available evidence seems to indicate that the district capitals were the
seats of influence for the upper stratum families. The regression analysis in
Table 10 lends strength to this observation. Several independent variables were
selected to study their effects on Governorate Committee membership, as the
dependent variable. None of the independent variables seems to have had as
much effect on the appointment of Governorate Committee members as
membership in the district council ($p = .005$) with a coefficient of .40. Holding
the 'Umda post also appeared to be related to membership in the Governorate
Committee ($p = .02$) with a coefficient of .13. These findings suggest that it
was more likely to find members in the ASU's Governorate Committee who
were district council members in the local government and also connected by
family ties with village leaders. Nonetheless, high status in the local govern-

TABLE 9   Families' NU Rank versus ASU Rank

| NU Scale of Elective Status | ASU Scale of Elective Status | | | | | Total Families |
	No Rank	Comm. Memb.	Unit Officer	Dist. Officer	Govt. Comm. Memb.	
No Rank	9a 2.4	1 1.0	2 5.0	0 1.1	0 2.5	12
Committee Member	7 10.8	6 4.3	31 22.7	3 4.9	7 11.3	54
District Officer	1 3.0	1 1.2	5 6.3	3 1.3	5 3.1	15
MP, 1957 or 1960	3 3.8	0 1.5	4 8.0	3 1.7	9 4.0	19
Total Families	20	8	42	9	21	100

x^2: 46.68, DF = 12, Prob. = 0.0001

a The upper figure in each category is the obseved occurrence, the lower figure is the expected frequency of occurrence (see methodological explanation in appendix A).

ment appeared to be most decisive in the selection of individuals to serve on the Governorate Committee.

The above conclusion, however, reveals a curious anomaly in the pattern of rural elite influence reflected in the inverse relationship between local power and external influence. This anomaly in the diffusion of rural influence will become apparent by examining the effects of several independent variables on the changes that had occurred in family representation in the local committees following the ASU elections—see dependent variable RDIFF in Table 11 representing the difference in family representation on the ASU committees in comparison with the NU committees. Two variables, 'Umdas and Shaykah, had significant (p = .005) effects on RDIFF, with coefficients of 1.62 and .98, respectively. If a family member had one 'Umda, then, on average, it gained 1.62 committee members relative to a family without 'Umdas. Similiarly, each additional Shaykh a family had was worth roughly one extra committee seat gained or one fewer seat lost. Total family landownership (TOTFLOS) was probably related to RDIFF, although its coefficient (– .48) was not significantly different from zero. Families with greater amounts of land in 1966 experienced more of a decline in committee membership, up to roughly one-half seat per unit. Higher administrative posts were not related to RDIFF; the coefficient for

TABLE 10   Multiple Regression Using Membership on The ASU's Governorate
Committees (GVCMP) As the Dependent Variable

Independent Variable	Coefficient	Significance	Standard Error
Intercept	– .22	.0100	.08
Governorate Council Member (MEMGC)	– .07	.4701	.10
District Council Officer (ODC)	.40	.0057	.14
Number of 'Umdas (NUMDA)	.13	.0228	.06
Number of Shaykhs (NSHK)	– .04	.2555	.03
Family size in the NU Committees (NUFRACT)	– .13	.3552	.14
Family Adult Population (FP)	.02	.0004	.005
Lower/Upper Egypt (UPLOW)	.11	.1877	.08

MEMGC was – .10. Finally, district officeholding (ODC), family adult
population (FP), and regional location (UPLOW) did not appear to have an effect of the same magnitude as was noted for the traditional offices of *'Umda*
and Shaykh.

In sum, the adaptive capacity of the traditional elites to the ideological
and political changes at the center was manifested at every level of the local
government and party apparatus. On the local level, the real force behind the
traditionalization of the party apparatus was the *'Umda* class, despite the

TABLE 11   Multiple Regression Using Change in Family Representation on Party's
Local Committees as the Dependent Variable (RDIFF)

Independent variable	Coefficient	Significance	Standard Error
Intercept	1.34	.3924	1.56
Governorate council member (MEMGC)	– .10	.9180	.96
District Council member (ODC)	1.04	.4412	1.35
Number of 'Umdas (NUMDA)	1.62	.0042	.54
Number of Shaykhs (NSHK)	.98	.0023	.31
Total family landownership (TOTFLOS)	– .48	.1654	.34
Family population (FP)	.04	.4392	.05
Upper/Lower Egypt (UPLOW)	.34	.6582	.76

[a] Measurement units for the independent variables may be reviewed in appendix A.

reorganization of local government on the basis of a new electoral procedure and limited tenure. The available data shows that administrative and party reorganization in the early 1960s proved ineffective in limiting traditional authority in the villages. On the provincial level, the HCLF data reveals that the upper stratum families, distinguished by descendancy from ancestors who dominated the prerevolutionary parliaments, continued to exert influence over high levels in local government and the party, despite tight screening procedures imposed on the selection of key party officials. At the local level, the families that traditionally controlled the 'Umda post continued to enjoy unmitigated influence in the local communities. It will now be interesting to observe the effects the agrarian reforms had on social and political stratification in the countryside.

THE AGRARIAN REFORMS AND THE
EMERGENCE OF MULTIPLE OWNERSHIP WITHIN THE FAMILY

Many scholars have strongly argued that, because of the agrarian reforms, large landownership ceased to exist.[35] The breakup of large holdings in the agrarian structure was generally regarded to be of crucial significance, and from it some questionable conclusions about changes in the rural social structure were drawn. The first of these conclusions was that the Nasserist regime, through implementation of the agrarian reforms, had uprooted the old class of big landowners. These elite were now condemned as "feudal" owners whose relations with the peasants were based on the most primitive tenurial system and who were for the most part absentee owners.[36] Secondly, it was asserted that the major beneficiary of the agrarian policy was the rural middle class. Many scholars remarked on the steady improvement in the circumstances of medium-sized landowners,[37] and, as a social class, it was described as the "privileged class" or the "rich peasants" or the "capitalist farmers"[38] to underscore the shift of the center of political and economic gravity from the large landowners to this "new privileged stratum of rich peasants."[39]

These conclusions were derived for the most part from gradations, somewhat uncertain, of landownership in official statistics. These statistics divided landownership into large, medium, and small holdings. Some of the serious limitations on use of these records has been pointed out by several authors.[40] One drawback in the official statistics was the distortion of the extent of landed property concentration. A landowner with pieces of land in several villages was not counted in the official data as one owner, but as several. Also, many landowners produced fictitious bequests as part of their attempts to transfer excess property to family members. It was common knowledge that many of the big owners evaded the agrarian reforms by resorting to such fraudulent measures. Needless to say, an entirely different picture of property concentration would have emerged had the official statisticians and those who had made extensive use of them concentrated on property distribution within the family unit. Few examined the possibility that the swelling in the ranks of the intermediate strata was a consequence of land, held among closely related family members being divided as part of the big landowners' attempts to preserve their large estates.[41]

As revealed by the minutes of the HCLF, the family unit was an important consideration in the implementation of political and economic objectives. The social and political significance of the traditions of mutual aid and solidarity in the peasant community were fully understood by the authorities. Some of the HCLF members pointed out how the big landowners had responded to the pressures of the agrarian reforms without violating specific regulations on land ceilings. As remarked by 'Abdel Muhsin Abu al-Nur, HCLF member and deputy premier of agriculture, irrigation and land reform, almost all land-holdings were within the legal limits set by the reforms, but the problem of peasant exploitation and elite control over village affairs persisted, mainly because of the large number of family members who held land as a result of property redistribution.[42]

It is not surprising that the HCLF imposed collective family responsibility. However, the HCLF members had a different understanding of what con-stituted a family unit than the one adopted when the agrarian reforms were implemented. The HCLF definition was based on the extended family system, which included the patriarchal head of the family, *Rab al-'A'ilah*, as well as col-laterals and affines defined by proximity of relationship to the family head. By contrast, the family unit during the implementation of the agrarian reforms was defined as the nuclear family, that is, married couples and their minor children. As I have pointed out earlier, the HCLF members became aware of the political significance of kinship solidarity, hence the decision to expand the scope of the investigations to include members of the larger family. The impact of the agrarian reforms on relations within the extended family was another reason for abandoning the narrowly based definition of the family unit. When the agrarian reforms were first conceived, the general aim was to create a com-munity of small farmers with economically viable holdings.[43] The Nasser regime hoped to realize this objective by forcing the upper stratum families to sell land they held in excess of the limit set by the agrarian reforms to small farmers or to divide a maximum of one hundred faddans among dependent children. It was naively thought that large estates would be parcelled out when the dependent children became adults with independent households.[44] The outcome was quite the opposite. It has been argued that "instead of breaking up the traditional network of the joint families and kinship groups, the reform has strengthened their interaction and widened the scope of their functions."[45]

A short review of the agrarian reform laws and their effects on land distribution will show that large concentrations of property persisted even within the nuclear family. The first agrarian reform law (1952) imposed a maximum holding of two hundred faddans per individual and allowed the transfer of one hundred faddans to children, but no attempt was made to restrict ownership within the total family unit. The combined ownership of the nuclear family, however, became the subject of later legislation. In 1958, an amendment to the 1952 agrarian reform law limited family ownership to three hundred faddans, but the amendment applied only to future acquisition of property either through inheritance or contracts. The amendment, therefore, did not affect families whose combined ownership was in excess of three hundred faddans at the time of its adoption. In the same year, landholding, al-Hiyazah (owned and leased land), was also limited to three hundred faddans. This restriction was clearly aimed at rich peasants who expanded their holdings by taking advantage of the recent reduction in rent. Another attempt to break up property concentration within one family was the abolishment of the Waqf. With this decision, one of the factors that accounted for the continuity of large estates in the first half of the twentieth century was eliminated.[46]

With the radicalization drive of July 1961, a second agrarian reform law was enacted limiting individual ownership to one hundred faddans. Interestingly, family ownership was completely ignored by the new law. The only reference to the family unit was the imposition of a fifty-faddan limit on al-Hiyazah i.e., landholding operated as one unit and registered with the local agricultural cooperative. The failure to restrict family ownership led to a great deal of controversy among jurists. The basic issue was whether the limit imposed on family ownership in 1958 was still in force. This controversy was not settled by the declaration of al-Mithaq, following the conclusion of the National Conference of Popular Forces convened in 1962. The Mithaq stated that the ultimate objective of the agrarian policy was to limit individual ownership to fifty faddans and family ownership to one hundred faddans by 1970. It was hoped, as Nasser declared at the conference, that by 1970 the concentration of land within one family would be broken up by natural processes. The dependent children would in time become adults with families and properties of their own.

The parcellization of land through the natural process did not take place as expected; therefore, a third agrarian reform law was enacted in 1969 that limited individual ownership to fifty faddans and family ownership to one hundred faddans. This last law left no ambiguity about the total amount of land a given family could own, but it had come about almost eighteen years after the army officers had seized power. In the meantime, the pattern of ownership within the family had been completely transformed. Multiple ownership emerged within the nuclear and extended family systems. Also, the consolidation of property under *al-Hiyazah*, usually exploited by the family head or *Rab al-'A'ilah*, became a major phenomenon of the postreform era. It is no surprise that the repeated efforts to break up property concentration led to greater combination and consolidation, especially among the upper stratum families.

The data on multiple, large landownership within traditionally influential families were derived from the list of persons subjected to expropriation under the three agrarian reform laws (1952, 1961, and 1969). In addition, we have used the HCLF data to identify family members who experienced expropriation in 1952 and 1961 and to determine their proximity of relationship to the *Rab al-'A'ilah* in order to exclude distant relatives. Figure 15 makes use of these factors in the study of one traditionally dominant family. The figure illustrates what is meant by multiple, large landownership within the family unit as defined by the HCLF.

The Zahran family established its political status toward the end of the nineteenth century. Muhammah 'Ali Salih was a member of the Legislative Assembly under British occupation. 'Abd al-Zahir 'Ali 'Ali Salih, the patriarchal head, was a senator and a Wafdist deputy in the parliaments under the constitutional monarchy. Also, Muhammad 'Abd al-Majid 'Uthman Salih (third degree relative of the family patriarch) was a Wafdist deputy and secretary of the Wafd Committee in 1950. In the postrevolutionary period, Fuad Ahmad 'Ali Salih held the post of *'Umda* as well as the post of ASU secretary at the basic unit. In 1968, he was elected to the ASU's Governorate Committee. The family also controlled the agricultural cooperative in the village.

Figure 15 shows two parallel effects of property distribution—from inheritance and from the pressures of the agrarian reforms. In regard to the former, the evidence clearly contradicts the generally held view that land being parcelled into small holdings as a result of inheritance would ultimately bring an end to the large estates. Note the formation of large estates among the descendants of 'Ali Salih (marked by the asterisk). 'Ali Salih's property was converted into *Waqf* towards the end of the nineteenth century. After the abolishment of the *Waqf*, the property was divided among 'Ali Salih's heirs on the basis of two shares for the male and one share for the female members. With few exceptions, the proportion of inherited property was much smaller

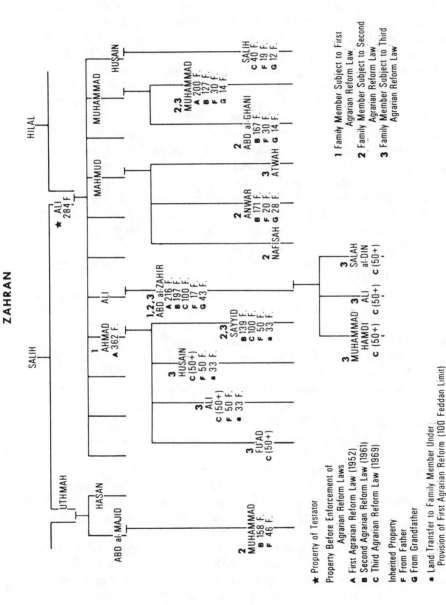

15. Effects of Islamic inheritance and agrarian reform laws on members of a rural elite family.

than the total amount of land owned by the descendants in different periods. In the Muhammad 'Ali branch, for example, one of the grandsons owned 200 faddans in 1952 and 127 faddans in 1961 before the implementation of the first and second agrarian reforms. His share of inheritance from his father, however, amounted to only a small portion of the total amount owned. This small proportion of inherited property in the large estates indicates that some of the rural elites had the resources and opportunities to expand their holdings by buying more land.

The second revealing aspect of the distribution of land among family members is the intergenerational effects of the agrarian reforms. The numerical symbols in the diagram distinguish the family members who were subjected to the agrarian reforms. The patriarchal head of the Zahran family, 'Abd al-Zahir, experienced expropriation three times. By glancing at the steady decline in his holdings from 1952 to 1969, one would assume, as many writers concluded after examining the official statistics, that large estates ceased to exist by 1969. We would, however, draw an entirely different picture if we considered the combined ownership of his immediate family members. We have no data on the actual amount of land owned by his sons before 1969; however, since all of them were subjected to expropriation under the third agrarian reform, we are quite certain that the amount of land each owned exceeded fifty faddans before this law was enforced. As many scholars asserted, property division among immediate family members was nominal. In sum, combined family holdings account for the continuity in the large concentration of property among rural elite families.

Table 12 shows in actual numbers the families and the landowners within the families whose properties were in excess of the limits defined by the

TABLE 12   Number of Families and Landowners within the Families Subjected to the Three Agrarian Reform Laws

| | Agrarian Reforms | | | Total without duplication |
	1952	1961	1969	
Families	32	47	50	64
Landowners	65	148	190	291
Average individuals per family	2.0	3.1	3.8	4.5

SOURCE: List of persons subject to Law No. 178/1952, Law No. 127/1961, and Law No. 50/1969. Evidence on the relationship of landowners within a given family is found in data from the Committee for the Liquidation of Feudalism.

agrarian reform laws and were therefore expropriated. Some family members had their lands expropriated three times, whereas others were affected twice or only once. The last column gives the totals without duplication. Among those investigated by the HCLF, then, 64 families had 291 members who were dispossessed of parts of their land as a result of the enforcement of the agrarian reforms. The biggest increase in the proportion of family members who experienced expropriation was in 1969, following the enforcement of the third reform law. The average number of affected individuals per family almost doubled in 1969 as opposed to 1952.

The map in Figure 16 shows the geographical distribution of families with multiple large landowners and the provincial variation in the application of the three agrarian reforms. The map differentiates families belonging to an upper group (four or more landowners) from those in a lower group (one to three landowners). Fayyum in Upper Egypt had a high proportion of families with multiple, large landowners in the upper group. Under the first agrarian reform law, which expropriated properties of over two hundred faddans, besides Fayyum, the families in al-Qalubiyya, Sharqiyya, and Kafr al-Shaykh were most affected. The families in all the other provinces fell in the lower group of one to three large landowners.

Under the second agrarian reform law, which limited individual owner-ship to one hundred faddans, we note that, in addition to those in Fayyum and al-Qalubiyya, the next families to appear with multiple owners in the upper group were in Asyut and Sohag in Upper Egypt and in the western sector of the Delta in the provinces of Beheira and Kafr al-Shaykh.

Under the third agrarian reform law, which limited individual ownership to fifty faddans, we note an increase in the proportion of families in the upper group of multiple owners in the provinces of Upper Egypt. Most of the families in Lower Egypt fell into the lower group of from one to three large landowners. A possible explanation for the increase in the number of owners within the families subjected to the 1969 agrarian reform is that, under the pressure of the successive agrarian reforms, the traditionally influential families had resorted to breaking up property concentrated in the hands of one individual and redis-tributing it among family members. The breakup of property was most prevalent among the upper stratum families I have identified as the descend-ants of members of the prerevolutionary parliaments.

Table 13 shows that a differentiation of families by political genealogy is significantly related to property concentration ($P = .0001$). Thus, it was more likely for families having prerevolutionary MP ancestors to contain one or more landowners subjected to the 1952 agrarian reform law, and it was less likely for families whose political influence did not extend beyond the local community to have large landowners. Also, as indicated by the ratios of the observed to the

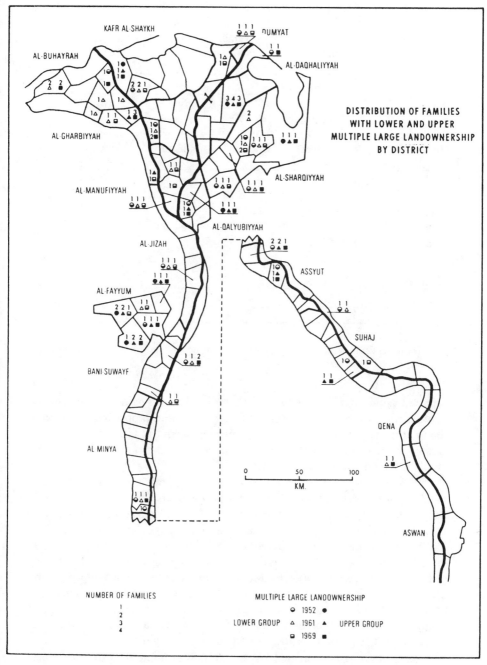

16. Distribution of families with multiple large landownerships by districts.

TABLE 13   Political Hierarchy Among the Families Investigated by the HCLF
correlated with degrees of property concentration

Political Hierarchy	Unexpropriated 1969 (owned <50 faddans)	Expropriated			Total families
		(owned >50 faddans)	1961 (owned >100 faddans)	1952 (owned >200 faddans)	
Locally Notable Families	23[a] 13.7	4 4.6	6 7.6	5 12.2	38
Postrevolutionary Elite Families	8 5.8	3 1.9	3 3.2	2 5.1	16
Upper Stratum Families	5 16.6	5 5.5	11 9.2	25 14.7	46
TOTAL Families	36	12	20	32	100

X^2: 30.0; DF = 6; Prob. = .0001

   [a]The upper figure in each category is the observed occurrence, the lower figure is the expected frequency of occurrence (see appendix A).

expected values, it was more likely for families that had gained parliamentary status in the postrevolutionary era to fall into the unexpropriated category or the intermediate stratum. In short, the pressure from the agrarian reforms was greater on members of the upper stratum than on the rural middle class or locally influential families.

If, as indicated earlier, the pressures of the agrarian reforms led to the break up of properties, then we should expect a greater number of large landowners within families of the upper stratum. Table 14 shows a strong relationship between political hierarchy and multiple, large landownership (P = .0001). In particular, we note that, of the families in the upper group of four or more large landowners, significantly more than expected were in the category of families with prerevolutionary MP ancestors, but fewer than expected appeared in the other two categories. Thus, we can conclude that the higher proportion of multiple, large landownership within the families of the upper stratum underscores the continuity of their large landownership status and reflects a greater property redistribution among family members.

By means of regression analysis, we can now examine the extent to which party-bureaucratic penetration of the rural areas affected the dominancy of the

TABLE 14 Political Hierarchy Among the Families Investigated by the HCLF correlated with Multiple Ownership

Political Hierarchy	Unexpropriated families small-medium owners	Families with multiple large landowners		Total families
		lower group (1-3)	upper group (>4)	
Locally Notable Families	23[a] 13.7	14 14.1	1 10.3	38
Postrevolutionary Elite Families	8 5.8	7 5.9	1 4.3	16
Upper Stratum Families	5 16.6	16 17.0	25 12.4	46
TOTAL Families	36	37	27	100

X^2: 39.2; DF = ; Prob. = .0001

[a] The upper figures in each category is the observed occurrence, the lower figure is the expected frequency of occurrence (see appendix A).

upper stratum families in the local government and party apparatus. It was observed earlier that local government was organized on a hierarchical order. On the local community level, the most prestigious posts were those of *'Umda*, Shaykh or deputy *'Umda*, and director of the agricultural cooperative. As pointed out by many authors, these posts reflected power relations within the village community. Outside the village, the District Councils and the Governorate Councils served as the higher administrative units in each province. To show the relationship between administrative influence and landownership, multiple ownership was regressed on the administrative positions of family members. According to the regression results in Table 15, only Governorate Council membership, the highest administrative post next to the centrally appointed governor, was significant (P = .0039), with a coefficient of 0.64. These results indicate that holders of high administrative positions were much more likely to belong to large landowning families.

Since we found earlier evidence of convergence in the upper hierarchies of the provincial administration and party organization, we should expect to find strong correlations between high party position and multiple, large landownership. Under the NU scheme, we note in the regression results shown in Table 16 that the occupation of district office was significantly (P = .007) related to

TABLE 15   Family Administrative Status Correlated with Multiple Ownership

Independent variable	Coefficient	Significance	Standard Error
Intercept	1.89	.0001	.13
Governorate Council member	0.64	.0039	.22
District Council officer	0.19	.5236	.30
cUmda	0.01	.9532	.12
Shaykh	– 0.04	.4725	.06
Agricultural Cooperative director	– 0.14	.4375	.18

multiple landownership, with a coefficient of 0.36. Given that many of the upper stratum families contained two or three district officers, the chances of these families falling into the upper group of four or more large landowners were much greater than for families whose influence was concentrated in the lower level of party organs. The multiple, large landownership status for families with NU district officers strongly confirms the view that they formed a higher order of status, as indicated by their descent from prerevolutionary ancestors and *'Izba* ownership.[47]

Let us now see to what extent party reorganization under the ASU affected the status of families with multiple, large landownership. I earlier argued that there was little change in the influence of families at both the local and provincial levels after reorganization of the local government and party apparatus in the early 1960s. I have futher argued that, despite tight screening, Nasser's selective procedures to fill party posts at the provincial level favored members of the upper stratum families.

Table 17 shows the relationship between the party status of families in the ASU hierarchy and multiple, large landownership. According to the regression results, officeholding on the local level was significantly (P = .0015) related to the dependent variable, with a coefficient of .50. Given that many of the families that maintained local influence had two or more basic unit officers, it is possible to argue with confidence that, following party reorganization in 1963 under the radicalization trend, the influence of the large landowners among the upper stratum families was reflected at the local community level. Although some of the upper stratum families were found in the upper party hierarchy, such families had fewer large landowners subjected to the agrarian reforms. The data shows that there was sufficient ground for the fear aroused by the Egyptian left that the large landowners were able to consolidate their posi-

TABLE 16   Family Status in the National Union Correlated with Multiple Ownership

Independent	Coefficient	Significance	Standard Error
Intercept	1.82	.0001	.13
MP (1957, 1959)	0.04	.7743	.15
NU District officer	0.36	.0070	.13
Percentage of family representatation on NU local committees	− 0.21	.4293	.26

tions in the local communities by capturing party offices which prompted the HCLF to bypass them in its investigations of feudal influence. (See Appendix B for a summary on the effects of property distribution.)

AL-HIYAZAT

More interesting than multiple landownership is the development of land-holdings, or *al-Hiyazat*, within the family unit, for this area of farming activity revealed the remarkable adjustment the big landowners were able to make to the new economic order imposed by the central authorities. *Al-Hiyazat* refers to the actual operational unit of cultivation held by one invidividual either as owner, as tenant, or as both.[48] As I noted earlier, the tenancy law of 1961 limited the operational unit of the farming area to fifty faddans. All land-owners and tenants were required by law to register their holdings at the local

TABLE 17   Family Status in the Arab Socialist Union Correlated with Multiple Ownership

Independent variable	Coefficient	Significance	Standard Error
Intercept	1.88	.0001	.12
Governorate Committee member	0.26	.1574	.19
District officer	0.12	.5883	.22
Basic unit officer	0.50	.0015	.15
Percentage of family representation on local ASU committees	− 1.67	.0001	.40

agricultural cooperatives. The law further prohibited cultivation by proxy, a prohibition clearly aimed at absentee owners.

The economic incentives for seeking membership in the local cooperatives laid in their provision of loans, either in cash or in kind, for seeds, insecticides, fertilizers, agricultural equipment, irrigation pumps, and a host of other farming needs. As shown in Table 18, some members of the upper stratum and local notable families held important positions in the local cooperatives. One of the important functions of the directors was to approve credits and verify the identity of landholders registered at the cooperatives.

To overcome the constraints on joining the cooperatives, the big landowners often resorted to registering their holdings in the names of family members or in the names of tenants and agricultural workers, while they themselves received the loans and supplies. Table 19 provides an example of the holdings within one family, as recorded at the local agricultural cooperative of Shabah in District Dasuq as of January 1966. (see Figure 17). The debts owed to the village cooperative are shown for each holding. The table shows that a total of 447 faddans was divided into fourteen holdings, and the size of each holding, with one or two exceptions, was within the range of ten to fifty faddans. As was revealed by the HCLF's investigators, however, the entire area was actually under family control and was operated as a single unit.

The above example suggests that little significance can be attached to individual holdings; they must be related to the farm area under family control. The statistical evidence on the decline of large landholdings (fifty faddans and over) and the increase in the farm are of medium-sized holdings (from five to less than fifty faddans) from 1950 to 1961 was generally based on individual holdings,[49] but no attempt was made to examine the distribution of holdings within the family unit.

Interesting differences between the upper stratum families and rural notables were disclosed by examining the distribution of landholdings by types

TABLE 18   Officeholding in Local Cooperatives by Descendancy Status

Descendancy Status	Director	%	Accountant/ Secretary	%	Board Member	%
Notable Families*	20	54.1	26	65.0	34	74.0
Upper Stratum Families	17	45.9	14	35.0	12	26.0
TOTAL	37	100.0	40	100.0	46	100.0

*Including postrevolutionary elite families.

TABLE 19   Distribution of Holdings within One Family

Relationship to Family Head	Size of Holding (Faddans)	%	Debts (in E£)	%
Head of the Family	48	10.1	1271	10.3
Grandson	49	10.3	1191	9.7
Grandson	51	10.7	916	7.4
Grandson	45	9.4	1965	15.9
Grandson	47	9.9	2283	18.5
Grandson	45	9.4	2726	22.1
Grandaughter	14	2.9	4	.03
Granddaughter	12	2.5	38	.3
Grandaughter	12	2.5	21	.2
Grandaughter	15	3.1	—	—
Grandaughter	20	4.2	600	4.9
Grandaughter	13	2.7	403	3.3
Daughter-in-Law	57	11.9	—	—
Daughter-in-Law	49	10.3	919	7.4
TOTAL	477	99.9	12337	100.03

of tenure. As indicated earlier, multiple, large landownership was more prevalent among upper stratum families. Many of the rich notables, however, expanded their holdings through tenancy arrangments following the drastic reduction in rent by government order. Therefore, it is no surprise to note marked differences between the two groups of families in the distribution of landholdings by types of tenure as shown in Table 20.

The area of pure ownership was much larger for the upper stratum families. Furthermore, they had fewer holdings in the mixed category (owned and leased) than did the notable families. Clearly, recourse to tenancy was less widespread among members of the upper stratum.

So far, this analysis has concentrated on the distinction between freeholds and leased holdings, with little attention to the relationship between the landlord and the land user or immediate cultivator. As indicated by Abdel-Fadil, land tenure systems in Egypt "embrace a complex set of relationships involving many forms and bundles of land-use rights."[50] It will be interesting to examine, in light of the HCLF data, the relationship between landlords and peasants in the operation of farms.

The official statistics traditionally divided farm holdings into three tenure systems: cash tenancy, sharecropping, and owner's self-operation. On the basis of the HCLF revelations, I have found it necessary to add a fourth, "mixed"

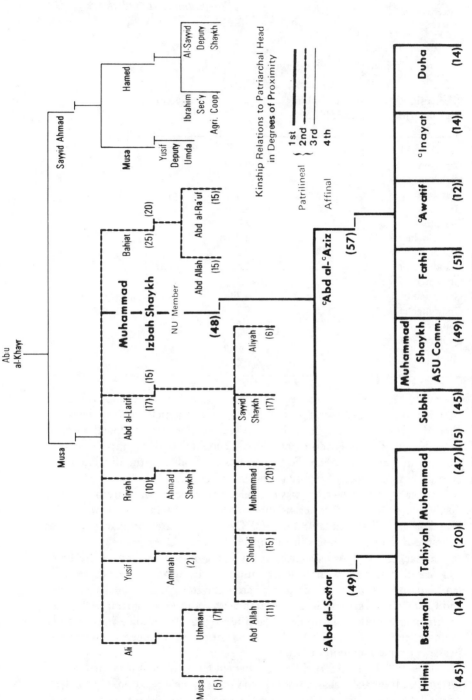

17. Distribution of landholdings registered with the local agricultural cooperative, 1966.

TABLE 20   Distribution of Types of Land Tenure by Descendancy Status

Descendancy Status	Pure Ownership				Ownership & Tenancy			
	Number of Holdings	%	Area of Holdings (Faddans)	%	Number of Holdings	%	Area of Holdings (Faddans)	%
Notable* Families	198	53.7	7172	41.6	110	76.9	2845	58.3
Upper Stratum Families	171	46.3	10077	58.4	33	23.1	2038	41.7
TOTAL	369	100.0	17249	100.0	143	100.0	4883	100.0

*Including postrevolutionary elite families.

type of relationship to account for the fact that many big landowners resorted to all three types of farm-holding relationships. The "mixed" type of tenure, both in the number and the area of holdings, clearly was most favored by the upper stratum and the locally notable families, mainly because of the official limits imposed on both landownership and landholding. Property "dispersion" by using the three tenure systems, when it was not possible to divide the land among family members, became one method of preventing the government from detecting the actual amount of land being exploited. As frequently mentioned in the reports to the HCLF, one of the abuses of tenancy relations was the refusal of landlords to issue written contracts to tenants; thus, only land within the legal limits, more often owner-operated, was registered at the local cooperatives. The excess land was leased to small farmers without benefit of written contracts.

The absence of written, contractual agreements between landlords and tenants was also meant to circumvent tenancy regulations pertaining to cash rent and sharecropping. The agrarian reform law of 1952 reduced rents to a maximum of seven times the land tax. The landlord's share of the produce under sharecropping was reduced to a maximum of 50 percent of the harvest, and all expenses were to be shared equally. As a result of these regulations, cash rents, which had reached astronomical heights in Upper Egypt before 1952, came down quite drastically. In Ashmon district, Minufiyya, for example, the rent per faddan plunged to E£ 20 from E£ 40, reached just before the passage of the agrarian reform in 1952. In Sohag, cash rents fell from E£ 70 to E£20. Nevertheless, because of the absence of written contracts, the HCLF revealed that landlords were leasing their lands at a much higher rate than the official limit. According to Saab, instances of rent violations were at 80 percent.[51] For example, in district al-Santah, Gharbiyyah, some landlords were receiving cash rents of E£ 25 per faddan, whereas the official limit was E£ 16. In fact, rents on a seasonal basis in this area amounted to E£ 60 per faddan. In Qalubiyya, the unofficial rent was even higher than in Daqahliyya (E£ 26) or in Gharbiyya (E£ 25). According to one account, some landlords in al-Qanatir were receiving cash payments of E£ 45 per faddan. In al-Minya, where the maximum rent per faddan was officially fixed at E£ 32, some landlords were receiving cash payments of E£ 55. Further to the south, particularly in Sohag, the unofficial rent per faddan attained the pre-1952 level of E£ 60 to E£ 70.

A more serious form of exploitation was the substitution of blank promissory notes, endorsed by tenants, for written contracts. Under the share-cropping system, the landlords held the tenants in perpetual debt and extracted what they pleased by virtue of their possession of these promissory notes. As revealed by the HCLF, in many instances, landlords received two-thirds of the crop, and, in addition, the cost of irrigating, ploughing, seeds, fertilizers, and harvesting were borne by the tenants. More often than not, landlords reserved for themselves the entire amount of any cash crops, such as cotton. A very prominent practice in Upper Egypt was the extortion of high prices by the landlords for use of their privately owned agricultural equipment, such as irrigation pumps and harvesters. In Minya and in Asyut, for example, the official, annual irrigation cost per faddan was fixed at E£ 9 and E£ 15, respectively. Some landlords in these provinces, however, were charging E£ 25 and higher for the tenant's use of their irrigation pumps. In Gizah, where the local agricultural cooperatives charged 70 piastres per hour for the use of one harvesting machine, some landlords were charging almost double that amount.

All of the above practices constituted flagrant violations of the agrarian reforms, and landlords using them were clearly running the risk of exposure and legal sanctions. Less risky from the legal point of view and economically more profitable was the system of owner-operated farms. As revealed by the HCLF, many landlords found it more to their advantage to evict tenants and turn their farms into lucrative orchards and vegetable gardens, using hired labor. In this method of farming activity, the exploitation fell upon the hired agricultural workers. A decree issued immediately after the 1952 law fixed a minimum daily wage of 18 piastres for men and 10 piastres for women. According to Saab, this decree was not evenly applied in the agricultural reform settlements.[52] As revealed by the HCLF, the maximum daily wage for agricultural workers was 10 piastres in Beheira, 15 piastres in Daqahliyya, 10 piastres in Minufiyya, and only 8 piastres in Bani Suwayf.

In light of the HCLF investigations, it can be asserted that no significant transformation occurred in the social and agrarian structures under the

Nasserist regime. The upper stratum families, the descendants of the large landowners in the prerevolutionary parliaments, were found to be among the largest landowners in the provinces despite the series of agrarian reforms. These conclusions run opposite to those of many social scientists who examined the social impact of the agrarian reforms. Many scholars, regardless of their ideological perspectives, argued that the provincial elites or members of the upper stratum not only lost a substantial proportion of their lands, but also lost their traditional, political influence in the provinces. It was further argued that the major beneficiary of the agrarian reforms was the rural middle class. If the elimination of the upper stratum had occurred, however, there would be no reasonable explanation for the conflict in Kamshish and the subsequent launching of the HCLF investigations. Perhaps the most revealing aspect of the latter's work was in its confirmation of the view that the influential family, after the imposition of successive agrarian reforms, experienced a radical transformation from within rather than from without.

THE URBAN CONNECTIONS OF THE RURAL ELITES

The influence of the rural elites was not confined to the countryside. The HCLF data reveals that kinship ties among traditionally influential families extended to the National Assembly, the army, the security apparatus, and the state bureaucracy. Except for the election to the National Assembly, recruitment into these institutions was not directly determined by local power considerations. HCLF data reveals that one of the manifestations of traditional influence over centrally located and managed institutions was the existence of informal and personal links between rural elites and some of the power elites, who turned the institutions under their control into nests of patronage.

The above revelations strengthen the argument against what has lately become a prevalent view among a number of scholars, that is, that there was a decline in rural clientelism, which was substituted by an alternative source of patronage based on positions within the bureaucracy.[53] The HCLF data reveals that rural-urban links were cultivated by the rural elites for the twin objectives of maintaining power and prestige on the local level and for fulfilling the traditional, intermediary role between the central authorities and the rural masses. The peasants traditionally feared the landowners, who had connections with the higher circles in the urban areas. In the eyes of the peasants, these landowners were *al-hukumah* (the government). On the other hand, the power elites themselves found it to their individual and collective advantage to cultivate rural support. As we have observed, during the prerevolutionary period, the cultivation of rural support became very intense whenever there was a plurality of competing political interests in the urban areas. Nasser eliminated the multiparty system, but factions, using the state institutions as leverage, emerged and were part of the HCLF deliberations. It is not surprising, therefore, that some of the rural elites enjoyed the protection of senior officials.

In the HCLF session of 19 May 1966, 'Amer warned the Executive Bureau secretaries and the directors of police in the provinces, who were about to launch the investigations, against falling into the traditional habit of extending courtesies, *mujamalat*, to influential persons. The investigators were ordered to report any state official who extended *mujamalat*, even if if involved him personally.[54] Some of the investigators heeded 'Amer's warning and included in their reports the names of high government officials who had personal connections with some of the rural elite families. Here are a few examples.

Muhammad Fahmi Abu Zaid was elected to the National Assembly as a representative of the peasant sector from Ashmon district in Minufiyya. The reports against Abu Zaid indicate he owned a medium amount of land, though together with rented land his holdings were in excess of the limits set by the agrarian reforms. The MCI report indicated that Abu Zaid was originally a landless peasant, a tenant of Fouad Muhi al-Din, National Assembly member and Executive Bureau Secretary in Qalubiyya. By 1966, Abu Zaid had accumulated a total of 327 faddans, of which only 42 faddans were owned. The reports further indicate that Abu Zaid enjoyed the protection of some National Assembly members, ministers, senior government officials, ASU secretaries, and the local police. For example, the report of Ibrahim Baghdadi, the governor of Minufiyya, contains a long list of senior government officials and members of parliament who protected or aided Abu Zaid in maintaining his influence. The list includes the former governor of Minufiyya, Muhammad Mutawwali, the former minister of the interior, 'Abdel Azim Fahmi, Executive Bureau secretary, Fouad Muhi al-Din, and some members of the intelligence and security forces in the province.

The report of the MCI, in addition to the persons mentioned in the governor's report, implicated Anwar al-Sadat who happened to come from the same province. The report alleged that Sadat assured Abu Zaid he would not lose his parliamentary immunity. The report further revealed that the former premier, Zakariya Muhi al-Din, pledged Abu Zaid that no harm would come to him. The commander of the MCI, Hasan 'Ali Khalil, nevertheless recommended to the HCLF that Abu Zaid be dismissed from the National Assembly and restricted to his place of residence either in Cairo or Alexandria, that the land held by him or owned by his wife and sons be seized, and that his associates and collaborators from the local ASU committee and the board of the agricultural cooperative be removed.

On 17 September, members of the HCLF met to discuss Abu Zaid's violations of the agrarian reforms and the complicity of local officials who helped him run for election as a peasant candidate. Opinions within the HCLF were divided on what form of action should be taken against a person who, besides his parliamentary immunity, enjoyed the protection of highly influential men. 'Abdel Mushin Abu al-Nur recommended postponement of any action until the parliamentary session was over. He said that "any action taken at this time might raise the ire of National Assembly members. We do not want to enter into a conflict with the Assembly now."[55] Abu al-Nur's plea for postponement was supported by other committee members, but the majority opinion was to take firm action. 'Amer, Gom'a, and Sami Sharaf were in favor of imposing a heavy punishment on Abu Zaid. The tricky problem was in dealing with the high state authorities who allegedly protected Abu Zaid. The junior local officials did not pose any problem. Yusif Hafez, deputy minister of the interior, announced during the parliamentary session that some police officers had been dismissed from service for their complicity in the forgery of land registration, an act that had enabled Abu Zaid to run for election as a peasant candidate.

The HCLF resolutions placed Abu Zaid and members of his family under sequestration, *al-Hirasah*, and dissolved the local ASU committee, the village council, and the board of the agricultural cooperative in the village. The HCLF also ordered the dismissal and transfer of nineteen provincial officials and the arrest of twenty-one persons who either belonged to the Abu Zaid family or were among his friends. These resolutions did not, however, include the loss of Abu Zaid's parliamentary seat. As for the higher state authorities the reports had implicated, 'Amer cautioned the HCLF members to keep this information a close secret because of the sensitivity of the issue and its political ramifications.[56] He promised to take up the matter with President Nasser. There the matter rested until Sadat assumed the presidency in 1970.

The National Assembly was not the only institution that came under fire. Let us not forget that all the assembly members were ASU members as well, and that the majority of them either held the post of ASU secretary on the village level or in the upper party hierarchy on the provincial level. As was observed earlier, one of the aims of socialism was to change the traditional social structure through use of the ASU. We have examined the failure of the Vanguard experiment and have observed that attempts to penetrate the local power structure gained momentum under 'Ali Sabri's mobilization drive through the apparatus of the Executive Bureaus. The top party *apparatchiki*, however, did not turn out to be "real socialists," as the left had suspected. The MCI reports disclosed embarrassing details about the collusion of party officials with traditionally dominant families in evading the agrarian reforms. The case of the Badawi family and its connection with Diya' al-Din Dawud, Executive

Bureau secretary in Dumyat, was one of the instances raised in the reports to the HCLF. The MCI report accused Diya' al-Din Dawud of helping the head of the Badawi family evade the agrarian reforms. According to the MCI director, Sa'ad Zaghlul Abdel Karim, Badawi resorted to the fictitious sale of land in excess of the limits set by the agrarian reform law to small farmers. The report further discloses that the signature of Dawud was found on one of the sale contracts. In reaction to this report, 'Amer ordered the ASU and the MCI to investigate Dawud's connections with the Badawi family. Nothing came of the investigations, however, for two years later Dawud was elected to the Supreme Executive Committee of the ASU.

In comparison with the number of reports on rural elite connections with the ASU *apparatchiki*, reports on rural elite connections with high circles in the military bureaucracy were quite rare indeed. Only one report offers just a brief glimpse of relations between Marshal 'Amer's brother, Hasan 'Amer, and a traditionally dominant family in Minya. The report came from the General Intelligence Bureau, over which 'Amer had no direct control. According to this report, 'Abdel Ghani was the ASU secretary in the village as well as the ASU treasurer on the provincial level. In the provincial administration, he was a member of the Governorate Council. In his village, Qillin, he acted as chairman of both the agricultural cooperative board and the social services unit. In short 'Abdel Ghani al-'Afiffi wielded political, social, administrative, and economic influence in the entire province. As if this information was not sufficient grounds to indict 'Abdel Ghani, the report also listed relatives and friends in his social network. The list included five members of the National Assembly, three of whom were relatives by marriage. All three belonged to families of pre-revolutionary parliamentary elites: the Tunis, Samhans, and al-Dirwis. The chairman of the city council of Malwi, Saif al-Nasr, also a member of a pre-revolutionary elite family, was listed among 'Abdel Ghani's relatives. On the village level, the report listed ten ASU committee members who were either family members or workers on his large estate.

It is interesting to note that neither the report of the governorate (provincial administration) nor that of the ASU's Executive Board in Minya brought 'Abdel Ghani's influential friends to the attention of the HCLF, friends who included the much sought after brother of the marshal. The subcommittee of the HCLF recommended the imposition of sequestration only on 'Abdel Ghani and his removal from the rural areas. It also recommended the dissolution of the agricultural cooperative board and the ASU committee in the village. Evidence on the final resolution of the HCLF on this particular case, however, is lacking.

Kinship ties provided direct evidence of rural elite influence over civil-military institutions. The most sensitive institutions from the standpoint of the security of the regime, were the military bureaucracy and the security services.

As shown in Table 21, both officers within the military-security complex and government officials came from rural elite families. What is surprising is that the upper stratum families had a larger number of military officers than did the rural middle class or locally notable families investigated by the HCLF. This finding contradicts the view that the purges carried out after the July revolution liquidated the influence of the large landowners or their descendants over the military establishment. The HCLF data further discloses that most of the military officers affiliated with the upper stratumn were doctors or engineers. Given the essential need for the services of professionals, one could assume that the regime tolerated their presence, despite the fact that some of them were descendants of prerevolutionary parliamentary ancestors. In the more sensitive area of public security, however, there were fewer officers belonging to the upper stratum families. On the whole, one could argue that the HCLF investigations of families with military officers effectively demoralized an important segment of the officer corps just a few months before the start of the fateful June War.

Another institution where rural elites had strong kinship ties was the government bureaucracy. In Table 21 I excluded members of the provincial bureaucracy, but included officials of the agrarian reforms and the provincial judiciary. At least five families had members holding the highly prestigious post of public prosecutor, and ten families had counselors in the central ministries. Ironically, some of the latter were instrumental in drafting the agrarian reform laws, and one of them, al-Sayyid 'Ali al-Sayyid, was the president of the State Council

Nowhere were the differences for families from prerevolutionary elites more apparent than in the National Assembly. Of the families investigated by the HCLF, the descendants of prerevolutionary parliamentary ancestors occupied a much higher proportion of asssembly seats than did the postrevolutionary elite

TABLE 21   Distribution of Military and Security Officers, Government Officials, and National Assembly Members by Descendancy Status

Descendancy Status	Military N = 41	Security N = 21	Government N = 63	National Assembly N = 23
Notables*				
Families	41.5	66.7	52.5	30.4
Upper Stratum	58.5	33.3	47.6	69.6

*Including postrevolutionary elite families. .

..s. This finding sustains the view that the upper stratum families continued to fulfill the mediating role between the center and the rural areas through representation in the postrevolutionary parliaments.

The existence of social links between an important segment of the power elites and traditionally influential families brings into question the disjunctive views on the relations between political power in the center and local influence in the peripheral areas. The HCLF data, in fact, underscores the significance of the role of rural elites in urban politics. Furthermore, the rural connections of some influential persons from within their institutional fiefs became a serious political issue during the factional rivalry that characterized urban politics in the 1960s. The HCLF activities split the political leadership into two opposing camps, foreshadowing the conflict between Sadat and Sabri's group following the dissolution of the HCLF. Of course, neither anticipated a power struggle, but with the advantage of hindsight, it is reasonable to argue that the political drama that began to unfold in the first year of Sadat's presidency was fundamentally related to the HCLF activities. The stage was set by the compromises made by Nasser in the period between the dissolution of the HCLF and Sadat's accession to the presidency in 1970. To this period I will now turn my attention.

Chapter Five
The Compromise

T HE JUNE WAR OF 1967 shook the foundations of the Nasserist regime. The regime stood weak and exposed before the world and before the eyes of its own people. The ignoble defeat plunged the Egyptian and Arab masses into a state of shock, from which they recovered only to face the new, bitter realities imposed by the much-detested enemy—the state of Israel. Accustomed to the braggadocio of their ruling class, the Arabs did not expect tiny Israel to defeat the mighty Arab armies.

As the dust settled on battlefields upon which little fighting had occurred, the Arab intellectuals began to offer explanations for the dismal failure of the leaders and their much-vaunted armies. The explanations for the defeat ranged from exposing the detrimental effects of traditional values to criticisms of the Arab individual. All possible explanations predicated on ideological confusion and inconsistencies, institutional failures, and personal aggrandizement by power hungry politicians were fully analyzed. As shown by Fouad Ajami in *The Arab Predicament*, however, the explanations themselves were heavily polemical. There was no frame of reference with which the various interpreters could reach a consensus.[1]

The reaction of the masses, by contrast, was spontaneous and unmediated. In Egypt, the unorganized masses responded directly to the concrete problems engendered by the June War defeat. These responses exposed the contradictions in Egypt's society as never before. A thoroughly weakened regime allowed the stirring of liberal aspirations that found expression in demands for an end to the repressive system of rule instituted by Nasser. The urban society, composed of workers, students, professionals, and bourgeoisie, apparently united in the post–June War period and demanded political freedom and effective participation. In the rural areas, the more numerous peasants reacted to the defeat by demanding full adherence to the revolutionary goals and preservation of the socialist gains; but, because of the weakness of the regime, the discrediting of its institutions, and the urban pressure for liberalization, the peasants were fighting a losing battle. The socialist crisis that had preceded the

June War defeat led to the abandonment of radical solutions and to the complete reversal of the decisions made by the HCLF.

Nasser assumed full responsibility in a speech delivered four days after the debacle. In this speech, Nasser announced his resignation and nominated Zakariya Muhi al-Din to take his place, a former RCC officer reputed to be pro-Western. The popular reaction to the resignation speech was swift and spontaneous. It was, by all accounts, an unorganized plebiscite fully expressing the popular will to hold on to Nasser's leadership.[2] Western observers were baffled by the fact that Nasser was able to maintain the leadership of his people even in defeat. The popular support demonstrated on 9 and 10 June gave Nasser a new mandate, which he urgently needed to begin the reconstruction of a bady shattered economy and to raise the morale of his armed forces. Nevertheless, Nasser showed a great deal of reluctance in responding to leftist demands for a people's war and for effective popular participation in the defence of the country.

The dissolutionment of the HCLF was one of the major consequences of the June War defeat. Its chairman, Marshal 'Amer, and three of its prominent members that belonged to 'Amer's faction—Shams Badran, Salah Nasr, and 'Abbas Radwan—permanently lost their political influence. Later, 'Amer committed suicide, and members of his faction, including some of the senior commanders, were twice tried under popular pressure for their responsibility in the defeat. Furthermore, as an indication of future trends, the new cabinet over which Nasser assumed the premiership included ministers who had come under the close scrutiny of the HCLF. Sayyid Mar'i, Hasan 'Abbas Zaki, and 'Aziz Sidqi joined the cabinet as the ministers of agriculture and agrarian reforms, of economy, and of industry, respectively. By including these men in the cabinet, Nasser was indicating the direction the desired change must take.

In the first cabinet meeting, Nasser remarked that the repressive measures of the HCLF were part of the causes of defeat. The committee sent "hundreds of innocent people to detention camps or to exile on groundless bases."[3] Therefore, Nasser pointed out, the first task of the government was to rectify previous mistakes. The starting point was to lift the sequestration imposed on the properties of the rural elites. According to the testimony of Sayyid Mar'i, the rehabilitation of the rural elites and the end of repression were enthusiastically embraced by the majority of the ministers attending the meeting. These ministers, however, were careful to draw a line between Nasser, who was originally responsible for the formation of the HCLF, and some of the HCLF members who had committed excesses against the rural elites during the investigations. The onus of blame naturally fell on Marshal 'Amer and members of his faction.

Nevertheless, two former members of the HCLF present at the cabinet meeting advised Nasser to exercise due caution in accommodating the rural elites in order to maintain state security. Both Sami Sharaf, minister of state, and Sha'rawi Gom'a, minister of the interior, expressed the opinion that a quick reversal of the policy of neutralizing the rural influence of the traditional elites was ill advised. The majority of the ministers, however, seemed to have won the argument in favor of immediately lifting sequestration when Nasser signed a decree ordering the restoration of properties belonging to 88 of the 334 families upon whom the decisions of the HCLF had been imposed. Mar'i stated that he received the decree on 26 July 1967 at the Ministry of Agriculture and happily set out to implement it with speed and dispatch. But he said he was careful to hand back the properties to its rightful owners without much fanfare, for any publicity might begin an unnecessary alarm among the peasants.[4] In a few days he was able to dispose of twenty cases. He was prevented from returning the property of the remaining sixty-eight cases, however, because of another change in policy.

The new policy revealed that both Sha'rawi Gom'a and Sami Sharaf enjoyed a considerable amount of influence, since they were able to convince Nasser to halt immediate and general desequestration and political rehabilitation of the rural elites. The new policy established two committees as part of a review process. One committee was headed by the former HCLF member and minister of labor forces in the new cabinet, Kamal Rif'at, whose main function was to review each case of desequestration from a political perspective. The second committee was technical and legal, composed of experts from the Ministry of Agrarian Reforms.

In a self-congratulatory note, Mar'i remarked that, just before Sadat assumed the presidency in 1970, the cases under sequestration remaining from the HCLF activities declined from 334 to only 25. This decline meant, in effect, a reduction in the amount of land under sequestration from 55,000 to 3,100 faddans. According to Mar'i, the remaining 25 cases were the only ones in which attempts to circumvent the agrarian reforms were uncovered. On the other hand, sequestration in the majority of the cases was imposed for "ambiguous political reasons such as hostility to the regime or feudalist behavior or sometimes for no reason at all."[5]

Mar'i further maintained that his enthusiastic responses to Nasser's desequestration order earned him the hostility of the centers of power, meaning 'Ali Sabri's faction. Because of his close connection with the landed elites, he was suspected of "collusion" and "complicity" with the forces of feudalism in the rural areas. He was therefore excluded from the political and technical committees. Moreover, he became the target of several criticisms at the meeting of the ASU's Central Committee, convened when the effects of desequestration began to reverberate from the rural areas.

Nasser's attention shifted to the reorganization of the political apparatus. The issue of political reorganization became more urgent under the incessant popular demand for change. Urban agitation for change reached a climax in February and March 1968. On 20 February the workers of the aircraft factory in Helwan declared a general strike, ostensibly in protest over the light sentences imposed on the air force officers held responsible for the crippling blow of the Egyptian air force on 5 June. The workers' strike soon spread and engulfed students at Cairo University. The protest slowly and inexorably penetrated the state institutions. The session of the National Assembly on 28 February was a memorable event, for speakers unreservedly expressed the view that the most urgent change to be made was the dismantling of the represssive state dominated by the secret police. The following month became the turn of the university professors and the judges. The latter, however, were more open in their criticisms of the political apparatus, particularly of the attempts by party leaders, including 'Ali Sabri, to undermine the autonomy of the judiciary. The judges declared in a meeting held on 28 March, just two days before the March 30 Statement, that they were opposed to politicization of judges. They further announced their full commitment to professional independence and, therefore, rejected the innovation of handling court cases with nonprofessionals in the people's courts. They also demanded the separation of the office of the public prosecutor from the executive authority.

Under popular pressure, the regime began to introduce changes to bring about a higher participation of nonmilitary professionals in the government. Thus, following his meeting with university professors on 6 March, Nasser brought to the cabinet, afterward dubbed the "cabinet of intellectuals," six new ministers from the national universities. By contrast, the former RCC officers who until then had served Nasser as his closest aides declined considerably in influence. Zakaria Muhi al-Din, Nasser's nominee for president only a year before, withdrew from politics permanently. Only Anwar Sadat remained in power as the head of the National Assembly, as well as Hussein al Shafi'i, who was appointed to the cabinet as deputy premier and minister of religious endowments.

By far the biggest change was announced in the March 30 Statement. The intended change was aimed at the country's political organizaton, the ASU. In this statement, Nasser pointed out the main faults that impeded the development of the political apparatus, including the "centers of power," — the factions that had emerged within the political apparatus and the hallowed principle of recruitment based on personal loyalty. Both these faults fed on each other, leading to self-aggrandizement and expansion of political influence by subordinates. As pointed out by Heikal in his assessment of the causes of the June War defeat, the state institutions, including the ASU and the government bureaucracy, had become the hosts of centers of power bent upon expanding their influence. Heikal disclosed that the recruitment procedure, based on selection, was conducive to the accumulation of influence in the hands of party leaders. Heikal was specifically directing his criticism against 'Ali Sabri's Executive Bureaus, formed during the mobilization period.[6]

The March 30 Statement also pledged political liberalization, supremacy of law, and reorganization of the ASU from top to bottom. Nasser, however, remained in favor of keeping the dual character of the ASU, although it had demonstrated its ineffectiveness during the period between the formation of the ASU in 1962 and 1965. Thus, in the March 30 Statement, Nasser affirmed the principle upon which the ASU would be based—an alliance of five classes and the preservation of party cadres. The ASU would give expression to the alliance of workers, peasants, intellectuals, national bourgoisie, and the security forces, while the Socialist Vanguard to be organized within the ASU would contain party cadres whose task was to bridge gaps between the social classes.

The ASU elections under the principles announced in the March 30 Statement did not much alter the distribution of power in the upper echelons of the political organization. In fact, contrary to the expressed desire of infusing new blood into the ASU and the state bureaucracy, there was an expansion in the influence of party leaders later identified as members of 'Ali Sabri's faction. Former HCLF members and party leaders 'Ali Sabri and 'Abdel Muhsin Abu al-Nur were elected to the Suprere Executive Committee. Sabri's position on the Supreme Executive. Committee was strengthened by the election of Labib Shuqayr and Diya' al-din Dawud. The former was a member of the Cairo Committee of the Socialist Vanguard under Sabri's control, while the latter was an Executive Bureau secretary in Dumyat. The influence of Sabri's group extended into the state bureaucracy and the National Assembly. Sha'rawi Gom'a, who was Sabri's right-hand man on the HCLF, retained his post as minister of the interior as well as his pivotal post in the ASU as secretary of organization affairs. In the National Assembly, Labib Shuqayr was elected speaker of the assembly, while former HCLF member, Kamal al-Din Al-Hinnawi, was elected to the post of deputy speaker.

Sayyid Mar'i, 'Aziz Sidqi, and Hasan 'Abbas Zaki entered the elections for the Supreme Executive Committee, but they were not elected. Mar'i claimed that the number of votes received by 'Ali Sabri and the election of three members of his faction were not indications of popularity, but were due to the fact that the elections were not free. Mar'i, however, was not able to produce any evidence to support his claim except by implying that the opponents of Sabri had no chance of winning the elections due to the overwhelming support Sabri enjoyed in the Central Committee—the party organ that elects the Supreme Executive Committee.[7] In fact, if there was any interference in the electoral procedure, it was carried out by Nasser himself. According to one source, Nasser decided to limit representation on the Supreme Executive Committee to only eight members just in time to block the election of a potential candidate identified as a member of Sabri's faction.[8] Despite the Central Committee's support of 'Ali Sabri, Anwar Sadat was also elected to the Supreme Executive Committee, receiving 119 votes in comparison to the former's 134 votes. A few months later (December 1969), Sadat was promoted to the rank of vice president. In February 1970, 'Ali Sabri lost his position in the ASU as secretary for organizational affairs.[9]

The ASU elections further revealed a decline in the influence of those closely associated in the past with the ASU's Ideological Affairs Committee. The so-called real socialists suffered an eclipse, as was indicated by the defeat of Khalid Muhi al-Din and Kamal Rif'at in the elections to the Supreme Executive Committee. Furthermore, prominent leftists in the ASU's Socialist Institute, such as Ibrahim Saad al-Din and Ahmad Hamrush, were not elected to the National Congress.

In the rural areas, the ASU reverted to its premobilization model. Although the majority of the Executive Bureau secretaries were elected as ASU secretaries at the provincial level, some of the influential elites belonging to the so-called feudal familites that had come under the HCLF investigations were elected as well. As is revealed by the data on the composition of district committees in 1968, members of fourteen families in this category were elected. In addition to family influence on the middle level of the party hierarchy, nineteen of these families had members elected to the provincial congresses. Twelve of these latter families had maintained district-level influence back in 1959 during the National Union period. The restoration of the political influence of the rural elite families is further supported by the election of members of "feudal" families to the National Assembly in 1969. Thirteen such families were represented in the assembly, adding weight to my argument that the restoration of the political influence of rural elites kept pace with the desequestration process that began soon after the June War defeat. These developments had a tremendous impact on the local community.

The consequences of the June War defeat had direct and immediate effects on the peasants. The defeat represented a direct assault on socialist gains and a fatal blow to the efforts of the regime to liquidate feudalism. Translated in concrete terms, the peasants who had benefited from the agrarian reforms, especially the recipients of small parcels from the estates of the big landlords, were thoroughly alarmed, as they feared that the reverses suffered by the regime would mean parting with the meager possessions they had recently acquired. The reinstatement of Nasser who, despite his ambivalence, was generally perceived as their main benefactor, could scarcely alleviate the fears evoked by a much-weakened regime. The peasants trusted their own instincts and began to mark time in expectation of orders to hand back the lands to their former owners. Nevertheless, some had sufficient will to resist. In this context, Kamshish once again played a pioneering role in putting pressure on the central authorities to reverse the trends engendered by the June War.[10]

It was pointed out in chapter 1 that the conflict in Kamshish was part of a general historical development, whose fundamental characteristic was the wide discrepancy between a wealthy minority of landed elites who wielded political influence continuously and a majority of small farmers and landless peasants. The tension between these two social strata increased considerably when the army officers seized power in 1952. Nasser gained political leverage against the influential landed elites by championing the cause of the small peasants. In Kamshish the contradiction between social forces was reflected in the history of conflict between the Fiqqis and the Maqlads. The reformist policy of the regime encouraged the Maqlads to work constantly toward undermining the economic and political influence of the Fiqqis. Due to these efforts, the conflict between the landed elites and the small tenants and farmers exploded in the Kamshish Affair and the formation of the HCLF in May 1966. The immediate cause, as was pointed out earlier, was the killing of Salah Maqlad and the suspicion that none other than the Fiqqis were behind his death.

The acquittal of the Fiqqis and the return of Muhammad al Fiqqi to the village began a reaction among villagers, who now awaited a similar fate. The authorities began to encounter resistance from peasants in the villages where former landlords were granted court injunctions to evict the peasants. The national press reported the eviction of tenants in Giza, Minufiyya, Sharqiyya, and Marsa Matrouh.[11] In the village of Ossim in the Giza governorate, an eviction order affected 289 tenants who cultivated 339 faddans that belonged to the Ghurab family before it was sequestered. In this instance, the peasants had acquired their tenancy rights over the land through the Department of Sequestration. Most of the tenants refused to give up the tenancy rights and, like the peasants of Kamshish, decided to resist. Sayyid Mar'i claimed that thirty-seven tenants voluntarily gave up their leases.[12] Rumors, however, began to circulate that these tenants were pressured. In some cases, tenants had formerly been conscripts in the army that had fought in Yemen. Their eviction would have had adverse effects on the efforts of the regime to raise the morale of the army.

Due to the sensitivity of the issue, Sayyid Mar'i intervened quickly to work out a compromise settlement between the landlords and tenants.

As the peasants in several parts of the country agitated against the courts' injunctions, the ASU's Central Committee met to discuss possible strategies for preventing an escalation of the conflict. From the discussions that took place during the 12 February session, though, members of the Central Committee apparently were sharply divided. The issues that drew sharp reactions from the members concerned socialism and counter-revolution. The socialists warning about counter-revolution—some of whom were later identified as members of 'Ali Sabri's faction—pointed out that landlords everywhere were abusing tenants with the help of the government. One member remarked that the Ministry of Agriculture not only favored landlords over tenants but also extended preferential treatment to the big landowners at the cost of the small owners. Another member pointed out that the government was even helping create a stratum of big landowners through the sale of orchards and lands up to the limit of one hundred faddans, even though the ASU charter had declared in 1962 that the one hundred-faddan limit would be reviewed with the possibility of further lowering the ceiling in 1970. Contrary to the spirit of the charter, then, no attempt was being made to slow the expansion of private property.

Sayyid Mar'i responded in the same session of the Central Committee to the warning about counter-revolutionary activities. He affirmed that security of tenure guarded by "due process of law" was necessary for keeping the peace in the rural areas and for increasing productivity. He further indicated the futility of the erstwhile policy of intimidating the landlords with threats of dispossession and sequestration. These threats would only undermine the right of private property and lower production.[13]

Nasser's position in the Central Committee's debate was indeed remarkable, for it brought to a close a decade of radical reforms whose climax was the HCLF. Nasser told an astonished audience that he had decided to put the brakes on socialism, despite his enthusiasm for it. The reason he gave for his decision was that public ownership led in many instances to loss of revenues, not because of the absence of the profit motive but due to bureaucratic mismanagement. Furthermore, Nasser rejected the claim that there was a counter-revolution. "We took the property of some individuals and nationalized the shares of others. But, as far as I know, the activities of these people are very limited. Indeed they do not constitute a threat and the feat of counter-revolution is exaggerated."[14]

Nasser stated that, as a general principle, landlords must not evict their tenants at will. He added, however, that this mandate must not be construed by tenants to mean they can flout their obligations under tenancy relations. Due process of law must be maintained in all cases where a peasant enters a contractual arrangement with a landlord. As for the cases stemming from the decisions of the HCLF, Nasser decided to let the political bureau of the Central Committee of the ASU, headed by Anwar Sadat, handle the cases on the basis of the committee's resolution prohibiting the eviction of tenants on desequestered lands.[15]

Nasser's decision struck a compromise between diametrically opposed claims. In the final analysis, his compromise did not satisfy anyone. The big landlords received the land back, together with the unwanted tenants. The anguish of the small peasant, in turn, is understandable since he reverted to the dependency status he had come to loathe. In Kamshish the sense of loss among the villagers was compounded by the fear of the return of the old feudal lords who had dominated their lives as far back as they could remember.

The contradictions of the regime reached a climax between the ASU's Central Committee meeting in February 1969 and Nasser's death on 28 September 1970. The resolution of the committee, which in effect nullified the eviction of tenants by court order, was followed shortly thereafter by a crackdown on the judicial system itself and the so-called independent judges. What came to be known as the "massacre of the judiciary" began with reports submitted to Nasser alleging that the Judges' Club was the center of intrigues against the regime. The reports said the regime and Nasser personally were the subject of criticisms by the judges who gathered at their club. The reports, originating from the political apparatus of the Socialist Vanguard under the control of members of 'Ali Sabri's faction, included a long list of persons accused of engaging in hostile activities. When the reports were brought to the cabinet for discussion, the minister of justice pointed out that the judges on the list were affiliated with families whose members had been subjected to the agrarian reforms and that they had close kinship links with the prerevolutionary politicians who had been excluded from political participation and whose properties had been put under sequestration. The statement was supported by the minister of the interior, Sha'rawi Gom'a, who was present at the cabinet meeting.[16]

Nasser's reaction to the statement of the minister of justice drove another nail into the coffin of the supremacy of law. Nasser declared that the "judges must maintain absolute neutrality in the implementation of laws. Since there are judges who profess hostility to the laws which embody the principles of the socialist measures, then under these circumstances they will let their personal inclinations and commitments to kinship and class position overcome the neutrality required of them."[17] The later "massacre of the judiciary" was actually precipitated by the election of officers at the Judges' Club in March 1969, during which government candidates failed to secure a majority vote. Most of the elected officers belonged to the independent judges, the subjects of the report that had been submitted to the cabinet meeting earlier. The blow against the independent judges was struck in August when a series of measures were adopted to reorganize the judiciary with the main objective of bringing it under tight government control. In the process of reorganization, two hundred judges were transferred to other posts in the huge government bureaucracy.[18]

The shifting position of the regime was reflected by its conduct vis-a-vis Israel and the big powers. The war of attrition across the Suez Canal brought swift Israeli retaliation. Perhaps for the first time in the history of Egypt, its cities in the Delta became exposed to the Israeli Air Force. The intensity of the Israeli air attacks in the first quarter of 1969 forced Egypt to rely more heavily on the Soviet Union, particularly in the field of air defence. By May 1970, however, Nasser seemed to be doubting the principle he had never tired of repeating to the masses, namely, that force alone was the means for getting back what was taken by force. In the traditional May Day speech in 1970, Nasser made his first overtures to the United States to put pressure on Israel to withdraw from the occupied territories and to recognize the rights of the Palestinians in return for peace. Nasser's overtures led to the Rogers' proposals, which Egypt accepted in July 1970 amid charges of sell-out by the radical regimes. In the Arab world, Egypt shifted from rhetoric about a popular war of liberation, which had found strength in Colonel Qadhafi's coup in Libya in September 1969, to a position of moderation. A new sense of realism about Egypt's capacity to fight a war with Israel and what could credibly be accepted from Arab regimes emerged at the Arab Summit Conference in Rabat in December. Perhaps the irony of all ironies was that Nasser died on 28 September 1970, just as he finished his last attempt at mending the fences between King Hussein of Jordan, who traditionally represented the conservative Arab regimes, and the Palestinians, who emerged as the revolutionary alternatives in the Arab world.

The internal and external contradictions of the Nasserist regime were left to Sadat to resolve when he assumed power in September 1970. To appreciate what Sadat was up against, it may be useful to recapitulate some of the problems that later proved to be his major trouble spots.

The social contradictions at the basis of the regime had important consequences for political development. Nasser's repeated attempts at undermining the social and political position of the rural elites climaxed in the formation of the HCLF. The activities of the HCLF, however, were aborted by the June War defeat. The period following the war saw the gradual restoration and rehabilitation of these elites. Although it is true that the defeat weakened the state and its capacity to carry out domestic policies, Nasser reversed his policy against the rural elites for more profound reasons. The main reason lies in the extensive influence of the rural elite themselves. In light of the evidence presented in the preceding chapters, there is no doubt that the activities of the HCLF hit the nerve center, if not the very foundation, upon which the state was erected. The rural elites had extensive kinship links that penetrated every branch of the government and the military bureaucracy. In fact, in light of the accumulated evidence on the social networks of the rural elites, it can be asserted that demoralization hit the government bureaucracy and the army roughly one year before the Israeli Air Force launched its devastating attack on the Egyptian airports on 5 June 1967.

The HCLF activities were bound to leave some impact on the rural areas. One consequence was that the revolutionary consciousness of the peasants in isolated areas was aroused. After more than a century of domination by a wealthy stratum of large landowners, the small peasants felt free while the HCLF was active. Once their consciousness was aroused, it was difficult to contain it. Nonetheless, because of the peasants' lifestyles and the isolation of peasant communities from one another, this revolutionary consciousness left no actual impact on the rural areas; hence, one can only provide instances of peasant rebellions, as in Kamshish, rather than talk about a broad social movement.

Political liberalization as promised in the March 30 Statement was intended to gain the support of the urban intelligentsia. Supremacy of the law and changes in government personnel on the basis of the principle of "the right man for the right job" however, clashed with actual implementation of policy. The hollowness of the state's claims was evident in the crackdown on the judges and the imposition of government control over the judiciary. Furthermore, with the exception of Marshal 'Amer's group in the army, the state institutions continued to be dominated by the same persons.

The uneasy balance and the delicate compromises were Nasser's response to the failure of the reforms. He attempted the almost impossible task of reconciling state interests with the demands generated from below for social change. The ensuing power struggle between 'Ali Sabri and Sadat was a continuation of these clashing forces.

Chapter Six
The Corrective Movement

O N SEPTEMBER 1970, THE ninth anniversary of the Syrian secession, Nasser died. On the same day, the speaker of the National Assembly, Labib Shuqayr, acting in accordance with the articles of the constitution regulating succession, declared Sadat as interim president. Following the recommendation of the Supreme Executive Committee of the ASU, the Central Committee met early in October and passed a resolution calling on the assembly to approve the nomination of Sadat as the only candidate for the presidency. The assembly thereupon convened in a session on 7 October and, after unanimously approving the nomination, called for a national plebiscite, the last of the constitutional steps for resolving the problem of succession. In accepting the nomination, Sadat said his government program was going to be none other than the March 30 Statement and that he was faithfully going to pursue Nasser's course. On 17 October 7.7 million people reportedly cast their votes in the national plebiscite, 90 percent of whom said yes to Sadat's candidacy.

In his first statement as president, Sadat said he was going to be president for everyone, regardless of the negative vote by a small minority. Sadat added that "the people must not give their full confidence to just one person after Abdel Nasser."[1] The members of the party and government upper echelon were in agreement with Sadat over the issue of collective leadership.[2] Sadat's desire to share responsibility was welcomed by the rival group. The speaker of the assembly, in his opening statement after Sadat assumed the presidency stressed the role of institutions in the decision-making process. A member of the Supreme Executive Committee of the ASU expressed the view that there was no alternative but the rule of existing institutions. Members of the opposing faction—'Ali Sabri, Sha'rawi Gom'a, Diya' al-Din Dawud, and Farid Abdel Karim—emphasized that a collective leadership seemed to emerge from the consensus established among all leaders during the process of nominating Sadat for the presidency.[3] They were comfortable in the thought that Sadat himself publicly endorsed the idea that the vacuum left behind by Nasser could be filled only "by the rule of the institution representing the unity of the popular forces."[4]

In the first few months of his presidency, Sadat projected the image that he was going to stick to the principle of collective leadership. His rivals were assured that they would stay in their posts exactly as Nasser would have wanted. 'Ali Sabri was appointed vice president, alongside Hussein al-Shafi'i, and was empowered to resolve some of the outstanding problems troubling Soviet-Egyptian relations, especially the thorny issue of supplying Egypt with electronic equipment to match American supplies to Israel. Sadat's conciliatory gestures toward Sabri's group were also apparent in the appointment of former HCLF member 'Abdel Muhsin Abu al-Nur as secretary general of the ASU. Sami Sharaf was given a cabinet post as minister of presidential affairs. The only perceptible change in the government was Heikal's resignation and return to his editorial post at *al-Ahram*. Thus far, it appeared that the succession problem had been resolved rather successfully through the constitutional mechanism and that Sadat had been able to win the support of his political rivals through compromise and accommodation. But it is one thing to win the presidency and another thing to have power and exercise it.

Factionalism ran deeply in the Egyptian political process. The factions resembled informal groupings of peers and followers who were like-minded and of the same social origins, sharing common political and personal interests. Many such groups were also united by kinship. These factions were not organized to overthrow the regime, only to consolidate their positions by using the state institutions as power bases. Several reasons have been given to explain the emergence of what has been described as the centers of power or cronyism.[5] According to one view, factionalism emerged as a natural consequence of the concentration of power under a personalist rule.[6] Nasser hesitated to share power with anyone except the most loyal and trusted subordinates. The principle of loyalty before competence restricted the number of power holders by the grace and permission of Nasser to the very few. Most of the trusted subordinates were members of the military junta that had overthrown the monarchy in 1952. By 1961, however, Nasser shifted the selective procedure in favor of second-string officers, whose promotions to key posts in the government were deeply resented by older members of the officer corps.[7] Resentment was the reaction to 'Ali Sabri's appointment as chairman of the Executive Council during the first cabinet reshuffle after the Syrian secession in September 1961. After this point, except for Marshal 'Amer in the army, Sadat in the National Assembly, and Zakariya Muhi al-Din and Hussein al-Shafi'i in the state bureaucracy, most of the original founders of the Free Officer's Movement either lost their political influence or were kicked downstairs.

'Ali Sabri's position was strengthened in 1965 when he was appointed secretary general of the ASU, replacing Hussein al-Shafi'i, one of the conservative officers who had participated in the July Revolution. The General Secretariat under Sabri included some of the members who were later either actively involved in HCLF activities or were implicated in the alleged conspiracy to overthrow the Sadat regime in May 1971. These members were Sha'rawi Gom'a, Kamal al-Din al-Hinnawi, 'Ali al-Sayyid 'Ali, 'Abbas Radwan, 'Abdel al-Fattah Abu al-Fadl, 'Abdel Majid Shadid, and 'Abdel Hamid Ghazi. The new General Secretariat did not include former RCC officers such as Anwar Sadat, Hussein al-Shafi'i, Kamal al-Din Hussein, or Hasan Ibrahim. The opportunity for Sabri to consolidate his position vis-a-vis other institutions arose when Nasser decided to revamp the party structure in May 1965 and to extend party control horizontally into the provinces as well as over some of the urban-based institutions.

During the mobilization period, the Executive Bureaus staffed by full-time party workers and the Socialist Vanguard began to penetrate the various branches of the government bureaucracy, the National Assembly, the military bureaucracy, and the security apparatus. The rationale for extending the authority of the party over other state institutions was derived from the principle enunciated by the Socialist Charter, which stated that "the Arab Socialist Union represents popular authority whose function is to lead, direct and exercise control in the name of the people."[8] Furthermore, the ASU's formula on party affiliation included the peasants, the workers, the "non-exploitative national bourgeoisie," members of the intelligentsia, the armed forces and the police. These ill-defined categories were welded together into a national coalition. Sabri was, therefore, in favor of creating a monolithic organization by incorporating all the elements defined by the Socialist Charter.[9]

Nevertheless, Sabri's inroads were resisted by all the institutions mentioned above. Nasser himself was in favor of separating the government bureaucracy from the party. The question of incorporating the government bureaucracy into the ASU came up during discussions on the creation of a party cadre of militant socialists in the mobilization period. Nasser's position on this issue was to remove all party activists from the state bureaucracy. Nasser reiterated his position in his meeting with the Executive Bureau secretaries in March 1966.[10] He said he was opposed to the combination of party and bureaucratic functions. The creation of an elite group of militant socialists was to be based on the principle of selectivity, and, unlike the party affiliates or the inactive members, they would devote their full attention to party functions. However, some exceptions were made. For example, Sha'rawi Gom'a continued to hold both party and government posts; hence, he became Sabri's link with the state bureaucracy, especially in the most sensitive area of maintaining internal security.

A major impediment to the extension of party authority was Marshal 'Amer and his group in the army. 'Amer himself was firmly set against the politicization of the army because, in his view, politicization would lead to a breakdown in discipline. In fact, the reverse took place when the army assumed activities normally the responsibility of the party apparatus.[11] The influence of the military over civilian affairs persisted with Nasser's encouragement, despite the occasional friction between him and Marshal 'Amer. In the period between the Syrian secession and the disastrous defeat of June 1967, the influence of the military increased under the pretext of wiping out corruption in the public sector of the economy and of maintaining the internal security of the regime.[12] Army intervention in civil society reached a climax during the HCLF investigations, followed by a perceptible decline as a consequence of the June War defeat.

Preceding the June War, the expansion of the role of the military in public affairs had wide social ramifications. To have a friend in the army or connections with military officers became a valuable asset. A network of patronage developed within the military bureaucracy, with Marshal 'Amer as the principal patron. However, the personal loyalty of key officers to 'Amer complicated his relations with Nasser and fellow officers who assumed civilian roles. When the Presidential Council, for example, decided to take from 'Amer the power of appointment of divisional commanders and above in retaliation for his dismal failure in Syria in 1961, all the top commanders of the army, the navy, and the air forces protested by offering their resignations. It has been suggested that after this episode, 'Amer began to show a degree of independence;[13] but his loyalty to Nasser remained beyond doubt. In 1964, Nasser appointed him first vice president.

Military intervention in civil society took a new turn when Nasser decided to let 'Amer take an active role in the affairs of the Socialist Vanguard by putting him in charge of a group of former communists and Marxists. This assignment was interpreted as an encroachment on Sabri's territory. A parallel step, however, was taken to counterweigh 'Amer's influence in the army. A branch of the Socialist Vanguard was formed within the military bureaucracy under the control of Shams Badran who, as director of budget and personnel, was well suited for the task of recruitment. Among the officers recruited by Badran were Muhammad Fawzi, general commander of the army after the June War debacle, and Muhammad Ahmad Sadiq, who replaced Fawzi in the wake of the Corrective Movement.[14] Whatever the merits of this role of the Vanguard in the army, the evidence overwhelmingly favors the view that 'Amer successfully kept the army isolated from the ASU.[15] In fact, as the HCLF investigations clearly show, the ASU was subordinate to the Military Police controlled by 'Amer. 'Amer himself was the chairman of the HCLF.

The extension of party authority was most deeply felt in the National Assembly, which Sadat as its speaker from 1960 to 1969 regarded as his personal fiefdom. In fact, the rivalry between Sabri and Sadat during this period presaged the struggle of power after Nasser's death. The rivalry was most intense when 'Ali Sabri was chairman of the Council of Ministers. According to Mar'i, Sabri was the source of tension between Nasser and the assembly, because he aroused Nasser's suspicions regarding the loyalty to the regime of some assembly members.[16] Sadat was considered the villain during this event because of his attempt to shield certain members for personal reasons.

Aside from personal conflicts, friction was bound to occur between the party and the assembly due to the deliberate ambiguities in the definition of relations between the two institutions. The Socialist Charter defined the National Assembly in relation to the party as being subordinate to the latter. The "National Assembly's function was the implementation of policies laid down by the Arab Socialist Union."[17] Assembly members deeply resented the right party leaders claimed in reviewing their eligibility in relation to party rules. The electoral procedures of 1964 stipulated that all candidates be working members of the ASU and that 50 percent of the assembly seats be reserved for peasants and workers. The socialist formula defined the peasant as the owner of a maximum of twenty-five faddans. Moreover, all those who had been subjected to the agrarian reforms or to the socialist decrees and property sequestration were disqualified. The ASU leader, however, was denied the right of selecting candidates for the assembly in the 1964 elections.

In the postwar period, the issue of whether or not the ASU leadership had the right to select National Assembly candidates became a point of contention between Heikal, Sadat's ally in the Corrective Movement, and Sabri's group. Heikal argued in favor of constitutional and practical autonomy for the parliament. Sabri's group, in the pages of *al-Gumhouriyya*, argued in favor of implementing the principles of the Socialist Charter, including party control over the assembly.[18]

The ambiguities in the relationship between the party and the assembly remained unresolved. This confusion allowed candidates to enter the assembly despite opposition from party leaders. This contention is supported by substantial evidence that some of the families that came under investigation by the HCLF had members in all the parliamentary sessions during Nasser's regime. Consequently, the assembly became the main target of criticism by 'Ali Sabri and his faction in the ASU leadership. The absence of firm control over the

selection procedure was blamed for the flagrant violations of the socialist formula. According to Sabri, many large landowners infiltrated the assembly as
peasant candidates (see the case of Abu Zaid in chapter 4). Most serious,
however, was the HCLF allegation that the elected large landowners enjoyed
the protection of senior officials, including Assembly Speaker Anwar Sadat.
The HCLF data reveals that the National Assembly was not the only institution
where the rural elites had either established links with its political elites or had
kinship ties with some of its members. Nevertheless, a major part of the HCLF
efforts focused upon some of the influential members of the National Assembly.
It is not surprising, therefore, to observe that the Corrective Movement not only
represented a conflict between the president and an opposing faction, but also
reflected a deeper conflict in the relationship between the assembly and ASU,
both of which claimed to be representative institutions.

The biggest problem Sadat encountered in the first few months of his
presidential term was the attempt of Sabri's group to control domestic and
foreign policies in the name of Nasserism. This problem was succinctly outlined
by Heikal in his famous *al-Ahram* editorials, which appeared weekly under the
catchy title of *Bisaraha* (frankly). In one editorial, Heikal accused Sabri and
company of perpetuating the myth of Nasser's omnipotence for self-serving
purposes.[19] He flatly rejected the notion that Nasserism needed self-appointed
interpreters or that Nasserism as a doctrine bestowed special privileges upon
anyone. These editorials were veiled criticisms of the attempt of Sabri's group
to control Sadat's policies by projecting themselves as the guardians of Nasser's
legacy, particularly as guardians of the ASU.

To free himself of the constraints of his political rivals, Sadat made several
moves, and each step along the way was designed to win the support of the
alienated section of Egyptian society. A top priority on Sadat's agenda was the
reorganization of the ASU, but any attempt in that direction was bound to be
resisted by the entrenched ASU leaders, since experience under Nasser had
taught them that reorganization of the political apparatus was synonymous
with purges. As pointed out by Sadat, the responsibility for reorganizing the
ASU elections was that of Sha'rawi Gom'a, who was still serving as minister of
the interior. Gom'a, however, voiced his objections to reorganization on the
grounds that the office term for members of the higher ASU committees had
not expired.[20] Thus, faced with the entrenched postion of the rival faction in
the ASU, Sadat took recourse to cultivating social support through the National
Assembly. In the meantime, he devised plans to neutralize the influence of the
faction in the army.

Part of Sadat's strategy to win social support was aimed at the landed
elites. In a dramatic move on 20 December 1970, Sadat issued a decree call-

ing for property desequestration and the return of land to its rightful owners. Sadat could legitimately claim that his decree was a continuation of Nasser's policy, which was initiated in the aftermath of the June War defeat and the dissolution of the HCLF. Few, however, had any doubts about the political motives of Sadat. According to a former member of the HCLF, General Muhammad Sadiq—whose support as chief of the army staff was crucial to Sadat during the events of May 1971—the desequestration decree aroused popular support because it "meant the removal of the oppression to which some people were subjects. It was a clear indictment of an era in which these oppressive measures were committed and a condemnation of the means of rule at the time."[21] General Sadiq—the only member of the defunct HCLF to support Sadat—was in fact exploiting the contradictions in Nasser's policies to condemn Nasserism. Sadat's desequestration decree was followed by a series of attempts through the cabinet and the National Assembly to enact the necessary legislation for regulating the desequestration process. These measures were taken in April and May as tensions between Sadat and Sabri reached explosive proportions.

Factional rivalry was brought into the open over issues that on the surface appeared to be related to foreign policy. These disagreements were over the extension of the cease-fire across the Suez Canal and the unity scheme with Libya, Syria, and the Sudan. Sadat began to reveal his predilection for one-man rule as he unilaterally decided issues of tremendous national importance.

The cease-fire across the Suez Canal was arranged under the American-sponsored Rogers' Plan. Nasser accepted the cease-fire resolution for ninety days, beginning on 8 August 1970. Sabri's faction interpreted Nasser's acceptance of the American mediation as a tactical maneuver to recover the occupied land by force. General Muhammad Fawzi has recently revealed that "a brief respite from the war of attrition was necessary to build the missile defence system to protect the Canal zone and the strategic areas in the interior."[22] He further pointed out that the "Granite Plan" for crossing the canal and occupying the strategic Mitla passes in Sinai was ready, but Sadat decided to postpone making the momentous decision for war, opting instead for a ninety-day extension of the cease-fire.

With the second cease-fire approaching its end, a joint session of the Higher Executive Committee and the National Defence Council met on 2 February 1971. The session was attended by all members except for Sadat and Prime Minister Mahmoud Fawzi. At this session, it was decided there should be no further extension of the cease-fire. According to Farid Abd al-Karim, the secretary of the Vanguard and the ASU secretary in the Giza province, the countdown for Zero-Hour began when the highest institutions in the country decided there was no alternative to war. There was full confidence in the ability of the Egyptian and Syrian armies to conduct armed struggle. Sadat, however, surprised members of the faction when he unfolded his peace initiative before the National Assembly on 5 February. Sadat called on Israel to withdraw its troops five kilometers from the east bank of the Canal, with the objective of reopening it for international shipping. He further revealed his interest in establishing peaceful relations with Israel in return for withdrawal from the occupied territories and recognition of the rights of the Palestinians. He also agreed on a one-month extension of the cease-fire.[23]

Sadat's initiative angered the Sabri faction since it ignored the decision of the Higher Executive Committee. It was quite apparent where Sadat was heading and on which of the superpowers he was betting heavily. Members of the faction were convinced that Sadat was seeking an alternative to war with Israel through United States mediation. Following the peace initiative, Heikal began a series of articles that progressively reflected Sadat's unfolding policy. Heikal's main thesis was that if American friendship was impossible, then efforts must be exerted at least to blunt the sharp edge of her intervention on the side of Israel. Members of the rival factions responded by pointing out that any attempt to neutralize the United States or to render less harmful its intervention in the Arab-Israeli conflict was not only wishful thinking but also naive and unrealistic. As far as the majority of 'Ali Sabri's faction was concerned, the United States was firmly committed to the Israeli cause.

Sadat's overtures to Israel and the United States were resoundingly rebuffed by the leaders of both countries. Israeli Prime Minister Golda Meir called the peace initiative an insult to Israeli intelligence, and United States President Richard Nixon let it be known that American mediation could not function under the pressure of a limited cease-fire. Indeed, nothing transpired until Sadat himself revoked the cease-fire on 6 March. He said, in a speech delivered that day, that Egypt was no longer bound by the cease-fire resolution. He also referred to a secret trip he had made earlier to the Soviet Union, from which he had returned fully satisfied in the support he received. Sadat proclaimed he would end the stalemate either through peace or war, hence, he called 1971 "the year of decision."

The following week, two articles appeared reflecting the heightened state of tension between Sadat's proxy, Heikal, and Ali Sabri.[24] Heikal wrote an article praising the armed forces for the forebearance they had shown so far in an intolerable situation, which he had aptly described several years earlier as "the state of no war and no peace." He went on to explain the complex factors in the regional and international arena and how a decision to break out of the stalemate must be weighed carefully. Any premature decision could only lead to a disaster. The response of the opposing faction came three days later in the pages of *al-Gumhouriyya*. Heikal's advice and praise were rejected on behalf of the army.

The next surprise Sadat sprang on his political rivals was the decision to hold a summit meeting with the leaders of Libya, Syria, and the Sudan to discuss the unification of the four countries. The meeting was held in Benghazi, and on 17 April an announcement was made on the formation of a Union of Arab Republics consisting of Egypt, Libya, and Syria. The Sudan had dropped out of the proposed union because of fear that it might complicate relations with the non-Arab population in the southern half of the country. Egypt's official name was changed from the United Arab Republic to the Arab Republic of Egypt.

Although Sadat announced the union in the presence of 'Ali Sabri, it became the litmus test in the power struggle between the two of them. The draft of the proposed union came up for discussion before the Supreme Executive Committee of the ASU on 21 April. According to Sadat, the majority of the committee members rejected the proposed union. The conflict was brought into the open at the ASU's Central Committee meeting on 25 April. Some of the committee members showed their support for Sabri by refusing to be stampeded into accepting the draft of the unification scheme presented by Sadat. Although the Central Committee after much hesitation did approve the union, Sadat was left unsatisfied. He concluded that the struggle for power must reach a climax the resolution of which would settle once and for all who had the final say in governing the country.[25]

The Arab Union, for the opposing faction, meant reorganization of the state institutions, meaning, in Nasserist parlance, the purging of unwanted elements. The opposing faction feared that Sadat was resorting to an old Nasserist ploy. With the advantage of hindsight, it can be asserted that Sadat himself was not serious about the union with Libya and Syria. The final drama of the proposed union was enacted on the floors of the National Assembly. Sadat wanted to appeal in person for the assembly's support, but he was informed he did not have to trouble himself. "The assembly itself was coming to him,"[26] meaning that the assembly members would not only approve whatever Sadat wanted, but were also coming in person to his home to demonstrate their unflagging support for the president. The assembly met on 29 April, approved the union, and adopted a resolution endorsed by 185 members (54 percent of the assembly), thereby affirming the assembly's support for Sadat's policies.

While the conflict was brewing with his political rivals, Sadat continued to hold meetings with top army officers. According to General Sadiq, Sadat's meetings with the officers were intended to "weaken the position of 'Ali Sabri's group and to gain a solid foot-hold for himself."[27] The meetings continued throughout the critical months of March and April. Recent revelations show that the army command was split. According to General Shazli, the majority of the Supreme Military Council members who met on 18 April under the chairmanship of General Fawzi were in favor of the union. The only exceptions were General Shazli and General Sadiq.[28]

Apparently, many highly placed individuals lent their support to Sadat for no apparent reason except their common antipathy for the opposing faction. Thus, individuals with varied poilitical outlooks, such as the ones held by Muhammad Abd al-Salam al-Zayyat, minister of state for parliamentary affairs, Heikal, and General Sadiq, were united by their fear of the alternative to Sadat's leadership, which would have had dire consequences for them. For this reason, scores of public figures were driven to support Sadat, even though they were skeptical of his political aptitude.

On Labor Day, two days after the National Assembly ratified the union with Libya and Syria, Sadat revealed to the workers of Helwan his determination to liquidate the centers of power who "had no legitimate claims to impose their will on the people." The very next day, 'Ali Sabri was dismissed, followed a few days later by Sha'rawi Gom'a. On 13 May, six ministers tendered their resignations, ostensibly in protest over the ouster of their colleagues. Their resignations precipitated a crisis that, as I will show below, both Sadat and the faction had expected. Sadat, however, made an implausible connection between the mass resignations and a conspiracy to overthrow the government. At this critical point, secret tapes were mysteriously discovered that the government alleged contained evidence of a plot to overthrow Sadat. On 14 May, the National Assembly met in an emergency session to deal with the crisis, while the Republican Guard under General Sadiq began its crackdown on the opposition. By 15 May, all the opposing top military, bureaucratic, and party elites had been arrested. The list of detainees included ninety persons.

Tapes containing telephone conversations, surreptitiously recorded, were produced by the government as evidence against the faction. Though they did not disclose clear evidence of a conspiracy, the tapes showed that the group led by Sabri was indeed acting and behaving as a faction. The tapes further revealed how urgently members of the faction viewed the need to consolidate power. In this context, the National Assembly became a critical element in the factional contest for support. The importance of the National Assembly was evident in the reactions of members of the faction to the assembly vote in favor of the proposed union on 29 April. According to Muhammad Fa'iq, Sadat's main source of confidence laid in the National Assembly. He summed up the situation to Sabri by saying that Sadat "concentrated his efforts on the Assembly.

All [deputies from] Upper Egypt and Beheira were taken. The National Assembly is in fact behind him. It seems that Labib Shuqayr [the speaker] is asleep all this time, and then the last straw is the cable signed by 185 deputies all giving support to Sadat. The [situation in the] assembly is bad, rather dismal."[29] Sabri responded by saying that all efforts must aim at gaining assembly backing. Fa'iq's response was that the number of deputies in the Socialist Vanguard was in the range of between 120 and 150. Thus, the estimate of support for the faction according to the figures provided by Fa'iq ranged from 33 to 42 percent of the assembly seats.

Sayid Mar'i's memoirs confirm the impression formed by the faction of Sadat's self-assurance concerning assembly support, although he himself tended to question Sadat's reasons for confidence. Mar'i wrote that he was called for an urgent meeting with the president to devise plans for diffusing the crisis brought about by the mass resignations of cabinet members on 13 May. He told the president that the situation was indeed very serious because the faction extended its control over "the army, the internal security, the mass media, the National Assembly, the Arab Socialist Union . . . etc."[30] Sadat, however, cut Mar'i short by saying that he was quite confident of the base of his support. He then asked Mar'i to perform an essential task at the assembly, which was to hold an emergency session the following day at his request. Mar'i did not divulge the nature of the task delegated to him by the president, except for making the cryptic remark that it was "concerning the unseating of the speaker and the few deputies moved by the centers of power."[31] He added that he was chosen for the task because of his on-going relations with assembly members.

One of the hitherto unresolved mysteries of the Corrective Movement was how Sadat was able to gather his supporters in the assembly at such short notice—how deputies whose home districts were distant from Cairo were able to respond to the call and converge on the capital in less than twenty-four hours. Even more implausible is the assertion that 280 deputies attended the emergency session. Mustafa Kamil Murad, the leader of the Liberal Party who was instrumental in gathering support for Sadat, tried in a recent article to shed light on this episode.[32] He revealed that, upon hearing of the mass resignations, he went straight to the home of President Sadat where he encountered a crisis atmosphere. Sadat remonstrated against the deputies who were supporting the opposing faction. Murad, assisted by a deputy from Giza by the name of 'Azmi Rashed al-Mikawi, drew up a list of thirteen deputies who were marked to lose their seats in the assembly. From the home of the president, Murad went to the broadcasting station to establish contact with deputies in their home districts through the telecommunications facilities. He was assisted by several deputies, including Yusif Makadi from Minya, Ahmad 'Abd al-

Akher and Muhammed Muzhar Abu Krishah from Sohag, Mohammed 'Uthman Ismail from Asyut, and Mohammed Hamed Mahmoud from Beheira—all of whome were later rewarded with cabinet posts and governorships. Three of the deputies mentioned by Murad belonged to traditionally influential families who had been investigated by members of the faction when the HCLF began its activities in 1966. Murad contended that the efforts of the deputies present at the broadcasting station were successful, since the next day a sufficient number of deputies arrived to establish the two-thirds quorum necessary for holding an emergency session. Murad's story has been disputed by Farid Abd al-Karim, who in a recent article disclosed that only fifty-two deputies gathered at the emergency session.[33] To establish a quorum, the signatures of deputies who supported Sadat but were not present at the meeting were forged, and their names were entered in the official minutes of the assembly. The charges of Abd al-Karim are quite serious since this assembly, by a majority vote, stripped eighteen deputies of their seats, including the speaker and his two deputies.

The majority of the ousted members represented urban districts, with Cairo losing the most representatives,—a total of eleven deputies. Rural support for Sadat is borne out by the provincial distribution of the official list of deputies who, supposedly, were present at the emergency session. Table 22 shows that support for Sadat was strongest among the deputies of Upper Egypt and the Western Delta. This distribution is not surprising given our earlier finding that traditional influence, as revealed by the HCLF data, was concentrated in Upper Egypt and in the northwestern part of the country. By contrast, traditional influence was weak in the eastern sector of the Delta. The weak support for Sadat in such provinces as Sharqiyya, Dumyat, and the Canal cities can be explained by the fact that these provinces were the homes of the leading members of the faction. Sharqiyya was the stronghold of 'Ali Sabri; Diya' al-Din Dawud belonged to Dumyat, and Muhammad Sabri Mubada had his base in Ismailiyya in the Canal Zone. Thus, from the distribution of the ousted members and the official list of Sadat supporters, it can be concluded that the faction derived support mainly from urban areas or from provinces in which kinship links had been established.

The urban support base for the faction can be further substantiated by noting the location of the ASU leaders who were the primary suspects in the alleged conspiracy to overthrow Sadat. The list of the accused included Sami Sharaf, minister of presidential affairs and head of the Vanguard for Eastern Cairo; Muhammad Muhammad Fa'iq, minister of information and head of the Vanguard for Western Cairo; Muhammad Sa'd al-Din Zaid, minister of housing and head of the Vanguard for Northern Cairo; and Hilmi Muhammad al-

TABLE 22   Provincial Distribution of the Official List of Sadat's Supporters in the People's Assembly[a]

Province	Total Seats	No. of Deputies Supporting Sadat	Percentage of Seats
Cairo	40	18	45.0
Alexandria	18	16	88.9
Canal Cities	10	3	33.3
Qalubiyya	14	12	85.7
Sharqiyya	24	12	50.0
Daqahliyya	26	15	57.7
Dumyat	6	2	33.3
Kafr al-Shaykh	12	11	91.7
Gharbiyya	22	19	86.4
Minufiyya	20	16	80.0
Beheira	22	21	95.5
Totals for Lower Egypt	214	145	67.8
Giza	16	12	75.0
Fayyum	12	6	50.0
Bani Suwayf	12	11	91.7
Minya	22	22	100.0
Asyut	18	17	94.4
Sohag	22	20	90.9
Qena	20	16	80.0
Aswan	6	3	50.0
Totals for Upper Egypt	128	107	83.6
TOTAL	342	252	73.7

SOURCE: Minutes of the National Assembly, 14 May 1971.

a Does not include the appointed members and the desert provinces (Wadi al-Jadid, Marsa Matruh, and the Red Sea). The official list of deputies included a total of 262 deputies.

Sa'id, minister of electricity and head of the Vanguard for Southern Cairo. In addition, key government officials who held just as prominent positions in the secret apparatus of the ASU were accused. The most distinguished officials were the head of the broadcasting station and the director of the Intelligence Bureau.

The majority of the National Assembly members seemed to exact full vengeance from their erstwhile tormentors when they convened on 31 May. They were to consider a government-sponsored legislation to impose sequestration on the property of prominent members of the faction.[34] The legislation was aimed at the property of "individuals who enriched themselves through influence derived from the holding of an official rank, a government position or parliamentary representation."[35] Another clause stated that sequestration would also be brought against individuals who "corrupted political life or exposed national unity to danger." According to the minister of justice, who introduced the proposed legislation in the assembly, these clauses were necessary to deal with the crisis of 15 May. He added, however, that the new legislation departed from previous sequestration measures, since it included an amendment stating that sequestration against any individual would be imposed only by a court order. Nevertheless, two innovations in the new legislation nullified any impartial prosecution of those public offenders specified in the above clauses. These innovations included the appointment of the socialist prosecutor general and the adoption of the jury system, the jury's selection being determined and controlled by the executive authority.

A special court, known as the "sequestration court," was set up to try the accused in the alleged conspiracy to overthrow Sadat under the new law. The court found 'Ali Sabri, 'Abd al-Muhsin Abu al-Nur, Shawr'ai Gom'a, General Muhammad Fawzi, and Muhammad Fai'q guilty of accumulating wealth through illegal means. All but Fa'iq were former members of the HCLF. Other former members of the HCLF, who were not part of the alleged conspiracy, were also brought before the sequestration court and found guilty. Most prominent among these were 'Abbas Radwan and Salah Nasr.

A revolutionary court was also set up under the chairmanship of Hafiz Badawi, the new speaker of the assembly, to try members of the faction under the criminal code. The trial of eleven members of the alleged conspiracy began in September 1971. All were found guilty of attempting to overthrow the government and were sentenced to various terms in prison.

The Corrective Movement brought many changes, all intended to sweep away the followers of the faction and to tighten Sadat's control over the government bureaucracy and the party. In the National Assembly, Sadat's nominee for the position of speaker, Hafiz Badawi, was elected by the deputies present at the emergency session held on 14 May. Mamdouh Salem, Sadat's strong man in the Intelligence Bureau, was promoted to the post of minister of the interior, replacing Sha'rawi Gom'a. Sadat's ally in the army, General Sadiq, replaced General Fawzi as the minister of war.

The game of musical chairs was naturally expanded to include the key posts in the ASU. In fact, Sadat went about reorganizing the ASU with almost indecent haste. The assets of the ASU were frozen on 21 May, presumably to prevent faction followers from siphoning off party funds under their control. This step was followed by a decree signed by Sadat calling for the reorganization of the ASU at all levels, from the village up. The National Assembly assumed the responsibilities of the ASU's Central Committee until a new committee could be elected. The general secretary of the ASU, 'Abdel Muhsin Abu al-Nur, was replaced by Muhammad Abdel Salam al-Zayyat, despite his strong leftist inclinations. The provincial secretaries, who formerly functioned as the Executive Bureau secretaries organized by 'Ali Sabri during the mobilization period, were replaced by provisional secretaries. Finally, the government ordered the complete cessation of the activities of the Socialist Vanguard or, as it was referred to in the wake of the Corrective Movement, the special spparatus of 'Ali Sabri. Full-time party work was abolished.

The party purges extended to include the unions and syndicates controlled by the ASU. These included the press syndicate, the Bar Association, the Teachers' Union, the Agricultural Professions Union, the Workers' Union of Petroleum and Minerals, and many more. Indeed, it was reported that a total of 277 associational groups were reorganized in June and July. In most cases, provisional councils were set up to replace the existing councils and were charged with union responsibilities until elections could be held. Predictably, when elections were held the following month, Sadat's supporters and loyalists were swept into the positions vacated by the opposing faction.

The extent of the changes in the upper hierarchy of the ASU was reflected in the results of the elections held in July. It must be noted that the main challenge to Sadat's authority before the Corrective Movement, the Higher Executive Committee, was abolished. The elections also eliminated Sadat's rivals at the highest party levels in the provinces. Of the twenty-one provincial secretaries who served under 'Ali Sabri, only four were reelected. To indicate how these changes would affect the ASU role, Sadat informed the newly elected National Congress, which assembled on 23 July, that the "ASU would henceforth serve, not rule." The limited role allowed for the ASU was also apparent in the decision to free the National Assembly from ASU control. As announced by al-Zayyat, elections to the assembly were to remain free and open to anyone who wished to become a candidate. Thus, the prerequisite of ASU membership for National Assembly candidacy was abolished.

The Corrective Movement (*harakat al-tashhih*) was the watershed between two eras. Later the *harakat al-tashhih* became known as the Corrective Revolution (*thawrat al-tashhih*) to mark the revolutionary change brought about on 15 May. Today the occasion is simply referred to as the People's Assembly Day. Under whatever name the occasion is celebrated, there is little doubt that Sadat's crackdown on 'Ali Sabri's faction was the first in a series of steps aimed at dismantling the institutions and reversing the policies that had come to be identified closely with Nasser. But, as in all movements caught between two ill-defined eras, there was a great deal of uncertainty and confusion. Sadat went before the National Assembly, which he had renamed the People's Assembly, to announce that he was firmly set on pursuing Nasser's course, and that his action against a handful of individuals was only intended to correct any deviations from the glorious 23 July revolution. No one at that time doubted Sadat's sincerity in invoking the name of Nasser and what he stood for. Many rushed to support Sadat because they sincerely believed he symbolized continuity. To the few knowledgeable persons within the inner circle of ruling elites, however, a choice had been made between the politically inept Sadat and Sabri, the ruthless organizer. Self-interest drove them to support Sadat. Under conditions of change, though, any compromises are bound to be transient. Indeed, many individuals such as Sadiq, Heikal, and Zayyat lived to regret the role they played in consolidating Sadat's power.

Sadat's base of support extended far and deep. The National Assembly's support may not have been critical, but it symbolized by its action on 15 May the link Sadat had established with the traditional elites, whose kinship ties penetrated the state institutions. By contrast, the support underlying the faction was predominantly urban. The ASU under 'Ali Sabri was like a giant with feet of clay. Thus, Sadat, confident of his base of support, could easily ride roughshod over his political rivals in the party. The significance of the Corrective Movement lies in its demonstration of the political influence of the rural elites, despite preceding attempts to weaken their hold and position in the rural areas. Furthermore, the Corrective Movement contained the seeds of the liberalization trends apparently begun in reaction to Nasser's repressive policy. Members of 'Ali Sabri's faction were held responsible for Nasser's repression, including the activities of the HCLF against the rural elites.

Following the Corrective Movement, Sadat appealed to all social groups alienated by Nasser's policies—the rural elites, the urban intelligentsia, the Muslim Brotherhood, the Wafd, and even some of the former communists and Marxists. But before deNasserization began in earnest, the Corrective Movement continued to derive its legitimacy from the March 30 Statement announced by Nasser in the aftermath of the June War defeat. Thus, in justifying his action against his political rivals, Sadat said in a speech before the People's Assembly on 20 May 1971 that his rivals had participated in the repression during the previous regime, meanwhile absolving Nasser of all blame. He pointed out that most of the prominent members of the faction were former intelligence officers who were running a police state. Sadat also drew attention to their responsibility in alienating important sections of the society in rural and urban areas by denying them basic freedoms. In the rush of enthusiasm for Sadat, few bothered to reflect on the strange mixture of the liberal image Sadat was projecting and the conservative spirit of the village he invoked, where disrespect of elders and defiance of their authority were condemned.

Chapter Seven
Undoing Nasserism

F
AMILIARITY WITH EGYPTIAN CULTURAL nuances was perhaps the only means to detect the early signs of deNasserization. In May 1971, Sadat expressed solemn faith in the Nasserist model and in the Corrective Movement, which, in his opinion, was no more than a correction of deviations from the right path. He declared that there was no turning away from the goals set by the "immortal" leader. A few years later or, to be exact, in the *October Paper* of 1974, the Open Door policy or *siyasat al-infitah* came to be identified in the public mind with deNasserization.

Sadat turned out to be a more shrewd and skilled manipulator than 'Ali Sabri and company. He felt his people were ripe for change, but he could express change only in the negative or oppositional sense. The term "opening" or *infitah* was a negation of what was perceived to be a closed system, *inghilaq*, under Nasser.[1] The term "permanent" constitution was coined in 1971 as a put down for the various "provisional" constitutions adopted under Nasser. The offical slogans of faith and science were raised in opposition to the alien beliefs upon which Nasserism supposedly thrived.

There was no dearth of articulators and opinion makers with the capacity and the will to equip these efforts at negating Nasserism with the necessary ideological weapons. In the wake of the Corrective Movement, the dean of Egyptian letters, Tawfiq al-Hakim, gave full expression to a general indictment of a regime that for eighteen years had robbed the individual of his reasoning and critical faculties. Following the publication of al-Hakim's *'Awdat al-Wa'y*[2] or the "return of consciousness," voluminous writings appeared to reveal the darkest side of Nasserism, its evils and malevolence. Naturally, a few individuals, mostly on the Egyptian left, rose in defense of Nasser, but their voices were drowned by the malcontent in the society.[3]

The release of political prisoners among Nasser's sworn enemies, the *Ikhwan* and Wafdists, and Sadat's denunciation of the repressions perpetrated in the name of Nasserism set the stage for razing the Nasserist edifice to the ground and launching a new beginning. Nevertheless, the deradicalization trend under Sadat could only be carried out in stages, a fact his predecessor had discovered when attempting the opposite strategy of dispossessing the dominant classes. Sadat also came to realize that there were limits on how far he could go in depriving the subordinate classes of their socialist inheritance. To the ruling elites, the socialist gains were a small burden they were willing to tolerate in order to maintain the stability of the political system. The burden was alleviated when outside powers provided help in the form of loans and foreign aid.

The undoing of Nasserist Egypt began with the desequestration measures of 1971. Sadat's first objective was to wipe out the remaining traces of the HCLF. This goal is understandable since the prominent members of the HCLF were the leading members of the opposition. To discredit them and to win the support of their erstwhile victims among the rural elites, Sadat left no doubt as to where he stood in relation to the HCLF. In his memoirs, Sadat wrote he was completely opposed to the activities of the HCLF.[4] He was not one of its members, and hence, he had no idea how it had arrived at its decisions and why. He recalled instances when he had tried to intervene and, on some occasions, had succeeded in reversing the penalties imposed by the HCLF against the rural elites. He recalled that, during one of his visits to his home village of Mit Abu al-Kom, a young engineer surprised him by revealing that some of the notables in Sadat's own district, that is, under his very nose, had had property put under sequestration. He said he knew each one of them and had no reason to suspect they were against the 23 July revolution. He had felt the HCLF was making a big mistake, and he was determined to rectify it. He therefore put pressure on Marshal 'Amer to rescind the HCLF's decision, but was frustrated that he was powerless to bring about a complete cessation of the HCLF's activities against the notables because of the pervasive influence of Marxists and communists.

The Kamshish Affair was, in Sadat's opinion, nothing but a Marxist fabrication. The persons supposedly combating feudalism (Salah and Shahinda) exploited this issue in order to expose the Egyptian village to Marxists and communists. According to Sadat, these elements infiltrated the Egyptian village during this period, and "they even took Sartre to Kamshish in order to show off what they had accomplished."[5] Sadat concluded that there had been no need for the HCLF since feudalism in Egyptian villages had been liquidated a long time ago.

The desequestration process was much more difficult and complex than Sadat had imagined it would be. This difficulty was because the Nasserist regime had only gradually imposed sequestration against landed and urban property owners, and each stage had been determined by different sets of laws and conditions. The complexity was made worse because of Nasser's inconsistent policy toward the property owners and because the motive behind sequestration differed according to circumstances. Consequently, three types of sequestration had emerged.[6] The first one immediately followed the enactment of the socialist decrees of July 1961 and was conceived as a means to bring about a speedy change in the social order. Sequestration was imposed in accordance with the provisions of law no. 162/58, enacted during the state of emergency declared after the Suez Canal crisis of 1958 and used to strip foreign nationals of their Egyptian holdings. This type of sequestration, which affected the largest number of wealthy families, ostensibly ended with the promulgation of the provisional constitution in 1964. Law no. 150/64 was enacted in March 1964 to end sequestration measures adopted under emergency law no. 162/58. It transferred all properties to state ownership with compensation payments not exceeding a limit of E£ 30,000 in negotiable bonds.

The second type of sequestration coincided with the increasing security concerns of the regime, caused by the discovery of plots and other adverse activities. It may be recalled that during this period the activities of the Muslim Brotherhood had assumed a new intensity. Sequestration was thus used as an instrument to disarm subversive elements. Law no. 119 was enacted in 1964 to deal with these subversive elements, whose activities threatened the security of the regime.[7] The third type of sequestration coincided with the activities of the HCLF following the Kamshish Affair and the rise in the influence of the left.

The number of families subjected to sequestration between 1961 and 1966 as a consequence of the socialist decrees and the security needs of the state totaled 4,000, and the total assets seized inlcuded 122,000 faddans, 7,000 urban properties, 1,000 business establishments, and over E£ 30,000 in stocks and bonds.[8] It must, however, be asserted that the majority of the families were put under sequestration between 1961 and 1964, when the socialist measures were most intense. During the third type of sequestration (resulting from the activities of the HCLF), according to the testimony of Sayyid Mar'i, a total of 334 families and 55,000 faddans were affected.[9]

The distinction drawn by jurists between the above types of sequestration is critical for understanding the conflicting claims and how legislators proceeded to settle them under Sadat. Of the three types, the most unfortunate victims were the families who came under sequestration between 1961 and 1964. Although the sequestration measures against them ended with the enactment of law no. 150/64, the cases of many families, involving as many of 1688 families, remained unsettled when Sadat assumed power due to numerous bureaucratic bottlenecks and legal complications.[10] The families affected by law no. 150/64 were unfortunate in another sense because their properties were confiscated against payment of compensation not exceeding E£ 30,000, whereas the properties of families affected later, that is, the families subjected to sequestration for security reasons after 1964, were restored in full.

The deputy speaker of the assembly, Jamal 'Utaifi, emerged in the early 1970s as the chief articulator of state legislation, upon whom fell the task of providing justifications for the actions arbitrarily taken by the state against the propertied classes. 'Utaifi expressed the opinion that sequestration between 1961 and 1964 was applied to bring about desired social change, although he did not regard the measure as a sound one because of the temptation to misuse it or to exploit it for power aggrandizement.[11] 'Utaifi was willing to countenance sequestration as long as the motivation was to protect society from excessive wealth held by a small minority. For this reason, he did not believe there was any justification for the imposition of sequestration after March 1965, because by then the motive was not social change but was that of inflicting severe punishment upon a cross-section of society, which included small farmers and workers. 'Utaifi therefore made the remark that sequestration affected families more severely after 1964 than before. He was convinced that the only redeeming feature of sequestration was in its ability to dissolve class differences, and that any other motive deserved to be condemned.

'Utaifi was hoping to end speculations that the desequestration measures announced by Sadat would snowball into something larger than what the regime had intended. Such a possibility was drawn by 'Utaifi himself when he said that the families who lost their properties as a consequence of law no. 150/64 would demand they be treated on an equal footing with the families whose properties were put under sequestration after 1964 for security reasons. To put an end to all these speculations and to nip in the bud any hopes entertained by the former proprietors, 'Utaifi declared there will be no turning back from the socialist measures and that no attempt would be made to undermine the agrarian reforms.

Clearly, despite the fanfare accompanying desequestration, the initial steps were narrow in scope and did not amount to any more than a confirmation of what had already been decided upon by the Nasserist regime. My data shows that the cases of only 152 families subjected to sequestration for security reasons after 1964 remained to be settled.[12] For the families subjected to sequestration before 1964 as part of the socialist transformation, law no. 49/71 was enacted that while upholding the provisions of law no. 150/64 including the payment of compensation of up to a limit of E£ 30,000, called for the removal of all obstacles impeding a speedy settlement of all outstanding claims.

While the People's Assembly was contemplating the passage of desequestration measures, steps were being taken by the government to release political prisoners and to end the political isolation or *al-'Azl al-Siyyasi* imposed by the previous regime against its perceived or imagined enemies. In August 1971, Mamdouh Salem, the minister of the interior, declared that there were 380 political detainees, the majority of whom were members of the *Ikhwan* or the Muslim Brotherhood.[13] He said that 134 persons would be released as part of the regime's program of political liberalization. In the same month, Mamdouh Salem also announced that the political isolation imposed on 13,000 individuals since 1962 would be eliminated.[14] Furthermore, 127 judges expelled in 1969 for attempting to preserve the independence of the judiciary against encroachments by 'Ali Sabri's party machine would be reinstated.[15]

The movement toward the right was not unopposed by the growing resistance of workers and students, although it did not constitute a cohesive movement with clearly defined objectives. Its outbursts were reactions to a deteriorating situation, in which the regime appeared to be completely helpless. The Sadat regime could not remove Israeli troops on the east bank of the Suez Canal, nor did it possess the capacity to alter the stalemate which Heikal had popularized by the phrase "no war and no peace." Egyptian frustration grew as the months and years passed without an end in sight. The impact was more severly felt among university students and youthful elements, who expressed their dissatisfaction by holding political rallies. Sadat seemed to add fuel to the fire by his habit of making promises he could not fulfill. He declared the year 1971 to be the "year of decision," meaning, the resolution of the Arab-Israeli conflict either by diplomatic means or by war before the year ended. The year 1971 ended, however, without a single shot being fired, giving rise to student and worker protests,[16] apart from the numerous jokes for which Egyptians are famous. Political agitation began in August at the steel complex in Helwan when workers went on strike to protest the steady erosion of the socialist gains made under Nasser.[17] Student protests were a continuation of the events of February 1968, sparked by the lenient sentences passed upon those responsible for Egypt's state of unpreparedness in the June War. The protests reached a climax in January 1972 following a speech by Sadat in which he appeared to contradict himself while offering lame excuses for his failure to make 1971 a decisive year.[18]

The regime had little trouble crushing student resistance but, to contain leftist elements on university campuses, the government encouraged the formation of Islamic groups, *jama'at*. This action began a dangerous trend that deeply affected communal relations with the Coptic minority and the Muslim majority. With hindsight, it can be seen that the growing tension between members of the two communities was closely connected with the use of religion as a political device to combat the left and with the gradual abandonment of the secularist tendencies rooted in Nasserism.[19] The first major sectarian conflict took place in a small town on the outskirts of Cairo in November 1972. The regime responded by passing legislation to preserve national unity.

Sadat's shift to the right was consistent with changes in the foreign policy orientation of the regime. There was a growing domestic disenchantment with Egyptian dependence on Soviet support. Members of the intelligentsia began to publicize their views on the need to lessen dependence on the Soviet Union and to normalize relations with the United States.[20] The deterioration in Soviet-Egyptian relations started with the Corrective Movement in May 1971. 'Ali Sabri was regarded as the "Soviet man" in the government, and his removal was interpreted as a major setback to Soviet influence and brought Kosygin to Cairo a few days later. Kosygin's emergency visit led to the Soviet-Egyptian Friendship Treaty and the reaffirmation of the traditional solidarity between the two countries. But neither the treaty nor the growing Egyptian dependence on the Soviet Union seemed to deter Egypt's shift to the right, both domestically and in its regional and international relations. Relations between the two countries deteriorated further when Sadat made his surprise move of expelling 20,000 Soviet advisers in July 1972. Analysts produced conflicting views on what led Sadat to take such a drastic step without even trying to gain some concessions from the United States.[21] The prevalent reason cited then was the Soviet unwillingness to accede to Egyptian demands for the supply of sophisticated military hardware to match American supplies to Israel. Nonetheless, changes in the international climate might also have influenced the new foreign policy orientation of the regime. The thawing of relations between the United States and the Soviet Union spelled an end to whatever little autonomy Third World powers enjoyed during the cold war through their exploitation of superpower phobias. In the era of detente, the Soviet leaders were reluctant to accede to the demands of their client state. They feared the situation in the Middle East might get out of control and lead to a dangerous escalation with the United States. The Soviets did not think the Arabs were ready for another war with Israel and, therefore, acted as a restraining influence. A few thoughtful analysts at that time pointed out the inevitability of war in the Middle East after the expulsion of the Soviet advisers.[22] But no one, least of all the United States and Israel, took the sabre rattling of Sadat seriously.

The Egyptians felt the Soviet Union stood to benefit from the continuing "no win" situation in which Egypt seemed to be hopelessly entrapped. The growing dependence of Egypt on the Soviets gave the latter the opportunity to extend their influence over the whole region, thus isolating the United States. The Egyptian intelligentsia and members of the armed forces frequently complained that the Russians were behaving like colonizers. They resented the haughty and arrogant manner of the advisers responsible for training Egyptian soldiers.[23] Another source of concern was the frequently expressed dissatisfaction over the quality of Soviet military hardware and spare parts. The general opinion was that Soviet supplies to Egypt lacked the sophistication of American supplies to Israel.[24]

In addition to the concerns above was Egypt's growing dependence on Soviet economic aid which reached alarming proportions between 1967 and 1973. During this period, Western aid shrank to a trickle — averaging only $10 to $12 million per year. In comparison, nonmilitary aid from the Eastern bloc amounted to more than $1.2 billion, financing development projects. The military aid was estimated to be about $4 billion.[25] Egypt was forced to pay part of her external debts in kind and by mortgaging its cotton crops. Under these circumstances, critics believed Egypt was gradually being transformed into a satellite of the Soviet Union.

The traditionally pro-Western and anti-Soviet Kingdom of Saudi Arabia and the Libyan leader, Colonel Mu'amar al-Qadhafi, were partly responsible for Egypt's new foreign policy orientation. It has even been suggested that Saudi Arabia was behind the tilt toward the United States.[26] In fact, the explusion of the Soviet advisers gave rise to much speculation about a secret deal between Cairo and Washington through Saudi mediation. Until Egypt, jointly with Syria, launched the fourth round of fighting with Israel in October 1973, however, Sadat's open and covert overtures received no response from Washington.

The October War was truly Sadat's most momentous decision, and to him goes the credit of finally breaking the prolonged stalemate with Israel. Unlike previous wars with Israel, the initiative in the October War seemed to lie in Egyptian hands during the first few critical days of fighting. Egyptian fighter's performance was a far cry from his conduct during the June War, which had given rise to the widespread belief that the Egyptian soldier lacked the courage and the will to fight — the qualities that made his Israeli counterpart famous. The recovery of part of the Sinai gave Sadat the opportunity to move out of the shadow of Nasser and to assert his own leadership.

In the *October Paper*, announced by Sadat in April 1974, the changes in Egypt's external relations and in its domestic policies were cast into a program meant to rival the Socialist Charter of 1962 and the March 30 Statement of 1968. Externally, Sadat believed Egypt must respond to the new opportunities created by the October War, including the rising oil prices. He appeared to suggest that Egypt was partly responsible for the steep rise in oil prices and was therefore eligible for a share in the huge revenues accumulated by the Arab oil-producing countries. The legitimacy of his claim was expressed by the phrase "blood money," meaning Egypt's sacrifices on the battlefields that resulted in the conditions of prosperity the Arab oil producers were enjoying. Sadat envisioned a prosperous future in which Egypt and the Arab oil producers would both participate. Egypt would provide the manpower and the oil producers would provide the capital to establish joint ventures. Free trade zones, new cities, and tourist centers were part of Sadat's schemes for the future, which needed a capital investment of $10 billion. These proposals constituted Egypt's response to the new opportunities created by the October War, ideas that became reflected in the Open Door Policy.

Internally, however, the *October Paper* reaffirmed the Nasserist model. Sadat was eager to stamp out any memory of Nasser, but not of the system he had imposed on his people. The *October Paper* recognized the legitimacy of the 1952 revolution, the agrarian reforms, and the Socialist Charter. Sadat admitted that some mistakes had been made, but the principles were sound because "the country was rescued from a violent class struggle, which many other countries have witnessed and are still witnessing. I would not be exaggerating if I say that the Revolution has saved the country from civil war."[27]

The *October Paper* was critical of the absence of political freedom during the Nasserist regime, but it confirmed the national alliance of popular forces as the medium of participation within the single-party organization. The multiparty system was rejected, and the only concession to the freedom of expression was the recognition of the existence of plurality of interests within the national alliance. Furthermore, the *October Paper* was critical of the public sector, it reaffirmed the Nasserist idea that the public sector would remain the main pillar of the economy upon which central planning would rest.

Riding high on the crest of the popularity resulting from the military and diplomatic breakthrough, Sadat seemed oblivious to the social consequences of the strategy he had earlier adopted for consolidating his power after the Corrective Movement. The *October Paper* fell short of the expectations Sadat had aroused by his appeal to the classes that had borne the full brunt of Nasser's socialist measures. On the other hand, nothing was done to allay the fears of workers and students, except for making a vague reference to adding an article to the permanent constitution stating that socialism was the basis of the regime. Because of his failure to respond to these demands, Sadat found himself, during the post–October War period, in the midst of sharp social contradictions.

In the *October Paper*, Sadat declared the supremacy of laws and due process. The dispossessed landed and urban elites appeared to challenge Sadat by resorting to the courts in order to redress their grievances, the most outstanding of which were the measures taken between 1961 and 1964 in the form of property sequestration. The dispossessed elites wanted the courts to declare that these measures were illegal because they contradicted the provisional constitutions promulgated in 1956, 1958, and 1964, whose articles upheld the sanctity of private property.[28] It was further argued that law no. 150/64, which had led to the nationalization of properties under sequestration with compensation payments not exceeding E£ 30,000, had no legal justification. A case brought before the Higher Constitutional Court in April 1974 claimed that dispossession contradicted the Socialist Charter, upon which socialism had been based in 1962.[29]

The mounting pressures on the courts to rescind the actions taken by the Nasser regime forced the government to intervene by sponsoring new legislation, the objective of which was to placate the dispossessed without alienating the subordinate classes that had benefited from sequestration. The new legislation originated in the People's Assembly Committee of Proposals and Grievances under the chairmanship of Mahmoud Abu Wafia, Sadat's brother-in-law and troubleshooter. To understand the legal complexity underlying the compromises that were reached, some measures introduced by the new legislation must be borne in mind. The first was the attempt to distinguish individuals who came under sequestration between 1961 and 1964 because of their dependent relationships to individuals who were the principal subjects of sequestration. The new legislation also introduced payment in kind as part of the compensation to be made, in addition to cash settlement. A further distinction was drawn between property that had remained under state control and property that had been divided into small parcels over which small farmers assumed ownership rights.

The above distinctions are important for understanding the provisions of law no. 69/74, which was enacted in July 1974. Article 1 provided for the liquidation of all sequestrations imposed between 1961 and 1964 in accordance with law no. 150/64, that is, the payment of compensation up to E£ 30,000. Article 2 granted dependents the full restoration of property acquired by means other than inheritance from sequestered principals. If conditions precluded the restoration of property, such as its sale to small farmers, the dependents would be entitled to the full face value of the sale contract.

For the properties acquired from sequestered principals, the law decreed restoration of property in kind up to E£ 30,000 per dependent but not exceeding a total of E£ 100,000 per family. The same provisions were granted to principals and their dependents when the former had not disposed of property to the latter and had continued to maintain sole rights of ownership. The value of sequestered property was to be determined on the basis of 70 times the land tax or 160 times the rates imposed on urban property. According to Ibrahim

Shirbini, the head of the Desequestration Department and the person responsible for drafting the law under discussion, the criteria for calculating compensation payments were least satisfactory for the large landowners, whose old tax rates were quite low due to the influence they had exerted during the monarchy.[30] According to figures released in 1981 — when the People's Assembly was considering yet another legislation to settle outstanding claims on sequestered properties — the total value of property compensation, including agricultural lands and urban properties, amounted to E£ 36 million, based on taxes imposed in 1949 for agricultural properties and taxes imposed in 1960 for real estate. Needless to say the value of compensation fell far below the current market value, much to the dismay of the dispossessed classes.

Furthermore, article 7 of law no. 69/74 dissolved all arrangements for the disposal of sequestered properties made between the Department of Sequestration and the Ministry of Agrarian Reforms. The article permitted the return of property to its former owner as long as it was unencumbered by a third party claim. No change of status was contemplated for farmers who obtained possession over confiscated property. According to Shirbini, this provision benefited the large landowners, the majority of whom owned orchards inappropriate for division into small parcels for distribution among small farmers and, hence, that remained under government control. Because parts of the properties of the large landowners from the rural upper stratum were unencumbered by third party claims, it was easier to return them to their former owners than properties that had been divided and on which the small farmers staked their claims.

The passage of the new desequestration law was received enthusiastically by the majority of the deputies in the People's Assembly.[31] They stood one after the other to pay tribute to Sadat, the Hero of the Crossing (of the Suez Canal in the October War), for having the courage to rectify past mistakes, punish the deviationist who strayed from the correct path of the 23 July revolution, and safeguard private property without causing harm to socialist sensibilities. Ironically, the deputies who had been most enthusiastic in expressing support for sequestration during the socialist era were suddenly transformed into ardent supporters of desequestration under the *infitah*. Sayyid Mar'i draws our attention to the political opportunists among deputies such as Hafiz Badawi, the speaker of the assembly after the Corrective Movement, Sayyid Galal, and Mustafa Kamil Murad, who, at the height of the crisis engendered by the Kamshish Affair in 1966, had denounced in no uncertain terms the feudalists that threatened the security of the Nasserist regime.[32]

The cupidity of the assembly deputies was prevalent even among representatives of the small peasants. For example, Ahmad Yunis was the representative of the small peasants from Beheira during the Kamshish Affair and the investigations of the HCLF. He was reelected to the assembly after the Corrective Movement in 1972. During the assembly debate over the crisis caused by the Kamshish Affair, Ahmad Yunis said that "those who claim that the news about the crimes committed by the feudalists were exaggerated are deluding themselves for the truth is greater than what has been reported."[33] The deputy then went on to point out what he regarded as the pervasive influence of feudalism in Beheira, in the companies of the public sector, and in the Egyptian press. In all these areas the sons of the feudalists continued to hold commanding positions that threatened the society, the revolution, and the acquired rights of the people. The views of the assembly deputy toward feudalism changed radically, however, during the assembly discussion of the new desequestration law. Ahmad Yunis remarked that the claims that feudalists and reactionaries were stirred by the Syrian secession into threatening the gains made by the workers and peasants were pure fabrications, invented by the authorities to cover up their own failures in Syria. The same farce was reenacted in Kamshish. The political apparatus of 'Ali Sabri and company committed the biggest crime by claiming that feudalists were behind the killing in Kamshish. "We [the assembly deputies] committed the folly of believing them. We are glad of the opportunity to rectify our past mistake. Kamshish was an illusion."[34]

The deputies who had themselves suffered the consequences of sequestration were in a vengeful mood. They were not satisfied with the generous terms of the new desequestration law. One deputy said that members of the committees formed to liquidate feudalism were still in the government and at the forefront of those now denouncing feudalism and the sequestration measures. The deputy argued that these opportunists must be held for questioning and be made to pay for their past mistakes.

The lone exception in this general call for retribution and the exaction of vengeance was Ahmad Taha, one of the very few Marxist deputies in the assembly. He warned against exaggerating the oppression inflicted by those who had offended the socialist sensibilites. He reminded the assembly that there was a greater oppression that the previous regime had tried to eliminate, that is, centuries of exploitation by a privileged minority. Ahmad Taha's remark was sufficiently provocative to cause an uproar in the assembly, which forced the government spokesmen to intervene to maintain some balance. The minister of state for cabinet affairs made it clear that the legitimacy of the Sadat regime was derived from the 23 July revolution. He admitted that some mistakes had been committed in the past, but that these should not be exploited to condemn a whole era. Jamal al-'Utaifi expressed similar views when he said that no further alterations in the reformist policies of the former regime were being contemplated. The socialist character of the state would be preserved. Indeed, the government was keen on preserving the rights of farmers and tenants over desequestered properties.[35] Landlords, for example, had no right to evict tenants protected by stringent tenancy regulations that, in addition to conferring security of tenure, kept rental prices very low. Naturally, the landlords felt cheated for having to content with unwanted tenants.

Dissatisfaction over the new desequestration law was related to the fact that there was little improvement in the situation of the propertied classes beyond what had already been granted through courts and presidential decrees since the Corrective Movement. As early as October 1971, the press began to publish news of properties handed back to their owners because sequestration was illegally imposed. Sequestration had been based on their dependent relationships with principals accused of harboring ill intentions against the Nasserist regime.[36] Among the first to benefit from the early desequestration measures were the Jazzar and Sha'ir families in Minufiyya, the Ghurab family in Giza, and the Sibahi family in Qena.[37] In short, the last desequestration law legitimized what had already taken place. Nevertheless, the number of families who received portions of sequestered properties increased in 1974, after the policy of *infitah* became the official doctrine of the state. In August, it was announced that 22,000 faddans under sequestration, including 5,000 faddans of orchards, were to be handed back to their owners in November.[38] In September, it was announced that 1700 faddans in Sharqiyya including 700 faddans or orchards were to be given back to eighty-six citizens.[39] Among the recipients were members of the famous Siraj al-Din family. Reportedly, this family was to receive 400 faddans of orchards in the Inshas area that were under the control of the Agrarain Reforms Bureau. Another report contended that nine members of the Siraj al-Din family would receive agricultural land, ranging in size between 10 and 40 faddans, in accordance with the last desequestration law.[40] Thus, unwittingly, Sadat set the stage for the return of the Wafd to politics, a matter to which I will turn my attention in chapter 9.

The final act in the desequestration process was the enactment of law no. 141/81, which coincided with President Sadat's crackdown on the secular and religious opposition in September 1981. This last piece of legislation declared that all the socialist measures taken under emergency law no. 162/58 and under laws subsequent to it were without any legal foundations. This action came after a series of court battles between the dispossessed classes and the government. A decision by the Supreme Administrative Court in 1979 had put the final touches on these court battles by declaring that emergency law no. 162/58, upon which all sequestration laws were subsequently based, was applicable only to corporations and not to individuals.[41] The court decision also nullified all subsequent legislation that limited the restoration of property. The opinion of the court was that such limitation was tantamount to confiscation.

According to Ibrahim al-Shirbini, the People's Assembly was moved to action by the anticipation of a great number of individuals who would be demanding the full restoration of their properties.[42] The main concern of the government was how to satisfy the claims of those individuals whose properties were already disposed of by sale or redistribution among small farmers. These properties could not be restored without encountering resistance, which the government was keen to avoid. Therefore, the new legislation confirmed the decision of the Supreme Administrative Court on the illegality of sequestration and decreed the principle of full restoration. As for properties toward which third parties had staked their claims, the new legislation included new clauses for generous compensations for the previous owners offering a 50 percent increase over the earlier compensation of 70 times the tax rate for agricultural property.[43] For urban property, there was also a 50 percent increase over its sale price in the amount of compensation. In all cases, a 7 percent return on investments was added retroactively from the date of the enactment of law no. 69/74, which was superceded by law no. 141/81.

The new legislation meant the restoration of 147,000 faddans to their former owners, land that the Ministry of the Agrarian Reforms had contracted out to small farmers. The land for which compensation was to be paid by the government amounted to 17,000 faddans, which the Ministry of Agrarian Reforms had distributed with full ownership rights among a total 7,500 families.[44] Nonetheless, both the tenants of the desequestered landlords and the small farmers who had received titles of ownership on sequestered properties began to mark time—another tale to be taken up in the next chapter.

The Open Door policy had a cumulative effect on the urban masses as well. It gave rise to a new nouveau riche, apparently consisting of middlemen, commission agents, and comprador merchants who thrived on imported goods. The flaunting of affluence by a small minority of the urban population accentuated the poverty of the masses. The first sign of trouble resulting from the *infitah* was labor unrest, which acquired a new intensity after the October War. In January 1975, the workers at Helwan Steel Complex took to the streets because of government refusal to consider the demands raised by their union. In August, Alexandria textile workers staged a two-week strike in defiance of a ban imposed by the authorities. In both instances the government blamed the Marxists and communists for infiltrating the workers' ranks and for influencing the minds of the poor and misled workers. In December, the government ordered that the funds of the General Union of the Egyptian Workers—the largest union in Egypt—be put under sequestration in accordance with law no.

34/71, enacted in 1971 by the Sadat regime to deal specifically with its political opponents.

Sequestration, in the social dialectic of power, had different purposes. Under Nasser it was predominantly used to dispossess the wealthy classes, although it was used against political opponents who were not necessarily wealthy. Under Sadat, sequestration became the means for suppressing political rivals, including the working class. The desequestration process was meant to placate the wealthy classes. As the Sadat regime moved to regulate and manage demands it had stimulated among property owners, however, it came to realize that there were limits to deradicalization. As will be shown in the next chapter, this recognition came much too late and only after the exacerbation of social contradictions, necessitating recourse to repression. Thus, ironically, Sadat returned to a policy whose reversal had been the cornerstone of the Open Door policy and the legitimizing source of deNasserization.

Chapter Eight
The Food Riots

THE EUPHORIA IN THE wake of the October War and the promise of the economic Open Door policy died suddenly amid the Food Riots on 18 and 19 January 1977, one of the worst Egyptian upheavals in recent memory. The working masses, from Alexandria to Aswan, spontaneously arose in reaction to the sudden decision of the government to increase the prices of some essential commodities as part of the austerity and belt-tightening measures ordered by Prime Minister Mamdouh Salem under pressure from the International Monetary Fund (IMF). These measures were thought to be essential if Egypt was to resolve its severe balance-of-payment deficits. According to some of the figures provided by David Hirst and Irene Beeson, the authors of Sadat's biography, the national debt stood at E£ 1,250 million in 1973 (excluding the military debt of some E£ 2,000 million to the Soviet Union). The debt was augmented by the annual deficit of E£ 249.8 million in 1973, E£ 670 million in 1974, and a whopping E£ 1,386 million in 1975. The financial crisis hit rock bottom in the second half of 1976 when the government faced a deficit totaling E£ 1.25 billion.[1]

Due to the economic *infitah*, Sadat found himself confronting the same choices that had confronted Nasser a decade earlier. To generate the necessary revenues, the government must either squeeze the rich by imposing stiff taxes on personal income and imported luxury items, or resort to the easy way out by relying on external borrowing. The first alternative was foreclosed, not only because the government machinery was one of the most inefficient in the area of tax collection among Third World countries, but because its implementation would have jeopardized the whole notion of *infitah*, which rested on the cultivation of bourgeois support. Sadat's circumstances, however, were much more favorable than his predecessor's since external credit was now available—a fact that explains his flexibility toward changing the economic structure to make it accessible to Western and Arab capital. As pointed out by Dessouki, "In the Fall of 1976 oil producing Arab states joined the United

States and the IMF in pressing for more fundamental changes"[2] in the country's economy. The chief obstacle (then and now) was the wide gap between the artificial prices of essential commodities in the local market, kept low by a subsidy system, and the international market price. In the winter of 1977, the government of Mamdouh Salem found no alternative but to order a cut in half the E£ 553 million subsidy. The immediate result was the January Food Riots that engulfed the whole country.

The policy of *infitah* deeply marked Egyptian society, the most obvious change being the emergence of a small minority able to derive immense profits from free imports and decontrols on foreign exchange. Boutiques and mini supermarkets sprang up in the more prosperous sections of the sprawling Cairo metropolis. In the public mind, the *infitah* not only meant a great variety of cheeses on the shelves of stores frequented by the upper classes, but it also meant congested streets thanks to restrictions being lifted on imports of cars and every other object on wheels. Gradually and inexorably, the cars and donkey carts began to impinge the sidewalks, leaving pedestrians to fend for themselves as well as their reflexes permitted.

The *infitah* also meant rationalizing the public sector, which had been operating at low capacity due to the lack of raw materials and spare parts, bueaucratic bottlenecks, mismanagement, and the encroachment of the private sector. The infusion of foreign capital did not contribute in any tangible sense to industrialization efforts. Foreign ventures were mostly concentrated in the tertiary sector. As many as seventy banks emerged, and several hotels were hurriedly constructed amid wild schemes to transform Egypt into a tourist haven, schemes that included building a golf course as part of the Pyramid Project in Giza.

The early confidence expressed in the *infitah* was based on the belief that Western know-how, Arab capital, and Egyptian manpower could successfully be brought together for the benefit of all parties. The optimism accompanying this expectation proved to be unrealistic due to the reluctance of foreign investors to enter into long-term projects. Many westerners feared that their investments would become "hostage" in a country whose political stability was questionable. Western businessmen also questioned Egypt's capacity to provide the infrastructure necessary to support an intensive industrialization program. The proverbial telephone breakdowns, transportation problems, and untrained labor were often cited to explain why foreign capital was hesitant to take the plunge, despite Egyptian inducements in the form of tax holidays, repatriation of profits, and allowing the bypassing of numerous bottlenecks in the huge and cumbersome bureaucracy.

The infusion of foreign capital was dependent on conditions the Egyptians could meet only at risk of popular displeasure, if not violence. Egypt was required to conform with IMF standards and begin to rationalize the economy, but the Sadat regime continued to waver between its social policy of feeding the hungry and economic rationalization. The contradictions between these two policies reached a climax on 18 and 19 January. On these two days, the masses took to the streets, and every object that reminded them of the authorities and the profiteers of the *infitah* were attacked. The police stations, the transporation system, and the casinos along the Pyramid Road in Cairo were objects of their fury. The government retaliated by calling in the security forces and the army. In the ensuing clashes, some 73 people were killed and 800 received injuries. Hundreds of individuals were also detained for instigating the riots or for looting stores and destroying public property. The government immediately blamed the left for organizing the riots, while the press began to circulate the official view of the existence of an underground communist organization that had planned and executed the riots. Some of the known members of the Tajamu' bore the brunt of the government clamp down, and, of the 1500 detainees, 140 were members of the Tajamu' falsely accused of either instigating or participating in the riots. It should be noted that the charges of a leftist conspiracy to overthrow the regime were received with a great deal of skepticism, since few believed there was any leftist group with the organizational capacity to launch a popular uprising on the scale and intensity of the Food Riots.

In the face of overwhelming popular opposition, the government was forced to rescind its decision to cut food subsidies. Although Sadat dismissed the whole affair as an "uprising of thieves," the events of 18 and 19 January were sufficiently traumatic to call for a complete reevaluation of the country's foreign and domestic policies. Any drastic changes, however, were more apparent in Egypt's external relations than in its domestic policies.

With the advantage of hindsight, it can be asserted that Sadat's peace initiative and visit to Jerusalem in November 1977, which led to a major reorientation of relations with Israel and the Arab countries, had its origins in Egypt's deteriorating economic conditions. To many informed observers, the road to Jerusalem had its beginnings in the Food Riots; however, during those critical days, few, even among insiders, were aware of the wider implications of the riots and of the solutions that lay ahead. There is some truth in David Hirst's observation that most Egyptians felt some bitterness tinged with envy over the miserliness of the Arab oil producers, who had not been generous to Egypt despite their huge wealth and Egypt's participation in enabling their prosperity, thanks to oil prices having quadrupled due to the pressure of the October War.[3]

The articulators of the official view in the mass media provided the main tenor of Egyptian grievances: "Egypt lost in a quarter of a century 40 billion Dollars as a result of its undertaking to defend Arab land and to resist enemy encroachments in four successive wars. Egypt bore this nationalist and common burden with as little support from the Arabs as the sum of four billion Dollars. The Arabs failed to rise to their historic responsibility by sharing equally the burden of a common cause."[4] Somehow, while formulating the balance sheet of twenty-five years of struggle during which the blood of many fine Egyptian men was shed, the official interpreters were able to convert the sacrifices into dollars and cents. The figures provided by Hazem el Biblawi accurately reflect the volume of Arab aid that preceded Sadat's peace initiative.[5] In addition to the military assistance program and other banking facilities, Arab aid amounted to $725 million in 1973, which then increased to $1,264 million in 1974. This sudden increase was spurred by the general Arab enthusiasm for Sadat's accomplishments during the October War. But this enthusiasm seemed to wane as Arab aid fell to $988 million in 1975 and declined even further to $625 million in 1976.

The Egyptian sense of betrayal was not relieved by the efforts of the oil rich Arabs to bolster the Sadat regime following the Food Riots. The Gulf Organization for the Development of Egypt (GODE) met to devise urgent plans to provide aid, but it added insult to injury by agreeing to commit barely $2 billion, to be capitalized over five years to finance development projects. This figure was $8 billion short of Egyptian assessments of developmental requirements. The alternative for Egypt was to sue for peace with Israel, while relying on American munificence. To show support for the shaken regime following the Food Riots, the United States acted immediately by shifting $190 million in already committed capital development funds to commodities that would enter the economy quickly. This gesture did not constitute an altogether mean effort on the United States administration, considering that its total assistance program amounted to $750 million in 1977.

The domestic situation proved much more complex and intractable than the simple formula *infitah* plus peace equals prosperity. At the heart of the problem were the social contradictions in the policies pursued by the Sadat regime, contradictions that caused the unrest that climaxed on 18 and 19 January. The government attempted to temporarily resolve the contradictions by reaffirming its social policy to feed the poor urban masses at the cost of economic rationalization. Given the popular backlash from the latter policy — its scope and intensity — even the IMF had to surrender to the pressures from the lower classes.

In a program aimed at dealing with the food crisis, a plan was submitted for popular consideration in a plebiscite held in February 1977 in which the government pledged not to tax peasants who owned less than three faddans or low income groups whose annual earnings did not exceed E£ 500. In the same plebiscite, however, the government demanded strict adherence to the laws, which prohibited damage to public property, strikes, demonstrations, and affiliation to underground or unrecognized political organizations. Any violations of these restrictions were made punishable by life imprisonment with hard labor.[6]

These measures dealt with the symptoms rather than with underlying causes. The root cause of the food crisis was, of course, the spiraling increase in food costs resulting from a perceptible decline in domestic production and a heavy reliance on imports. According to one estimate, Egypt in the second half of the 1970s was importing as much as 40 percent of its food requirements, of which 78 percent was wheat whose import costs represented more than one-half of the total American assistance in 1977. Here are some sobering figures that reveal the extent of Egypt's external dependence for feeding its fast-growing population:

> Egypt, which purchased abroad 7 percent of its foodstuffs in 1961, saw its imports increase to one-fifth of national requirements a decade later. Though as late as 1974 the country maintained a favorable net agricultural balance, by 1981–82, shipments of agricultural products from all foreign sources accounted for one-half of the total domestic food consumption.[7]

The critics of the former regime wasted no time in explaining the reasons for the decline in domestic food production. In their view, the stagnant agricultural sector was a direct consequence of the restrictions imposed by the agrarian reforms. These restrictions produced disincentives such as limits on landownership, depressed crop prices due to meddlesome government policies, and rent controls. These restrictions, according to the critics, favored the tenant over the landlord and the consumer over the producer in a flagrant violation of sound and rational economic principles. The advocates of *infitah* now called for another type of *infitah* for the countryside, aimed at restoring some balance in the rights of consumers and producers, tenants and landlords. The key to resolving these contradictions was to reverse the terms of the agrarian reforms. As pointed out by a deputy during the debates of the People's Assembly over a proposal to impose 100 percent increase in rents by 1979, the agrarian reforms were not a holy writ immune to man-made changes.[8]

The main criticsm of the agrarian reforms focused on the ceiling for landownership, which prevented more efficient, mechanized farming techniques. It may be recalled that the Nasserist regime adopted three successive agrarian reforms. The last one was adopted in 1969 and limited individual ownership to fifty faddans and family ownership to one hundred faddans. These measures were seen by the welfare-oriented regime as proper means for equitable land distribution. The concentration of land in a few hands was then considered the main reason for the lopsided development in landownership, and parcellization into small and medium-sized farms became the ideal. These perspectives changed after the emergence of the Open Door policy, and the argument against concentration of land was replaced by the diametrically opposite argument regarding the ill effects of fragmentation on production. The mass media decried the dwindling number of large landowners, who, for lack of incentives, had decided to divest themselves of their holdings.

In the absence of properly documented studies, it is difficult to ascertain the extent of the decline in large farms and the degree of property fragmentation. It should be noted that no official survey of land distribution has been undertaken since the 1960s. However, in a study based on a 1975 survey conducted by the Ministry of Agriculture of land holdings registered with the agricultural cooperatives, Harik concluded that

> the holders of 10 faddans or more are fewer now, 2% of total farm operators instead of 5.5% in 1961. The area of land they controlled declined sharply from 44.5% to 18% of the total area. In absolute figures they lost 1,676,600 faddans. It is clear from these findings that in the second stage of land reform, it was the rural middle class who started to lose ground to the landless and small farmers.[9]

Waterbury questions Harik's conclusions and provides evidence to show that the rich farmers remained at the top of the pecking order in the rural areas and that "since 1970 an active lobby in defense of the interests of the rural middle class has taken shape."[10] The immense advantages derived by the rich farmers under the umbrella of the *infitah* were reflected by their easy access to credit through the local agricultural cooperatives, which were replaced by a banking system in 1978. The rich farmers also possessed the capacity to move away from field crops (broad beans, lentils, peanuts, sesame, soya, and potatoes) and invest heavily in the freely marketed vegetable produce and fruits. The returns on the freely marketed crops were three to four time higher than for field crops. Besides, as of 1977, the orchards were free of taxes. When attempts were made in the same year to impose taxes upon the orchards, the People's Assembly quickly rejected them.

There are no reliable figures on the rich farmers' share of the production of freely marketed crops. According to 'Abdel Mu'ti, the orchards area expanded from 64,000 faddans in 1952 to 313,000 faddans in 1976, and the areas producing vegetables totaled 913,000 faddans in 1976, up from 652,000 in 1966.[11] Owners of over fifty faddans in the early 1960s controlled roughly 51 percent of all orchards. The stratum owning between twenty and fifty faddans possessed

15 percent, leaving a balance of 34 percent held by the lower middle strata.[12] It is unlikely that any drastic changes occurred in the distribution of fruit acreage, given the level of capital investments, the required lead-time, and the cost of maintenance around the year, which only the rich farmers could afford. A survey carried out in 1979 shows that 56 percent of the fruit acreage remained under the control of rich farmers.[13]

It is possible to argue, in light of some of the evidence presented above, that the small farmers were the ones who bore the main brunt of the depressed prices of field crops because of government regulations. As pointed out by Weinbaum, the government farm procurement policy produced an unfavorable trade balance between the rural and urban areas. In addition to the food subsidy, which largely benefited the urban masses, the low prices of the requisitioned crops amounted to a tax equivalent of 40 to 50 percent on the agricultural sector.[14] During 1974–75, the producers, the majority of whom were small farmers, transferred to the state E£ 1.2 billion net of input subsidy.

Nonetheless, neither the ceiling on landownership nor depressed prices caused as much concern to the deputies in the People's Assembly as rent control. This concern is not surprising since, as I have explained earlier, there were many loopholes for getting around the limits imposed on personal and family holdings. The low-priced farm procurement policy caused little concern for those who did not suffer its consequences. Rent control, however, belonged to a different order of reality. For one thing, tenancy relations as determined by the agrarian reforms affected all landlords, from the largest to the smallest. The majority of the tenants belonged to the lowest rural strata, the majority holding less than three faddans. This fact is the basis of the argument advanced mainly by Marxists—that the opposition between landlords and tenants reflects class conflicts, even though the former might include owners of as little as a fraction of a faddan, one *Qirat*.[15]

The rise in rents, to as much as a 100 percent increase, effective from 1979 could not have been applied without the vested interest of the deputies themselves. A deputy remarked during the assembly's discussion over the proposed increase in rents in a session held in June 1978 that only tenants benefited from the steep rise in the prices of all crops, while rents remained unchanged since the imposition of the agrarian reform law in 1952.[16] In the opinion of the majority of deputies, the Nasserist regime favored the tenants over the landlords with a whole string of regulations that restricted and steadily impoverished the latter. Not only had rents remained frozen at their 1952 level, the tenants had also been given security of tenure. The first crack in the tenancy regulations occurred in July 1975 after the enactment of law no. 65/75, which amended the tenancy regulations contained in the famous agrarian reform law no. 178/52. The amendment sought to increase rents on the basis of seven times the current tax rates instead of the old, lower rates. Landlords were also granted the right to evict tenants if they did not pay rents within the stipulated period. Furthermore, the conversion of tenurial relationships from cash rents to sharecropping was permitted under the new law. This action was seen as another way of placating the landlords, since sharecropping officially granted the latter one-half the produce, with the net of expenses shared equally by landlords and tenants. Most controversial, however, was the substitution of local committees for adjudication of disputes over rents with the regular judiciary. The former were closer to and often more sympathetic to the tenants than were the courts.

It should be noted, however, that the assembly was not prepared to countenance any changes in tenancy relations in the urban areas. For this reason, all rent increases only affected landed properties. As the independent deputy from Alexandria, Mahmoud al-Qadi, said with his characteristic cynicism, the deputies from the rural areas who constituted the majority would be at the forefront of opposition if any attempt was made to decontrol rents in the urban areas. His reasoning was that the deputies would be zealous about protecting the rights of their kinsmen residing in Cairo.

The new changes in tenancy relations affected 1.5 million peasants, who rented an area of 2.5 million faddans or roughly 43 percent of the cultivated land. According to Fouad Mursi, the arch critic of the Open Door policy, the new tenancy regulations reflected a desire on the part of the majority of the landlords to become self-cultivators and to convert their lands into capital intensive and more lucrative orchards and truck gardens.[17] He even predicted that the capitalist drive was likely to lead to a greater concentration of land in fewer hands, sharpen class differences in the countryside, and lead to a mass exodus of small tenants and farmers into the cities. He was also critical of the sharecropping system, strengthened by the new tenancy regulations. He pointed out that this backward tenurial system affected roughly one million faddans or one-sixth of the cultivated land in Egypt. The immediate consequences of the new regulations would be to increase the number of clashes between evicted tenants and the police.

The same words of warning were uttered by Abu al-'Azz al-Hariri, the outspoken Marxist deputy from Alexandria, in the assembly session of June 1978. He warned that rent increases would threaten peaceful coexistence in the rural areas and upset the delicate balance between the haves and the have nots. He went on to say that, if the government was keen on increasing its revenues, then it should not punish the tenants and the small farmers by more exactions. It should instead impose taxes on the owners of orchards, whose exemptions ran up to E£ 10,000. In the same month, this Marxist deputy and one of the three deputies forming the total parliamentary strength of the Tajamu' was ousted from the assembly by a decision adopted by the majority (see chapter 9). The real test of strength for the government and its majority in the assembly, however, occurred not as a result of the challenges posed by the left, but as a consequence of the emergence of the right, the illegitimate child of the policy of *infitah*. To this contest, I will now turn my attention.

Chapter Nine
Retraditionalization
behind the Liberal Mask

I N CONTRAST TO THE economic situation, Sadat's retraditionalization through use of a liberal formula was quite successful in producing its intended results, namely, consolidating the authority of the regime against its urban rivals. Sadat's rhetoric against the HCLF and the repressive policies of the former regime won the support of the traditionally influential families. Nonetheless, the strategy produced unintended results in that it brought rivals to the surface that attempted to expose the limits of the liberal formula and unmask the continuing traditional base of support to the regime, the support rooted in the rural areas. The rival claimants to power were urban-based and mainly centered around the New Wafd and the Muslim Brotherhood. The urban rivals were tolerated at the beginning as the step-children of the *infitah*, until the strategy of control and the liberal ideology could no longer be sustained together.

The irony of retraditionalization behind the liberal mask laid in the emergence of the Islamic's *Jama'at* and their adverse impact on social harmony. This group fits into the strategy of the regime, which aimed at isolating the urban left and even the Muslim Brotherhood from whose womb some of the *Jama'at* initially grew. It is not surprising that some of the *Jama'at* were regarded as the legitimate children of the regime, until the latter found it impossible to reconcile its strategy of combating the left with the increasing autonomy and hostility of the former.

The liberal and Islamic challenges went on simultaneously. In this chapter, I will focus on how retraditionalization was successfully achieved through use of the liberal formula, and on its limits given the New Wafd and the urban syndicates and associations. In the next chapter, I will concentrate on the emergence of the *Jama'at* as part of the strategy of power consolidation and its impact on community harmony. The liberal formula of the Sadat regime was an incrementalistic and gradualistic approach to the demands for participation, whose pressures were more visible in the urban than in the rural areas. But the hesitancy shown by the regime in response to the demands for participation was related to its own power strategy and to the limits imposed by the urban rivals. Indeed, the situation had not much changed since Nasser's time, when the single party was used as a vehicle for mobilizing rural support to exclude the urban-based political movements, such as the outlawed *Ikhwan* and the Wafd.

The liberal formula initially envisaged the recognition of a plurality of interests within the single party, the ASU. The modus operandi for the expression of these interests was the *manaber* (tribunes) — a formula announced in July 1975, conceived as a compromise between the single party and the multiparty systems. The tribunes were the left, right, and center of the ASU, expressing what was assumed to be the mainstreams of interests within the party. The left came to be identified with the ASU members who remained faithful to the Nasserist ideals, including the ex-communists and former Marxists. The right came to represent a few of the middlemen and the merchants of *infitah*, but not the old bourgeoisie or the *Ikhwan*. The majority of ASU members, however, came to identify their interests with the center, since it was obvious that it enjoyed the blessings of the authority and was led by Prime Minister Mamdouh Salem.

Elections to the People's Assembly were conducted on the basis of the new formula of interest representation, although some candidates were allowed to run as independents. In these elections, the government was careful to project the image of complete impartiality. Sadat himself declared that he was above partisan struggle. Mamdouh Salem also pledged to conduct "clean elections." Following the elections, Sadat ordered the conversion of the *manaber* into political parties. Table 23 shows the parliamentary strength of each party. The ruling party, the Arab Socialist Party of Egypt (Hizb Misr), secured an overwhelming majority. The left-wing Nationalist Progressive Unionist Party (Ta-

TABLE 23   Distribution of Seats in the People's Assembly by Party Affiliation in 1976[a]

Party	No.	%
The Arab Socialist Party of Egypt (Hizb Misr)	295	86.3
Independents	34	9.9
The Liberal Socialist Party	10	2.9
Nationalist Progressive Unionist (Tajamu')	3	0.9
TOTAL	342	100.0

[a] The table does not include the desert governorates, the seats created for women deputies, and the seats of appointed members, all of whom belonged to the ruling party.

jamu') and the right-wing Liberal Socialist Party held few seats in the assembly, since both parties derived their support from urban areas that did not carry much political weight in a representative system heavily biased toward rural areas.

By such unfamiliar and unconventional methods, Sadat launched the liberal experiment. Neither the *Ikhwan* nor the Wafd was allowed to express its interest in the new parliament.[1] The elections to the People's Assembly did, however, give rise to the phenomenon of independent deputies, who became most critical of government policies and, two years later, played a significant role in the emergence of the New Wafd. These deputies were elected mainly from urban districts and represented diverse political movements, including Nasserists, Marxists, Wafdists, and *Ikhwan* members. The independents even included deputies who had belonged to the Free Officers Movement, whose contributions to the 1952 revolution rivaled Sadat's. Most notable among these deputies were Kamal al-Din Hussein and Khalid Muhi al-Din, the leader of the Tajamu'.

The most remarkable aspect of the new assembly was that it contained one of the largest gatherings of *Kibar al-A'yan* families, who had dominated Egyptian parliamentary history. The majority of these families, however, came from Upper Egypt. These names are but a few examples: al-Shali (Aswan); Ma'tuq, Huzayin, and Khalifa (Qena); 'Abdel Akher, Abu Krishah, Hamadi, and Abu Satit (Sohag); Qurashi, Mahfuz, Tammam, Khashabah, and Sulayman (Asyut); Tuni, Sa'di, 'Ushari, Dirwi, Makhluf, Makadi, Jazzar, and Mustafa (Minya); al-Basil and Tantawi (Fayyum); and Azzam, Abu Hamilah, and Zomor (Giza). Deputies from the rural upper stratum families of Lower Egypt were comparatively fewer. Among these family names were Muhi al-Din (Qalubiyya); Shinnawi, 'Abdel Ghaffar, and Sha'ir (Minufiyya); Abaza, Mar'i, and Baligh (Sharqiyya); Mursi (Daqahliyya); and Abu Wafia, Mahmoud, and Salem (Beheira).[2]

Nearly all the above families had been subjected to the investigations of the HCLF and, therefore, stood to benefit most from Sadat's Corrective Movement. Logically, therefore, the assembly's first order of business was to conduct hearings on the abuses committed against rural elites during the Nasserist era. These hearings were held before the assembly's Complaints and Grievances Committee chaired by Mamhoud Abu Wafia, the deputy from Beheira, Sadat's brother-in-law and the secretary general of the ruling party.[3] The hearings were repeat performances of the Kamshish trial, albeit on a grander scale. Rural elites described in gruesome and minute details their plight during the HCLF investigations. Government officials, themselves responsible for managing confiscated or sequestered properties, joined in the chorus of condemnation. The state turned against itself in an orgy of self-flagellation once the politics of "scapegoatism" exhausted itself. Nonetheless, the loyalty test for the traditional elites in the People's Assembly was in the emergence of competitive urban interests.

The three parties—the left-wing Tajamu', the right-wing Liberal party, and the ruling party, Hizb Misr—were all state creations and led by former officers in the army and the police. Mamdouh Salem, the leader of Hizb Misr, was a police officer and one-time governor of Alexandria. The leader of the Tajamu', Khalid Muhi al-Din, was one of the free officers who had participated in the military coup of 1952 and who represented the leftist trend in the defunct Revolutionary Command Council (RCC). The Liberal party was led by former army officer Mustafa Kamel Murad, a close confidant of Sadat. Therefore, only with emergence of the Muslim Brotherhood and the Wafd that a real challenge to the authority seemed to be credible. Both movements had a large number of supporters, mainly in Cairo and Alexandria, who began to pressure the government to lift its ban on free participation. Lifting the ban on the Wafdists, enabling them to form their own party, was made possible by the election of a number of independent deputies who were former Wafdists. They were joined by Marxists, Nasserists, and *Ikhwan* members in opposing the total and unmitigated hegemony imposed by the Sadat regime.

Despite their absence from the political scene for nearly twenty-four years, Wafdist leaders have always seen themselves as the guardians of the nation, a notion whose legitimacy was derived from the 1919 mass revolt against British rule. In his first important public appearance at the Bar Association in August 1977, Fouad Siraj al-Din delivered a stinging speech to mark the anniversaries of the deaths of Sa'd Zaghlul and Mustafa al-Nahas.[4] This occasion has become an annual affair to demonstrate the Wafdist commitment to its cause. On this particular occasion, however, Siraj al-Din gave the impression that he had learned nothing and forgotten nothing, just like the emigres who returned to France after the collapse of the French revolution and the Bourbon restoration. He defended the *Pasha* class, citing the names of 'Urabi, Kamel, Zaghlul, and Nahas who were remembered for their nationalist fervor and contribution to the struggle for independence. Most alarming to the Nasserists and to the beneficiaries of the agrarian reforms and the socialist decrees was Siraj al-Din's denunciation of social and economic reforms under Nasser. He rejected the repeatedly stated belief that the reforms were absolutely necessary to rectify a lopsided development in landownership. In his opinion, there was nothing in the history of landownership in Egypt akin to European feudalism.

More invidious than his condemnation of the agrarian reforms was Siraj al-Din's comparison of the 1919 revolution with the military coup in 1952. He remarked that while the 1919 revolution created the Egyptian individual and awakened him from deep slumber, the 1952 revolution (let us call it a revolution for the moment) stifled the Egyptian individual and trampled upon his dignity. The 1919 revolution had risen to evacuate the British, while the 1952 revolution led to Israeli occupation of Egypt twice. The leaders of the 1919 revolution were tortured and maimed, exiled and rendered homeless, while the leaders of the 1952 revolution lived in palaces—palaces which were taken forcibly from their owners or built by unknown means.[5]

In the same vein, Siraj al-Din attacked the leaders of Hizb Misr, although he was careful to single out Sadat since, but for him, he would not have had the opportunity to speak his mind freely. At the end of his speech, he said that the party ranks were discussing the formation of a new party, but he did not disclose any details about its identity, program, or leadership. He left this information out deliberately since many questions were being raised among Wafdist ranks regarding the wisdom of participating in Sadat's liberal initiative.

Some of Wafdists were dubious about Sadat's liberalism. They pointed out in a discussion with Siraj al-Din that they doubted that Sadat was really serious about creating an opposition strong enough to challenge him or the party upon which he was dependent for support.[6] In addition, they pointed out the obstacles to free association and party formation. These critics were concerned that a positive response to Sadat's liberalization would be tantamount to acquiescence to the restrictions imposed. On the other hand, Siraj al-Din pointed out to the skeptics that there were advantages to be reaped from participating in politics, despite the limits being imposed. He said that not since the abolishment of political parties and restrictions being imposed on the freedom of the press had there been any opportunity for the Wafd to express itself. The law enacted in 1977 on party organization would entitle the new party to publish its own paper and organize public meetings that would reestablish its links with the masses. Participation in politics would thus help, in the long run, either to establish a genuine democracy or, in the event of the failure of the latter, to expose to the public that the democracy sought by Sadat was a sham democracy. At any rate, Siraj al-Din pointed out that the Wafd would lose nothing by participating in Sadat's liberal experiment. A green signal was given to 'Abd al-Fattah Hasan to muster the requisite number of deputies in the People's Assembly to make the formation of the new Wafd official.

'Abd al-Fattah Hasan was a member of the last Wafdist cabinet, as minister of defence, before the toppling of the monarchy. He was also one of the few independent deputies elected to the assembly in 1976 from his traditional district Bassun in al-Gharbiyya Province. He was behind the passage of a bill that allowed the formation of new parties, although several clauses had been added to limit the number to be formed. One clause stipulated that no party could receive official recognition without the minimum support of twenty deputies. 'Abd al-Fattah Hasan was so confident of winning the support of a larger group that he even proposed raising the requisite number to thirty-six.[7] But he said he was wary of the opportunists among the deputies of Hizb Misr who had no compunctions about selling their votes to the highest bidder. The deputies who finally agreed to endorse the New Wafd were committed Wafdists and sympathetic supporters who resisted all temptations and threats dangled before them by the ruling party.

Among the twenty-three known supporters of the Wafd in the assembly, there were fourteen independcents, seven belonging to Hizb Misr, and two affiliated with the Liberal Party. The majority of the independents represented the urban areas of Cairo and Alexandria. Of the few rural notables who supported the formation of the New Wafd, five came from al-Fayyum and all except one belonged to Hizb Misr. It has been pointed out that their defection was stimulated by differences with the local governor.[8] Whatever the merits of this statement, the availability of rural notables to competing political interests at the center is very significant. The rural-urban dichotomy and its impact on the electoral process within the liberal formula will be discussed at length shortly. For now, it is sufficient to say that the Wafd has been traditionally adept at bringing together diverse elements into an uneasy alliance. This ability was demonstrated by 'Abd al-Fattah Hasan's observation that the parliamentary group he was able to fashion included men with conflicting ideologies and social backgrounds. This group included men such as Shaykh Salah Abu Ismail, a Muslim fundamentalist, Ahmad Taha, a Marxist, and Hilmi Murad, formerly of Misr al-Fatah. There was no common denominator to unite these men except their opposition to the ruling party; nevertheless, they were badly needed to overcome the restrictions on party formation.

The social backgrounds of the members of the constituent body of the New Wafd reveal the elitist character of the party. The 105 members (excluding the 103 additional persons included to fulfill the official stipulation of 50 percent representation for workers and peasants) included men of high reputation in the fields of law, the press, medicine, engineering, education, and business. In addition, there were several retired senior army officers, rural notables, and *'Ulama'*. Perhpas more revealing than the occupational breakdown was the family backgrounds of the constituent elements. Those familiar with the social history of Egypt will recognize that the main supporters of the New Wafd belonged to the rural *A'yan*. These family names included Abaza, Saif al-Nasr, al-Fiqqi, al-Jazzar, Hashish, Siraj al-Din, Badrawi, Nahas, Lamlum, Shari'i, 'Allam, and so on. Reading the names of the constituent members of the New Wafd was like going throught a "Who's Who" for the monarchical period.[9]

The next step in the complicated process of gaining official approval was to obtain the recommendation of a committee composed of three ministers (who included Mustafa Khalil, then serving as secretary general of the ASU), three judges, and the minister of justice. The committee first objected to the proposed name of the party (Siraj al-Din said the ministers were afraid the chosen name of the party would evoke the memory of the old Wafd). The second objection was over Siraj al-Din's nomination by party rank and file for the leader position. As for the name of the party, Siraj al-Din said that, with a name like the New Wafd, the "support of at least sixty percent of the electorate is guaranteed given the strong sentiment for the Old Wafd among the people." As for the second objection, Siraj al-Din said that the Wafdist members had expressed unreserved confidence in his leadership. According to him, the members' insistence on his leadership increased in direct proportion to the increasing pressures from the government for him to relinquish his leadership. He explained the steadfastness of members over his leadership in light of the conviction that the overwhelming electoral success of the Wafd in the past laid not so much with the organizational capacity of the party as with the personality of leaders such as Sa'd Zaghlul and Nahas Pasha. Confronted with the strong loyalty of the Wafdists toward their leader, the committee had no alternative but to approve the new party under its chosen leader by a majority vote.[10]

Having fulfilled all the required conditions for establishing a new party, the New Wafd was declared official in February 1978. Sadat put his final stamp of approval on the formation of the new party and appointed Siraj al-Din to the Central Committee of the ASU, which was still in existence despite the creation of the multiparty system. The party's official existence, however, lasted little over three months; for this reason, Siraj al-Din dubbed it the "one hundred-day party." What happened between the formation and the dissolutionment of the New Wafd reveals how demands for liberalizaton were dealt with when they became threatening to the regime.

The government-controlled press and the ruling party mounted a vicious campaign against the New Wafd. The favorite line of attack was that the New Wafd represented *mujtama' al-bashawat*, the society of the *Pashas*, who wanted to put the clock back. Even those who took part in the de-Nasserization campaign were compelled to join in the approval of Nasser's socialist achievements, including the much-vaunted agrarian reforms and the suppression of the old bourgeoisie. The government was also compelled to take steps to silence some of its arch-critics in the People's Assembly. By means of its overwhelming majority, the government was able to secure the dismissal of Shaykh 'Ashur, the outspoken Muslim fundamentalist from Alexandria and one of the co-sponsors of the New Wafd.[11]

According to Siraj al-Din, Sadat changed his attitude towards the New Wafd after the former delivered a speech in Alexandria on 12 May. Siraj al-Din observed that the popular response to his speech was overwhelming. No fewer than forty to fifty thousand, mostly young men, gathered to listen to his speech, despite the bad weather. Furthermore, in the two and a half months following the formation of the New Wafd, 959,000 joined the party. This tremendous popular response was deeply unsettling for the government and ruling party. They were surprised that, after twenty-five years during which the Wafd was nothing but a memory, the public was ready to embrace it. Siraj al-Din confidently declared that the Wafd was bound once again to become a mass party, and he even speculated that by 1980 the party would gain 90 percent of the seats in the assembly.

Sadat's response to Wafdist inroads into the stability and continuity of the regime was swift and decisive. Sadat was forced to give up the democratic pretenses and reimpose some of the repressive measures for which Nasser was so thoroughly denounced. On the anniversary of the Corrective Movement, and only two days after Siraj al-Din's Alexandria speech, Sadat reimposed a law enforced during the Nasserist era that prohibited all those who held cabinet posts during the monarchy from engaging in politics. The law was aimed specifically at Siraj al-Din and 'Abd al-Fattah Hasan among the prominent Wafdists. This action was followed by a new press law, which was tantamount to an infringement of the right of legitimate parties to publish their own newspapers.

In the opinion of Siraj al-Din, partisan activities under the shadow of these draconian laws became impossible. The New Wafd faced the dilemma either of functioning without its chosen leader—and under laws that curtailed the role of the opposition—or of defying the authority by noncompliance. The first option was rejected by Siraj al-Din in a meeting of the Higher Board of the Wafd, because it would have meant acquiescence in a sham democracy. The second option was also rejected, because his continuation in politics as a leader of his party would have been a clear violation of the law. Thus, there was no solution to the dilemma except the self-dissolutionment of the party.

Siraj al-Din pointed out that Sadat would have preferred the New Wafd to stay in politics without its traditional leaders and within the rules defined by the government. Sadat wanted a weak party that would provide a semblance of democracy to the regime without challenging its ultimate authority. The dissolutionment of the New Wafd left the liberal experiment in shambles, the legitimacy of the government questioned, and the ruling party under Mamdouh Salem on a shaky foundation. In May 1978, Sadat found himself torn between the urge to silence his critics and the desire to maintain a semblance of democracy. The question was how long he could continue to resist the pressure for true participation. But before the dam burst, Sadat took steps to fill the vacuum created by the dissolutionment of the New Wafd.

The regime attempted to fill the vacuum by reorganizing the ruling party and by helping create a new opposition party that would draw upon the followers of the New Wafd. Thus, the National Democratic Party (NDP) replaced Hizb Misr as the ruling party, with Sadat as its president. Both Mamdouh Salem and Hizb Misr disappeared into political oblivion. To create a loyal opposition, twenty deputies belonging to the ruling party were loaned to a new opposition party, the Labor Party, fulfilling the legal stipulation that requires the support of at least twenty deputies for the formation of political parties. The secretary general of the defunct Hizb Misr, Mahmoud Abu Wafia, Sadat's brother-in-law and troubleshooter, was loaned to the Labor Party as its first deputy president. Ibrahim Shukri, one of the prerevolutionary leaders of the Egyptian Socialist Party, assumed the position of president.

The regime had been shaken by the challenge posed by the New Wafd. The way to overcome such a setback was to ensure total victory in the 1979 elections to the People's Assembly. With this objective in mind, the NDP took steps to instill party discipline while selecting strong and loyal candidates. The NDP, contrary to an established electoral pattern, limited the number of official candidates to the number of seats in the assembly with the exception of 20 seats which were left to candidates of opposition parties as part of a deal struck behind the scene to ensure parliamentary representation for the latter (see the wide difference in Table 24 of the number of official candidates in 1979 in comparision with the 1976 elections).[12] A primary goal in limiting the official candidates was to strengthen party control over the bureaucracy and the syndicates, apart from the traditional support of rural elites. The NDP list of candidates included such loyal elements as Prime Minister Fouad Muhi al-Din, who replaced the discredited Mamdouh Salem, Deputy Prime Minister Mustafa Khalil, and Minister of the Interior Nabawi Ismail. One other important consideration in drawing up the list of candidates was to include the prominent members of the labor unions and syndicates. In the 1979 elections, some of the syndicate leaders were not only party members but were also cabinet ministers. The notable individuals on the list were the presidents of the Egyptian Medical Association, the Engineering Syndicate, the Agricultural Worker's Union, the Egyptian Labor Union, and the Professional National Councils. Needless to say, any increase in the number of government officials or syndicate leaders on the list of party candidates would limit the number of seats for which the local elites could normally compete. The majority of government officials and syndicate leaders were closely bound to urban interests and far removed from the direct concerns of their constituencies.

The limited number of official candidates gave rise to an increase in the number of independents, as shown in Table 24. A contributing factor to this increase was the decision of the ruling party to limit official candidates in a bid to strengthen party affiliation and to instill party discipline. This step, however, fell short of producing a party slate, and the electoral procedure continued to adhere to the traditional two-member districts with election by absolute majority of the votes cast. The rural notables naturally expressed preferences for the traditional system since it maximized their autonomy and enabled them to tap personal contacts and local solidarity ('asabiyat) to support their bid for an assembly seat. Nevertheless, the official party list of candidates eliminated a large number of notables who preferred to run as independents rather than join the minority parties.

When the official list of candidates was announced, the NDP leaders stressed that those who refused to submit to the party's will and, instead, ran as independents, would lose party membership.[13] It was also announced that party members who ran as independent candidates would not be allowed to rejoin the party, even if they won the elections. These measures were taken so as not to encourage what the semi-official newspapers described as "political opportunism."[14] This criticism which was specifically directed against the local in-

TABLE 24   Comparing Candidates by Political Affiliation in the Assembly Elections of 1976 and 1979

Parties (1976)	No.	%	Parties (1979)[a]	No.	%
Independents	897	54	Independents	1029	62
Egypt Arab Socialist (Hizb Misr)	527	32	National Democratic (NDP)	322	20
Liberal Socialist	171	10	Liberal Socialist	76	5
Tajamu'	65	4	Tajamu'	31	2
			Labor Socialist	185	11
			National Front	7	0.4
TOTAL	1660	100%		1650	100%

SOURCE for the 1976 candidates: Mark N. Cooper, *The Transformation of Egypt* (London: Croom Helm, 1982), 205.

a The breakdown of candidates for the 1979 elections does not include the electoral districts in the desert governorates, seats reserved for women candidates, and appointed members.

fluential notables or *A'yan* because of their constantly shifting loyalties which prevented the growth of party cohesion.

Nevertheless, the ruling party went against its declaration by allowing the independents who won against its own candidates to rejoin the party quietly. Table 25 compares the actual results of the election, based on the official list of candidates, with the final results as they were officially announced. Most striking is the decline in the proportion of independents and the proportionate increase in the number of NDP deputies in the assembly. Interestingly, the majority remaining independent, despite mounting pressures to join the ruling party, represented urban districts. The candidates who ran against the official NDP candidates but later joined the ruling party derived support from local connections and prestige. Some of the independents were incumbents fighting to retain their parliamentary seats against party candidates. Ironically, most seats left to the minority parties, as part of the arrangement between the ruling party and the leaders of the opposition, were won by independents who subsequently jointed the NDP. Thus, there may be some validity to the statement made by the Labor Party that the arrangement with the NDP leadership did not contribute much to the electoral success of the opposition parties.

The reason the NDP leadership allowed those who ran as independents to rejoin the party can be understood only in light of the fact that the regime always believed that absolute consensus was the only basis for its legitimacy (see Table 26).[15] Sadat had no qualms about stating that he did not expect the Labor Party to win more than twelve or thirteen seats.[16] Interestingly, these numbers approximate the strength of the Labor Party in parliament after the defection of several deputies to the NDP.

Sadat's next step in consolidating his rule was to launch a major constitutional innovation in the form of an upper chamber, the *Majlis al-Shura* (Advisory Council). This institution matched the consultative assemblies established in the second half of the nineteenth century. But there were some am-

TABLE 25   Comparison of Actual and Official Electoral Results in the 1979 Elections

Affiliation	Actual[a]		Official	
	No.	%	No.	%
NDP	240	70.2	301	88.0
Independents	65	19.0	10	2.9
Minority parties	37	10.8	31	9.1
TOTAL	342	100.0	342	100.0

[a] Based on the official list of candidates

TABLE 26   Distribution of People's Assembly Seats in 1976 and 1979 by
Party Affiliation[a]

1976	No.	%	1979[a]	No.	%
Egyptian Arab			National Democratic		
Socialist (Hizb Misr)	295	86.3	(NDP)	295	86.3
Independents	34	9.9	Independents	10	2.9
Liberal Socialist	10	2.9	Liberal Socialist	3	0.9
Tajamu'	3	0.9	Tajamu'	0	0.0
			Labor Socialist	34	9.9
TOTAL	342	100.0		342	100.0

[a] The table does not include the desert governorates, the seats created for women deputies, and the seats of appointed members, all of whom belong to the ruling party.

biguities in the new council's functions and in its relationship to the People's Assembly. It was officially maintained that the council would function only in an advisory capacity. The opposition parties, however, were skeptical about the new experiment.[17] Some feared that the council would become another instrument in the hands of the regime to mobilize support, silence criticism, and establish additional means to legitimize its unpopular policies. These fears were reinforced when it was announced that the Advisory Council would replace the ASU as the legal guardian of the official media, especially for the major newspapers and periodicals. A Press High Board, consisting of members of the Advisory Council, was established to confirm the appointment of the editorial staffs for the press and to issue publication licenses.

Most alarming to the opposition was the adoption of a new electoral procedure for electing the Advisory Council. The new procedure, endorsed by a plebiscite, introduced for the first time in the history of Egypt the method of voting by party slate, but, to the intense displeasure of the opposition, the procedure rejected proportional representation.[18] The new electoral procedure thus eliminated two major problems encountered in the recent elections to the People's Assembly. First, the lack of discipline and cohesion within the NDP was resolved through voting by party slate. Secondly, the principle of winner-take-all of the votes cast in the provinces assured the ruling party a complete monopoly over the new council, while eliminating not only the opposition parties but also the independents.[19] Naturally, the opposition parties boycotted the elections in September 1980. After observing the successful results of the elections, the leaders of the ruling party began to entertain the idea of extending the new electoral procedure to include elections to the People's Assembly and to the local councils.[20] In the meantime, Sadat turned his attention to the syndicates.

Through its monopoly of deputies in the People's Assembly, the government passed several laws that steadily eroded whatever little autonomy was enjoyed by associations and that effectively silenced its critics. Sadat himself showed increasing impatience with any criticism of his peace policy with Israel, since he interpreted any such criticism as questioning the legitimacy of the regime. Of all the associations, however, Sadat bore a special grudge against the legally constituted council of the Bar Association. This animosity is no surprise since the legal profession has always been the bête noire of the authority.

The judiciary and the lawyers have long maintained a high reputation of impartiality, which infuriated Nasser. In the March 1954 crisis, when all parties were dissolved and the trade and labor unions brought under effective government control, the Bar Association stood alone in its demand for an end to dictatorship and the restoration of democratic life. Perhaps a more dramatic example of the deep-seated desire to preserve autonomy against government control is the so-called "massacre of the judges" in 1969. Roughly two hundred judges were dismissed because they opposed 'Ali Sabri, then secretary general of the Arab Socialist Union, who attempted to bring the judiciary under tight party control.[21] The dismissed judges have since been declared the defenders of the independence of the judiciary.

Under Sadat, judges dismissed hundreds of cases prosecuted by the government for political reasons and handed out particularly lenient sentences in many others. The last straw in the building tension between the judiciary and the executive authority was the sentence made by the Supreme Council of State Security that declared the innocence of those on trial for participating in the Food Riots of January 1977. In the face of mounting criticism, Sadat promulgated a vaguely worded Law of Shame, which could be applied to a multitude of political sins, to be administered by a special court dominated by party deputies in the People's Assembly.

Sadat reserved special treatment for the recalcitrant council of the Bar Association. This council was openly critical of the legislation that curtailed freedom of association and expression of opinions. The Bar Council was particularly incensed by the pressure the government brought to bear on the Wafdist leaders to dissolve the newly constituted party. This anger is hardly surprising given the traditional intimacy between the Wafd and the Bar Association. All the leaders of the Wafd — Sa'd Zaghlul, Mustafa al-Nahas, and Fouad Siraj al-Din — were lawyers. Furthermore, slightly less than half of the constituent body of the New Wafd belonged to the law profession. The president, the two vice presidents, and the secretary general of the new party were lawyers.

In a meeting with lawyers of the Alexandria branch of the Bar Association, Sadat indicated his displeasure with the Bar Council because it contained Wafdists, Marxists, and communists critical of his policies.[22] Sadat, however, managed his little coup against the legally constituted council with the help of lawyers on the government payroll. According to one report, lawyers converged on Cairo from all the provinces on 16 June 1981, only to find the gates of the Bar Association firmly closed before them. They stormed the gates and declared themselves in session. Thereupon, they adopted a resolution declaring their unwavering support for Sadat's leaderhsip, their withdrawal of confidence in the council, and their opposition to the Marxists, communists, and Wafdist reactionaries who had infiltrated their association.

Sadat followed this little coup by addressing a letter to the People's Assembly in which he declared that the Council of the Bar Association involved itself in matters not in the public interest and certainly not in the interest of maintaining a popular consensus.[23] Sadat pointed out, as an example, the council's adoption of a line conflicting with the peace process that had been approved by a popular referendum on 19 April 1979.

The People's Assembly, in turn, passed a law approving the dissolution of the Council of the Bar Association, called on the socialist prosecutor general to investigate members of the dissolved bar council, and appointed a temporary committee to supervise the activities of the association until the election of a new council under a new law approved by the assembly.

Members of the opposition, including the remaining independent deputies, denounced the assembly's action as unconstitutional. According to Mohammad 'Asfur, the arch critic of the Sadat regime, the assembly went beyond its constitutional mandate with its meddlesome legislation and interference in the internal affairs of autonomously constituted associations.[24]

Sadat followed what has by now become a familiar pattern in Egyptian parliamentary history. He packed the People's Assembly and *Majlis al-Shura* with party-bureaucratic elites, with leaders of various associations and syndicates co-opted by the regime, and with influential rural elites. By doing so, Sadat was able to shelve the issue of participation being demanded by the urban supporters of the Wafd and the Muslim Brotherhood, as well as by other elements to the right and left of the political spectrum.

What Sadat did not realize was that the pressure for participation was building to the point of explosion. There were other related issues that fueled the spirit of discontent. The liberalization of the economy (*siyasat al-infitah*) opened the floodgates to import businesses, whose income fattened the pockets of a small segment of a comprador class. Inflation under the impact of *infitah* drove up prices, making the purchase of essentail commodities beyond the means of people with fixed incomes. Many officials in the huge government bureaucracy were obliged to seek additional sources of income in the private sector. The importation of luxury goods, which only a few in the society could buy, further widened the gap between the wealthy classes and the majority of the urban population. Thus, the liberalization policy in the economic sector contradicted the restrictions that prevented the emergence of genuine liberal politics.

Under these political and economic crises, the peace treaty with Israel became the focal point to unite the alienated elements among the intelligentsia. Ironically, even the leaders of the Labor Party, who had initially accepted the peace treaty, joined with the intellectuals in the Tajamu', the leaders of the Muslim Brotherhood, the Wafdists, and the independents, who generally considered themselves part of the progressive mainstream, to form a national front. The choice before Sadat was either to pursue the illusion of political liberalization while continuing to tighten his control over the state's institutions, or to allow a genuine multiparty system to emerge. He opted for the first course.

The crackdown on the critics of the regime began in early 1981 in successive and relentless waves. The suppression of dissident journalists and writers began with interrogations held at the office of the socialist prosecutor general. The main charges against them were based on their views as they were publicly revealed in the foreign press. More distressing to the regime was that some of the critics were elected to the Council of the Press Syndicate in March. A few months later, it was the turn of the Bar Association, whose council was dissolved in June becasue it was composed of a large number of Wafdist supporters. The confrontation between the Bar Association and the regime sharply polarized the independent lawyers and brought to their side the minority parties and the outlawed political movements. In the meantime, one of the ugliest communal riots between Muslims and Copts in recent memory erupted in June at al-Zawiya al-Hamra, a lower-class district in Cairo. The incident left an ugly scar on a social system that had traditionally upheld the unity and amity of members of the Muslim and Christian communities. As will be noted in the next chapter, the incident reflected the limits of retraditionalization in the regime's appeal for support against its urban-based rivals.

Chapter Ten
The Political Expediency
of Religion

THE ISLAMIC MILITANT PHENOMENON, which claimed the life of President Sadat, was the unintended result (as we have already witnessed) of retraditionalization in the composition of state institutions. Islam was part of Sadat's appeal to traditional values, an appeal he made early in his presidency while shoring up his defenses against the Nasserists and Marxists. There was a clear distinction, however, in Sadat's appeal to the traditional *A'yan* in the name of village values and in his appeal to youth on university campuses in the name of Islam. Both appeals were made to consolidate power against urban rivals, but their consequences were diametrically opposite. We have already observed that, thanks to the support of influential *A'yan* in the People's Assembly, Sadat was able to ride roughshod over the urban opposition gathered around the Wafd. Sadat appeared to be in full command, even though the wily Siraj al-Din was able to call his liberalization bluff.

The appeal to Islamic values as part of Sadat's strategy of containment did not produce its intended results. Instead of control and order, it produced autonomous groups or Islamic *Jama'at* whose activities threatened to tear the social fabric and undermine communal harmony between the Coptic minority and the Muslim majority. The suppression of the militants took place shortly before the assassination of President Sadat. My contention is that none of these events would have occurred if sociological, anthropological, and psychological conditions pertaining to the rural migrants and their attitudes toward the authority had been absent. I will restrict my analysis to the Jihad group that claimed the life of President Sadat and was partly responsible for the escalation of communal conflict at Zawiya al-Hamra shortly before the crackdown on the militants in September 1981.

Tremendous social and regional transformations have taken place in Egypt over the past thirty years. In sheer demographic terms, the population totaled 40 million in 1978, of which 42 percent were under the age of fifteen. The demographic changes had their greatest impact on urban areas because of rural migration from densely populated provinces, giving rise to severe housing shortages and constant breakdowns in public services. Population density in Cairo was estimated to be two thousand inhabitants per square kilometer, making the city one of the most crowded in the world. If present growth rates are maintained, the city's population is expected to reach 20 million by the year 2000. By contrast, the population of rural areas declined from 81 percent in 1960 to 56 percent in 1976. Minufiyya accounts for the largest number of rural migrants who have settled in urban areas. It is followed by the more densely populated and industrially underdeveloped provinces of Upper Egypt, including Sohag and Qena. Some rural migrants managed to secure employment in the gulf following the oil boom. But most were attracted by the construction boom in Cairo in the mid-1970s, where even the cemeteries were converted into places of residence.

The psychological profile of the Islamic *Jama'at*, as drawn by observers in the field, has generally been expressed in terms of the theory of alienation. Individuals uprooted from their traditional moorings and finding themselves in an alien environment turn toward religion as a means of consolation and comfort. The therapeutic value of religion, however, ends when it becomes an instrument of social protest, and then there is no dearth of Islamic legitimizing formulae to justify the activities of those who feel they are on the outside and terribly wronged. One legitimizing principle is that of enjoining the good and prohibiting the evil. This principle becomes "an unconditional duty incumbent on every individual Muslim—which means that no Muslim, even one who lacks proper knowledge of religious principles, is exonerated from the obligation to do all he can to secure the adherence of his fellow Muslims to those principles."[1]

The *jama'at* further justify their presence on political and ethical grounds.[2] The various leaders of the different *Jama'at* mobilize their followers in response to what they perceive as the moral laxity of the times and the defeatist spirit, a consequence of the June War defeat of 1967. The *Jama'at*, however, are groups and coteries with varied internal cohesion and rituals, whose attitudes are reactions to the circumstances in which they find themselves. These attitudes were visible in the strong reaction against the secularist tendencies of the Nasserists, rooted in the ideas of nationalism and socialism. Their leaders expressed severe disappointment with the traditional *'Ulama'* for their failure to combat atheism and corruption and to stem moral degeneration. In this moral vacuum, marked by the absence of the traditional leadership of Islam vested in the *'Ulama'*, some of the leaders of the fraternities came to believe that their mission was as sacrosanct as religion itself.[3] Thus, a distinguishing feature of the *Jama'at* is their willingness to take an activist role and to adapt doctrinal matters to political objectives.

Of the activists, the extremists are those mililtant *Jama'at* that invoke *jihad* (struggle) as a fundamental obligation. These *Jama'at* have come to be known by their adopted or externally imposed names, such as al-Takfir wa al-Hijra and the Jihad group held responsible for plotting Sadat's assassination. Their militant doctrine harks back to that of the earlier Kharijites, who drew "perilous conclusions about a man's inner faith on the basis of external acts."[4] On the basis of this doctrine, the Islamic militants justify rebellion against Muslim rulers whose actions do not conform with Islamic laws. These militants must be distinguished from other *Jama'at*, who express moderate views on relations between faith and behavior, and from those with a *sufi* outlook who preach withdrawal and cultivation of inner spirituality.

Political movements to the left and right of the political spectrum during Sadat's rule shared the belief that the *Jama'at* received official encouragement. A critic of the Sadat regime once remarked that "the Islamic *jama'at* enjoyed privileges reminiscent of the privileges granted to foreigners under the Capitulation."[5] Many liberals likewise believed that the role of the *Jama'at* at the early stages of Sadat's rule was in harmony with the political goals of the regime, which included the neutralization of all political opposition.

Curiously, although both the *Ikhwan* and the Tajamu' opposed the Islamic militant phenomenon, both felt that its adherents were misguided youths whose extremism or false consciousness prevented them from taking the proper course. The competition over the rural migrant is not surprising since he was viewed the "natural candidate" for both the *Ikhwan* and the Nasserist left. We have already observed the effects of these competing ideologies on the life of Salah Husain Maqlad, leading us to the conclusion that Nasser succeeded not only in driving the *Ikhwan* underground but also in winning its constituency. The resentment of the *Ikhwan* persisted despite the conciliatory gestures of the Sadat regime. Omar Tilmisani thought that the officially sponsored *Jama'at* were created to counterbalance his movement.[6] By contrast, the Tajamu' believed that the "false consciousness" of the militants was the direct result of the interventionism of the state and not a result of its own organizational failure.

Rather than undermining the influence of the left or the right, the militant activities of the *Jama'at* spread to provincial cities and to peripheral areas of Cairo, where they encountered some resistance from militant Copts. Also, contrary to the impressions of the threatened political movements, the *Jama'at* were diverse, divided entities, lacking common political objectives, and their relations with the state and the *Ikhwan* were varied and conflicting.[7] While some *Jama'at* forged links with the state, others fell under the influence of the *Ikhwan*.[8] Nevertheless, many groups either turned their attention to other worldly interests or took to extremism in order to establish by force the kingdom of God on earth.

Despite their diversity, the majority of the *Jama'at* had a common ancestry. They were rooted in the *Ikhwan* movement, and many *Jama'at* members were either former members of the *Ikhwan* or came from the same social origins.[9] Furthermore, the notion of *takfir* (the appellation of unbelief), which served as the basis of the militant doctrine of rebellion against the established authority, was inspired by the writings of the *Ikhwan* leader, Sayyid Qutb.[10] Because of these common bonds, many observers erroneously concluded that the *Jama'at* and the *Ikhwan* were one and the same. Sadat himself denounced the mililtant *Jama'at* declaring them to be the secret army of the *Ikhwan*.

Fundamental differences emerged between the *Ikhwan* leadership and the militant *Jama'at* after 1971.[11] The cultivation of religious values by Sadat and the affirmation of the Islamic character of the state had come in response to the challenge posed by leftists and Nasserists. In a bid to placate the right, Sadat ordered the release of *Ikhwan* leaders and followers who had served long prison sentences during the Nasserist regime. He even permitted the *Ikhwan* to reorganize and publish its journal, *al-Da'wa*. The new leadership under Tilmisani seemed reconciled to the role of advisor to the authorities and to confining the activities of the movement to propagation of Islamic values.

The growing disenchantment of the militants with the *Ikhwan* was based on the conviction that the *Ikhwan* leaders, the majority of whom belonged to the older generation, had grown tired of the repression they had suffered for at least three decades and were ready to compromise true beliefs in order to win some favors from the political authority. Although the *Ikhwan* was able to win to its side the Islamic *Jam'at* that dominated student unions in the Egyptian universities, many *Jama'at* that had adopted the concept of *takfir* rejected the *Ikhwan* leadership.[12]

In contrast to the *Ikhwan* and the moderate *Jama'at*, the militants believed that Sadat's attempts to establish Islamic rule were a sham. Most of them adopted the extreme position that Sadat was not a Muslim ruler nor did his rule represent a step toward the establishment of Islamic rule. They defended the purity of their beliefs and attacked the Muslim Brotherhood for its willingness to reach a modus vivendi with the authorities. It was even rumored within militant circles that Tilmisani was cooperating with the security department, something he came close to admitting in an interview with *al-Musawwar*.[13] Also, the groups in the universities originally encouraged by the state could not escape the stigma of their former association.

After 1973, the government came to the realization that the Islamic *Jama'at* were a bad idea after all. This revelation occurred long after Sadat had gotten rid of his rivals identified with the left during the Corrective Movement of May 1971. The brief successes in the October War further consolidated the regime and even brought to it a measure of popularity. These successes obviated the need for a strategy heavily dependent on appealing to the right in order to suppress the left. But, in the meantime, the Islamic *Jama'at* had gained an autonomy and momentum that laid beyond state control, and some were able to forge links with rural migrants of similar origins on the outskirts of Cairo and in the provincial cities of Upper Egypt.

The Islamic militants launched a series of attacks on what they considered symbols of authority beginning with the Military Technical College in 1974. The scope of their hostilities was expanded to include those conservative *'Ulama'* who were critical of the militant doctrine. For example, a former minister of al-Awqaf was kidnapped and killed in 1977 by al-Takfir wa al-Hijra. The discovery of each group by government authorities led to its immediate suppression, but this action did not prevent the emergence of similarly inclined groups. It must be remembered that these groups were not connected with each other in any formal sense. The last group to emerge was the Tanzim al-Jihad, which figured prominently in the period between the sectarian disturbances at Zawiya al-Hamra in June 1981 and Sadat's assassination in October of the same year.

There is little to substantiate the claims of spokesmen of the regime after Sadat's assassination that Tanzim al-Jihad was an organized group. Press accounts show that the Tanzim was composed of groups whose leaders shared similar political views, but there is little evidence of the existence of a formal organization. The official view is that the Tanzim originated in 1974, when some followers of the group liquidated after its attack on the Military Technical College reorganized. The new group (which came to be known as the Jihad) was liquidated in 1978 after a bloody confrontation with security forces in Alexandria. More than eighty persons were detained and subsequently released. The following year, security forces arrested 134 people on charges of belonging to the Jihad group, but they were all released for lack of evidence. Thus, as a result of constant harassment by the police, the Jihad followers were supposedly divided into groups flung as far apart from each other as Alexandria and Naga' Hamadi. One of the Jihad leaders, Muhammad 'Abdel Salam Farag, assumed responsibility for reorganizing the splinter groups. This history of the group explains why the Tanzim is often referred to as the Jihad Tanzim. In April 1982, Farag was the only civilian executed after a military tribunal established his guilt in the assassination of Sadat.

The effectiveness of the Tanzim must, however, be attributed to nonrational and informal types of organizational skills. Their methods included traditional means, especially personal contacts with military officers, kinship ties, and the availability of the Ahli (private) mosques as grounds for establishing contacts. To these organizational skills could be added the ability to escape detection by the security forces.

The Tanzim's relationship to the military establishment and to parallel Islamic groups loomed during the interrogations held by the Office of the Public Prosecutor. (Transcripts of the interrogations are accessible to the public.) Official concern was concentrated on finding out the extent to which the Tanzim members infiltrated the military apparatus or acted in concert with other Islamic *Jama'at* in the plot to assassinate President Sadat. During one of the sessions, Colonel 'Abbud, the high-ranking military officer in the Tanzim, insisted there were no formal contacts with other Islamic *Jama'at*, although he admitted that some of the Tanzim members did participate in the summer camps and the meetings held by university-affiliated *Jama'at*.[14] Nevertheless, Colonal 'Abbud was unequivocal on the issue that the Tanzim acted independently. He also pointed out that his group was not ready to stage a popular Islamic revolution. As we will observe later, there was an element of truth in his statement that the Tanzim had been forced to act prematurely when the activities of some individuals within the Tanzim were uncovered by the security forces.

The recruitment of civilians was carried out by a select group of leading members of the Tanzim. According to 'Abbud, there were five leaders in Greater Cairo and parts of Giza who frequented local mosques to recruit potential members. There was no division of labor and no territorial division of responsibility within the Tanzim. Recruitment could be carried out anywhere and by any responsible members. Nevertheless, 'Abbud pointed out that most Tanzim members were recruited at mosques in the localities where the rank and file of the Tanzim lived. He also mentioned that the activities of the Tanzim had not spread outside local neighborhoods because the group was still at the embryonic stage. But he added that the Tanzim had plans to spread out in order to realize the objective of a popular Islamic revolution.

Mohammad 'Abd al-Salam Farag, the civilian leader of the Tanzim in Cairo, revealed that he and other members set out to cultivate the support of military officers because of their specialized knowledge in the use of firearms and because they could easily get hold of weapons and ammunition. On the other hand, 'Abbud denied that any special efforts to recruit army officers and servicemen were made. He believed the Tanzim feared exposure since internal security within the military apparatus was very tight and that it had not intended to launch a military coup. The aim was a popular revolution. However, a number of officers joined the Tanzim through the initiative of civilians, either through kinsmen and friends in the service or through contacts established at local mosques. Farag said he asked officers to join the Tanzim whenever there was an opportunity, once they satisfied him that they were committed to promoting the cause of the Jihad. It is not surprising to note that, of all the civilians in the Tanzim, Farag bore a major responsibility for recruiting the officers who took part in the assassination of President Sadat.

The officer who played a decisive role in the assassination was Khalid al-Islambuli. There is strong evidence showing that he conceived of the assassination plot only a few days before the fateful day—6 October (the day of the annual military parade in observation of the Egyptian "victory" in the October War of 1973).[15] He sought the cooperation of the Tanzim leaders for forming a team to carry out the plot in a meeting attended by Farag and some of the group leaders of Upper Egypt. Farag enlisted the support of a reserve army officer from his own home town, while Islambuli brought to the team his friend and kinsman, 'Abd al-Hamid 'Abd al-Salam, a retired, noncommissioned officer who ran a bookstore. The fourth man to join the team through Farag's mediation was Hussein 'Abbas, also a noncommissioned army officer. 'Abbas' sister's husband was the member of the Tanzim responsible for military training and was apprehended on 25 September while carrying a suitcase full of explosives. Interestingly, there is no evidence that connects all four members of the assassination team to the Tanzim prior to when Islambuli thought up the assassination plot. In fact, it has been pointed out that the two members recruited by Farag met Islambuli for the first time shortly before the plot was carried out.[16]

Kinship ties were also important; some members of the Tanzim were closely related to each other. For example, 'Abbud and Tariq al-Zomor, both heading the indictment list of the public prosecutor, are first cousins, and the former is married to the latter's sister. There are also intermarriages between Tanzim members and other militant groups, such as the marriage relationship between one of the leading members of the Tanzim in Asyut and Shukri Mustafa, the leader of the group widely known as al-Takfir wa-al-Hijra who was executed for his role in the assassination of the former minister of al-Awqaf in 1977. In fact, because of the social bonds and similarities in political outlook between Shukri Mustafa's group and some members of the Tanzim in Asyut, the latter were wrongly identified in the Egyptian press as members of al-Takfir wa-al-Hijra.

In addition to the extensive friendship and kinship relationships, the militant *Jama'at* began to establish societies for learning the *Qur'an* and social centers that attracted rural migrants in the neighborhoods on the periphery of the metropolis.[17] These attempts at attracting supporters by no means had any mass appeal and were confined to isolated localities. Judging from the successes of the 'Usar (fraternities) established by the Islamic *Jama'at* on university campuses for providing mutual aid and support, the attempts of the militants at emulating them in their own localities were bound to have some impact. According to the mayor of Delinjat, the city in which Farag grew up and remained active, the distribution of clothes and meat increased the popularity of the militants among the poor and the needy.

Perhaps the one key element that brought the militants together was the proliferation of Ahli mosques in the localities of the various groups of Tanzim. Many observers note that the recent Islamic resurgence was accompanied by an increase of both private mosques and independent preachers and Imams. According to one estimate, the number of Ahli mosques in 1970 was 20,000, by 1981 that number had more than doubled.[18] Thus, of the total 46,000 mosques in Egypt in 1981, only 6,000 of them were under the control of the Ministry of Religious Endowments, al-Awqaf, and maintained by 3,000 officially approved Imams.[19] The minister of al-Awqaf admitted that his ministry lacked the resources to keep an eye on the private mosques. Part of the problem was the decline in the number of Azhar graduates, and the fact that many of them found the job of Imam unattractive because of the low pay.[20] Some of the Ahli mosques became famous when their Imams established reputations for being independent of the authority. The militants were frequently in contact with popular Imams such as Mahalawi in Alexandria and Hafiz Salamah in Suez.[21]

The Ahli mosques also proved to be a haven for the militants to establish and renew contacts. Farag, for example, was approached by Islambuli after he had concluded his regular sermon at the local mosque in Bolaq al-Dakrur. This encounter took place roughly six months before the assassination of President Sadat. At the time of the meeting, Islambuli was seeking an apartment to rent and asked Farag to help him. Afterwards, each met the other's friends and kinsmen. Most of the confession statements indicate that the impression formed from listening to the sermons of various group leaders stimulated individuals to join the Tanzim. For example, the person who led the attack on Christian jewelry stores in Naga' Hamadi confessed that his thinking was influenced by the sermons of the group leader in Asyut. The various groups in Tanzim can be identified not only by the leaders or the locality, but also by the mosque group members frequented.

The mosques surrounding Greater Cairo included Omar Ibn Abd al-Aziz in Bolaq al-Dakrur, al-Anwar in 'Ain Shams, Al-Tawhid in al-Haram, and Masjid al-Gharbi in Nahia. These mosques were included in the list of sixty-five mosques across the country brought under control of the Ministry of al-Awqaf in September 1981.[22]

The popularity of the militants was confined to those areas where state authority was absent. The crackdown on sectarian and secular opposition in September, just one month before the assassination of President Sadat allows us to ascertain the validity of the statement from the minister of the interior— that the militants, whom he identified as members of the secret Muslim Brotherhood in a bid to implicate the latter as a militant movement, were being shadowed by the security forces.[23] It was generally assumed that the September list of 1,536 detainees included all the known enemies of the regime. This figure, however, does not include those detained before the September crackdown. By comparing this list with the list of the Tanzim's membership, drawn up by the public prosecutor's office, we can see how effective the security apparatus was and gain some insight into the possible motives behind the suicidal plot on the life of the president by the militants on 6 October and the ensuing clashes with the security forces in Asyut.

Of the 302 members of the official list of the Tanzim, only 27 (8.9 percent) were on the September list, 20 of whom came from Fayyum, Minya, Asyut, Sohag, and Qena. These individuals headed the indictment list of the public prosecutor as the principal organizers of the plot to overthrow the regime.[24] Interestingly, although orders for their arrest were issued during the first week of September, almost all these men remained at large and, hence, could participate in the assassination plot and, subsequently, in the clashes with the security forces in Asyut. These individuals, however, should not be confused with the twenty-two members of the Tanzim who were listed as fugitives on the official list. There is some evidence indicating that some of these fugitives were overseas workers.

In addition to the group leaders identified in the September list, a number of Tanzim members had relatives on the list who were actually detained in September, thus embittering these members and driving them into acts of desperation. Khalid Islambuli's brother, for example, was among the detainees. According to an eyewitness, Khalid broke down upon hearing about his brother's detention and swore to avenge the misfortune that had befallen the family.[25]

The connection between the September crackdown and the identification of members of the Tanzim reveals interesting information on the capability of the security apparatus to keep the ringleaders of militant movements under surveillance. In the most traditional areas south of Bani Suwayf, the security apparatus was most successful in identifying, although not in apprehending, the leaders of the militant *Jama'at*. By contrast, the security apparatus failed to penetrate the northern belt of Greater Cairo or its southern tip that overlaps Giza.[26] As an astute observer of the political scene in Cairo remarked, the regime kept a close watch on the activities of the Islamic *Jama'at* that observed the limits on political action, but it was highly negligent toward the militants whose activities were less visible and yet very dangerous.[27]

There is sufficient evidence to suggest that the most active militant groups affiliated with the Tanzim were concentrated in the Upper Egyptian region. Table 27 shows that their number was decisively higher there than in Lower Egypt. There is little doubt that the rates of development in Upper Egypt have generally lagged behind the rest of the country. This delay can be attributed to several factors, including the scarcity of resources, especially of land available for agricultural production; the persistence of traditional influences, as reflected in the extended family system which is dominated by the patriarchal figure; and the policies of the central government, which has traditionally treated the region with benign neglect. However, in recent years the provincial cities have experienced a tremendous expansion, thanks to the opening of universities and the increased rate of construction stimulated by the infusion of hard cash from the remittances of migrant workers in the Persian Gulf.

Provincial capitals, such as Asyut and Minya, represent the cutoff point in rural-urban discontinuities. These areas were the first in a predominantly traditional region to come under the impact of rapid urbanization. Hence, they are the most likely places to witness social instabilities, manifested by sectarian and political violence. Asyut's urban population has doubled in the past two decades. The proportion of urban population for the whole province is 45 percent, compared to Minya's 34 percent. In absolute terms, Asyut appears to have a larger urban population than Minya (214,000 compared to 146,000).[28]

Part of the explanation for the greater urban population in Asyut is the increase in the enrollment of students at Asyut University. The available statistics show that student enrollment jumped from roughly 15,000 students in

TABLE 27   Distribution of Tanzim Members by Region

Region	No.	%
Greater Cairo	73	26.1
Upper Egypt	183	65.4
Lower Egypt	24	8.6
TOTAL	280	100.1

Note: Drawn from the list of Tanzim members issued by the office of the public prosecutor. Excerpts of the statement and the list were published in *al-Ahram*, 9 May 1982. The total does not include the twenty-two members listed as fugitives.

1971–1972 to 28,000 in 1976–1977. By comparison, the number of students enrolled at Minya University in 1976–1977 did not exceed 10,000.

Both Asyut and Minya have had a higher number of communal disturbances and instances of state repression than any other provincial capitals. According to one report, Minya's experience with religious extremism began in 1975.[29] The report attributed the phenomenon to the militant penetration of the educational system and some of the 2,000 mosques, only one-fourth of which were under the control of officially approved Imams. Some of the militants of Minya joined their co-religionists in Asyut in a show of solidarity whenever a confrontation took place between militants and the security forces. One such confrontation, which took place in November 1980, ended in violence and in the interruption of studies at Asyut University.[30] All through the late 1970s and during 1980 – 1981, house-to-house searches for hidden weapons were conducted in parts of Asyut and Minya, thus increasing the tension. This tension culminated in the bloodiest clashes ever to take place with securtiy forces in Asyut two days after Sadat's assassination.

Members of the Tanzim were concentrated in those very areas experiencing the unsettling effects of urbanization or, as will be mentioned later, in areas that have expanded so that they have become part of the metropolis. A breakdown of the list of Tanzim members by provinces and areas will be most revealing. The provincial distribution of Tanzim members (Table 28) shows that Greater Cairo and Giza had the highest concentration. Within Greater Cairo, the major areas of Tanzim activitiy were Mataria, Zeitun, Rod-al-Farag, and al-Sahel. All these areas lie in the northern belt, which "has been the receptacle for most of the twentieth-century rural migrants."[31] A few members were found in the northeastern extensions of Heliopolis in al-Wayli and 'Ain Shams. By contrast, no significant militant activities were found in the older and more stable communities in the popular sections of the city, such as Misr al-Qadima or Sayyida Zeinab.

In Giza, Bolaq al-Dakrur held the highest proportion of Tanzim members. This section of Giza is near Cairo University and is one of the most densely populated areas. Most of the inhabitants of Bolaq al-Dakrur live in substandard housing units that are steadily deteriorating under pressure from the constant influx of rural migrants. One such migrant was Farag, the chief architect and ideologist of the Tanzim, whose followers in Bolaq al-Dakrur, according to one newspaper, included seventy persons.

The area near the pyramids, al-Haram, also contained a large proportion of militants. This area has witnessed a tremendous residential expansion in the past decade through the conversion of agricultural land into urban property. Some of the choicest pieces of real estate went to influential persons. The

TABLE 28   Distribution of Tanzim Members by Provinces

Province	No.	%	Province	No.	%
Greater Cairo	73	26.1	Bani Suwayf	10	3.6
Giza	67	23.9	Sharqiyya	10	3.6
Asyut	37	13.2	Fayyum	9	3.2
Sohag	25	8.9	Daqahliyya	5	1.8
Minya	23	8.2	Beheira	4	1.4
Qena	12	4.3	Others	5	1.8
TOTAL				280	100.00

Pyramid's Plateau itself was converted into a resort area in which some of the richest and most influential persons, including the president, built little huts and villas that distorted the scenic beauty of the area. Nightclubs also became an endemic features of the Pyramid Road. Thus, the inhabitants of the villages of Nahia, Kirdasa, and Saft al-Laban—in which some of the most active militants grew up, including 'Abbud al-Zomor and his large family—might have been dismayed by the brutal assault on their lifestyle and traditional values.[32]

The most destabilizing event to occur was the influx of numerous families who were forcibly evacuated from the center of Cairo to make room for the construction of luxury hotels and tourist centers. The families were relocated to al-Zawiyya al-Hamra, the scene of ugly communal riots in June of 1981, and to 'Ain Shams beyond the airport. 'Ain Shams was near the housing complex, Alf Maskan, in which Khalid Islambuli's sister lived and where some of the group leaders met to plot the assassination.

In the provincial areas, the militants were mostly residents of provincial capitals such as al-Minya, Asyut, and Sohag. Some came from nearby villages and were either unemployed or nonagricultural workers. However, as Table 29 shows, the largest proportion of militants were students; the age distribution indicates a similar pattern. The very low percentage of farmers supports the view that Islamic militancy is an urban phenomenon, found especially in areas that have been suddenly transformed, whether through growth of provincial cities or through incorporation of villages into the Cairo metropolis.

The overwhelming majority of militants did not come from the traditional rural elite, who provided the main base of support for successive regimes in Egypt, nor did they represent the influential urban middle and upper middle classes. The militants were predominantly from a special segment within the lower middle classes that held low-income jobs. What makes this segment

TABLE 29   Distribution of Tanzim Members by Occupation and Age

Occupation	No	%
Students	123	43.9
Workers	41	14.6
Professionals	35	12.5
Unemployed	30	10.7
Shopkeepers	16	5.7
Govt. officials	15	5.4
Police and military	14	5.0
Farmers	6	2.2
TOTAL	280	100.0

Age Categories	No.	%
<20	49	17.5
21–30	196	70.0
31–40	30	10.7
>40	5	1.8
TOTAL	280	100.0

special is its political awareness, relatively high literacy rate, and higher mobility patterns. Even the unemployed militants had the benefit of technical education.

The leadership of the Tanzim groups was a curious mixture of people with different backgrounds and social origins. Ironically, however, of the *A'yan* families Sadat attempted to win over by declaiming the atrocities of the HCLF, the members of two families became accessible to the militants. The participation of these individuals, Colonel Abbud al-Zomor and Lieutenant Khalid al-Islambuli, was most effective in the execution of the assassination plot.

'Abbud al-Zomor (age 35) was the highest-ranking army officer in the Tanzim, holding the rank of colonel in army intelligence. His participation in the assassination was the main reason for the alarm expressed over the penetration of the militants into the most sensitive areas of the military hierarchy. 'Abbud's uncle was a general who died in the October War of 1973. Another uncle is a member of Majlis al-Shura, the advisory council. His father was the *'Umda* (mayor) of the family village, Nahia, in Giza until he was replaced by another family member. Other close patrilineal relatives continue to maintain influential positions. There are three members in the army at the rank of major. Moreover, one family member is the secretary of the Imbaba district (Giza governorate) branch of the governing National Democratic Party. The family is also linked through intermarriage with some of the older and well-established families, such as the Ghurabs and Mikawis in the same district. Both families, along with the Zomor family, had long-standing records in Egyptian parliamentary history before and after the July 1952 revolution. The regime's attempt to curry favor with the Zomor family, as part of its efforts to placate the families victimized by the activities of the HCLF, was evident from a newspaper report claiming that Abbud's mother was sent on pilgrimage to Mecca at the state's expense. Furthermore, Tariq al-Zomor was granted 5,000 pounds as part of the state's contribution to building a mosque in Nahia.[33]

The social profile of Khalid al-Islambuli, the army officer who led the assassination team, is similar to that of 'Abbud. Islambuli came from a family in Malawi, in al-Minya governorate, whose members generally had received the benefit of higher education, mainly in the law profession. His father is a legal consultant for the sugar factory in Naga' Hamadi, and his uncle is a retired judge. In fact, there are strong grounds for the belief that the family continues to enjoy political and social influence. For example, the post of chairman of the Minya District Council is held by a close family member.[34] Moreover, the family has a very high-ranking officer in the army;[35] thus, the evidence strongly disproves allegations made earlier that the family was alien to Egyptian society because of its Turkish descent. The available data show that the militant within the family was Khalid's brother, who went to Mecca twice for pilgrimage although he was a student. He was detained by the Asyut police for shouting anti-Sadat slogans outside the railway station in 1979. This incident may explain why he was arrested in the crackdown on the opposition in September 1981.

By contrast, the majority of the Tanzim leaders belonged to lower middle class origins, some of whom had close connections with the Muslim Brotherhood (although its present leadership not only denies the existence of any links but also denounces publicly the activities of the militants). Despite denials, the history of the *Ikhwan* remains inextricably intertwined with past violence and political assassinations in Egypt.[36] There were two examples of links between the *Ikhwan* and such violence. First, members of the *Ikhwan* who were serving long prison sentences under Nasser's rule became militant, or developed what has been described as a Manichaean view of the outside world.[37] The second link emerged when the *Ikhwan* leaders denounced the militants in an effort to demonstrate their moderation to President Sadat and strike a modus vivendi with the regime. At this point, some of the young descendants of the *Ikhwan* became disenchanted with the moderate *Ikhwan* and, consequently, took a militant position. Shukri Mustafa, the leader of the Takfir wa-al-Hijra, belonged to the first group, while Mohammad 'Abd al-Salam Farag, the chief architect and ideologist of the Tanzim, belonged to the second group.[38]

Farag's father was an employee of the Ministry of Health. He was a distinguished member of the Muslim Brotherhood and had been arrested several times. Before settling in Delinjat (Beheira Province) he lived in a small village in the Imbaba district in Giza. During the twenty-five years of his stay in Delinjat, relations were cemented with a local merchant through marriage. Farag graduated with a degree in electrical engineering, joined Cairo University's administrative staff, and settled in nearby Bolaq al-Dakrur. His chief distinction, however, is his authorship of *al-Farida al-Gha'iba* (literally, "The Absent Obligation," meaning *jihad* or struggle) — a text of forty-five pages that the authorities claimed was the constitution of the Tanzim.[39] *Al-Farida* called on Muslims to exercise *jihad* as a fundamental religious obligation. The authorities interpreted this directive as an incitement to revolt with arms against the constitutionally established government.

The convergence of Islamic militancy, the *Ikhwan*, the Coptic militants, urban pressure, and the political use of religion in the strategy of the Sadat regime was reflected by the communal clashes at Zawiya al-Hamra, which then precipitated the crackdown on secular and sectarian opposition in September 1981. Zawiya al-Hamra, in the northeastern part of Cairo, comes under the administration of the local Council of North Cairo. Politically, the area is under the control of the Local Committee of the National Democratic Party (NDP) in al-Sharabiyya district. The area (about forty faddans) was originally a *Waqf* property, which became state land when *Waqf* properties were abolished. Encroachments on state land increased as more settlers came to live in the area. The first settlers came from Upper Egypt in 1945, but since then rural migrants have come from differing parts of the country. Some of the new migrants forged common links with the old settlers, but the community, given its heterogeneous character, began to feel growing tensions from increasing population density. A local Coptic priest remarked that most of the trouble began after the arrival of rural migrants from Minya.[40] As I pointed out earlier, the Minya province has a long history of sectarian conflict. Apparently, the rural migrants brought to the city their ancient prejudices and petty feuds.

The immediate cause of the sectarian conflict was the government's decision to use the little space left in Zawiya al-Hamra to relocate the inhabitants of slums in other parts of the city. In 1979 a decision was made by the governor of Cairo to pull down the slums of Eshash al-Torgoman (Ishash al-Turjuman) and 'Arab al-Mohammadi and to relocate their inhabitants in Zawiya al-Hamra and in a new settlement on the outskirts of Heliopolis. Eshash al-Torgoman was a slum area in the center of the business district in Cairo, while the 'Arab al-Mohammadi slum was in the eastern part of the city, close to 'Ain Shams University. The areas were vacated to make room for the construction of business offices and upper class residence. Two sociologists, who observed the attitudes of the slum dwellers before their evacuation, said they were very resentful for many reasons, including the loss of livelihood which they had earned by providing menial services in the area.[41] They were also embittered by the prospects of a breakdown in their social relations, since they were relocated in two faraway places. Furthermore, it was observed that coercion was used to evacuate the inhabitants. It is no surprise then, as a sociologist concluded, that after the settlers arrived in Zawiya al-Hamra they nursed bitter feelings because of their alienation.[42]

The evacuation began in 1979 and was carried out in two stages that ended in 1981. The plan involved resettling 5,000 families or 30,000 individuals.[43] A sociologist who visited Zawiya al-Hamra before the sectarian clashes observed that families who came from Eshash al-Torgoman were living under appalling conditions due to lack of space. Her estimate was that, on the average, there were seven individuals per room and that in the majority of cases there were two or three related families in the same apartment.[44]

Sadat, however, gave a different version. He told *Mayo*, the official publication of the National Democratic Party, that two years before, when he was in Alexandria, he had summoned the minister of construction, Engineer Hasaballah al-Kafrawi, and he had given him the following instructions:

> Listen, for thirty years, from before the 23 July revolution to this day, we have been facing a big problem called the problem of Eshash al-Torgoman and 'Arab al-Mohammadi in the center of Cairo. It is a major problem and it gives a very bad picture of the people's standard of living. I have summoned you to tell you that the time has come to solve this problem immediately. I will no longer allow the continuation of this problem. . . . Al-Kafrawi acted immediately. He chose al-Zawiya al-Hamra and decided to move the inhabitants of Eshash al-Torgoman and 'Arab al-Mohammadi there. Last year I went to al-Zawiya al-Hamra, toured the area, entered some houses and talked to their owners. I was really pleased to see happiness in the faces of the new residents. They had left their shacks and now lived in healthy houses in an area that was rebuilt in accordance with the modern system.[45]

Contrary to the impressions formed by the president, the inhabitants of Zawiya al-Hamra were deeply affected by the policies adopted by the government. In particular, *infitah*, the economic liberalization policy, had led to a spiraling increase in the cost of living, while the gap widened between the few individuals able to profit from selling imported goods on the one hand and the deprived majority on the other. The Islamic fraternities sharpened religious differences by disseminating information on the level of prosperity achieved by Coptic businesses under the umbrella of *infitah*. (It should be noted that during the riots at Zawiya al-Hamra some of the shops owned by Copts were looted or destroyed.)

There are different versions of the reasons behind the outbreak of sectarian conflict. Sadat, in one of his speeches, contended that the clashes began as a petty feud between two neighbors, which was then exploited by religious extremists and politicians to advance political goals[46]. In typical fashion, Sadat blamed communists and misguided members of the opposition for fomenting the sectarian disturbances. Actually, it was the ruling party (NDP) that was engaged in the deadly game of promoting political objectives at the cost of national consensus. At that time, the NDP's local committee, composed of parliamentary deputies and party officials, was still excited by the victory it had won against the opposition during the elections to the People's Assembly a month earlier. The ruling party's local committees normally become active during election times, after which their activities subside until they come to a complete standstill. In the case of Zawiya al-Hamra, however, the pre-electoral tension had lingering effects. Such effects were evident in the local committee's ill-advised intervention to settle a dispute between a Muslim and a Copt over a piece of land of about 1800 square meters.[47] The reasons it gave for intervening were explained in a leaflet distributed in the area two days before the outbreak of violence.

The leaflet was addressed to the people of al-Sharabiyya district and al-Zawiya al-Hamra. It began with a quotation from the *Hadith*: "Let sedition lie asleep for God curses whoever awakens it." The NDP then went on to say that on "12 and 13 June a citizen claimed a piece of land on the basis that he had a court ruling [in his favor]. The security forces intervened in cooperation with the NDP to examine the claim and found that it was invalid. The local Popular Council of North Cairo had already decided to let a poultry firm use part of the land for the purposes of the firm and the rest was to be utilized for building a mosque." The leaflet ended by saying that the "NDP is vigilant and attentive in the interests of the masses, [works to] instill spiritual values and maintain law and order." The names of the secretary general of the NDP, two members of the People's Assembly, and local community members were appended at the bottom of the leaflet.

The decision of the Local Council undoubtedly infuriated the Coptic family, whose right to the disputed land was upheld by a court of law. Blinded by fury and outrage, the Coptic family members opened fire on Muslims gathered on the disputed land for the evening prayers. Moderate and extremist *Jama'at* were quickly mobilized. In the ensuing clashes, 17 people were killed and 112 injured, and a total of 171 shops and public places were ransacked or destroyed. Sources at the Ministry of the Interior said that 266 persons were arrested; some of them were carrying stolen property. The minister of the interior personally appealed to Omar Tilmisani and other fundamentalist leaders closely connected with the *Jama'at* to step in to calm the situation and soothe the embittered Muslims. A High Council of the Permanent Islamic Propagation Conference was established to monitor the situation closely and to recommend action to the minister of the interior. The council included two prominent *Ikhwan* leaders—Omar Tilmisani and Mohammad al-Ghazali—and 'Abdul Latif Mushtahri and 'Attiyeh Khamis, among other Muslim leaders.

The *jama'at* who rejected the militant doctrine and were closely connected with the *Ikhwan* held a conference at Zawiya al-Hamra on 20 June. As can be shown from the recorded speeches, however, there was little in their denunciation of Copts that distinguishes them from the militants.[48] They too seemed to have succumbed to the evils of uncompromise. Hilmi al-Jazzar, speaking on behalf of the *Jama'at* in the Egyptian universities, attributed the "Christian militancy to the absence of Islamic rule which alone could put an end to aggressions committed against the Muslims." He called on Muslims to boycott Christian businesses as a means of preventing them from accumulating money in order to arm themselves.

The speakers at the conference repeated the allegations made by Sadat in his speech on the anniversary of the Corrective Movement. Most inflammatory, however, was the speech of Shaykh Hafiz Salama, the independent Imam from Suez and a leading critic of Sadat. He said that Sadat's own words revealed the existence of a conspiracy hatched in the Vatican and in New York against Islam. Another leading member of the *Jama'at* in the Egyptian universities, Essam al-'Aryan, said that Shenouda (the head of the Coptic Church) was playing the same role as was Major Sa'd Haddad in Lebanon so that sufficient havoc would be created in the country to invite foreign intervention under the pretext of protecting the minority.[49] He added that the Copts had never given up their old ambition of establishing a state with Asyut as its capital. Some Christians were fully armed and some were trained in Lebanon, as was declared by the president. As evidence of the preparedness of the militant Copts, al-'Aryan pointed out that the Christians used firearms in their attack in Zawiya al-Hamra, while Muslims fought back with sticks and any sharp instrument they could get hold of.

Essam al-'Aryan, however, admonished those responsible for the destruction of homes and shops, because in his opinion such activities exposed the weaknesses of the Islamic movement. He added that, at any rate, the government would no doubt compensate the owners as it had in the past when owners of casinos and nightclubs were compensated. (He presumably was referring to the destruction of places of entertainment during the Food Riots of January 1977.)

The resolutions of the conference called on authorities to dismiss Shenouda, disarm the Christians, stop the building of churches, bring to trial the attackers at Zawiya al-Hamra, and put an end to the missionary activities The conference also called on Muslims to stay away from Christian shops and places of business. It can hardly be said that these resolutions were hammered out by a moderate group prepared to defuse the conflict. On the contrary, there is good reason to suspect that the moderate *Jama'at* were rivaling the extremists in showing their hostility to the Copts. Somehow, in the fracas caused by the Zawiya al-Hamra affair, the Islamic teachings that extol the virtue of tolerance and call on Muslims to respect the integrity of Christians were forgotten.

The speakers at the conference did, however, distinguish themselves from the more radical groups present in the audience. It was revealed at the conference that militant elements were exerting pressure behind the scenes for strong measures against Christians. Shaykh 'Attiyeh Khamis, for example, announced that some extremists had tried to pressure the leaders of the community to take a more militant stand. He called them presumptuous in thinking that they were more zealous about Islam than the traditional leaders of the community. He further condemned them as a superficial bunch of youths devoid of sound understanding of the principles of faith. Similarly, the chairman of the Local Council of North Cairo, speaking at the conference, warned against subversive elements who were splitting the Muslim movement. (It was not clear who these speakers meant until the identities of members of Tanzim al-Jihad became known publicly when the autonomous group responsible for President Sadat's assassination was revealed. Through signed confessions, each member revealed his role, beginning with attacks on Copts in Upper Egypt and Cairo and ending with the assassination.)

Sadat reached the limit of his tolerance in September. Security officers were sent out to arrest all urban dissidents without discrimination. The number of detainees in the first week reached 1536, including members of all sectarian and secular political movements as well as some of the middle level leaders of recognized minority parties. Bishops, priests, Shaykhs, Imams, secular party leaders, and nondescript vagabonds were put behind bars. Shahinda and her colleagues in the Tajamu' were already in prison when they were joined by men such as Fouad Siraj al-Din, Tilmisani, Abdel Salam Zayyat, Milad Hanna, Ismail Sabri Abdullah, Hilmi Murad, Shaykh Mahalawi, and Shaykh Kishk. These men represented diverse ideologies and political movements. Their only commonality was their opposition to Sadat's controversial domestic and foreign policies. At any rate, they were not united to overthrow the regime as it was claimed. The outspoken Coptic and Muslim philanthropic groups and societies were closed, and their journals and bulletins banned. Journalists and university professors were either imprisoned or transferred because of their criticism of Sadat. Indeed, Sadat's repressive policy was unprecedented, since it affected such a wide cross-section of the society.

In the weeks following the September crackdown on the secular and sectarian opposition, the streets of Cairo were jammed with trucks loaded with peasants from the provinces, who had been quickly mobilized by the NDP to demonstrate support for the regime. Sadat went to the People's Assembly, where his condemnation of sectarian violence received a standing ovation. Nonetheless, the repressive measures, that Sadat paid for with his own life, revealed in a painful way the limits of retraditionalizaiton carried out in the name of Islam.

Chapter Eleven
Conclusion

T
HE EGYPTIAN POLITICAL ORDER has weathered many storms, including the developmental crisis of participation, distribution, and ideology. Until this writing, the persistence of the political order continues to contrast sharply with the increasing social and economic problems. The anomaly between a continuous political order and unstable social and economic conditions has been explained by concepts that run counter to the forces underlying the crises of development. These concepts including the use of second stratum, the strategy of mobilization of rural support and neutralization of urban rivals, and the application of the retraditionalization process after each major social conflagration.

The application of these ideas to a study of Egypt demands a different understanding of the concept of power than the narrowly defined one in the conventional, elitist approach to the study of politics in the Middle East. Power, in this work, engulfs the whole society, from the village level and the local areas upward to the center. The main assumption behind this definition of diffused power is that the ruling elites are not devoid of the will to exercise their authority and express their policy preferences, nor are they free of social constraints. Rather, the political process is determined by the dialectical relationships between these two fundamental variables.

The first concept used in explaining the persistence of the political order is based on my reinterpretation of Leonard Binder's thesis of the second stratum, which he defines as the instrument of rule without which the ruling class cannot rule. Behind the concept of the second stratum lies the cultural-geographical specificities, of which the most politically significant is the rural-urban dichotomy. The empirical referent for Binder's second stratum is the rural middle class—the class that constituted the social base of support for the Nasserist regime. In this work, however, I have expanded the time frame for the second stratum to include the pre- and post-Nasserist eras. Furthermore, I have widened the scope of its empirical referent by including the rural strata above and below the rural middle class, that is, the large landowners or *Kibar al-A'yan* and the small farmers.

The second concept used to explain stability is the strategy of mobilization and containment. This strategy, in its original form, is part of Binder's thesis that that Nasserist regime mobilized the rural middle class through the use of the single party in order to exclude the urban-based political movements represented by the Wafd and the Muslim Brotherhood from participation. A necessary dynamic quality is missing however, in Binder's thesis, since he assumes that social support for the Nasserist regime was confined to one rural stratum defined as the rural middle class. The strategy of mobilization and containment through history reveals that successive rulers mobilized different segments of the rural population, depending on circumstances in urban areas as well as on the political orientations of the rulers themselves. As this work has demonstrated, the hierarchical structure of the second stratum provides the necessary tool for explaining the paradox of harmony and conflict that has determined the relations of the ruling class with its instrument of rule.

Although the bulk of the rural middle class continued to support Nasser, neither *Kibar al-A'yan* nor the small farmers can be dismissed from consideration. In the 1950s, Nasser's policy toward the *A'yan* was ambivalent, despite agrarian reforms. During the radical trends of the 1960s, the small farmers came forward to occupy the central stage. At no time, however, did the *Kibar al-A'yan* totally disappear from the political scene, as it has been generally assumed. The absence of any revolutionary change in the countryside is directly related to the process of retraditionalization.

Retraditionalization is the concept that reveals the stabilizing role of the influential traditional elites in the strategy of the ruling class. It is not surprising that retraditionalization coincided with regime-level changes amid rural and urban instabilities at critical historical junctures. These critical moments included the 'Urabi revolt in 1881 followed immediately by the British occupation, the 1919 revolt leading to the establishment of the constitutional monarchy, the 1952 military coup and the substitution of the monarchy by a republican regime, the 1967 June War defeat that marked the retreat from radicalism, and the 1971 Corrective Movement and the 1977 Food Riots leading to the suppression of urban radicals. All these decisive events were followed by a retraditionalization process which reflected the political ascendancy of the influential *A'yan* by their representation in the parliamentary institutions.

In the majority of cases, retraditionalization was preceded by peasant militancy and ambiguous political behavior by the most influential elites. Before the British occupation in 1882, some of the *Kibar al-A'yan* supported

'Urabi but, later, were forced to turn against him as peasant militancy began to threaten the social order. Similarly, the 1919 revolt was led in part by influential *A'yan*, but their revolutionary zeal was lost as soon as peasant militancy began to be directed against them. The 1952 military coup was also preceded by peasant unrest, to which the military officers later responded by an iron fist policy tempered by inadequate reforms measures that largely left the rural *A'yan* in an influential position. This ambivalent position of the regime toward the *A'yan*, however, changed during the radicalization trends of the 1960s. Both the Kamshish Affair and the HCLF were preceded by developments in urban areas, where the regime identified its goals with leftist demands for change though it continued to feel threatened by the underground movements of the Wafd and the Muslim Brotherhood. The formation of the HCLF was a response to these demands for change, but its activities revealed the paradox inherent in attempting to bring about change with instruments that resisted change.

The results of the HCLF investigations showed that the bureaucracy, the military establishment, the representative institutions, and the single party were not immune from traditional influence. In fact, the hierarchical structure of the provincial bureaucracy was the mirror image of the rural structure. The families at the top of the social order maintained their influence at the highest echelons of the provincial bureaucracy. The same results were found in the party hierarchy and in the National Assembly. These families were also distinguished by multiple ownership, which, as I have shown, was a devise used to break up properties (as was required by the agrarian reforms) within the family structure rather than outside it. A further distinguishing feature of the families at the top of the social hierarchy in the rural areas was the continuity of their traditional influence as indicated by their descendancy from prerevolutionary, parliamentary ancestors. These families, to which I have alternately referred as the *Kibar al-A'yan* or the upper stratum, continued to maintain their traditional influence in all spheres, despite regime-level change. In all the aforementioned manifestations of local influence, the kinship bond and the adaptive capacity of the rural elites produced the objective conditions that resisted change. If there is any testimony to the persistence of traditional influence, it is the fact that the HCLF activities against the rural elites provided the legitimizing basis of the strategy of mobilization and containment in the 1970s.

Retraditionalization reflected the attempts of the ruling elite to reproduce the conditions that would ensure their continuity and the stability of the political order. Nonetheless, the costly consequences of these attempts were apparent in the crises of development. These crises were of participation, distribution, and ideology. Historically, the participation crisis goes back to the early period of the monarchy, when the king resorted to all available means to augment his authoritarian rule. The palace-created political parties in addition to the Azhar *'Ulama'* were part of the means used to thwart the Wafdist rivals, who were riding high on a crest of popularity. A pluralistic society run on the principle of a competitive party system continued to be frustrated by the apparent willingness of the influential *A'yan* to side with the king and the minority parties. Their support leads us to conclude that authoritarianism does not speak with a single voice, nor is it a self-sustaining phenomenon.

The problem of participation after the overthrow of the monarchy was partially resolved by mobilizing the rural elites through use of the single party, while the urban-based political rivals were subjected to the alternating policy of co-optation and repression. The left, composed of Marxists and communists, were the object of repression in the 1950s, followed by co-optation in the mid-1960s. The reverse order took place with the Muslim Brotherhood. The military junta at the outset cooperated with the latter within the limits they defined. But the cooperation ended, and repression was instituted when the Brethren decided to go beyond the limits drawn by the officers. Only the Wafd remained the object of total and unmitigated repression until Sadat launched the Open Door policy.

Sadat's liberal experiment was a copy of the prerevolutionary party system, with all the paraphernalia of electoral manipulation and limited participation for the opposition. Sadat was able to maintain a policy based on limited participation as long as the ruling party continued to enjoy the total support of the rural elites, and as long as the urban-based political parties accepted their limited role. None of these conditions could be fully satisfied given the opportunistic behavior of the rural elites toward urban-based competition over the rural vote. It is rather ironic that, in both the prerevolutionary party competition and during the limited participation initiated by Sadat, pluralism led to the enhancement of traditional and local influence.

The redistribution policy was closely linked with limited participation, since both had been determined by the strategy of mobilization and containment. This link is not surprising in light of the differentiated impact the agrarian reforms had on the landed elites due to prerevolutionary developments. It has been observed that the resident *A'yan* had developed their intermediary role through affiliation with competing political interests in the urban areas. They were not particularly noted for strong party loyalty however, and were prone to side with the party closely identified with the authority, unlike the absentee owners who threw their weight behind the Wafd in opposition to the king and minority parties. The conclusion derived from the dichotomous development of the landed elites is that the resident *A'yan*, through their extensive local kinship connections, preserved their traditional authority and local autonomy, important considerations in explaining the differentiated impact of both the agrarian reforms and the strategy of mobilization and containment on the landed elites during the Nasserist era.

Redistribution became a pressing issue before the outbreak of the military coup in 1952, reflected in rural unrest and migration into urban areas. Skyrocketing rental prices and the steep rise in land values were among the factors that drove rural migrants into the cities, where they joined the extremists among the Muslim Brotherhood and Misr al-Fattah. Rural unrest was further manifested by sporadic revolts by peasants on large estates. The agrarian reforms, launched by the military immediately upon its assumption of power, were designed to stabilize the countryside and neutralize extremism in the urban areas. The reforms succeeded in reducing rents, shifting the parameters of land distribution, reversing the processes of absenteeism and rural migration into the cities, and undermining the economic position of rival urban elites among the Wafd and the minority parties. Nonetheless, the reforms left the traditional social structure in the countryside largely intact.

The distribution crisis in the 1960s emerged as a consequence of the clash between the egalitarian ideology of the ruling class and its ruling strategy. The dilemma Nasser faced in the mid-1960s was how to balance the requirements of a stable political order with his desire to appeal to the small and landless peasants. Radicalization seemed to run contrary to retraditionalization—the regime's instrument of power consolidation against the relentless urban rivals. Nasser's ultimate decision was to sacrifice the egalitarian principle in favor of political stability. His shift toward the right was justified by the need to provide the necessary security as a precondition for economic growth. Furthermore, the revelations of the HCLF demonstrated the limits of radicalization, beyond which any changes in the agrarian structure would have meant changes in the instrument of rule. The substitution of law and order for egalitarianism, the dissolution of the HCLF, and the rescission of all its measures were all intended to reverse the radicalization trends. The lower classes, though, remained unresponsive to the new rhetoric of law and order, since the rhetoric of social change continued to exert such an overwhelming appeal.

The distribution crisis under Sadat was the culmination of the paradoxes inherent in the requirements of stability versus the policy preferences under a particular ideology. The Open Door policy was tailored to fit the deNasserization process, albeit deradicalization, behind the mask of economic growth, rationalization of the public sector, and infusion of foreign and domestic investments into the private sector. The limits of these policy objectives were determined by the lower classes, as was clearly manifested by the Food Riots in the urban areas in 1977. The dilemma Sadat faced was either to accelerate the process of deradicalization and thus subject himself to the wrath of the classes divested of their "socialist inheritance" or to put a halt to deradicalization and thus earn the displeasure of the upper strata in the rural and urban areas. He resolved the dilemma by attempting to balance the demands generated from below with the pressures to pursue the Open Door policy to its logical conclusion. Although he was inclined to follow the latter course, he hesitated because of its ill effects on the stability of the political order.

The distribution crisis under both Nasser and Sadat was directly related to developments in Egypt's external relations. Superpower rivalry to win Middle Eastern clients by means of aid and arms supplies allowed the ruling elites to postpone urgently needed domestic reforms. Some of the hardest choices were avoided because of the availability of an external solution. On two occasions, however, the Egyptian rulers found themselves facing the painful task of dealing with social contradictions under domestic and external pressures. Nasser's "socialist crisis" probably would not have occurred had he been able to maintain growth and equity. Sadat's "liberal crisis" would have probably been avoided had the International Monetary Fund been less sanguine about the virtue of a capitalist economy and more lenient toward a welfare-oriented policy.

The ideological crisis was neither the result of the poverty of ideas nor the outcome of cognitive failure on the part of the populace. On the contrary, Egypt has established a long tradition as the sanctuary of ideologists escaping the tyranny of their home countries. It is not surprising that Egypt has often been described as the articulate society. The openness of the society to diverse ideas and competing ideologies, coupled with the strategy of mobilization and containment, produced the ideological crises. The army officers did not come to power armed with a ready-made ideology. They adopted an eclectic view of the prevailing ideologies and often embraced the ideology of their opponents as part of the process of power consolidation. In this sense, ideology does not reflect a constitutive will, but a negating will, since it is conceived with the primary purpose of disarming opponents and winning their constituencies. Given the shifting nature of the ruling strategy, there was little consensus on what constituted the dominant value system. Ideology as the handmaiden of mobilization and containment is necessarily an ideology that lacks coherence, and its impact on the masses is confusing.

A historical review of the official ideologies beginning with the army seizure of power will reveal a bewildering array of contradictions. In the early 1950s, the army officers espoused different ideologies, although the ideology of the Muslim Brotherhood was most predominant. This predominance is not surprising given the popularity of the *Ikhwan* among the lower middle class elements, to whom the army officers appealed for support. The liquidation of the Muslim Brotherhood gave rise to a new ideology in the 1960s that had a superficial resemblance to Marxist and Leninist thought. It came to be identified with the appeal to the lower classes and the suppression of the urban and landed bourgeoisie. The ideological contradictions reached a climax under Sadat because of the heterogeneity of the classes to which he had appealed for opposing his rivals among Nasserists and former Marxists. He appealed to them in the name of liberalism and traditional values rooted in Islam, which were set in opposition to socialism and heretical beliefs.

The ideological crisis manifested itself at two levels. At the ruling elite level, the ideological crisis was apparent in the inconsistencies between the requirements of a stable political order and the expressed ideals. After the dissolution of the HCLF, the rhetoric of law and order clashed sharply with the revolutionary ideals of social change. Under Sadat, the ideological confusion was in the attempt to justify a repressive policy, while continuing to uphold a belief in liberalism. The reemergence of the Wafd—a symbol of the prerevolutionary order and the Pasha class—gave rise to the rhetoric of redistribution (the idealized principle of Nasserism) as part of liberalism and traditional values.

At the mass level, the ideological crisis occurred as a direct consequence of the unrealistic assumption on the part of the ruling elites that the constituency to which they appealed would remain ideologically confined within the limits drawn by the rulers. Both Nasser and Sadat found themselves confronting those who pitted the purity of their beliefs against the official ideology prevailing at the time. Nasser resisted the so-called "real left" or the Marxists and former communists, as the latter attempted to push Nasser's radicalism further to the left by recognizing class struggle—something he was unwilling to do since it would call into question the social base of support for the regime. The dissolution of the HCLF signalled not only an end to radicalism but also a pulling away from it.

The challenges confronting Sadat were much more complex. Sadat's appeal to liberalism, traditional values, and Islamic values was meant to draw the support of practically all those classes who had been repressed by Nasser against the Nasserists and Marxists. Nasser succeeded somewhat in keeping the Marxists and former communists under tight control and supervision, since the majority were employed by the state and were carefully watched by the party *apparatchiki* or the official left. In contrast, Sadat's liberal appeal aroused the political aspirations of the Wafd, which then attempted to constitute itself officially and appeared to challenge the political hegemony of the ruling party. Furthermore,

Sadat's appeal to religious values gave rise to the political aspirations of the *Ikhwan*, and also brought to the surface the Islamic groups or *Jama'at* who gradually gained autonomy and strongly appealed to the rural migrants. The ideological confusion climaxed when Sadat cracked down on secular and sectarian opposition in the name of both liberalism and traditional values.

The interrelationships between the concepts upholding the political order (the second stratum, mobilization and containment, and retraditionalization) and the concepts that illuminate the diametrically opposed factors, those factors that militate against political stability (the crises of participation, distribution, and ideology), were revealed by the convergences and divergencies between the local community and the ruling class. Only within the realm of the immediate and the concrete can one appreciate the subtleties, nuances, and resultant contradictions in the relations between the substructure and the superstructure. As we have noted in the chapter on Kamshish, deep resonances are often found within small noises. On the other hand, little meaning can be attributed to intercommunal relations in the absence of consideration of wide and more complex relationships of power of which they are a part.

Social relations in the village community evolved around a pattern of control and domination in opposition to autonomy and resistance. The system of domination was based on traditional authority and landownership concentrated in the hands of a few individuals united by ties of kinship. Opposed to them were the small farmers and the landless peasants, who from time to time expressed deep dissatisfaction by rebelling openly against their immediate oppressors. Relations within this system of control and domination appeared to alternate between stages, which exposed the intertwining relations between the ruling strategy and differentiated rural classes. Retraditionalization and radicalization were the bipolar extremes in a strategy of rule whose objective manifestations at the local community level became apparent in the reassertion of traditional authority or, conversely, in the rising influence of the small farmers and peasants. Between these bipolar extremes, resistance to social change and political ambivalence by the ruling elites laid behind the series of compromises to blunt the edge of social contradiction by means of political neutralizaiton and token reform.

The army seizure of power in 1952 and the formation of the HCLF marked the bipolar extremes of retraditionalization and radicalization in the strategy of the ruling class. The army intervention signalled the limit of retraditionalization, and the dissolution of the HCLF in 1967 was the watershed of radicalization. In both instances, we have noted the parallel developments of property concentration in the hands of a small minority and the attempt at redistribution through parcellization among the small peasantry. In both instances, we have also noted the parallel developments of political participation for the wealthy upper stratum and the opposite tendency of peasant mobilization. Ideology was brought into full play to express these mutually exclusive goals and purposes in the political orientation of the ruling class.

None of the above shifts, necessitated by the requirements of stability, went unresisted by members of the local community. Retraditionalization was resisted by the peasant masses, and radicalization was opposed and hindered by the upper stratum. The former was apparent in peasant agitation for social change, and the latter was reflected in the resistance of the bureaucracy and the party apparatus, that is, the instrument of rule, to change. Resistance was further apparent in the conflicting interpretation of the official ideology, which has led us to conclude that neither the dissemination of ideology was uniform nor was this ideology free from resistance and counterpressures. As we have observed in the Kamshish Affair, the attempt to reconcile parochial interests with the official ideology lacked symmetry and coherence. The checkered political career of the "martyr" of Kamshish revealed how the attempt at reconcilation was frustrated by local rivalry, by conditions of inequality, and by vested interests in the bureaucracy. If anything can be learned from Kamshish, it is that signification is multiple. Symbols mean different things to different people. They are twisted, changed, and taken out of context to suit particular interests.

In sum, stalled societies do escape the horrors of revolutionary upheavals and civil wars, but at the cost of postponing the necessary political and social reforms. With the increase in rural migration into urban areas and with the mounting costs of feeding the urban population, the likelihood is greater for the crises of development to become far more overwhelming than the attemtps to reproduce the conditions of political stability through retraditionalization.

Postscript

I N THE FIRST FEW months of his presidency, Mubarak cultivated the illusion that he was on the side of all groups and classes with the exception of the extremists among the Islamic *Jama'at* and the Coptic minority. He presented an olive branch to domestic opposition and, in the Egyptian spirit of letting bygones be bygones, invited the leading members of the secular and religious opposition who were imprisoned by Sadat during the September 1981 crackdown to the presidential palace on the day of their release from prison in November 1981. Mubarak made it clear that there would be no return to repression. He promised that he would let the opposition express its legitimate interests and that he would hold regular meetings to exchange views with its leading members. But, with characteristic indecisiveness, Mubarak wavered over rescinding the laws that curtailed personal freedoms and refused to end the state of emergency imposed after Sadat's assassination.

Mubarak further assured the entrenched interests in his administration and the foreign powers, including the Israelis, that he was continuing along the path taken by Sadat and that he would honor and abide by the spirit of Camp David. He was eager to impress upon his Arab detractors that there would be no turning back and that they must reconcile themselves to existing realities. Yet, Mubarak started talking about nonalignment in tones reminiscent of Nasser, paid official visits to nonaligned countries, attended in person the nonaligned conference in New Delhi, and withdrew the Egyptian ambassador from Tel Aviv after the Israeli invasion of Lebanon in June 1982. He has also provided diplomatic and military support to Iraq during her five-year war with Iran. These steps were apparently taken to curry favor with moderate Arabs.

Internally, Mubarak carefully began to distance himself from the influential members of the ruling party—the National Democratic Party (NDP)—who acquired a great deal of notoriety in the public eye because of the corrupt and illegitimate means by which its members have amassed wealth. Some of them were close relatives of Sadat, including his brother 'Essmat al-

Sadat. Under the slogan of *al-Tahara* (purity), the new regime began to pro-
secute the "fat cats" in the private sector and in its own ruling party. The first to
be put on trial was Rashad 'Uthman, the NDP's secretary for food security in
Alexandria and a member of the People's Assembly. Afer Rashad 'Uthman, it
was the turn of Sadat's brother, who revealed the names of ministers and
bureaucrats who aided and abetted him. These revelations led to a minor
cabinet reshuffle in April 1982; however, only five ministers made their exit
much to the disappointment of those who were clamoring for radical changes.

Mubarak's fight against corruption coincided with a unique conference
held in November 1981, attended by social scientists and experts to discuss
hypocrisy as a widespread social and political disease.[1] There could not have
been a more timely subject for discussion because of the intensification of the
struggle over Mubarak's "soul," to use Saad al-Din Ibrahim's euphemism in his
description of the various "social forces" that attempted to win Mubarak over to
their way of thinking.[2] There were Nasserists who continued to espouse the
dreams of reforms and social justice. There were also the Wafdists, who believed that the panacea for all Egyptian ills was the establishment of a
democratic order. More ingenious Egyptians within the intellectural community, who identified themselves as social democrats, firmly believed in the
possibility of reconciling Nasser's social justice with Sadat's liberalism. Sayyid
Yassin, for example, argued in favor of fusing the most positive aspects of
Nasser's socialism and Sadat's policy of *infitah*, that is, social justice and
democracy.[3]

Most opposition members, however, encouraged by the fight against corruption within the ruling party, entertained the hope of persuading Mubarak
to distance himself from the rank and file of the NDP, while the latter fought
hard through the media and behind the scenes to keep Mubarak firmly on their
side. The opposition voiced the opinion that Mubarak should not identify
himself with any party and should instead become an arbiter among all parties.
The NDP's leadership responded by correctly observing that it was wishful
thinking on the part of the opposition to hope to separate Mubarak from the
party that he himself had helped create under the direction of Sadat.[4]

Mubarak's reaction to this intensified struggle was to confirm his decision
to continue Sadat's path. He warned against digging up the past, *Nabsh al-
Madhi*, and rejected the insinuation made by the opposition that fighting corruption meant discarding the Open Door policy. He also confirmed his belief
in the NDP when its rank and file convened a conference in January 1982 to
confer upon him the leadership of the party. There was open recognition on
both sides that they needed each other. On the other hand, under the pretext
that the economic order needed urgent attention, Mubarak turned a deaf ear to

the opposition's demands for freedom to organize and express freely its legitimate interests. Some of the hopes Mubarak had aroused for an early end to repression were dissipated, which caused Fouad Mursi to warn that the countdown for another September—an allusion to Sadat's crackdown on the opposition in September 1981—had begun.[5]

A conference was convened in February 1982 to discuss economic problems and to suggest remedies for the widening social gaps. The conference ended with recommendations that reaffirmed the mixed nature of the economy. The recommendations included the continuation of the policy of *infitah* as well as centralized control and planning, although the conference emphasized the productive aspects of the policy of *infitah* and recommended curtailment of the importation of luxury goods. The food subsidy was to be maintained, but no attempt was made to devise plans for ensuring that subsidies went to those whom they were meant for in the first place. As it now stands, the food subsidy is available to everyone, including the affluent classes. With the increase in the urban population and the lowering of agricultural production, direct subsidies amounted to $2 billion in 1984, the wheat subsidy alone coming to $400 million. Contradictions remain in place in the countryside, too. Agricultural production is impeded by two parallel markets. One market is a free market for cash crops, the other market being that for traditional, government-regulated field crops, whose prices are kept below the free market rate. Rent controls gave rise to another serious contradiction, which manifested itself in tension between tenants and landlords. In sum, the socialist and capitalist modes in the relations of production continue to coexist in an uneasy tension and imbalance. The economic system cries out for reform but, as Mousa Sabri cautioned, sound economic policies do not necessarily go hand in hand with sound political considerations.[6] For the time being, the Mubarak regime has opted to follow its predecessor's policies by maintaining both the *infitah* and a welfare-oriented system, the combined effects of which are reflected in severe balance-of-payment deficits that increase Egyptian dependence on American and Western support.

The contrast between a continuous political order and unstable social and economic conditions will become more obvious when we examine the changes introduced by Mubarak into the political system. It should, however, be borne in mind that the final outcome of these changes was the affirmation of the existing political order. The changes were apparent in the new electoral procedures under which the elections to the People's Assembly were held in May 1984. The new procedures reduced the electoral districts from 176 to 48 and, for the first time in the electoral history of Egypt, introduced proportional representation and voting by party slate in place of elections by absolute majority in the traditional, two-member districts. The new electoral procedures were viewed by the opposition parties as a hopeful sign for securing adequate representation in the assembly elections in May 1984, despite a clause that limited party representation to 8 percent of the votes cast. As a result of these changes, the number of seats in the assembly increased from 382 to 448. The distribution of seats continued to reflect a rural bias, but becasue of the introduction of proportional representation and voting by party slate, some observers formed the erroneous impression that the electoral system would no longer be influenced by traditional powers.

Furthermore, the Mubarak regime allowed the New Wafd to reconstitute itself under the leadership of the old guard of prerevolutionary elites after numerous court battles. The regime continued to deny official recognition to the Muslim Brotherhood, but did not oppose the electoral alliance forged between it and the New Wafd. The other parties, which contested the May elections, were the ruling NDP, the Labor Party, the Liberal Party, and the left-wing Tajamu'. All four parties were Sadat's creations between 1976 and 1979, and they never totally escaped the stigma of their origins. The major departure from previous patterns was the emergence of the New Wafd as a political force, a move that led some Egyptians to entertain the hope that Egypt was at the threshold of a far-reaching change.

The alliance between the New Wafd and the Muslim Brotherhood was a marriage of convenience to improve the former's electoral chances, but it was consumated at the cost of liberals and secularists, who then defected. Judging from the results of the elections, apparently the Wafdist leadership miscalculated the strength of the Muslim Brotherhood among the urban lower middle classes and rural migrants. Nonetheless, the Wafdists were not the only ones who found the appeal to religion too strong to resist. All the parties that contested the elections, including the NDP, committed themselves to upholding the *Shari'ah* (Islamic laws). The NDP further appealed to the ideals of the 23 July revolution (1952) against the Pasha class and the bourgeoisie, who stood behind the New Wafd. During the heat of the campaign, Nasser's voice and pictures appeared in the government-controlled mass media, following a long absence. Amid this ideololgical confusion, Heikal, in his usually eloquent style, cast a shadow of gloom over Egypt's future. He said Egypt had lost confidence in her capacity to regain her sense of direction.[7] His statement may be so, but I suspect that the real reason for his despair was that the political course seemed to be predetermined, as the results of the assembly elections show.

The results of the asssembly elections reaffirmed the political formula the army officers had devised since assuming power in 1952. The NDP won an overwhelming majority (390 seats). No minority party, including the Labor Party, the Liberal Party, and the Tajamu', secured 8 percent of the votes cast nationally. The only opposition party to emerge in the assembly was the New Wafd in alliance with members of the Muslim Brotherhodod. Together they won fifty-eight seats, with the majority of the seats going to the New Wafd. Roughly half of the Wafdists strength in the assembly was derived from urban areas, the remaining seats being won in scattered rural areas.

The election returns were the subject of a valuable study by Ali al-Din Hillal in al-Ahram's Institute for Political and Strategic Studies.[8] His study shows that the opposition derived its strength primarily from the urban areas. Of the votes cast, the opposition received 38 percent in Cairo, 36 percent in Suez, and 32 percent in Alexandria. These areas also registered a low voter turnout: 20 percent in the Suez, 23 percent in Cairo, and 28 percent in Alexandria. By contrast, voter participation was strongest in the rural areas. Of the densely populated areas, Minufiyya had the highest voter turnout (55 percent), followed by Qalubiyya (53 percent), Beni Suwayf (49 percent), Gharbiyya (47 percent), and Qena (43 percent).

There is no doubt that the overwhelming victory of the NDP was due to the support it received from the rural areas. Behind this victory was the NDP's mobilization of traditional elites. However, the noticeable increase in the number of traditional elites, some of whom were direct descendants of pre-revolutionary parliamentary members going as far back as the nineteenth century, may be attributed not only to the mobilization strategy of the NDP but also to the fact that the New Wafd was competing for the same constituency. There is even evidence to suggest that members of the elite families were split by party competition for their votes and support. Nonetheless, the NDP won the support of the majority of the rural notables because, in their eyes, it was the government party. Neither changes in the electoral procedures nor the reemergence of the New Wafd seemed to affect the political formula based on traditional support from the rural areas.

The hegemony of the NDP must also be attributed to the weakness of the political right and left. The New Wafd continues to function under a leadership that has not divorced itself from the past or learned anything since it lost power to the army officers. The leaders of the New Wafd evoke memories of a bygone age, long buried under the historical heap. The New Wafd won a substantial number of seats largely on its nationalist-secularist past. It was a strange spectacle indeed when, in a recent gathering of Wafdists, men in the audience shouted "Long live the Wafd, the enemy of the British" and "Down with (British) occupation." The party's future orientation is unclear, particularly in light of its electoral alliance with the *Ikhwan*.

The return of the Wafd is likely to lead to polarization between the Nasserists—the beneficiaries of the agrarian reforms and the socialist decrees and the employees of the public sector—on the one hand, and the old class of bourgeoisie and the new class that has prospered thanks to Sadat's economic liberalizatoin, on the other. Wafdist leaders have privately expressed the concern that polarization could open the door to direct military intervention or suppression by the government in the name of preserving the "gains of the 23 July Revolution."

The swing of the pendulum toward the socialist direction must await a change in the political orientation of the authorities. The Tajamu' lacks the organizational strength and the followers to make this change a distinct possibility. As revealed by the conference of the peasants union in April 1983, there are deep divisions between small landowners and tenants, worsened by changes in tenurial relations and by higher rents. Although Shahinda often blames the government and the secret police for the weakness of the party in the rural areas, she also recognizes that the left is dominated by intellectuals who know more about abstract theorizing and pedantic logic than about organizing peasants. She cited this reason when explaining why she lost to the NDP candidate in her own district at the May 1984 election to the People's Assembly. But she continues to hope, since, for her and for the small band of peasants clustered around her, the Kamshish Affair as yet remains unfinished.

Appendixes

A. Methodological Note

Expected Value

To examine the relationship between the categories of the dependent and independent variables, we have used the expected value as a basis of comparison for the observed value. A difference of five or more generally indicates a strong relationship between the categories. The expected value is computed as follows:

$$\text{Expected value} = \frac{(\text{Row total}) \times (\text{Column total})}{\text{Grand total}}$$

Scaled Variables

We have constructed several scales to differentiate the families by status in the provincial administration and party organization, and by family size and total amount of landownership in 1966. Family position on each unit of the hierarchically structured provincial administration and party organization was determined by the highest status achieved by a family member.

The scaled units for the provincial administration from the lowest to the highest level are as follows:

0	1	2	3	4
No Administrative Rank	Shaykh	'Umdah	District Council Officer	Governorate Council Member

The scaled units for the NU organization from the lowest to the highest level are:

0	1	2	3
No Party Rank	Committee Member	District Officer	National Assembly Member (1957, 1959)

The scaled units for the ASU organization from the lowest to the highest level are:

0	1	2	3	4
No Party Rank	Committee Member	Basic Unit Officer	District Officer	Governorate Committee Member

The families have also been differentiated by the number of adult members. The scaled units for family population (FPS) are:

1	2	3	4
<10	11–20	21–30	>31

The scaled units for total family landownership in 1966 (TOTFLOS) are:

1	2	3	4	5	6
<5	5–50	50–100	100–200	200–500	>500

Units of Measurement Used in the Multiple Regression:

AFRACT = Family fraction in ASU committees.

Family fraction = $\dfrac{\text{Family total on ASU committees}}{\text{Total ASU committee membership}}$

ASCBU = Number of ASU basic unit officers

ASUDO = 1, if family has ASU district officer
0, if no ASU district officer

DAGCP = 1, if family had director of agricultural cooperative
0, if famiy had no director of agricultural cooperative

DS 2 = 1, if family had prerevolutionary M.P.
0, if no prerevolutionary M.P.

DSO = If family had no prerevolutionary or postrevolutionary M.P.

FP = Number of family members

FPS = Scaled units of family population

GVCMP   =   1, if family had member in ASU governorate committee
      0, if no member in ASU governorate committee

LRL 4   =   1, if subject to land reform, 1952
     0, if not subject to land reform, 1952

LRL 2   =   1, if subject to land reform, 1969
     0, if not subject to land reform, 1969

MEMGC   =   1, if family had a member in the governorate council
      (administrative unit)
      0, if no member in the governorate council

MPNU   =   1, if family had M.P. under NU
     0, if no M.P. under NU

NSHK   =   Number of Shaykhs within a family

NUDO   =   Number of NU district officers within a family

NUFRACT   =   Family fraction in NU committees

$$\text{Family fraction} = \frac{\text{Family total on NU committees}}{\text{Total NU committee membership}}$$

NUMDA   =   Number of *'Umdas* within a family

ODC   =   1, if family had district officer (administrative unit)
    0, if no district officer

TOTFLOS   =   Scaled units of total family landownership in 1966

B: Factors Influencing Patterns of Property Distribution

To study the factors influencing the patterns of property distribution within the rural elite families, a regression of the dichotomous dependent variable of multiple large landownership, upper and lower groups of large landowners (LOWN), was performed with the degrees of property concentration as reflected by the application of the land reform laws (LRL), descendant status (DS), adult family population (FPS), total family landownership in 1966 (TOTFLOS), and regional distribution (UPLOW) as independent variables. The families not subjected to the land reform laws (LRL = 1) and the families in the categories of small or medium property owners (LOWN = 1) were removed to avoid circularity between the independent and dependent variables.

  Furthermore, since it was suspected that the families upon whom the first land reform law was enforced in 1952 (LRL = 4) and the families with prerevolutionary M.P. descendants (DS = 2) would emerge as important, dummy variables, LRL4 and DS2, were introduced. Similarly, dummy variables were constructed for the families subjected for the first time to the third land reform law in 1969 (LRL = 2), and also for the notable families that maintained local influence only (DS = 0). These dummy variables were denoted LRL2 and DSO. The middle level group of families, that is, the families subjected for the first time to the second land reform law in 1961 (LRL = 3) and the families with postrevolutionary M.P.'s (DS = 1), were used as reference groups.

The regression equation was as follows:

LOWN: 1.67 + .22 LRL4 - .28 LRL2 + .28 DS2 - .08 DSO
         (.35)   (.12)   (.15)   (.16)   (.17)

         - .03 FPS + .11 TOTFLOS + .13 UPLOW
          (.06)   (.07)   (.11)

The variables LRL4, LRL2, DS2, and TOTFLOS had coefficients approaching significance at the .05 level, although none actually attained that level. However, the overall F value (6.22) and 7 and 56 degrees of freedom (P = .0001) indicates that, taken as a group, the independent variables had explanatory power. The above equation could predict into which group of multiple land ownership (LOWN = 2 or LOWN = 3) a given family would fall.

We will use the above regression equation to predict into which group the Zahran family (See Figure 15) falls. As we have observed earlier, the Zahran famiy had at least one family member subject to the first agrarian reform law, thus indicating a high concentration of individually owned property (LRL4). Furthermore, the family had ancestors in the prerevolutionary parliament (DS2), with a score of 3 on the scaled variable (see Appendix A) of adult family population (FPS), and with a score of 6 on the scaled variable of total family landownership in 1966 (TOTFLOS). Also, the family is an Upper Egyptian family (UPLOW 1). The predicted value for the Zahran family may be computed as:

LOWN = 1.67 + .22 + .28 - .03(3) + .11(6) + .13 = 2.87

Since the resultant value is closest to 3, one would predict that the Zahran family would fall into the upper group of multiple large landownership

(LOWN = 3), indicating four or more landowners who were subjected to one or more land reform laws.

C. The Secret Correspondence of Kamshish

Administrative Control
No W/31/2637
10/May/1966

Subject: Complaints of National Union members in Kamshish regarding the violations of the agrarian reform law by al-Fiqqi family

To: Abd al-Fattah Abu al-Fadl, Secretary of the General Secretariat for Membership Affairs in the ASU

Please be informed that: 1. complaints were received from a number of National Union members in Kamshish against al-Fiqqi family during 1960 and 1961. The complaints were investigated by Mohammad Zuhdi, deputy prosecutor, appellate court in Cairo, at that time.

2. The Administrative Control investigated the complaints over violations of the agrarian reform laws and the results were sent in a report to the director of the Office of the Prosecutor in the State Security, no. 2047 dated 1 July 1961. The report pointed out the possibility of collusion between the owners and those who were entrusted with the task of implementing the agrarian reform laws. There were also criminal activities which go under the penal code.

3. A copy of the report was sent to Mahmud Abd al-Nasir, director of the office of Kamal Rifaat, Minister of State, no. 205 (top secret) dated 13 July 1961, for information and necessary action.

4. A complaint was received from Salah Mohammad Husain and Mrs. Shahinda Shawqi Maqlad and others from Kamshish, Minufiyya. These complaints were sent to the deputy secretary in the Ministry of Agrarian Reforms at that time, no. 3304 dated October 1961, for investigation and response. The matter was expedited by other letters, no. 3757 dated 30 October 1961, no. 146 dated 9 January 1962 and no. 2678 dated 23 June 1962, although the results of the investigation were not received.

5. A complaint by Salah Mohammad Husain and others against Ahmad Abdullah and his brother for violating the agrarian reform law no. 127 dated 1961

was sent to us from the General Director of Agrarian Reform Bureau on 24 October 1961. The complaint was forwarded to Mohammad Zuhdi, the director of the prosecutor office in Cairo in a letter no. 3868 dated 6 November 1961 for informaiton and necessary action.

6. Attached is a copy of the report of the Administrative Control containing the results of the investigation mentioned in paragraphs 2 and 3.

Director of Administrative Control
Kamal Mohammad al-Gharr

[All the documents related to the HCLF's investigations and the Kamshish Affair upon which this study is based are in the possession of the author.]

General Investigation Bureau
Internal Activities Branch
Section of Combating Communism

Top Secret

Memorandum

— We have been informed that Salah al-Din Mohammad Husain Maqlad and some of those who mix with him among the inhabitants of Kamshish in Al-Minufiyya Governorate hold seminars for raising socialist consciousness in the village. The sessions are attended by some of the peasants.

— The aforementioned and his friends raise in the discussions during these meetings the following topics:

* They call for the collectivization of agricultural and the abolitionment of private property. They are calling for the establishment of cooperative farming parallel to the Communist countries.

* They maintain that the socialist thinking in the Arab Republic is very close to the Marxist ideology and that its recognition of private property is temporary, dictated by the peculiarities of the present stage.

— They disseminate these opinions among the inhabitants which have caused harm and confusion. There is a feeling of anxiety caused by the belief that this was a communist activity.

Comment

1) Salah al-Din Mohammad Husain belonged to the dissolved Muslim Brotherhood. His place of residence was restricted by a military order on 26 Nov. 1953. He was arrested by military order on 23 Nov. 1954 and released on 25 Feb. 1956. He was exempted from the Presidential decree of

political disenfranchisement. He was arrested on 9 September 1965 and released on 14 September 1965.

2) The aforementioned and his friends who organized these activities are antagonistic to the feudal al-Fiqqi family in Kamshish and previously some of the communists exploited the hatred of the village inhabitants toward al-Fiqqi family to recruit some youth who are enthusiastic for the communist movement.

General Investigation Bureau
Internal Activities Communism

Information originating from Minufiyya
No. 351
Registration No. 33637

(Top Secret) 9742/66

To Mohammad Abd al-Fattah Abu al-Fadl
Member of the Secretariat General for Membership Affairs in the Arab Socialist Union

Subsequent to our letter No. 5504/66 dated 2nd March 1966 in regard to the attempts of Salah al-Din Mohammad Husain and some of his associates from the village Kamshish, district Tila in al-Minufiyya Governorate, to disseminate ideas in conflict with our socialism during the consciousness raising seminars in this village causing confusion and leaving bad effects on the inhabitants, we would like to inform you that, although Mustafa 'Azb member of the National Assembly and the Executive Bureau in the Governorate and Mohammad Abu Shadi, Secretary of the ASU in District Tila, explained our socialist ideas in a seminar held in the village on 11 March, it was apparent that Salah al-Din Mohammad Husain insisted after the conclusion of the discussion in telling the peasants that our socialism is influenced by Marxist thought.

As a result, a dispute took place among the inhabitants. They were divided into two camps. One camp supported Salah al-Din Mohammad Husain and the other camp opposed him. They exchanged accusations since the first camp called the second camp reactionary, while the second camp called the first camp communist.

The camp opposing Salah al-Din Husain began to boycott the seminars. They boycotted the one held on 18 March to raise the socialist consciousness because they were controlled by Salah al-Din's associates. Most of this session was used to attack the other camp. The followers of Salah al-Din terrorized their opponents. Some of them carry sticks. It was also reported that on the day of the seminars on the 11th, Salah al-Din fired one shot from inside one of the homes with the purpose of terrorizing his opponents.

We see that the continuation of the hold that the associates of Salah al-Din have on the consciousness raising sessions through violent means will lead to dangerous divisions among the ASU members in the villages as well as cause harm to internal security. The team led by Salah al-Din includes the following:

Shawqi Abdullah Sharif	Official in the social security unit in Shibin al-Kom who has communist inclinations
Ahmad Ali Rajab	Peasant
Badrawi Ahmad Aman	Sports director in the Agricultural Institute, Shibin al-Kom
Kamal Attiya	Elementary school teacher, Secretary of the ASU in the village
Abdel Hameed Attiya	Peasant and brother of the former

We are of the opinion that the consciousness raising sessions should be held under the supervision of the Executive Bureau and the General Secretariat in the Governorate.

> Liwa'
> Director of General Investigation Bureau
> Hasan Talaat

From the Department of General Investigation/Internal activities/ *Communism*/ top secret. No. 5504.66

To: Mohammad Abd al-Fattah Abu al-Fadl, Member of the Secretariat General of the Arab Socialist Union.

We are enclosing a memorandum on the activities of Salah al-Din Mohammad Hussain and on some of those who mix with him of the inhabitants of the village Kamshish in al-Minufiyya Governorate. For your information.

> Liwa'
> Director of the General Investigation
> Bureau
> Hasan Talaat

[It was received in the Secretariat for Membership Affairs on *2 March 1966*]

D. Samples of the Confidential Reports Submitted to the Higher Committee for the Liquidation of Feudalism

Military Criminal Investigation

Memorandum
In regard to the feudalist Ahmad Hasan Abdun
From Ghazalat Abdun—Faqus District Sharqiyya Governorate

First: Investigations
1. Ahmad Hasan was a Wafdist deputy before the revolution. He was occupying the post of the 'Umda of Ghazalat Abdun until the end of 1955. He is politically disenfranchised from the Arab Socialist Union. He was dismissed from the 'Umdiyya because of his criminal activity.

2. His Children
Hasan Ahmad Hasan Abdun: student at the Cotton Institute in Alexandria. He was elected to the 'Umdiyya post unopposed. No one dared to nominate himself for this post. He is occupying the post of secretary of the Arab Socialist Union in the village.
Ali Ahmad Hasan Abdun: Student and dependent.
Alsayyid Ahmad Hasan Abdun: Student and dependent.
Dawlat Ahmad Hasan Abdun: Married.

3. His Brothers:
1. Abdel Rahman Hasan Abdun: Deputy 'Umda and Shaykh al-Balad.
2. Imam Hasan Abdun: Member of the Committee of Twenty of the Arab Socialist Union.

4. His Relatives:
1. Ismail Ghunaim Abdun. His cousin (brother's son). Member of the National Assembly (elected from) Faqus district.
2. Ahmad Abu Abdun. His cousin (brother's son). One of the wealthy members of the Faqus community and owns several buildings there.
3. Mahmoud Nadim Abdel Mu'ti Hussein. His cousin (his father's sister son). Chairman of the city council of Faqus.

Second: His property before the (enactment) of law 127 for the year 1961:
[A detailed account of lots bought or disposed of in the Zimam of Ghazalat Abdun omitted by the author]

Total: 156 Faddans [fractions omitted by the author]

Third: (the application) of law 127 for the year 1961.
In accordance with law no. 127 for the year 1961, the aforementioned gave the following list of lots he decided to keep:
[A detailed account of lots in Zimam Ghazalat Abdun is omitted]

Total: 100 Faddans
Property earmarked for confiscation: 18 faddans [fractions omitted] of fallow land in Sam'ana village in Faqus district.

Fourth: Comparison between his property mentioned above [i.e., before the application of law 127/61] and his testimony [following the application of law 127/61]. After comparing his property before and after the application of the law, it became apparent that the aforementioned violated the law by omitting to mention 37 faddans [fractions omitted] possessed by him, but registered under different names.

Fifth: [A detailed account of property bought and disposed of in the names of the children is omitted since their totals are stated in summary form in clause six below.]

Sixth: Family landownership: From the above it becomes obvious that family ownership is as follows:
156 faddans owned by Ahmad Hasan Abdun
 55 faddans owned by Hasan Ahmad Hasan Abdun
 31 faddans owned by Ali Ahmad Hasan Abdun
 31 faddans owned by Alsayyid Ahmad Hasan Abdun
 13 faddans owned by Dawlat Ahmad Hasan Abdun
290 Total [the discrepancy in the total is due to the omission of fractions by the author]

Seven: Landholdings [The unit actually cultivated and registered with local agricultural cooperative. Landholdings *hiyazat* include both owned and leased-in property.]
After reviewing the records of the agricultural cooperative in Ghazalat Abdun the lots stated below were found to be registered in the names of the following:
138 faddans, lot no. 56, held by Ahmad Hasan Abdun in Zimam Ghazalat Abdun.

38 faddans, lot no. 1, held by Ahmad Hasan Abdun in Zimam Sam'ana.

55 faddans, lot no. 9, held by his son Hasan Ahmad Hasan Abdun in Zimam Ghazalat Abdun.

23 faddans, lot no. 2, held by his uncle Ahmad Abdun Muhammad of the property owned by Ahmad Hasan Abdun in Ghazalat Abdun.

3 faddans, lot no. 47, held by Imam Ahmad Abdun Muhammad, cousin of the owner of the property of Ahmad Hasan Abdun.

6 faddans, lot no. 246, held by Abdun Hasan Abdun, brother of the owner, of the property of Ahmad Hasan Abdun in Ghazalat Abdun.

2 faddans, lot no. 31, in the name of Hasan Muhammad Timraz, steward of the owner, of the property of Ahmad Hasan Abdun in Ghazalat Abdun.

---

268 faddans [discrepancy in the total is due to the omission of fractions by the author.]

This is in addition to area amounting to 22 faddans owned by others which came under his control as stated by Muhammad al-Bazz Ibrahim, the clerk at the agricultural cooperative in Ghazalat Abdun. Appendix no. 4.

Eight: His Exploitaton of Peasants

1. Tenancy contracts do not exist between him and the peasants and he exloits them in the worst manner because he appropriates all the crops, while leaving to them only meager amounts of rice and wheat.

2. He submitted to the agricultural cooperative two weeks ago sharecropping contracts, when he sensed that the state was taking steps to liquidate feudalism. The contracts were for a three-year duration from 1966 to October 1969, according to the testimony of Muhammad al-Bazz, the clerk at the cooperative. Appendix 4 and 6.

3. He controls the irrigation [facilities] adjoining his property and a water pump.

4. He imposes forced labor on peasants to work in [his] orchards without payment of wages or against very low wages. Whoever opposes him is punished by beating and torture to be followed by his expulsion from the land and the villages, as stated by Abdel Azim Ibrahim Muhammad. Appendix 3.

Nine: Terrorist and Criminal Behavior:

Ahmad Hasan Abdun is famous in Faqus district for his criminal behavior and recurrent aggression against citizens in the village and its surrounding areas. The following are few examples:

1. He was accused of killing Muhammad al-Qalshani Ibrahim from the village of Ghazalat Abdun approximately ten years ago. The latter vanished from sight and no traces of him were to be found until now. No one came forward to

testify against him out of fear. The investigations were suspended for lack of evidence. He took possession of the land belonging to the slain peasant which amounts to more than four faddans of the village Zimam.

2. He beat and tortured the farmer Hasan Ahmad Ali, known as Hasan Naqah, who was his private guard, by shoving a wire into his anus which led to bleeding and death. This incident took place because the victim refused to comply with the wishes of the feudalist's wife who was known for her bad behavior. This took place five years ago and no one in the village dared to lodge a complaint against him.

3. He also beat and tortured the farmer Abdel Wahid al-'Aryshi who died as a result of his injury. The reason was a dispute over a demand made by the victim for the conversion into hiyazah a plot of land he was cultivating, but owned by the feudalist. This incident took place some four years ago and no one in the village dared to complain [to the authorities].

4. He beat and tortured the lawyer Abdel Azim 'Idrawis by burying him up to the shoulders in a cemetery at night. He was rescued by his relatives. But as a result of this incident the aforementioned lawyer lost his mind. He now lives as an insane person in the village of Ghazalat Abdun. This incident took place three years ago.

5. He beat and tortured the farmer Abdel Hafiz Ali Alsayyid by tying him to his car and dragging him along the village roads until he reached the front of his store. The victim was bare and he was beaten and maimed in front of his mother. This took place because the victim demanded the conversion into hiyazah a plot of land he was cultivating that belonged to the feudalist.

6. He beat and tortured Amna Mahmoud, wife of the farmer Abdel Aziz Abdel Qadr, during the holy month of Ramadan, by forcing her to break her fast. He then beat her children, while her husband was lying sick. They were expelled from the village and went to settle in 'Izbat al-Manshiyya. This incident took place following the demand of the victim for the conversion into hiyazah of a plot of land he was cultivating but belonged to the feudalist.

7. He beat the citizen Ahmad Yusif in the mosque while he was praying. He also assaulted his wife and, when Muhammad Ali Abdel 'Al, the teacher in the 'Izbah, intervened to protect his aunt, he, too, was assaulted by hitting him with a liquor bottle which he held in his hand.

8. He led a group of regular and private guards as well as members of his gang in an attack on the 'Izbat of Haj Ibrahim Najm, close to the village of Ghazalat Abdun. They fired several rounds of ammunition to terrorize the peasants. The attack was caused by an old dispute between him and the owner of the 'Izbah over a piece of land.

9. He goaded the wife of the fruit seller Abdel Latif Ali to run away from her marital abode and coaxed her to stay with him for a long time until her husband was forced to divorce her. Thereupon, the feudalist married her and she continues to be his wife until now.

10. He assaulted the farmer Ahmad Marihli and his son Abdel Raziq and forced them to flee the village because they demanded that the [plot which they had cultivated] and owned by the feudalist be made into a landholding [hiyazah].

11. He had a dispute with his relative Muhammad al-Bazz, the clerk at the agricultural cooperative, because the latter resisted his requests for greater quantity of fertilizers than his alloted quota. He put the warehouse of the cooperative on fire causing damage amounting to 180 pounds which were paid by the aforementioned clerk. This incident took place in 1963. He also instigated some of his aides to let the water flow into the warehouse that caused some damage to the stocked fertilizers with the purpose to mete out vengeance on the cooperative's clerk.

Despite all these criminal incidents and the knowledge of the village inhabitants of their occurrences, no one dared to accuse him out of fear.

Ten: The results [of the investigation]

1. The aforementioned violated the agrarian reform law no. 127 for the year 1961 since he did not mention in his testimony the lands possessed by him amounting to 37 faddans.

2. He holds together with his sons and daughters 290 faddans. Exploiting his tenants by making out fictitious holdings in their names [at the agricultural cooperative] which enabled him to possess greater quantities of fertilizers than what he was entitled to receive. This he was able to achieve by forcing the farmers to affix their stamps on the receipts.

3. He was able to get his son, the student in the Cotton Institute in Alexandria and where he is now residing, appointed to the 'Umda post in the village as well as the post of Secretary of the Arab Socialist Union so that he will continue to impose his authority and omnipotence on the peasants as described above.

4. The aforementioned exploits the peasants and indulges in criminal activities against them in order to realize his objectives as mentioned before.

Opinion

1. Imposing sequestration on Ahmad Hasan Abdun and his family and his removal together with his family from the rural areas.

2. Dismissal of Hasan Ahmad Hasan Abdun from his post as 'Umda of the

village of Ghazalat Abdun as well as from the post of the secretariat of the Arab Socialist Union.

3. Handing over usurped lands to their owners as stated in the land registers.

4. Dismissal of the following:

— Abdel Rahman Hasan Abdun   Deputy 'Umda and Shaykh al-Balad.

— Imam Hasan Abdun   Member of the Committee of Twenty in the village

5. Removal of Ahmad Abu Abdun and his family from the rural areas.

6. Sequestration of the property of Ahmad Abu Abdun and its distribution among peasants on tenancy basis under the supervision of the agricultural cooperative society.

Submitted for consideration

Colonel Hasan Ali Khalil
Commander, Military Criminal Investigations
Signature

The Arab Socialist Union
The Executive Bureau
Beheira Governorate

Report
On the Hinnawi Family in the Village of Kafr Awanah
in Itay al-Barud District

The investigations on the Hinnawi family in the village of Kafr al-Awanah in District Itay al-Barud showed that it constitutes in its collectivity occupations and administrative feudalism [since] some of them occupy administrative positions. Other [family members] are members of the Committee of Twenty of the Arab Socialist Union and the board of the Agricultural Cooperative in the village, as follows:

1. Said Abdel Latif al-Hinnawi   'Umda
2. Abdel Aziz Khalid al-Hinnawi   Shaykh al-Balad
3. Hashim Hasan al-Hinnawi   Shaykh al-Balad

Second: Members of the Arab Socialist Union

1. Said Abdel Latif al-Hinnawi	Secretary
2. Muhammad Hasan Hussein al-Hinnawi	Member
3. Subhi Kamil al-Hinnawi	Member
4. Halim Khalid al-Hinnawi	Member
4. Hashim Muhammad Hasan al-Hinnawi	Member
5. Ahmad Rafiq Abdel Latif al-Hinnawi	Member

Third: Members of the Agricultural Cooperative Board

1. Subhi Kamil al-Hinnawi	Chairman
2. Abdel Latif al-Hinnawi	Member

Other Family members

Major Mustafa Shalabi al-Hinnawi	Air Force
Major Hussein Hamdi al-Hinnawi	Armed Forces
Lt. Abdel Majid Fadl al-Hinnawi	Armed Forces
Lt. Sharif Labib al-Hinnawi	Armed Forces
Abdel Latif Fadl al-Hinnawi	Cadet in War College
Ashraf Labib Shalabi al-Hinnawi	Cadet in War College
Major Baligh Shalabi al-Hinnawi	Security Department
Amin Abdel Latif al-Hinnawi	Legal Consultant
Muhammad Disuqi Abdel Latif al-Hinnawi	Attorney
Mahmoud Abdel Latif al-Hinnawi	Director/Ministry of Agriculture

It was revealed that the total ownership of the family in agricultural lands amounts to 530 faddans out of the village total zimam of 629 faddans. The remainder is distributed among nine families in the village. It is obvious that the family exerts administrative, occupational and agrarian influence and that it controls all the administrative affairs that concern the inhabitants of the village. It may be observed that none of the family members were subject to the agrarian reforms laws because none of them exceeded the ceilings decreed by law.

It has also become clear that they have violated the agrarian reform law in regard to tenure relationships and this subject was the source of many disputes between themselves and the tenants. Not a single one of the decisions adopted by the Arab Socialist Union was implemented by them until now.

Ibrahim Adam
Secretary
Executive Bureau
Beheira Governorate

The Higher Committee for the Liquidation of Feudalism
Top Secret

Governorate: Minya
District: Maghagha
Village: Abu Busht

Name: Amin Ahmad Bahr

Results of the investigations: Based on reports and documents received from the following sources:
− − − The Governorate of Minya
− − − The Arab Socialist Union in Minya
− − − The General Intelligence Bureau

The case represents:
− − − Criminal Behavior
− − − Domination
− − − Exploitation

Recommendations of the Branch Committee: − Imposing sequestration on Amin Ahmad Bahr and his removal [together] with his family from the rural areas.

Detention of the following:
1. Amin Ahmad Bahr
2. Jamal Sadiq Ahmad Ali

Dismissal of the following:
1. Amin Ahmad Muhammad Abdel Samad Bahr/'Umda
2. Muhammad Ahmad Abdel Samad Bahr/Shaykh al-Balad
3. Abdel Wahab Ahmad Salman/Shaykh al-Balad
4. Hafiz Abdel Latif Ali/Shaykh al-Balad
5. Abu al-'Ata Ibrahim/Deputy Shaykh al-Ghafar
6. Ahmad Radi Muhammad/regular ghafir
7. Muhammad Ibrahim Radi/regular ghafir

Transfer of the following to posts outside the governorate:
1. Abdel Azim Abdel Samad Bahr
− Dissolution of the agricultural cooperative in Abu Busht
− Dissolution of the committee of the Arab Socialist Union in Abu Busht
− Establishment of a police station in the village

E. Families with Local Influence Investigated by the HCLF in 1966

FAMILY	VILLAGE	DISTRICT	PROVINCE
Zaid	Zarqun	Damanhur	Beheira
Sakhi	Kafr al-Jadid	Shubrakhit	—
Syrafi	Qlishan	Itay al-Barud	—
'Allam	Kafr al-Hajah	— —	—
'Umran	— —	— —	—
Hinnawi	Kafr 'Awanah	— —	—
Jibali	Nuqrash	— —	—
Quni	Nabirah	— —	—
Niqroud	Al-'Awamer	— —	—
Nassar	Tawd	Kom Hamadah	—
Darwish	Al-Minshya Al-Jadidah	Dilinjat	—
Salem	Abu Shushah	—	—
Saleh	Al-Bustan	—	—
Maqrahi	Zawiyat Muslim	—	—
Bassiuni	Mansha't Bassiuni	Karf al-Duwwar	—
'Amer	Mansha't 'Amer	— —	—
Minyawi	Derut/Qasr	Mahmoudiyya	—
Zidan	Abu al-Matamir	Abu al-Matamir	—
'Ukashah	Hararah	Hosh 'Isa	—
Munji	Shubra Badin	Mansurah	Daqahliyya
Khokha	Zafar	Sinblawin	—
Sayyid	Minyat al-Nasr	Dikirnis	—
'Arishi	Mit Salsil	—	—
Sodah	Kafr al-Kurdi	—	—
Qaddah	Birimbal	—	—
Suwaylm	—	—	—
Mursi	Karf al-Jinainah	Talkha	—
Far	Abisto	—	—
Hilal	Belgas	Belgas	—
Abu Gazyah	Abu al-Gharr	Kafr al-Zayyat	Gharbiyya
Buryk	Kafr Ya'koub	— —	—
Shalabi	— —	— —	—
Rizq	Bahbit al-Hijarah	Samanud	—
'Awad	Samanud	—	—
'Allam	Sajin al-Kom	Qutur	—
Hijazi	Minyat Tokh	Al-Santah	—

FAMILY	VILLAGE	DISTRICT	PROVINCE
Shitat	Mashtul al-Suq	Bilbis	Sharqiyya
Tahawi	Tahawiyya	—	—
Baligh	Al-Suds	Hihya	—
Mikawi	Mahidiyya	—	—
Tubayli	Talrak	Kafr Saqr	—
Badran	Al-Ghabah	Abu Kabir	—
Mahmoud	Qarajah	— —	—
'Abdun	Ghazalah	Faqus	—
Omar	Samakkin	Husainiyya	—
'Ashur	'Umdan	Kafr al-Shaykh	Kafr al-Shaykh
Yusif	Al-Khadimiyyh	— —	—
Rajab	Al-Rizqah	Fuwah	—
Bakr	Al-Bina	—	—
Shita	Mandourah	Disuq	—
Abu al-Khyr	Shabah	—	—
Jawish	Rawdah	—	—
Dufrawi	Dakma	Shibin al-Kom	Minufiyya
'Aql	Saqiyat	Ashmon	
	Abu Shaarah	—	—
Yusif	Baraniyya	—	—
Zaid	Jirys	—	—
Fiqqi	Kamshish	Tila	—
Ghazi	Bum	—	—
Susa	Minawahlah	Bajur	—
Shalqani	Basus	al-Qantar	Qalubiyya
'Allam	Sandabis	—	—
'Udah	Qarqashandah	Tukh	—
Nimr	Kufr 'Alim	Qalub	—
Zahir	Sunaniyyah	Dumyat	Dumyat
Badawi	Sharbas	Fariskwar	—
Ghurab	Ossim	Imbaba	Giza
Zomor	Nahia	—	—
Azzam	al-Shubak	Badrashin	—
Bihnisawi	Tarfayah	—	—
Shaghmim	Nasiriyyah	Fayyum	Fayyum
Saleh	Bani Saleh	—	—
Tantawi	Mansha't Tantawi	Sinuris	—
'Awad	Tarsa	—	—

FAMILY	VILLAGE	DISTRICT	PROVINCE
Jibali	Qasr al-Jibali	Ibshiway	—
Taalib	Shaalan	—	—
Maabad	Abu Kisa'	—	—
Basil	Qasr al-Basil	Atsa	—
Saif al-Nast	Abu Jandir	—	Fayyum
Jammal	Mansha't Jammal	Tamiah	—
Sulayman	Mansha't Sulayman	Samsata	Bani Suwayf
Mishri	Myana	Ahnasiya	— —
Minshawi	Bani Manin	Fashan	— —
'Afifi	Qalba	Malawi	Minya
'Ushairi	Qalandul	—	—
Islambuli	Malawi	Malawi	—
Bahr	Abu Busht	Maghagha	—
Shafi'i	Saila Sharqiyya	Matai	—
'Abd Allah	Bani Hakim	Samalut	—
'Abdel Baqi	Hussaniyya	Abu Qirqas	—
Darwish	Al-Mandarah	Derut	Asyut
Shalqami	Derut	—	—
Qurashi	Qudiyat al-Islam	—	—
Mahfuz	Hawatka	Manfalut	—
Shalh	Mandarah Qibli	—	—
Mahran	Badari	Badari	—
Darwish	Shaturah	Tahta	Sohag
Fawaz	Kharfa	Girga	—
Abu Satit	'Alywah	Bilina	—
Abu Krishah	Awlad 'Ali	Mansha'h	—
Huzayn	Isna	Isna	Qena

Notes

NOTES TO THE INTRODUCTION

1. Clement H. Moore, "Authoritarian Politics in Unincorporated Society: The Case of Nasser's Egypt," *Comparative Politics* 6(1974):193–218.
2. Amos Perlmutter, *Egypt: The Praetorian State* (New Brunswick, N.J.: Transaction Books, 1974).
3. Robert Springborg, "Patrimonialism and Policy-Making in Egypt: Nasser and Sadat and the Tenure Policy for Reclaimed Land," *Middle East Studies* 15 (1979):49–69. See also by the same author *Sayyid Mir'i: Family Power and Politics in Egypt* (Philadelphia: The University of Pennsylvania Press, 1982).
4. Shahrough Akhavi, "Egypt: Neo-Patrimonial Elite," in *Political Elites and Political Development in the Middle East*, ed. Frank Tachau (New York: Halstead Press, 1975), 69–113.
5. John Waterbury, *The Egypt of Nasser and Sadat: The Political Economy of Two Regimes* (Princeton, N.J.: Princeton University Press, 1983), 32–40.
6. Ibid., p. 15.
7. Leonard Binder, *In a Moment of Enthusiasm: Political Power and the Second Stratum* (Chicago: The University of Chicago Press, 1978), 12.
8. Ibid., p. 26.
9. The distinctions are more visible in Morocco and Algeria than in Egypt, a fact that formed the basis of the policies of the French colonialists and the national leaderships. See Elbaki Hermassi, *Leadership and National Development in North Africa: A Comparative Study* (Berkeley: University of California Press, 1975).
10. Fouad Ajami in A. Gouda and Robert Tignor, eds. *The Political Economy of Income Distribution in Egypt* (New York: Holmes and Meier, 1982), 512–13.
11. Binder, *In a Moment of Enthusiasm*, 26.
12. Ibid., p. 36.
13. Ziad Keilany, "Land Reforms in Syria," *Middle Eastern Studies* 16(1980):221.
14. Hanna Batatu, "The Egyptian, Iraqi, Syrian Revolutions: Comparisons," *Perspectives on the Middle East 1983: Proceedings of a Conference*, eds. William G. Miller and Philip H. Stoddard (Washington, D.C.: The Middle East Institute, 1983), 70–71.
15. Waterbury, *The Egypt of Nasser and Sadat*, 37–38.

16. Binder, *In a Moment of Enthusiasm*, 7.

17. Ibid., p. 26.

18. Shaul Bakhash, "Revolutions in the Middle East and North Africa in Comparative Perspectives," in Miller and Stoddard, eds., *Perspectives on the Middle East*, 16. Iran is the only country in the Middle East whose agrarian reforms can be considered revolutionary for their impact on the social structure. I believe that behind the Shah's success in carrying out radical agrarian reforms was the absence of the structural limitation that inhibited Nasser. Recently, a scholar has pointed out that a rural middle class in Iran was conspicuous by its absence and that landlord absenteeism had become rampant. See Eric J. Hooglund, *Land and Revolution in Iran: 1960–1980* (Austin, Texas: University of Texas Press, 1982), 34.

19. Binder argues that the RMC was a compliant instrument in the hands of the ruling elites since it was neither conscious of its class interests nor did it act as a collectivity. His use of the concept of class is therefore, as he puts it, a bit of ordinary language. Binder, *In a Moment of Enthusiasm*, 31.

20. The official statistics do not reflect the actual size of landholdings under cultivation, which often include leased-in land and freeholds together. Nor do these statistics reflect the extent of property concentration resulting from cultivation of lands nominally divided among family members, or of illegally held properties. See Mahmoud Abdel-Fadil, *Development, Income Distribution and Social Change in Rural Egypt 1952–1970* (Cambridge, England: Cambridge University Press, 1975), 13.

21. Waterbury rejects Binder's thesis that the RMC, in a moment of enthusiasm, embraced the Egyptian revolution, became its embodiment, and served as a "referent or source of values for the Nasserist elite." According to Waterbury, the RMC was merely tolerated and not infrequently harassed. He draws this inference from the activities of the Higher Committee for the Liquidation of Feudalism (HCLF). Paradoxically, Waterbury draws the opposite conclusion from the activities of the HCLF by asserting that the RMC was not only conscious of its class interests but was able to affect regime-level changes, both of which Binder denies. Waterbury draws attention to the role of the Zomor family investigated by HCLF in 1966, considered by him to be a prototype of Binder's family sets: an artificial construct created by Binder to draw the characteristics of the rural elite families. See Waterbury, *The Egypt of Nasser and Sadat*, 274 and 303. Binder believes that the purpose behind the formation of the HCLF was consistent with that of party mobilization under Ali Sabri. Because of the Kamshish Affair, the left put pressure on the regime to bring an end to the conditions of exploitation in the rural areas and to start a social revolution, which could have alienated the RMC. The left was certainly threatening the political formula upon which the stability of the regime rested. Thus, the HCLF was formed to absorb the leftist pressure and to blunt its growing criticism of the regime for allowing conditions of exploitation to persist. Binder draws parallel conclusions from his examination of the experiment of the socialist Vanguard, organized on the Leninist model. In both instances, Marshal Amer, who opposed radical solutions, was appointed to keep a close watch on the activities of the radicals and to keep elements among former communists and Marxists under control. Binder, *In a Mo-*

ment of Enthusiasm, 342–43. See also by the same author, "The Failure of the Egyptian Left," *Asian and African Studies* 14 (March 1980): 20–34.

22.   In his critique of the dichotomous ruling elite model, Iliya Harik observes that "less significance has been attributed to leaders' relations to one another or to their power base, strategies, and interrelations at various levels in society. When the concept of power is conceived as a dyadic relationship whereby one actor induces or forces compliance from another, the power network of which their relationship is a part is overlooked." *The Political Mobilization of Peasants: A Study of an Egyptian Community* (Bloomington: Indiana University Press, 1974, 26.

23.   Batatu, "The Egyptian, Iraqi, Syrian Revolutions", 67–80.

24.   Lisa Anderson, "Qadhafi's Islam," in *Voices of Resurgent Islam*, ed. John L. Esposito (Oxford: Oxford University Press, 1983), 139.

25.   Hanna Batatu, *The Old Social Classes and the Revolutionary Movements of Iraq's Old Landed and Commercial Classes and of its Communists, Ba'thists and Free Officers* (Princeton: Princeton University Press, 1982), 1004–7.

26.   Wilfred S. Blunt, *Secret History of the British Occupation of Egypt* (New York: Howard Fertig, 1967), 13.

27.   Waterbury, *The Egypt of Nasser and Sadat*, 325.

28.   See Anouar Abdel-Malek, *Egypt: Military Society* (New York: Random House, 1968), 68–70.

29.   The historian Gabriel Baer has asserted that peasant rebellions have occurred in every generation in the past two hundred years. See *Studies in the Social History of Modern Egypt* (Chicago: The University of Chicago Press, 1969), 108.

30.   See Hermassi, *Leadership and National Development in North Africa*, 128–30.

31.   The concept of the intermediate state is used by Michal Kalecki to describe these developments, to which a passing reference was made by Samir Radwan in Dharm Ghai et al., *Agrarian System and Rural Development* (New York: Holmes & Meier, 1979), 200. See also M. Kalecki, "Observations on Social and Economic Aspects of "Intermediate Regimes." *Coexistence* 1(1967): 1–5.

NOTES TO CHAPTER ONE

1.   Ahmad Majdi Hejazi, "Al-Bina' al-Tabaqi fi al-Qariya al-Misriyya" (M.A. Thesis, Sociology Department, Ain Shams University, 1975), 140–45.

2.   Data on the parliamentary elections are derived from Muhammad Subhi, *Ta'rikh al-Hayat al-Niyabiyya. fi Misr* (Cairo: Dar al-Kutb, 1974).

3.   Barakat, *Tatawwr al-Milkiyya al-Zira'iyya. fi Misr Wa-Atharuh 'Ala al-Harakal al-siyasiyya 1813*–1914 (Cairo: Dar al-Thaqafah, 1977), 412.

4.   Ibid., p. 414.

5.   Sabri Abu al-Majd "Watha'iq Jadidah fi Qissat Khiyanat Thawrat 'Urabi," *al-Musawwar*, 23 September 1966, pp. 17–18.

6. Hejazi, "Al-Bina' al-Tabaqi," 140–41.

7. Ibid., pp. 141–43.

8. Ibid., pp. 140–151.

9. Shahinda Maqlad, "Tajribat al-'Amal al-Thawri," al-Tali'ah, September 1966, p. 49.

10. Aziz al-Fiqqi, in an interview with this author, maintained that Shahinda was a jariyyah (slave) of his grandfather and not his wife. When I repeated this claim before some peasants gathered in Kamshish, there was loud protest.

11. Hejazi, "Al-Bina' al-Tabaqi," 140–45.

12. Ibid., pp. 151–55.

13. Shahinda, "Tajribat al-'Amal al-Thawri," 50.

14. Ibid., pp. 50–51.

15. Hejazi, "Al-Bina' al-Tabaqi," 196.

16. These incidents were reported in the national journals, Akher Sa'a, 12 August 1953, and al-Musawwar, 14 August 1953.

17. Data on the alleged political affiliations of Salah Hussain and records of his arrest are derived from the official confidential report sent by the Internal Security Department, al-Mabahith, to Muhammad Abdel Fattah Abu al-Fadl, the ASU's secretary for organization and membership affairs. The report carried no. 5504/66 and was dated March 1966.

18. Data on the Fiqqis' landownership is derived from the confidential reports of the office of Administrative Control submitted to Muhammad Abdel Fattah Abu al-Fadl, the ASU's secretary for organization and membership affairs. The latter was interviewed by this author in October and November, 1982.

19. Ahmad Rajab Harhash, "Kamshish," al-Tali'ah, September 1966, p. 46. Report to Abu al-Fadl, the ASU's secretary for organization and membership affairs from the Internal Security Department. The report carried no. 5504/66 and was dated March, 1966.

20. Shahinda, "Tajribat al-'Amal al-Thwari," 51.

21. Harhash, "Kamshish," 46. See also Rose al-Yusif, 15 February 1965, p. 15.

22. Hejazi, "al-Bina' al-Tabaqi," 163–69.

23. Ibid., p. 230.

24. Hejazi conducted a survey in Kamshish after the Kamshish Affair and in another village, which did not have a history of large landownership. He found that the ASU committee was more effective in the latter than in the former. The police station was the main source of authority in Kamshish. Ibid., p. 252.

25. Che Guevara visited Minufiyya on 8 March 1965 and was present at the ASU conference at Shibin al-Kom. He concluded his official visit and left Egypt on 11 March. The description of the visit is based on an interview with Shahinda on 5 April 1983.

26. See the text of the letters exchanged between the Kamshish Ideological Affairs Committee and the ASU's secretary for organization and membership affairs in Muhammad Rashad, Sirri Jiddan: Min Malafat Lajnat Tasfiyat al-'iqta' (Cairo: Dar al-Ta'awun, 1977), 29–50

27. Lutfi al-Kholi, "Thermometer Kamshish," al-Tali'ah, June 1966. See also Salah Hafiz in Akher Sa'a, 11 May 1966.

28. Mohammad Anis. "Shahid la Qatil," *al-Gumhouriyya*, 13 June 1969.
29. In an interview published in *al-Sha'b*, 8 June 1982, Sha'rawi Gom'a denied Nasser had any prior knowledge of the torture that took place in Kamshish.
30. Based on an interview with this author, 5 April 1983.
31. The reaction of the peasants in Kamshish to desequestration is based on an interview with Shahinda by this author on 19 April 1983.
32. The proceedings of the court were published in *Al-Ahram* on 23 May 1968. The sentences were published on 9 July 1968. A background story on the conflict in Kamshish was the subject of an article in al-Musawwar, May 1968.
33. See Philip Galab, "Man Qatal Man Fi Kamshish," *Rose al-Yusif*, 16 December 1974.
34. Interview with Shahinda by this author on 19 April 1983.
35. The peasant claims of ownership of sequestered lands were supported by Hejazi, "Al-Bina' al-Tabaqi," 169.
36. See *Al-Ahram* and *al-Akhbar*, 10 and 11 August 1976.
37. Ibid., 18 January 1978.
38. See, for example, *Akhbar al-Yaum*, 14 August 1976.
39. Based on an interview with this author on 19 April 1983 in Cairo.
40. See *al-Ahram*, 29 January 1978.
41. Ibid., 22 March 1978.
42. See *al-Akhbar*, 22 January 1982.

NOTES TO CHAPTER TWO

1. The HCLF investigations included both absentee and resident owners. A common denominator of the former families was the absence of strong local kinship connections, as revealed by the investigations. A large number of absentee owners were urban bourgeoisie who used land as an investment. These families were the industrialists, merchants, and urban property holders. Among the families that came under investigations of the HCLF were the cotton merchant families Yusif, 'Abd Rubbuh, Balba', Yahya, and Barakat. The list also included the banker 'Allam and the industrialist Wisa. The most numerous of the absentee owners were the foreigners, members of the Coptic minority, and professionals. Of the Coptic families, the Ghali family came under investigation of the HCLF. There were, in addition, several Coptic families originally from Upper Egypt investitaged. The large number of absentee owners among Copts is not surprising, given that many of them turned toward the more profitable commercial and industrial enterprises rather than concentrating on agriculture. The Khayats and Wisas were more successful as traders and industrialists than as agriculturists with large investments in land. Furthermore, the large number of absenteeism among the Copts might also be related to the fact that, traditionally, the Coptic minority distinguished itself as a class of artisans, professionals, and accountants.
The HCLF's reports also covered nonindigenous landowners and members of the professional class, including doctors, engineers, and lawyers who were for the most part

absentee owners. The families with substantial holdings in Beheira were the Rufa'ils, Tumbas, and Qasiris. These families, I suspect, were of Syrian-Lebanese origins and were residents of Alexandria. The professionals included the Matinis, Sulaiman, Salib, and Khalifa families whose properties were also located in the Beheira provinces.

2.   For the transformation of the village community under Sa'id, see Gabriel Baer, *Studies in the Social History of Modern Egypt* (Chicago: The University of Chicago Press, 1969), 27–29.

3.   'Ali Pasha Mubarak, *al-Khitat al-Tawfiqiyya al-Jadida*, (Cairo: Bulaq Press, 1886–1889), vol. 10, p. 84.

4.   Ibid., vol. 14, p. 127.

5.   See Rif'at al-Sa'id, *al-Asas al-'Ijtima'i li-Athawarah al-'Urabiyya* (Cairo: Madbuli Press, 1966) 127.

6.   Mubarak, *Khitat*, vol. 14, 116.

7.   'Ali Barakat, *Tatawwr al-Milkiyya al-Zira'iyya fi Misr wa-Atharuh 'Ala al-Harakah al-Siyasiyya 1813–1914* (Cairo: Dar al-Thaqafa, 1977), 270.

8.   Baer, *Studies in Social History*, 49–50.

9.   Quoted by Ra'uf Abbas Hamid, *al-Nizam al-'Ijtima'i fi Misr fi Zill al-Milkiyyat al-Zira'iyya al-Kabirah* (Cairo: Dar al-Fikr, 1973), 91.

10.   Gabriel Baer, *A History of Landownership in Modern Egypt, 1800–1952* (London: Oxford University Press, 1962), 59.

11.   Mubarak, *Khitat*, vol. 13, 46.

12.   Wilfred S. Blunt, *Secret History of the British Occupation of Egypt* (New York: Howard Fertig, 1967), 49.

13.   Alexander Schölch, *Egypt for the Egyptians, the Socio-Political Crisis in Egypt 1878–1882* (London: Ithaca Press, 1981), 78.

14.   Ibid., p. 80.

15.   Al-Sa'id, *Al-Asas al-'Ijtima'i*.

16.   Schölch, *Egypt for the Egyptians*, 310.

17.   Ibid., p. 270.

18.   Ibid., p. 241.

19.   Afaff Lutfi al-Sayyid, *Egypt and Cromer: A Study in Anglo-Egyptian Relations* (London: John Murray, 1968), 17.

20.   Evelyn Baring (Lord Cromer), *Modern Egypt* (London: MacMillan and Co., 1908), 409.

21.   Barakat, *Tatawwr al-Milkiyya al-Zira'iyya*, 420–34.

22.   Al-Sayyid, *Egypt and Cromer*, 36.

23.   Al-Sa'id, *Al-Asas al-'Ijtima'i*, 212.

24.   Cromer, *Modern Egypt*, 193.

25.   Eric Davis, *Challenging Colonialism: Bank Misr and Egyptian Industrializatoin, 1920–1941* (Princeton, N.J.: Princeton University Press, 1983), 54.

26.   Asim al-Disuqi, *Kibar Mullak al-Aradhi al-Zira'iyya wa dawruhum fi al-Mujtama' al-Misri* (Cairo: Dar al-Thaqafa, 1975), 211.

27.   Davis, *Challenging Colonialism*, 46.

28.   Ibid., p. 59.

29.   Abdel Azim Ramadan, *Sira' al-Tabaqat fi Misr: 1837–1952* (Beirut: Al Mu'assassah al-Arabiyya, 1978), 91.

30.   Davis, *Challenging Colonialism*, 50.

31.   Disuqi, *Kibar Mullak al-Aradhi*, 255–56.

32.   Ramadan, *Sira' al-Tabaqat fi Misr*, 75.

33.   Quoted by Disuqi, *Kibar Mullak al-Aradhi*, 260.

34.   Baer, *Studies in Social History*, 101–2.

35.   Baer, *A History of Landownership*, 145.

36.   John Anderson, "Representative Systems and Ruralizing Elections" (M.A. thesis, University of Chicago, 1976), 101. See also Leonard Binder, *In a Moment of Enthusiasm: Political Power and the Second Stratum* (Chicago: The University of Chicago Press, 1978), 121–43. Anderson emphasized the urban character of the property owners among the Wafdist supporters, even if they were primarily Latifundists.

37.   Zaheer Quraishi, *Liberal Nationalism in Egypt* (Delhi: Jamal Printing Press, 1967), 114.

38.   Baer, *A History of Landownership*, 109–15.

39.   Ibrahim Amer, *Al-Ardh wa-al-Fallah: Al-Mas'lah al-Zira'iyya Fi Misr* (Cairo: al-Dar Misriyya, 1958), 89–90.

40.   Baer, A History of landownership, p. 109.

41.   Mahmoud Abdel-Fadil, *Development, Income Distribution and Social Change in Rural Egypt* (London: Cambridge University Press, 1975), 4.

42.   Disuqi, *Kibar Mullak al-Aradhi*, 77.

43.   Ramadan, *Sira' al-Tabaqat fi Misr*, 177.

44.   Amer, *Al-Ardh wa-al-Fallah*, 106–7.

45.   Henry Ayrout, *The Fallaheen* (Cairo: R. Schindler), 29.

46.   Ibrahim Zaki al-Sa'i, *Ta'rikh al-Minufiyya* (Cairo: Dar Loran, n.d.), 52–53.

47.   Baer, *Studies in Social History*, 102.

48.   Quoted by Baer, Ibid., p. 103.

49.   Anouar Abdel-Malek, *Egypt: Military Society* (New York: Random House, 1968), 68.

50.   In *'Awdat al-Ruh*, Tawfiq al-Hakim expressed the fervent belief that the only way out of the malaise in which Egypt was hopelessly ensnared during the 1930s was for a leader to come who would unite all into one. This call was repeated several times, and many were convinced that only a strong man with a strong will could end the anarchy.

NOTES TO CHAPTER THREE

1.   Mahmoud Abdel-Fadil, *Development, Income Distribution and Social Change in Rural Egypt 1952–1970* (Cambridge, England: Cambridge University Press, 1975), 9.

2.   Abdel Azim Ramadan, *Al-Sira' al-'Ijtima'i wa-al-Siyasi fi Misr: 'Abdel Nasser wa-Azamat Mars* (Cairo: Rose al-Yusif, 1976), 42.

3.   Abdel-Fadil, *Development, Income Distribution*, 12–13.

4.   Saad Gadalla, *Land Reform in Relation to Social Development in Egypt* (Columbia: University of Missouri Press, 1962), 62.

5.   Anouar Abdel-Malek, *Egypt: Military Scoeity* (New York: Random House, 1968), 74–75.

6.   Ramadan, *Al-Sira' al-'Ijtima'i*, 51.

7.   Ibid., pp. 52–52.

8.   Abdel-Malek, *Egypt: Military Society*, 70.

9.   Sayyid Mar'i, *Awraq Siyasiyya* (Cairo: Al-Maktab al-Misri, 1979), 299.

10.   P.J. Vatikiotis, *The Egyptian Army in Politics: Pattern for New Nations?* (Bloomington: Indiana University Press, 1961), 79.

11.   Ibid., p. 68.

12.   Ibid., p. 45.

13.   Mar'i, *Awraq Siyasiyya*, 304.

14.   Ramadan, *Al-Sira' al-'Ijtima'i*, 79–83.

15.   Vatikiotis, *The Egyptian Army in Politics*, 98.

16.   Abdel-Malek, *Egypt: Military Society*, 149.

17.   Ibid., p. 118.

18.   Ibid., p. 367.

19.   Leonard Binder, *In a Moment of Enthusiasm: Political Power and the Second Stratum* (Chicago: The University of Chicago Press, 1978), 76–787. The term 'Izba refers to a small village wholly owned by a landlord whose acreage usually amounts to fifty faddans.

20.   Abdel-Malek, *Egypt: Military Society*, 131–132.

21.   The failure to restrict family ownership led to a great deal of controversy among jurists. The basic issue was whether the limit imposed on family ownership in 1958 was still in force. This controversy was not settled by the declaration of *al-Mithaq*, following the conclusion of the National Congress of Popular Forces convened in 1962. The *Mithaq* stated that the ultimate objective of the agrarian policy was to limit individual ownership to fifty faddans and family ownership to one hundred faddans by 1970. It was hoped, Nasser declared at the conference, that by 1970 the concentration of land within one family would be broken up by natural processes. The dependent children would in time become adults with families and properties of their own. According to Doreen Warriner, the main motive behind the agrarian reforms was the creation of a community of small farmers patterned on the liberal ideal. See *Land Reform and Development in the Middle East: A Study of Egypt, Syria and Iraq* (London: Oxford University Press, 1967), 10. See also Nasser's speech at the National Congress of Popular Forces, May 16 session 1962.

22.   Abdel Latif al-Baghdadi, *Memoirs* (Cairo: Al-Maktab al-Misri, 1977), 152.

23.   The Congress of Popular Forces defined a peasant as an individual who owned less than twenty-five faddans. This definition remained in force until Ali Sabri began to publish his radical views in *al-Gumhourriyya* between 23 December 1966 and 31 March 1967. In Sabri's view, the real *fallah* was the small owner of less than five faddans, since this group, together with the agricultural workers, constituted the majority of the population in a country of roughly 10 million. The small owners amounted to 3.3

million, while the owners of twenty to twenty-five faddans totaled only 29,000, according to statistics obtained in 1965. Nasser settled the controversy by declaring, in a speech on 1 May 1966 in Kafr-al-Duwwar, that the *fallah* was the owner of less than ten faddans whose only source of livelihood was the cultivation of the land.

24.   The sequestration measures were liquidated by a Presidential Decree No. 119 in 1964. According to this decree, all sequestered properties were to be handed over to the Agrarian Reform Bureau, while compensations not exceeding E£ 30,000 were to be disbursed to the former owners. Commercial establishments of less than E£ 30,000 were ordered to be restored to their former owners. See Ibrahim al-Shirbini, *Tasfiyyat al-Hirasat* (Cairo: Al-Ma'rifa Press, 1964).

25.   The social and political implications of sequestration measures were examined by a number of scholars, but they never received a systematic treatment. See the comments of Muhammad Abdel Salam al-Zayat in *al-Ahram*, 10 May 1971. See also the views of jurist Jamal al-'Utaifi in *al-Ahram*, 12 May 1971.

26.   John Waterbury, *The Egypt of Nasser and Sadat: The Political Economy of Two Regimes* (Princeton, N.J.: Princeton University Press, 1983), 339.

27.   For the organization of the ASU, see R. Hrari Dekmejian, *Egypt Under Nasir: A Study in Political Dynamics* (Albany: State University of New York Press, 1971), 274–75.

28.   Binder, *In a Moment of Enthusiasm*, 312.

29.   Elsayd M. Zaki, *An Outline of the Local Administration System in the United Arab Republic* (Cairo: Ministry of Local Government, 1965).

30.   Voices were raised at the sessions of the National Congress of Popular Forces for abolishing the *'Umda* system because "the 'Umdas and Shaykhs were shielding the feudalists and they were exploiting the peasants by taking away sources of their livelihood." *Minutes of the National Congress of Popular Forces* (Cairo: Government Printing Press, 1962, session on 10 December 1961), 206.

31.   See *al-Ahram*, 17 July 1980.

32.   The Soviet position regarding the controversial theory of "noncapitalist development" was expounded by V. G. Solodovinkov. The author underscored the Marxist-Leninist character of the controversial theory. Underdeveloped countries could skip the "capitalist stage in the natural periods of social development" by creating the material conditions that "can eventuate into the building of a socialist society." See "Classics of Marxism and Non-Capitalist Development," *Africa in Soviet Studies* 1 (1971): 194–203.

33.   See Ahmad Hamrush, *Qissat Thawrat 23 Yulyu* (Beirut: Al-Mu'assasah al-Arabiyya, 1974), 244.

34.   Binder, *In a Moment of Enthusiasm*, 332.

35.   Hamrush, *Qissat Thawrat 23 Yulyu*, 240–43.

36.   Ibid., p. 244.

37.   For the text of Nasser's statement on the organization of the Socialist Vanguard see *al-Tanzim wa-al-Harakah* (Beirut, 1975).

38.   Hamrush, *Qissat Thawrat 23 Yulyu*, 246.

39.   The reports were forwarded by Abdel Fattah Abu al-Fadl, secretary of the ASU's Subsecretariat for Organization and Membership Affairs, in the period between March

and August 1965, roughly one year before the Kamshish Affair. The reports levied charges against several families in Giza (the Ghurab family), Beheira (Muhanna and Nuwar families), Qalubiyya (the Shalqani family), Dumyat (Badawi family), and Bani Suwayf (the Mahmud family). The charges ranged from committing acts of violence to escaping from the agrarian reforms and to infiltrating and controlling the ASU committees on the local level. The Subsecretariat recommended to the authorities an action to be taken against the offending families. But, as revealed by the reports, some of the families used their connections with high state officials to thwart any effort aimed at reducing their influence. For the texts of the reports, see Muhammad Rashad, *Sirri Jiddan: Min Malafat Lajnat Tasfiyat al-'Iqta'* (Cairo: Dar al-Ta'awun, 1977), 28–35.

40.   Hamrush, *Qissat Thawrat 23 Yulyu*, 256–58.

41.   Members of the Socialist Vanguard remained anonymous since their main function became information gathering on subversive elements. This purpose was apparent from the directive dated 24 August 1965, which was circulated among the Vanguard members. The directive revealed to the members that there was evidence of subversive activities by members of the outlawed Muslim Brotherhood, acting in cooperation with "imperialist and reactionary forces in the Arab world which are harboring ill feelings towards us. Investigations led to the arrest of members of two groups operating in Cairo and Daqahliyya. Arms and explosives were found hidden in these areas." The directive ended by reminding members of the duties in doubling their efforts by establishing closer links with the masses and in countering the effects of the lies being spread among them. The directive further reminded the members of their duty to provide the authorities with information on subversive elements. See Jamal Salim, *Al-Tanzimat al-Sirriyya li-Thawrat 23 Yulyu fi 'Ahd Jamal 'Abdel Nasser* (Cairo: Faniyya Press, 1982), 213–14.

42.   Hamrush, *Qissat Thawrat 23 Yulyu*, 256–58.

43.   Salim, *Al-Tanzimat al-Sirriyya*, 114.

44.   Ibid., p. 123.

45.   Ibid., pp. 120–24.

NOTES TO CHAPTER FOUR

1.   Leonard Binder, *In a Moment of Enthusiasm: Political Power and the Second Stratum* (Chicago: The University of Chicago Press, 1978), 334.

2.   R. Hrair Dekmejian, *Egypt Under Nasir: A Study in Political Dynamics* (Albany: State Univerity of New York Press, 1971), 239.

3.   Diya' al-Din Bibars, "Al-Sira' al-Sirri Bayna al-Mabahith wa-al-Mukhabarat," *Rose al-Yusif*, 11 November 1975.

4.   Ahmad Hamrush, *Qissat Thawrat 23 Yulyu* (Beirut: Al-Mu'assasah al-Arabiyya, 1974), 246.

5.   Ibid., p. 196, 216, and 219.

6.   For the published portions of the HCLF's minutes, see Muhammad Rashad, *Sirri Jiddan: Min Malafat Lajnat Tasfiyat al-'Iqta'* (Cairo: Dar al-Ta'awun, 1977), 62–207.

7. Ibid., p. 66.

8. Ibid., p. 95.

9. Ibid., p. 67.

10. Ibid., p. 95.

11. Ibid., p. 87.

12. The Socialist Charter, *al-Mithaq*, limited individual ownership to one hundred faddans. But the general aim was to make this amount of land the upper limit for the whole family unit, defined narrowly as the parents and their dependent children, to be realized gradually by 1971.

13. Rashad, *Sirri Jiddan*, 114.

14. Ibid., p. 94.

15. Ibid., p. 63.

16. Hamed Ammar, *Growing Up in an Egyptian Village* (New York: Octagon Books, 1966), 47.

17. Henry Ayrout, *The Egyptian Peasant (Boston: Beacon Press, 1968)*, 20.

18. Binder, *In a Moment of Enthusiasm*, 75–77. Binder arrived at these tentative statements on the family characteristics of rural notables by examining members of the National Union Committees. In the lists of NU members for sixteen agricultural provinces, Binder found, with some frequency, two or more similar names in the same village committee. Assuming that two or more identical nominal elements indicated membership in the same family, Binder created family sets. Each family set included two or more members, depending on how many individuals with similar names were found in the same basic unit UN committee. Three basic characteristics can be clearly observed in Binder's family sets. The first is that although a number of identical nominal elements indicate close relationships between the NU committee members included in the family sets, given the nature of the evidence the exact relationships are unknown. Secondly, the NU committee members included in the family sets had occupations not representative of occupations in the village. Binder, therefore, assumed that members of the family sets possessed the resources and opportunities to get themselves elected in their own right. Finally, since many family-set members had ancestors in the prerevolutionary parliaments, Binder assumed that the elite status of the influential families was a persisting phenomenon. Of the 29,936 NU committee members, rougly one-fifth were included in the 2,223 family sets.

19. The traditional concept of kinship solidarity was challenged by community studies carried out in Lower Egypt. These studies revealed that kinship groups in the Delta were smaller, kinship solidarity tended to be weaker, and community relations appeared to be more competitive. Harik's study of a village in Beheira indicates that village pluralism emerged to take the place of traditional patterns of relationships among local community members as a result of external influences, represented by party-bureaucratic penetration of the rural areas. Social change, according to Harik, was reflected in the shift of emphasis to personal merits and achievements rather than to hereditary status and ascribed rights. He also asserted that membership in a kinship group did not seem to bestow on an individual either special privileges or disadvantages. He suggested, therefore, that individuals rather than social classes or primary groups should be the

focus of interest in efforts to make sense of the village scene. See *The Political Mobilization of Peasants: A study of an Egyptian Community* (Bloomington: Indiana University Press, 1974), 214–16.

20. The reader must bear in mind the crucial distinction between *al-'A'ilah* and al-'Usrah. The former refers to the extended family system, the latter, to the nuclear family. The immediate family of the patriarch represents a sublineage structure within the traditionally influential family, *al-'A'ilah*. Its patriarchical head is referred to as *Rab al-'A'ilah* or *'Amid al-'A'ilah* (dean of the larger family), in deference to his traditional role of authority within the extended family system. Identification of the family patriarch and his kinship relations to the influential members in the local community was the primary objective of the HCLF investigations.

21. Rashad, *Sirri Jiddan*, 171–80.

22. Ibid., p. 82.

23. Ibid., pp. 160–61, Kamal Rif'at, suggested that deportation must be imposed on individuals and not on the whole family. Rif'at feared the hostility of the new generation toward the regime if they were made to suffer for offenses committed by the older generation.

24. Ibid., p. 152, Marshal 'Amer, in the session of 11 June 1966, explained that the task before the HCLF was more than simply a question of investigating the large landowners who had evaded the enforcement of the land reform laws, because "those who were subject to the land reform law of 1952 cannot be loyal to the revolution. Although their activities at present are not marked by overt hostility, once they are given the opportunity, they will act against the regime. If we recall the events of 1954, we will realize that those who threatened the revolution were the feudalists upon whom the land reform law of 1952 was enforced.

25. Ibid., pp. 158–80. There were two motions before the HCLF in its 11 June session. One motion demanded the imposition of property sequestration on all family members (the nuclear family of the patriarchal heads) and their banishment from the village. The second motion demanded that property sequestration and removal from the rural areas be imposed on individuals only. Of those attending the session, fourteen members voted in favor of the first motion, ten favored the second. Marshal 'Amer temporized by voting in favor of imposing the first motion on very large landowners who were subjected to the 1952 agrarian reform law. At the same time, he held the position that the imposition of collective responsibility must be determined on the basis of case-by-case investigations. It is interesting to note that those who identified themselves with the left, like 'Ali Sabri, Sha'rawi Gom'a, and Sami Sharaf, cast their votes in favor of the first motion.

26. Ibid., p. 158.

27. Ibid., p. 166.

28. Ibid., p. 166.

29. Ibid., p. 134.

30. Ibid., p. 135.

31. Ibid., p. 173.

32.   Gabriel Baer, *A History of Landownership in Modern Egypt, 1800–1952* (Oxford: Oxford University Press, 1961) 63, 140–42.

33.   Ibid., pp. 93–94.

34.   Binder, *In a Moment of Enthusiasm*, 248.

35.   Mahmoud Abdel-Fadil, *Developming, Income Distribution and Social Change in Rural Egypt 1952–1970* (Cambridge, England: Cambridge University Press, 1975), 116. Also Fathi 'Abd al-Fattah, *al-Qaryah al-Mua'asirah*, (Cairo: Dar al-Thaqafah, 1975), pp. 24–25.

36.   'Abd al-Fattah, ibid., p. 215, argues that following the implementation of the agrarian reforms, the former large estate owners had to manage the farms themselves and discard the outmoded and primitive forms of tenancy arrangement in favor of intensive and market-conscious agricultural exploitation. See also Anouar Abdel-Malek, *Egypt: Military Society* (NewYork: Random House, 1968), 74–75.

37.   'Abd al-Fattah, ibid., p. 118, argues that the agrarian reforms benefited the rural middle class. According to the statistics provided by him, medium ownership increased both in acreage and in the number of owners. The number of owners of five to fifty faddans was 148,000, or 5.3 percent of total landowners, and these owners possessed roughly 30.0 percent of the cultivated land in 1952. In 1965, the number of owners in this category increased to 168,000; but their percentage of total landowners (5.2 percent) and their percentage of total land under cultivation (30.3 percent) remained roughly the same as in 1952. Abdel-Fadil, *Development, Income Distribution*, 118, similarly argues that the class of rich peasants in the intermediate strata has, since 1952, increased its area of owned land by a net purchase of 161,000 faddans, which forms 19.8 percent of current farm areas.

38.   Fouad Mursi, *Hadha al-Infitah al-'Iqtisadi* (Cairo: Dar al-Thaqafah, 1976), 270, maintains that the most notable phenomenon in the postreform era has been the continuing growth of rural capitalism at the cost of semi-feudal large landowners at the beginning and, more recently (under the Sadat regime), at the cost of the small farmers.

39.   Abdel-Fadil, *Development, Income Distribution*, 121.

40.   Ibid., pp. 12–13.

41.   Several HCLF members pointed out that the *A'yan* or rural notables continued to farm the same amounts of land they held before the enactment of the agrarian reform law in 1952. The reason for this unchanged situation was that the transfer of land to relatives or even *ghafirs* was purely nominal. This covert action was indicated by the amount of crops they were able to turn over to the local authorities for cooperative marketing. See the minutes of the HCLF's session on 19 May 1966, in Rashad, *Sirri Jiddan*, 70.

42.   Ibid., pp. 83–84.

43.   Doreen Warriner, *Land Reform and Development in the Middle East: A Study of Egypt, Syria, and Iraq* (London: Oxford University Press, 1962), 10, maintains that the liberal ideal of a community of small farmers with economically viable holdings was the motivating force behind the agrarian reforms. See also Abdel-Fadil, *Development, Income Distribution*, 23.

44.   Nasser's speech at the National Conference of Popular Forces. See *Minutes of the National Conference* (Cairo: Government Printing Press, 1962, session on 6 May 1962), 146. The same argument was made by Ali Sabri at the HCLF session on 6 June 1966. Sabri observed that there was nothing wrong with the transfer of property to dependent children. After all, all parents are drawn by the instinct of securing the future for their children. At any rate, the dependent children of 1961, having acquired property of their own, would eventually establish independent households. See Rashad, *Sirri Jiddan*, 149.

45.   Saad Gadalla, *Land Reform in Relation to Social Development in Egypt* (Columbia: University of Missouri Press, 1962), 62. The same observation was made by Abd al-Hamid Ghazi, ASU secretary of peasant affairs, at the HCLF session on 23 May 1966 in response to a remark made by Ali Sabri, the secretary general of the ASU. Ghazi said that it was wrong to assume that parcelling out land among family members would prevent the family head from exercising his traditional control over family property. See Rashad, *Sirri Jiddan*, 86.

46.   Baer, *A History of Land Ownership*, 79.

47.   Binder, *In a Moment of Enthusiasm*, 140.

48.   Abdel-Fadil, *Development, Income Distribution*, 14–15.

49.   Ibid., p. 14.

50.   Ibid., p. 17.

51.   Gabriel S. Saab, *The Egyptian Agrarian Reforms 1952–62* (London: Oxford University Press, 1967), 143.

52.   Ibid., p. 146.

53.   According to Springborg, the political elite who came into power in the post-1952 period did not owe their recruitment to rural clientage networks. The connections to the top "became after 1952 more than equal to a plethora of ties spreading downward." Robert Springborg, "Sayed Bey Marei and Political Clientelism," *Comparative Political Studies* (October 1979): 260. See Clement H. Moore, "Clientelist Ideology and Political Change: Fictitious Networks in Egypt and Tunisia," in *Patrons and Clients in Mediterranean Societies*, eds. E. Gellner and J. Waterbury (London: Duckworth, 1977).

54.   Rashad, *Sirri Jiddan*, 73.

55.   Ibid., p. 269.

56.   Ibid., p. 270.

NOTES TO CHAPTER FIVE

1.   Fouad Ajami, *The Arab Predicament* (Cambridge: Cambridge University Press, 1980).

2.   See, for example, Mahmoud Hussein, *Class Conflict in Egypt* (New York: Monthly Review Press, 1973), 265.

3.   Sayyid Mar'i, *Awraq Siyasiyya* (Cairo; Al-Maktab al-Misri, 1979), 530.

4.   Ibid., p. 531.

5.   Ibid., p. 533.

6.   See Heikal's interview with Fouad Matar, *Muhammad Hasanain Heikal: Bisraha 'An Abdel Nasser* (Beirut: Dar al-Qadaya, 1975).

7.   Mar'i, *Awraq Siyasiyya*, 578–79.

8.   R. Hrair Dekmejian, *Egypt Under Nasir: A Study in Political Dynamics* (Albany: State University of New York Press, 1971), 279–80.

9.   *Al-Ahram*, 4 February 1970.

10.   The reaction of the peasants in Kamshish to desequestration is based on an interview with Shahinda by this author on 19 April 1983.

11.   See *Akhbar al-Yaum*, 15 February 1969.

12.   Mar'i, *Awraq Siyasiyya*, 582–83.

13.   The debates of the ASU's Central Committee were published by Mar'i, ibid., pp. 581–91.

14.   Ibid., p. 590.

15.   *Akhbar al-Yaum*, 15 February 1969.

16.   Mar'i, *Awraq Siyasiyya*, 601.

17.   Ibid., p. 602.

18.   See Salah Muntasir, "Ghazwi al-Qada'," *al-Ahram*, 20 March 1983.

NOTES TO CHAPTER SIX

1.   See *al-Ahram*, 18 October 1970.

2.   Interview with 'Ali Sabri in *al-Ahram al-'Iqtisadi*, 3 January 1983, pp. 12–17. See also the *al-Ahram* opinion on sharing power responsibilities, 22 October 1970.

3.   Diya' al-Din Dawud, *al-Ahram*, 18 October 1970.

4.   See also recent revelations by Diya' al-Din Dawud in *al-Ahali*, 28 July 1982.

5.   According to Robert Springborg, "Sayed Bey Marei and Political Clientelism," *Comparative Poltical Studies* (October 1979): 261, cronyism results from an aggregation of personal connections within modern institutions, better understood as lopsided friendships.

6.   See Tariq al-Bishri, *al-Dimuqratiyya wa-al-Nasseriyya* (Cairo: Dar al-Thaqafa, 1975), 28–29.

7.   Ahmad Hamrush, *Qissat Thawrat 23 Yulyu* (Beirut: Al-Mu'assasah al-Arabiyya, 1974), 211, 218–219.

8.   Jamel Salim, *al-Tanzimat al-Sirriyya: Thawrat 23 yulyu fi 'Ahd Jamal 'Abdel Nasser* (Cairo: Faniyya Press, 1982), 52.

9.   Sabri's stand on the incorporation of the army, the police, and members of the judiciary was made known publicly in serialized articles published by *al-Gumhouriyya*, the organ of Sabri's group in opposition to Heikal's group in *al-Ahram*. The articles calling for the incorporation of the army in the ASU were published in five consecutive days from 12 to 17 March 1967.

10.   *al-Tanzim wa-al-Harakah*, (Beirut: n.p., 1975), pp.26–27.

11.   Hamrush, *Qissat Thawrat 23 Yulyu*, 216.

12.   Ibid., pp. 218–219.

13. Ibid., p. 214.

14. Ibid., p. 215.

15. R. Hrair Dekmejian, *Egypt Under Nasir: A Study in Political Dynamics* (Albany: State University of New York Press, 1971), 254.

16. Sayyid Mar'i *Awraq Siyasiyya* (Cairo: Al-Maktab al-Misri, 1979), 622. Despite the strong kinship ties between Sabri and Mar'i, the latter sided with Sadat. Later on Mar'i solidified his political alliance with Sadat through his son's marriage to Sadat's daughter.

17. Salim, *al-Tanzimat al-Sirriya*, 52.

18. *al-Gumhouriyya*, 7 January 1967.

19. Mohammad Heikal, "'Abdel Nasser Laysa 'Usturah," in *al-Ahram*, 6 November 1970. See also, Ibid., 13 November 1970. These articles should be read in conjunction with articles published later, in the wake of the Corrective Movement. See, for example, *al-Ahram*, 21 May 1971.

20. See the published excerpts of telephone conversations surreptitiously recorded by members of Sabri's faction in *October* 2 January 1977. See also Sadat's speech at the National Assembly on 20 May 1971.

21. See excerpts from General Sadiq's memoirs in *al-Sha'b*, 18 May 1982.

22. See General Fawzi's response to the allegations made by General Sadiq in *al-Sha'b*, 1 June 1982.

23. See Sadat's *al-Bahth 'an al-Dhat* (Cairo: al-Maktab al-Misri, 1978), 232.

24. Heikal's column in *al-Ahram*, 12 March 1971. See also the response to it by Sabri's faction in *al-Gumhouriyya*, March 1971.

25. Sadat, *al-Bahth 'an al-Dhat*, 231.

26. Mar'i, *Awraq Siyasiyya*, 646–47.

27. Excerpts from General Sadiq's memoirs in *al-Sha'b*, 18 May 1892.

28. Lt. General Saad El-Shazli, *The Crossing of the Suez* (San Francisco: American Mideast Research, 1980).

29. Mamdouh Rida, *15 Mayo: Al-Thawra wa al-Mustaqbal* (Cairo: Dar al-Ta'awun, 1977), 315.

30. Ma'ri, *Awraq Siyasiyya*, 652.

31. Ibid., p. 653.

32. Statement by Mustafa Kamil Murad in *al-Ahrar*, 17 May 1982.

33. Statement by Farid Abdel Karim in *al-Ahali*, 11 May 1983.

34. The leading members who sponsored the imposition of sequestration on members of Sabri's faction were Abdel Fattah Azzam and Yusif Makadi, both from families investigated by the HCLF in 1966. See the *Minutes of the National Assembly*, 31 May 1971.

35. See law no. 34/1971 regarding regulations for the imposition of sequestration.

NOTES TO CHAPTER SEVEN

1. See Gouda Abdel Khalek, ed., *al-Infitah* (Cairo: al-Markaz al-'Arabi, 1982), 24.

2. Tawfiq al-Hakim, *'Awdat al-Wa'y* (Cairo: Dar al-Shuruq , 1974).

3. The following represents only a small sample of the reassessment literature on the Nasser era: Muhammad 'Udah, *al-Wa'y al-Mafqud* (Cairo: Dar al-Thaqafah, 1975); Rif'at al-Sa'id, *Awraq Nasiriyya* (Cairo: Dar al-Thaqafah, 1975); Sami Jawhar, *al-Samitun Yatakallamun* (Alexandria: al-Maktab al-Misri, 1975); Karam Shalabi, *Harb al-Kalimat* (Cairo: n.p., 1975).

4. Anwar Sadat, *al-Bahth 'an al-Dhat* (Cairo: al-Maktab al-Misri, 1978), 179–80.

5. Ibid., pp. 185–86.

6. See *al-Akhbar*, 6 July 1974.

7. See Ibrahim Shirbini, *Tasfiyyat al-Hirasat* (Cairo: al-Ma'rifa Press, 1964).

8. Figures provided by John Waterbury, *The Egypt of Nasser and Sadat: The Political Economy of Two Regimes* (Princeton, N.J.: Princeton University Press, 1983), 339.

9. Sayyid Mar'i, *Awraq Siyasiyya* (Cairo: Al-Maktab al-Misri, 1979), 532.

10. Quoted by a deputy during the People's Assembly debate. See the assembly's minutes, session 41, 2 July 1974.

11. Ibid.

12. Quoted by a deputy during the People's Assembly debate. See the assembly's minutes, 2nd session, 30 November 1971.

13. See *al-Ahram*, 20 August 1971.

14. The names of the released political detainees were published in *al-Ahram 23 August 1972.*

15. See *al-Ahram*, 22 October 1971.

16. Ibid., 30 August 1971.

17. David Hirst and Irene Beeson, *Sadat* (London: Faber & Faber, 1981), 123.

18. Ibid., pp. 122–29.

19. See Hamied Ansari, "Sectarian Conflict and the Political Expediency of Religion," *The Middle East Journal* (Summer 1984): 397–418.

20. See Heikal's column in *al-Ahram*, 27 August 1971. See the letter sent to President Sadat on 4 April 1972, which was signed by leading Egyptian political and literary figures. Published in *al-Nahar* of Beirut, 12 July 1972.

21. See Hirst and Beeson, *Sadat*, 137.

22. See, for example, the *Guardian*, 19 July 1972.

23. See *Christian Science Monitor*, 20 July 1972.

24. Hirst and Beeson, *Sadat, 129*–30.

25. See *Times*, 19 July 1972.

26. The Soviet attack on Saudi Arabia and other reactionaries for causing the Soviet-Egyptian rift appeared in *Pravda*, 18 August 1971 and in *Izvestia*, 28 August 1972.

27. *The October Working Paper* (Cairo: Ministry of Information, State Information Service) April 1974, p. 13.

28. See *al-Ahram*, 8 June 1974.

29. The Higher Constitutional Court under the chairmanship of Badawi Hamoudah ruled in favor of reopening the cases regarding sequestration before the enactment of law no. 150/64. See *al-Ahram*, 8 June 1974.

30. Based on an interview with Ibrahim Shirbini by this author on 2 June 1983.

31. See the minutes of the assembly, session 41, 2 July 1974.

32. Mar'i, *Awraq Siyasiyya*, 503–4.
33. Ibid., p. 503.
34. Minutes of the assembly, session 41, 2 July 1974.
35. See *al-Ahram*, 29 October 1974. See also ibid., 30 June 1974.
36. Ibid., 8 October 1971.
37. Ibid., 21 October 1971.
38. Ibid., 12 August 1974.
39. Ibid., 4 September 1974.
40. Ibid., 19 February 1975.
41. Ibid., 17 May 1981.
42. Interview with Ibrahim Shirbini on 2 June 1983.
43. See the minutes of the People's Assembly on 6 September 1981, a session convened to discuss law no. 141/81.
44. See *al-Ahram*, 12 September 1981. Also, *al-Ahram*, 31 May 1981.

NOTES TO CHAPTER EIGHT

1. David Hirst and Irene Beeson, *Sadat* (London: Faber & Faber, 1981), 229.
2. Ali E. Hillal Dessouki, "Policy Making in Egypt: A Case Study of The Open Door Economic Policy," *Social Problems* (April 1984), 414.
3. Hirst and Beeson, *Sadat*, 237.
4. See Rushdi Saleh's views in *Akher Sa'a*, 26 January 1977, p. 4.
5. See *al-Ahram*, 17 July 1980.
6. See *Akher Sa'a*, 9 February 1977, p.7.
7. Marvin G. Weinbaum, "Egypt's Adjustment to a Global Market Economy: The Role of the U.S. Economic Assistance," paper delivered at the 1983 annual meeting of the American Political Science Associaiton, 1–4 September 1983.
8. *Minutes of the People's Assembly*, 11 June 1978.
9. Iliya Harik, *Distribution of Land, Employment and Income in Rural Egypt* (Rural Development Committee, Cornell University, 1979), 42–43. Quoted by John Waterbury, *The Egypt of Nasser and Sadat: The Political Economy of Two Regimes* (Princeton, N.J.: Princeton University Press, 1983), 270.
10. Waterbury, *The Egypt of Nasser and Sadat*, 282.
11. Abdel Basit 'Abdel Mu'ti, *Tawzi' al-Faqr fi al-Qarya al-Misriyya* (Cairo: Dar al-Thaqafah, 1979), 34.
12. Ibid., p. 38.
13. Quoted by Waterbury, *The Egypt of Nasser and Sadat*, 290.
14. Weinbaum, "Egypt's Adjustment to a Global Market Economy," 16.
15. See Waterbury's analysis of Abdel Mu'ti in *The Egypt of Nasser and Sadat*, 284–85.
16. See *Minutes of the People's Assembly*, 11 June 1978.
17. See Fuoad Mursi, *Hadh al-Infitah al-'Iqtisadi* (Cairo: Dar al-Ma'mun, 1976), 178–81.

NOTES TO CHAPTER NINE

1. The Muslim Brotherhood's position regarding political participation was rather ambiguous. Its leadership announced that it had no political ambitions and that it was neither scheming nor dreaming of sharing power. Nonetheless, the leaders of this Muslim fundamentalist movement expected to be called upon to render advice to the ruler on doctrinal issues. See *al-Da'wa*, 26 June 1981, p. 15.

2. The author is highly indebted to Abu Saif Yusif, deputy in the People's Assembly 1976–1979, for his insightful information on the deputies during an interview on 2 August 1977.

3. The information on the hearings held by the People's Assembly Committee on Complaints and Grievances was graciously provided by Fouad Siraj al-Din in an interview with this author on 20 February 1983.

4. Roughly five hundred were present at the meeting of the Bar Association on 23 August 1977, to which this author was invited. Most of the people present represented the Egyptian professional class and members of the intelligentsia. At the podium stood the old Wafdists in their impeccable white suits. True to his style, Siraj al-Din sat puffing on his cigar.

5. The speech has since been printed and is widely circulated under the title *Limaza al-Hizb al-Jadid*, by Fouad Siraj al-Din, (Cairo: Dar al-Shuruq, 1977).

6. Based on an interview with Siraj al-Din by this author at his residence in Garden City, Cairo, on 30 November 1982.

7. Based on an interview with the late 'Abd al-Fattah Hasan by this author on 20 August 1977.

8. See Raymond A. Hinnebusch, "The Reemergence of the Wafd Party: Glimpses of the Liberal Opposition in Egypt," *International Journal for Middle East Studies* 16 (1984): 99–121.

9. For a complete social history of the old and well-established families, see Asim al-Disuqi, *Kibar Mullak al-Aradhi al-Zira'iyya wa dawruhum fi al-Mujtama' al-Misri* (Cario: Dar al-Thaqafa, 1975).

10. Interview with the late 'Abd al-Fattah Hasan by this author on 3 December 1982.

11. Before the dissolutionment of the assembly, the following members lost their seats as a result of a majority vote in the assembly: Kamal al-Din Hussain (2 May 1977), Shaykh 'Ashur Nasr (21 May 1978), 'Abd al-Fattah Hasan (27 June 1978), and Abu al-'Azz al-Hariri (27 June 1978). It should be noted that 'Abd al-Fattah Hasan was the principal force behind the mobilization of deputies to form the New Wafd. Kamal al-Din Hussain was dismissed because of his famous letter to Sadat immediately after the Food Riots of January 1977 in which he asked the president to step down. Shaykh 'Ashur Nasr was dismissed for his criticism of the quality of bread. Abu al-'Azz al-Hariri was a member of the Tajamu' from Alexandria.

12. Ibrahim Shukri's explanation of the arrangement worked out between the NDP and his own Labor Party for apportioning electoral districts came in reaction to Sadat's speech on 15 May 1981. Sadat said that the ruling party created the opposition. Shukri denied there was any prior agreement with the government to let the Labor Party have

thirty seats in the People's Assembly. He did, however, acknowledge that the ruling party did not contest six electoral districts in al-Beheira as well as the districts the NDP did not hope to win. Shukri glossed over the fact that the NDP allowed him to run unopposed in his district, Shirbin in Daqahliyya. Only Khalid Muhyi al-Din, the leader in the Tajamu' was opposed by NDP candidates. See *al-Sha'b*, 26 May 1981.

13.   See *al-Ahram*, 2 June 1979.

14.   Ibid., 8 May 1979.

15.   In comparison with the 1976 assembly, the 1979 assembly had only nine independents. The most notable was Mumtaz Nassar from Asyut, a lawyer by profession who fought fiercely for the independence of the judiciary and who made countless speeches on the floor of the assembly denouncing the curtailment of civil liberties. The other notable independent was Salah Abu Ismail, a former member of the Muslim Brotherhood, who was relentless in pursuing the objective of legislative enactment according to Islamic laws.

16.   See *al-Sha'b*, 26 May 1981, and the speech of President Sadat on 15 May 1981.

17.   The objections of the Tajamu' were based on the following points: (1) one-third of the *Majlis'* members were appointed by the president; (2) it had an advisory function only; (3) the *Majlis* was another vehicle for seating party loyalists; (4) it provided a means for the executive to control the press; and (5) election to the *Majlis* was determined by absolute majority and not proportional representation. See *al-Taqaddum*, 21 June 1980; and also *al-Sha'b*, 9 June 1981.

18.   The new electoral system under which the *Majlis* was elected included voting by party slate province-wide instead of having two-member districts. Rather than adhering to the principle of proportional representation demanded by the minority parties, the authorities adopted absolute majority as the basis for election. See *al-Sha'b*, 12 May 1981.

19.   The results of the elections were quite predictable. The NDP lists won in all the governorates. The lists included 140 voting members, 82 alternate members, and 70 appointed members. Among the last category were seven former ministers, nine writers and journalists, nine university professors, five presidents of the professional unions, six representatives of banks and private companies, five members of the judiciary, six heads of NDP committees, five members of the Liberal party including its leader Mustafa Kamel Murad, six members of sporting clubs, and, finally, two former members of the People's Assembly.

20.   The organ of the ruling party, *Mayo*, wrote in early May 1981 that studies were under way for organizing the next elections to the People's Assembly and the rural councils on the basis of the new electoral system. See *al-Sha'b*, 21 April 1981 and 12 May 1981.

21.   See interview with the independent deputy, Mumtaz Nassar, in *al-Musawwar*, 29 July 1983, pp.40–41.

22.   See the account of Hilmi Murad in *al-Sha'b*, 30 June 1981.

23.   See Fathi Radwan's comment on Sadat's letter to the People's Assembly in *al-Sha'b*, 28 July 1981.

24.   See *al-Sha'b*, 21 July 1981.

NOTES TO CHAPTER TEN

1.   Hamid Enayat, "Iran: Khumayni's Concept of the Guardianship of the Juris-consult," in *Islam in the Political Process*, ed. James Piscatori (London: Cambridge University Press, 1983) p. 161.
2.   For a fuller discussion of the *Jama'at* see this author's article, "The Islamic Militants in Egyptian Politics," *The International Journal of Middle East Studies* 1(16): 123–44.
3.   See Muhammad Abdel Qudus' interview with Essam al-'Aryan in *al-Da'wa*, November 1980, p. 46.
4.   Fazlur Rahman, *Islam* (Chicago: The University of Chicago Press, 1979), 131.
5.   Salah Hafiz in *Rose al-Yusif*, 26 October 1982, pp.7–9.
6.   Interview with Omar Tilmisani in *Al-Ahrar*, 15 February 1982.
7.   See the interview of Shaykh Jad al-Haq, the Rector of al-Azhar, in *al-Liwa' al-Islami*, 20 July 1981.
8.   From the internal journal *al-Taqaddum*, 25 June 1981 and 19 August 1981.
9.   It is difficult to know the exact number of Islamic fraternities or how many in-dividuals joined them. According to *al-Ahrar*, 2 January 1982, there were, altogether, thirty different types of Islamic fraternities. A report in *al-Musawwar*, 29 January 1982, said that inside al-Liman—Egypt's most notorious prison camp—there were ninety-nine different Islamic groups. President Sadat, presumably relying on figures provided by the Ministry of the Interior, said that militants among the Islamic fraternities numbered in the range of 7,000 to 8,000. Undoubtedly, Sadat's figures included members of both the militant and moderate fraternities.
10.   See Sayyid Qutb, *Ma'alim fi al-Tariq* (Cairo: Dar al-Shurug, 1981).
11.   Hamied Ansari, "The Islamic Militants in Egyptian Politics," *International Journal of Middle East Studies* 16 (1984): 136–40.
12.   See the critique of the militant doctrine by the leader of the Islamic fraternities at Cairo University in *al-Da'wa*, November 1980.
13.   Interview with Omar Tilmisani in *al-Musawwar*, 22 January 1982. See also denials of complicity with the Ministry of the Interior in *al-Da'wa*, March 1981. Hilmi al-Jazzar, the leader of the Islamic *Jama'at* who was most closely associated with the *Ikhwan*, said he was personally requested by the Minister of the Interior to go to Minya to calm Muslim feelings after the sectarian clashes there. See *al-Da'wa*, June 1980, p. 61.
14.   The minister of defense, Abu Ghazalah, denied the existence of a Tanzim secret apparatus in the military services; however, he did acknowledge reports that an unspecified number of army personnel had been either retired or transferred to civilian posts. See *Akher Sa'a's* interview with the defense minister, 11 April 1982.
15.   Khalid Islambuli was selected to participate only eleven days before the annual military parade on 6 October.
16.   See *al-Ahram*, 25 March 1982.
17.   Based on an interviwew by this author with Kamil Zuhayri, the former president of the Egyptian Press Syndicate, on 24 November 1981.
18.   See *al-Gumhouriyya*, 8 September 1981.
19.   See *al-Liwa' al-Islami*, 25 February 1982.

20. Interview with Shaykh Zakariya al-Burri, the minister of al-Awqaf, in *Mayo*, 2 November 1981.

21. Shaykh Hafiz was the head of Jamiyyat al-Hidaya al-Islamiyya in Suez. He delivered sermons at both al-Shuhada' mosque in Suez and al-Nur mosque in Cairo. Both mosques were private. The latter was a popular meeting place for militants. Shaykh Salamah was one of the most outspoken critics of the peace treaty with Israel. In one of his sermons, he described the treaty as the treaty of surrender, '*Istislam*. Among the accusations levied against him by the regime was his alleged role in the sectarian conflict in al-Zawiyya al-Hamra in June 1981. President Sadat called Shaykh Salamah "the mad Imam."

22. See *al-Gumhouriyya*, 9 September 1981.

23. See *al-Ahram*, 23 September 1981. After Sadat's assassination, the minister of the interior, Nabawi Ismail, acknowledged that the September crackdown did not go far enough so to include all members of all Islamic groups: "Although the backbone of the extremists was broken, some elements remained at large." See *al-Musawwar*, 30 October 1981.

24. This statement was confirmed by the statement of the governor of Asyut, who asserted that the assault by militants against the security forces was led by the Amirs from the group who were on the wanted list since 5 September 1981. See *al-Musawwar*, 23 October 1981.

25. See *al-Ahrar*, 2 November 1981. Also, ibid., 26 October 1981.

26. The security forces penetrated the group led by Colonel Abbud al-Zomor and were actually able to videotape the transaction between one of the militants in the group and an underground arms dealer. Sadat himself viewed the tape just a few days before the actual assassination on 6 October.

27. Information from Kamil Zuhayri in an interview with this author on 24 November 1981.

28. Data on population and other social indicators are derived from the 1978 census conducted by the Central Agency for Statistics and General Mobilization, Cairo, Egypt.

29. *Akher Sa'a*, 11 November 1981.

30. See *al-Ahram*, 18 November 1980.

31. John Waterbury, *Egypt, Burdens of the Past, Options for the Future* (Bloomington, IN: Indiana University Press, 1978), 17.

32. Interestingly one of the first decrees issued by President Mubarak shortly after assuming office was the demolition of all constructions on the Pyramids' Plateau, including the presidential villa.

33. See *al-Ahrar*, 2 November 1981.

34. Obituary notice in *al-Ahram*, 23 March 1982.

35. Khalid al-Islambuil's aunt's husband is an army general. See *al-Ahrar*, 26 October 1981.

36. See the discussion of Sabri Abu al-Majd in *al-Ahram*, 22 January 1981.

37. Hasan Hanafi, "The Relevance of the Islamic Alternative in Egypt," *Arab Studies Quarterly* 1 & 2 (Spring 1982): 61.

38. The militant group known as al-Takfir wa-al-Hijra was liquidated in 1977. See Saad Ibrahim, "Anatomy of Egypt's Militant Islamic Groups: Methodological Note and Preliminary Findings," *International Journal of Middle East Studies* 12 (1981): 423–53.

39. See *al-Ahrar*, 14 December 1981. The paper claimed that it was publishing the unabridged version of the text.

40. See *al-Musawwar*, 19 July 1981.

41. Aly Fahmi and Madiha el-Safty, "Anxiety and Deviance in the Arab City," unpublished paper presented at the Tenth International Congress on Social Defense, Salonika, 28 September to 2 October 1981.

42. Madiha El-Safty, "Sociological Perspectives on Urban Housing," *Cairo Papers* (The American University in Cairo, 1983).

43. See a repot in *Akher Sa'a*, 23 May 1979. Also see *Akhbar al-Yaum*, 19 May 1979.

44. El-Safty, "Sociological Studies in Urban Housing." See also the criticism raised by the Labor Party member of parliament Hamdi Ahmad in *al-Sha'b*, 21 July 1981.

45. See *Mayo*, 22 June 1981.

46. See text of Sadat's speech in *al-Ahram*, 15 September 1981. See also *Mayo* 7 September 1981, and Al-'Sha-'b, 30 June, 1981.

47. According to Milad Hanna, a prominent member of the left-wing Nationalist Progressive Unionist Party (Tajamu'), the local committee of the NDP had no business meddling in matters best left in the hands of the courts of law, but the shortsightedness of the NDP was due to its political opportunism. See *al-Taqaddum*, 26 June, 1981. He also confirmed that the Copt had a legal claim to the land under dispute.

48. To my knowledge, these speeches have never been published. Nevertheless, apart from the secret police, who recorded the speeches of leading members of the fraternities on various occasions, the militant members or what came to be known as Tanzim al-Jihad recorded them. As revealed by the transcripts of the interrogations of members of Tanzim al-Jihad, a machine to mass-produce cassettes was bought in an effort to emulate the Iranian revolution.

49. Essam al-'Aryan, a medical doctor aged twenty-seven, was born in Nahia village, Imbaba district, in Giza. To this village also belonged Colonel Abbud al-Zomor, the member of the Tanzim al-Jihad with the highest military rank, who stood trial for his part in the plot to assassinate President Sadat. Al-'Aryan was married to the sister of one of the accused for the attack on the Military Technical College in 1974. He was the former Amir al-'Am of the Islamic fraternities of the Egyptian universities. Although he gave regular sermons in which he preached the enforcement of Islamic laws, he rejected the militant doctrine of *takfir*. For an explanation of this doctrine, which distinguishes the moderates from the extremists, see my article, "The Islamic Militants in Egyptian Politics."

POSTSCRIPT NOTES

1. Statement by Dr. Usama al-Bazz in *al-Misa'*, 23 November 1981. See also the criticism levied by Ibrahim Saada against the hypocrites who change with every new president in *Mayo*, 15 March 1982.
2. See also David Ottaway's coverage of a lecture by Saad al-Din Ibrahim at the American University in Cairo in the *Washington Post*, 3 July 1983.
3. *Al-Ahram*, 11 December 1981.
4. *Al-Musawwar*, 11 December 1981.
5. *Al-Ahali*, 11 May 1983.
6. *Al-Akhbar*, 10 February 1982.
7. *Al-Ahali*, 4 November 1984.
8. See Professor Ali al-Din Hillal's article in *al-Ahram*, 16 June 1984.

Bibliography

Abdel-Fadil, Mahmoud. *Development, Income Distribution and Social Change in Rural Egypt: 1952–1970.* London: Cambridge University Press, 1975.

'Abdel Fattah, Fathi. *Al-Qarya al-Mua'asira.* Cairo: Dar al-Thaqafah, 1975.

Abdel-Malek, Anouar. *Egypt: Military Society.* New York: Random House, 1968.

'Abdel Mu'ti, 'Abdel Basit. *Tawzi' al-Faqr fi al-Qarya al-Misriyya.* Cairo: Dal al-Thaqafah, 1979.

Ajami, Fouad. *The Arab Predicament.* New York: Cambridge University Press, 1981.

— — —. "The Open Door Economy: Its Roots and Welfare Consequences," In Abdel Khalek Gouda and Robert Tignor, eds., *The Political Economy of Income Distribution in Egypt.* New York: Holmes and Meier, 1982. pp.469–516.

Akhavi, Shahrough. "Egypt: Neo-Patrimonial Elite." In Frank Tachau, ed., *Political Elites and Political Development in the Middle East.* New York: Halsted Press, 1975. pp. 69–113.

'Aluba, Muhammad 'Ali. *Zikrayat 'Ijtima'iyya wa-Siyasiyya.* Cairo: The Arab Center for Research and Publication, 1982.

'Amer, Ibrahim. *Al-Ardh wa-al-Fallah: Al-Mas'lah al-Zira'iyya fi Misr.* Cairo: Dar al-Misriyya, 1958.

Ammar, Hamed. *Growing Up in an Egyptian Village.* New York: Octagon Books, 1966.

Anderson, John. "Representative Systems and Ruralizing Elections." M.A. thesis, The University of Chicago, 1976.

Anderson, Lisa. "Qadhafi's Islam." In John L. Esposito, ed., *Voices of Resurgent Islam.* Oxford: Oxford University Press, 1983. pp. 134–49.

Ansari, Hamied. "The Islamic Militants in Egyptian Politics." *International Journal of Middle East Studies* 16(1984). pp. 123–44.

— — —. "Sectarian Conflict and the Political Expedience of Religion." *The Middle East Journal* 3(1984). pp. 397–418.

— — —. "Mubarak's Dilemma: The Contradictions of Two Regimes." *Current History* (January 1985). pp. 21–24.

Ayrout, Henry. *The Fallaheen.* Cairo: R. Schindler.

— — —. *The Egyptian Peasant.* Boston: Beacon Press, 1968.

Baer, Gabriel. *Studies in the Social History of Modern Egypt*. Chicago: The University of Chicago Press, 1969.

———. *A History of Land Ownership in Modern Egypt, 1800–1952*. London: Oxford University Press, 1962.

Bakhash, Shaul. "Revolutions in the Middle East and North Africa in Comparative Perspectives." In William G. Miller and Philip Stoddard, eds., *Perspective on the Middle East, 1983: Proceedings of a Conference*. Washington, D.C.: The Middle East Institute, 1983. pp. 55–63.

Barakat, 'Ali. *Tatawwr al-Milkiyya al-Zira'iyya fi Misr wa-Atharuh 'Ala al-Harakah al-Siyasiyya: 1813–1914*. Cairo: Dar al-Thaqafah, 1977.

———. *Ru'yat 'Ali Mubarak li'Ta'rikh Misr al-'Ijtima'i*. Cairo: Al-Ahram Center for Political and Strategic Studies, 1982.

Batatu, Hanna. "The Egyptian, Iraqi, Syrian Revolutions: Comparisons." In William G. Miller and Philip Stoddard, eds., *Perspectives on the Middle East, 1983: Proceedings of a Conference*. Washington, D.C.: The Middle East Institute 1983.

———. *The Old Social Classes and the Revolutionary Movements of Iraq: A Study of Iraq's Old Landed and Commercial Classes and of its Communists, Ba'thists and Free Officers*. Princeton: Princeton University Press, 1982.

Bibars, Diya' al-Din. "Al-Sira' al-Sirri Byna al-Mabahith wa-al-Mukhabarat." *Rose al-Yusif*, 11 November 1975.

Binder, Leonard. *In a Moment of Enthusiasm: Political Power and the Second Stratum*. Chicago: The University of Chicago Press, 1978.

———. "The Failure of the Egyptian Left." *Asian and African Studies* 14 (March 1980). pp. 20–34.

Blunt, Wilfred S. *Secret History of the British Occupation of Egypt*. New York: Howard Fertig, 1967.

Baring, Evelyn (Lord Cromer). *Modern Egypt*. London: MacMillan and Co., 1908.

Davis, Eric. *Challenging Colonialism: Bank Misr and Egyptian Industrialization, 1920–1941*. Princeton: Princeton University Press, 1983.

Dessouki, Ali E. Hillal. "Policy-making in Egypt: A Case Study of the Open Door Policy." *Social Problems* (April 1984).

Enayat, Hamid. "Iran: Khumayni's Concept of the Guardianship of the Jurisconsult." In James Piscatori, ed., *Islam in the Political Process*. London: Cambridge University Press, 1983. pp. 160–80.

Gadalla, Saad. *Land Reform in Relation to Social Development in Egypt*. Columbia: University of Missouri Press, 1962.

Galab, Philip. "Man Qatal Man fi Kamshish." *Rose al-Yusif*, 16 December 1974.

Ghai, Dharm ed. *Agrarian System and Rural Development*. New York: Holmes and Meier, 1979.

Hamid, Ra'uf Abbas. *Al-Nizam al-'Ijtima'i fi Misr fi Zill al-Milkiyyat al-Zira'iyya al-Kabirah*. Cairo: Dar al-Fikr, 1973.

Hamrush, Ahmad. *Qissat Thawarat 23 Yulyu*. Beirut: Al-Mu'assasah al-'Arabiyya, 1974.

Hanafi, Hassan. "The Relevance of the Islamic Alternative in Egypt." *Arab Studies Quarterly* 1 and 2 (Spring 1982). pp. 54–74.

Harik, Iliya. *The Political Mobilization of Peasants: A Study of an Egyptian Community*. Bloomington: Indiana University Press, 1974.

———. *Distribution of Land, Employment and Income in Rural Egypt*. Ithaca: Rural Development Committee, Cornell University, 1979.

Heikal, Mohamed. *Autumn of Fury: The Assassination of Sadat*. New York: Random House, 1983.

Hermassi, Elbaki. *Leadership and National Development in North Africa: A Comparative Study*. Berkeley: University of California Press, 1975.

Hinnebusch, Raymond. "The Reemergence of the Wafd Party: Glimpses of the Liberal Opposition in Egypt." *International Journal of Middle East Studies* 16(1984). pp. 99–121. Vol 16 March 1984 No. 1.

Hirst, David, and Beeson, Irene. *Sadat*. London: Faber & Faber, 1981.

Hooglund, Eric. *Land and Revolution in Iran: 1960–1980*. Austin: University of Texas Press, 1982.

Hussein, Mahmoud. *Class Conflict in Egypt*. New York: Monthly Review Press, 1973.

Ibrahim, Saad Eddin. "Anatomy of Egypt's Militant Islamic Groups: Methodological Note and Preliminary Findings." *International Journal of Middle East Studies* 12(1981). (pp. 423–453). Vol 12, Dec. 1980 No. 4.

Jawhar, Sami. *Al-Samitun Yatakallamun*. Maktab al-Misri, 1975.

Keilany, Ziad. "Land Reforms in Syria." *Middle Eastern Studies* 16(1980). pp. 209–24.

Landau, Jacob. *Parliaments and Parties in Egypt*. Tel Aviv: Israel Press Ltd., 1953.

Landes, David. *Bankers and Pashas*. Cambridge: Harvard University Press, 1958.

Mar'i, Sayyid. *Awraq Siyasiyya*. Cairo: Al-Maktab al-Misri, 1979.

Matar, Fouad. *Muhammad Hasanain Heikal: Bi-Saraha 'an Abdel Nasser*. Beirut: Dar al-Qadaya, 1975.

Minutes of the National Congress of Popular Forces. Cairo: Government Printing Press, 1962.

Minutes of the People's Assembly. Cairo: Government Printing Press, 1971, 1976, and 1978.

Moore, Clement H. "Authoritarian Politics in Unincorporated Society: The Case of Nasser's Egypt." *Comparative Politics* 6(1974). pp. 193–218.

———. "Clientelist Ideology and Political Change: Fictitious Networks in Egypt and Tunisia." In E. Gellner and J. Waterbury, eds., *Patrons and Clients in Mediterranean Societies*. London: Duckworth, 1977. pp. 255–273.

Mubarak, 'Ali. *Al-Khitat al-Tawfiqiyya al-Jadida*. CAiro: Bulaq, 1886–1889.

Mursi, Fouad. *Hadha al-'Infitah al-'Iqtisadi*. Cairo: Dar al-Thaqafah, 1976.

Perlmutter, Amos. *Egypt: The Praetorian State*. New Brunswick, N.J.: Transaction Books, 1974.

Quraishi, Zaheer M. *Liberal Nationalism in Egypt*. Delhi: The Jamal Press, 1967.

Qutb, Sayyid. *Ma'alim fi al-Tariq*. Cairo: Dar al-Shuruq, 1981.

Rafi'i, 'Abdel Rahman. *'Asr Ismail*. Cairo: Dar al-Ma'arif, 1982.

Ramadan, 'Abdel Azim. *Al-Sira' al-'Ijtima'i wa-al-Siyasi Fi Misr: 'Abdel Nasser wa-Azmat Mars*. Cairo: Rose al-Yusif, 1976.
— — —. Sira' al Tabaqat fi Misr: 1837–1952. Beirut: Al-Mu'assasah al-Arabiyya li-al-Dirasat wa-al-Nashr, 1978.
Rashad, Muhammad. *Sirri Jiddan: Min Malafat Lajnat Tasfiyat al-'Iqta'*. Cairo: Dar al-Ta'awun, 1977.
Rida, Mamdouh. *15 Mayo: Al-Thawra wa-al Mustaqbal*. Cairo: Dar al-Ta'awun, 1977.
Saab, Gabriel S. *The Egyptian Agrarian Reforms, 1952–1962*. London: Oxford University Press, 1967.
Sadat, Muhammad Anwar. *Al-Bahth 'an al-Dhat*. Cairo: Al-Maktab al-Misri, 1978.
Safran, Nadav. *Egypt in Search of Political Community*. Cambridge: Harvard University Press, 1961.
Sa'i, Ibrahim Zaki. *Ta'rikh al-Minufiyya*. Cairo: Dar Loran, n.d.
Said, Rif'at. *Al-Asas al-'Ijtima'i li-Athawrah al-'Urabiyya*. Cairo: Madbuli Press, 1966.
— — —. *Awraq Nasiriyya*. Cairo: Dar al-Thaqafah, 1975.
Salim, Jamal. *Al-Tanzimat al-Sirriyya li-Thawrat 23 Yulyu fi 'Ahd Abdel Nasser*. Cairo: Faniyya Press, 1982.
Sayyid-Marsot, Afaff Lutfi. *Egypt and Cromer: A Study in Anglo-Egyptian Relations*. London: John Murray, 1968.
— — —. *Egypt's Liberal Experiment, 1922–1936*. Berkeley: University of California Press, 1977.
Shalabi, Karam. *Harb al-Kalimat*. Cairo: n.p., 1975.
Shazli, Saad. *The Crossing of the Suez*. San Francisco: American Mideast Research, 1980.
Shirbini, Ibrahim. *Tasfiyyat al-Hirasat*. Cairo: Al-Ma'arif Press, 1964.
Siraj al-Din, Fouad. *Limaza al-Hizb al-Jadad*. Cairo: Dar al-Shuruq, 1977.
Solodovinkov, V. G. "Classic of Marxism and Non-Capitalist Development." *Africa in Soviet Studies* (1971).
Springborg, Robert. "Patrimonialism and Policy-Making in Egypt: Nasser and Sadat and the Tenure Policy for Reclaimed Land." *Middle East Studies* 15 (1979). pp. 49–69.
— — —. "Sayed Bey Marei and Political Clientelism." *Comparative Political Studies* 12 (October 1979). pp. 259–288.
— — —. *Sayyid Mar'i: Family Power and Politics in Egypt*. Philadelphia: The University of Pennsylvania Press, 1982.
Udah, Muhammad. *Al-Wa'y al-Mafqud*. Cairo: Dar al-Thaqafah, 1975.
Vatikiotis, P. J. *The Egyptian Army in Politics: Pattern for New Nations?* Bloomington: Indiana University Press, 1961.
Warriner, Doreen. *Land Reform and Development in the Middle East: A Study of Egypt, Syria and Iraq*. London: Oxford University Press, 1962.

Waterbury, John. *Egypt: Burdens of the Past, Options for the Future.* Bloomington: Indiana University Press, 1978.

——— . *The Egypt of Nasser and Sadat: The Political Economy of Two Regimes.* Princeton: Princeton University Press, 1983.

Zaki, Elsayd M. *An Outline of the Local Administration System in the United Arab Republic.* Cairo: Ministry of Local Government, 1965.

NEWSPAPERS

Al-Ahali
Al-Ahram
Al-Ahram Al-'Iqtisadi
Al-Ahrar
Akhbar
Akhbar al-Yuam
Akher Sa'a
Al-Da'wa
Al-Gumhouriyya
Al-Liwa' al-Islami
Mayo
Al-Musawwar
Al-Nahar
October
Rose al-Yusif
Al-Sha'b
Al-Tali'ah
Al-Taqaddum

Name Index

Subject Index

Absenteeism, 62, 80

Agrarian reforms: under Khedive Ismail, 61; purposes of, 6–7; failure of, 7–8; calls for in 1940's, 77; Agrarian reform laws (1,2,3,), 119, 124–129, effects on Kamshish, 28–30, 31–32, 33; first law, 79–81; second law, 87, 89; sequestration laws announced, 88–90; emergence of multiple ownership, 118–129; evasion of by large landowners, 119–120; cooperatives, 130; violations of, 133–135; social and agrarian impact of, 134–135; and Nasser's desequestration order, 143, 147–149; and decline in domestic production, 189–192; impact on landownership and tenancy relations, 189–192; denounced by Wafd, 198; during Nasserist era, 234–235

Agricultural production, 189–192; under Mubarak, 243

Ahli mosques, 218

al-Ahram, 154, 158

al-Akhbar, 46, 48

Alexandria, 183, 218

Algeria, 3, 5, 12–13

Amanat al-Fikr wa al-Da'wa, 94, 99

Anglo-Egyptian treaty, 73

'Arab al-Mohammadi, 226

Arab Socialist Party of Egypt, 196, 198, 199, 203

Arab Socialist Union (ASU); replaces National Union, 32; creation of, 88; organization of, 90; creation of Socialist Vanguard, 92; impact on rural areas, 93–94; as part of effort to wipe out feudalism, 98; under Sabri's leadership, 99; committees excluded from HCLF investigations, 105–106; hierarchical order of, 113–117;

reorganization after Syrian secession, 114; effect of reorganization on upper stratum, 128–129; use of to change social structure, 137; collaboration with rural elites, 138; reforms of announced in March 30 statement, 144–146; and desequestration, 149; relationship to National Assembly, 157–158; attempts by Sadat to reorganize, 158; effects of Corrective Movement on, 167–169; as envisaged by Sadat's liberal formula, 196–197; replaced as media censor, 206

Arab Summit Conference (Rabat), 150

al-'Asabiyya al-'A'iliyya (kinship solidarity), 102–105

Asuyt, 69, 124, 134, 164, 219, 220–223

Asyut University, 220–221

'Awdat al-Sa'y, 171

al-Awqaf (Ministry of Religious Endowments), 218al-Azhar, 70

al-'Azl al-Siyyasi (political isolation), 83

Baghdad Pact, 85

Bani Suwayf, 134

Bar Association, 84, 167, 207–209

Beheira, 163, 164, 81, 180; in HCLF investigations, 108; multiplelandownership in, 124; wages for agricultural workers, 134; "Blue Shirts", 71

Bolaq al-Dakrur, 218, 221

Britain; occupation of Egypt, 12, 59, 66–67, 69; impact on Egyptian parliament, 62–63; Anglo-Egyptian treaty, 73

Buhut (Gharbiyya), 76

Cairo University, 144

Caisse de la Dette Publique, 64